PRAISE FOR *SPEED BUMP: CARTOONS FOR IDEA PEOPLE,* ALSO AVAILABLE FROM ECW PRESS

"Funny at any speed. With his knack for steering straight for the funny bone, Dave Coverly's new *Speed Bump* cartoon collection takes readers on a laugh-filled joyride. Dave's real philosophy seems to be 'anything to get a laugh,' and in the case of *Speed Bump: Cartoons for Idea People*, it's one of those rare philosophies that actually works 99 percent of the time. For this reason, the book should not be read by surgeons (especially brain surgeons) in the operating room, or by anyone operating heavy machinery."

— Ted Kreiter, *The Saturday Evening Post*

"There's no single theme to *Speed Bump: Cartoons for Idea People*, no basic philosophy — but his 'outtakes' appear in over 200 newspapers around the country and *Speed Bump* is a fine survey which gathers these into themed chapters, includes the author's introduction to each, and even presents a small portion of color cartoons with the black and white winners. Dave Coverly is funny and pointed: *Speed Bump* is running in its 10th year and has been nominated for numerous awards, so place this book at the top of the list."

— "Bookwatch," *Midwest Book Review*

"Overall, this book rates a solid three belly laugh out of four, on the guffaw scale."

— Tumbleweed, PenguinComics.net

"More than 200 pages where tons of press illustrations have been collected, as they are called here in France, always with a caustic tone in their retorts, depicting typical middle Americans, animals who are a little human, and corrupt politicians. Dave Coverly gives them joy and scorches on white paper all their fantasies and desires through humor, opening the eyes of the public. We also discover a 32-page color section of rare delicious black humor, where the author does not go easy, making us clear on his position as an observer of contemporary society. If authors like Aural, Cabu, Plantu, Lefred-Thouron, or Gébé give you another vision of society or simply, if you like any of them, then check this out. Great art, very beautiful graphics in a very European style, and a craving to show it all. Check this out immediately if you are familiar with the English language . . ."

— Philippe Duarte, Underground Society Webzine, France, http://undersociety.free.fr

Just one %$#@
Speed Bump™
after another . . .

Dave Coverly

ECW Press

Published by ECW PRESS
2120 Queen Street East, Suite 200, Toronto, Ontario, Canada M4E 1E2

LIBRARY AND ARCHIVES OF CANADA CATALOGUING IN PUBLICATION

Coverly, Dave
Just one %$#@ speed bump after another: more cartoons / by Dave Coverly.

ISBN 1-55022-700-9

1. American wit and humor, Pictorial. I. Title. II. Title: Just one speed bump after another.

NC1429.C68A4 2005   741.5'973   C2005-904373-3

Cover and Text Design: Tania Craan
Layout: Gail Nina
Production: Mary Bowness
Printing: Transcontinental

DISTRIBUTION

CANADA: Jaguar Book Group, 100 Armstrong Avenue, Georgetown, ON, L7G 5S4
UNITED STATES: Independent Publishers Group, 814 North Franklin Street,
Chicago, Illinois 60610

PRINTED AND BOUND IN CANADA

ECW PRESS
ecwpress.com

For Alayna and Simone

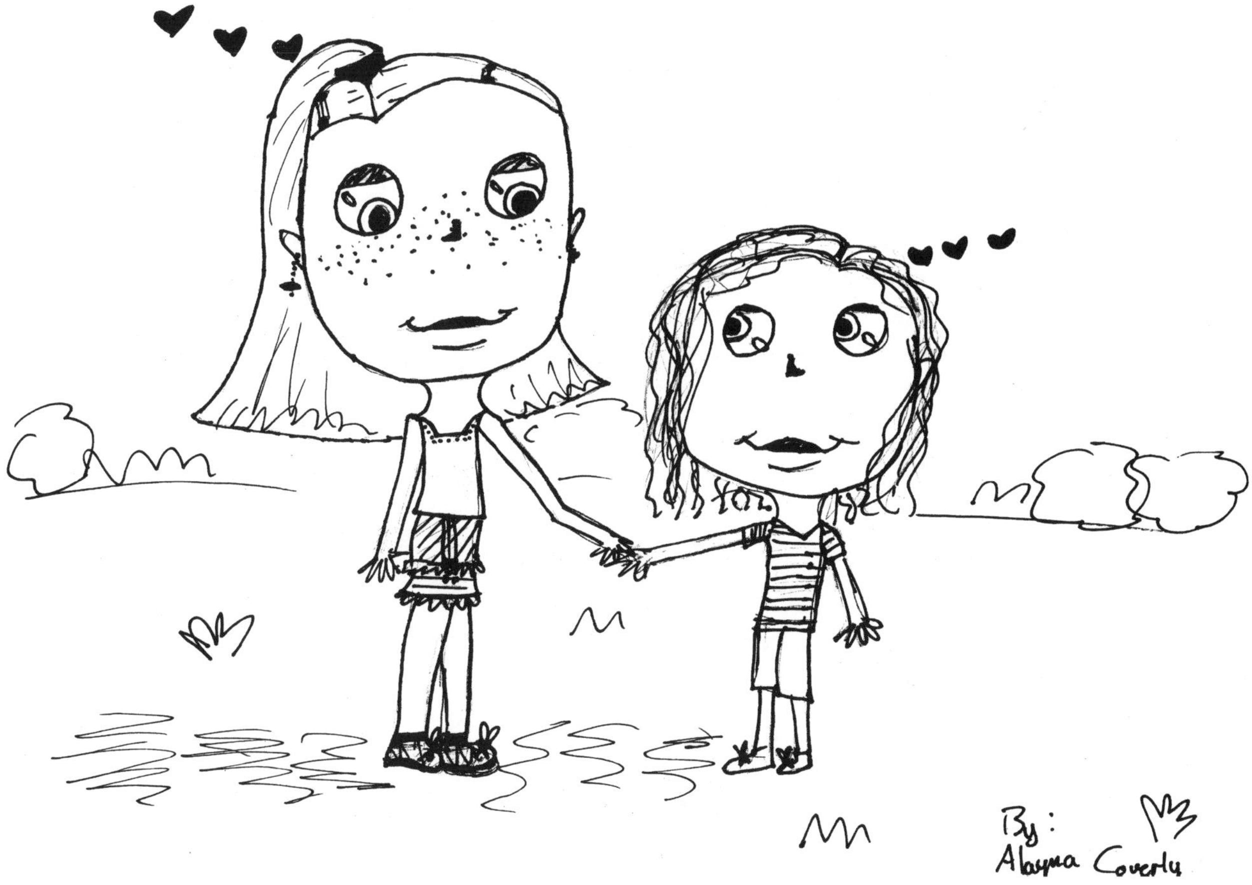
By:
Alayna Coverly

INTRODUCTION

I get asked the same questions all the time: Is it fun, sitting around in your underwear all day, doodling your life away? Do you have a real job? How do you make any money drawing your little cartoons?

But enough about my parents.

When I was in 5th grade, I spent most of my free time in class drawing comic strips. My teacher, Mrs. Lam, was complicit in this exercise, even encouraging. To this day I remember her notes in the margins, written in cursive in red ink and embellished with stars and smiley faces ("That's Funny!!" "Oh, I hate when that happens, too!" "Yes!"). She declared I had a "knack" for this.

So when the parent/teacher conference rolled around, she told my parents, "I think Dave is going to be a cartoonist."

Everyone laughed except Mrs. Lam. "Seriously," she said, in that no-nonsense teachery way, "Dave is going to be a cartoonist."

So they also became encouraging, and I never looked back. And now, whenever I show up at their house to borrow money, they get a big kick out of telling this story again.

Of course, it's one thing to recognize the moment you want to be something; it's another to recognize the moment you've become it.

I was returning to Michigan from a trip to Toronto with a friend. At the border, we stopped at the guard station to show our IDs and answer questions. Traffic was almost non-existent that day, so the two guards, one veteran and one young guy, looked to be killing the time by hanging out and chatting. After I rolled down my window and told them where I'd been, the conversation went like this:

Veteran: "Were you in Toronto for business or pleasure?"

Me: "Mostly business. I was at a cartooning function."

Vet: "You're a cartoonist?"

Me: "Yeah."

Young Guy: "No %$#@!"

Me: "Yep."

Vet: "Whaddaya draw?"

Me: "It's a cartoon called 'Speed Bump.' Runs in the *Free Press*."

YG: "No %$#@!"

Me: "Uh-huh."

Vet: "All right then."

Long Pause. Vet reaches back, grabs something under the counter. He hands me a small pad of paper and a pen.

Vet: "Draw something."

Me: "What? Draw what?"

Vet: "Anything. Whatever you draw."

Me: "I don't really have any characters. I just draw, you know, jokes. Like you see in magazines."

Vet: "All right."

I draw a picture of a dog wearing a business suit holding a beer bottle. I have no idea why. I'm feeling caught off-guard, so to speak. I pass the drawing back through the window to him.

Vet to Young Guy: "Take a look at that!"

YG: "No %$#@!"

Vet: "Hey, he really is a cartoonist!"

YG to Vet: "You oughta keep that."

Vet: "Well, dam', you really are a cartoonist! Go on, fellas, have a nice day."

Me: "Thanks. Here's your pen."

So it took one lousy drawing to get back into the U.S. And they never even asked for ID.

True story. No %$#@.

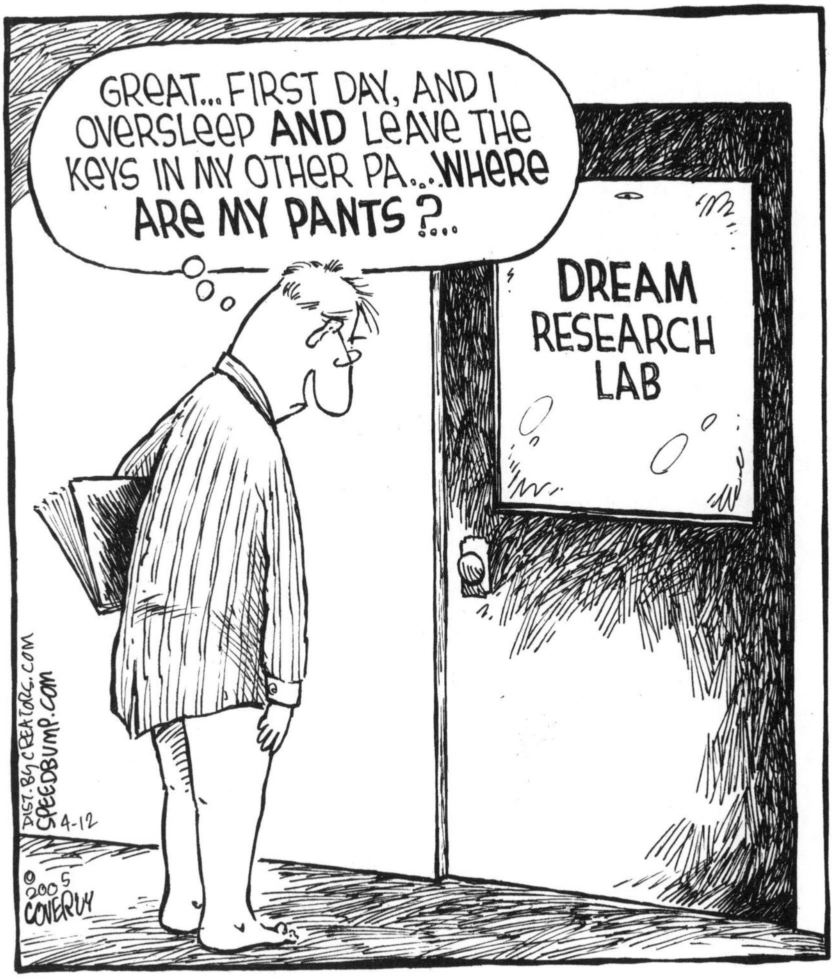
GREAT... FIRST DAY, AND I OVERSLEEP AND LEAVE THE KEYS IN MY OTHER PA... WHERE ARE MY PANTS ?...
DREAM RESEARCH LAB
DIST. BY CREATORS.COM
SPEEDBUMP.COM
4-12
© 2005 COVERLY

Kids

On first glance when you read Dave Coverly's cartoons about kids and parents, you think, "Hey! That's funny stuff." It's only when you reread them that you really start to understand what a truly disturbed person Dave must be. He populates his cartoons with hirsute children, abandoned babies on park benches, preschoolers being pushed out into the job market by their mothers and fathers, parents preparing their offspring for a life of psychotherapy, freaks of nature . . . I could go on, but you get the idea.

They say, "Write what you know" and from his cartoons, you have to wonder about the dark recesses of Dave's parental mind. Despite all this, or perhaps to his wife's credit, Dave's own children seem to be bright and well-adjusted.

Having drawn a comic strip about parenting and kids for the last fifteen years, I can tell you that people will write and complain at the slightest hint that a parent has left their child alone for a moment in a somewhat potentially dangerous situation. I can't imagine what Dave's mail must be like, for he leaves his cartoon progeny in settings that would leave today's obsessive parent apoplectic. It's a good thing he doesn't draw cartoons on this subject all the time, otherwise organizations would be sprouting up all over demanding his hide. On second thought, that might not be so bad. Competition on the comics page is fierce, and there's only so much room.

A note on the art of Dave Coverly: these unsettling depictions of family life occur in the most innocuous settings, all beautifully drawn in Dave's dense, thatchy, and understated style, which is the envy of many cartoonists. Just add my name to the I Hate Dave Coverly Fan Club.

Rick Kirkman
The guy who draws "Baby Blues"

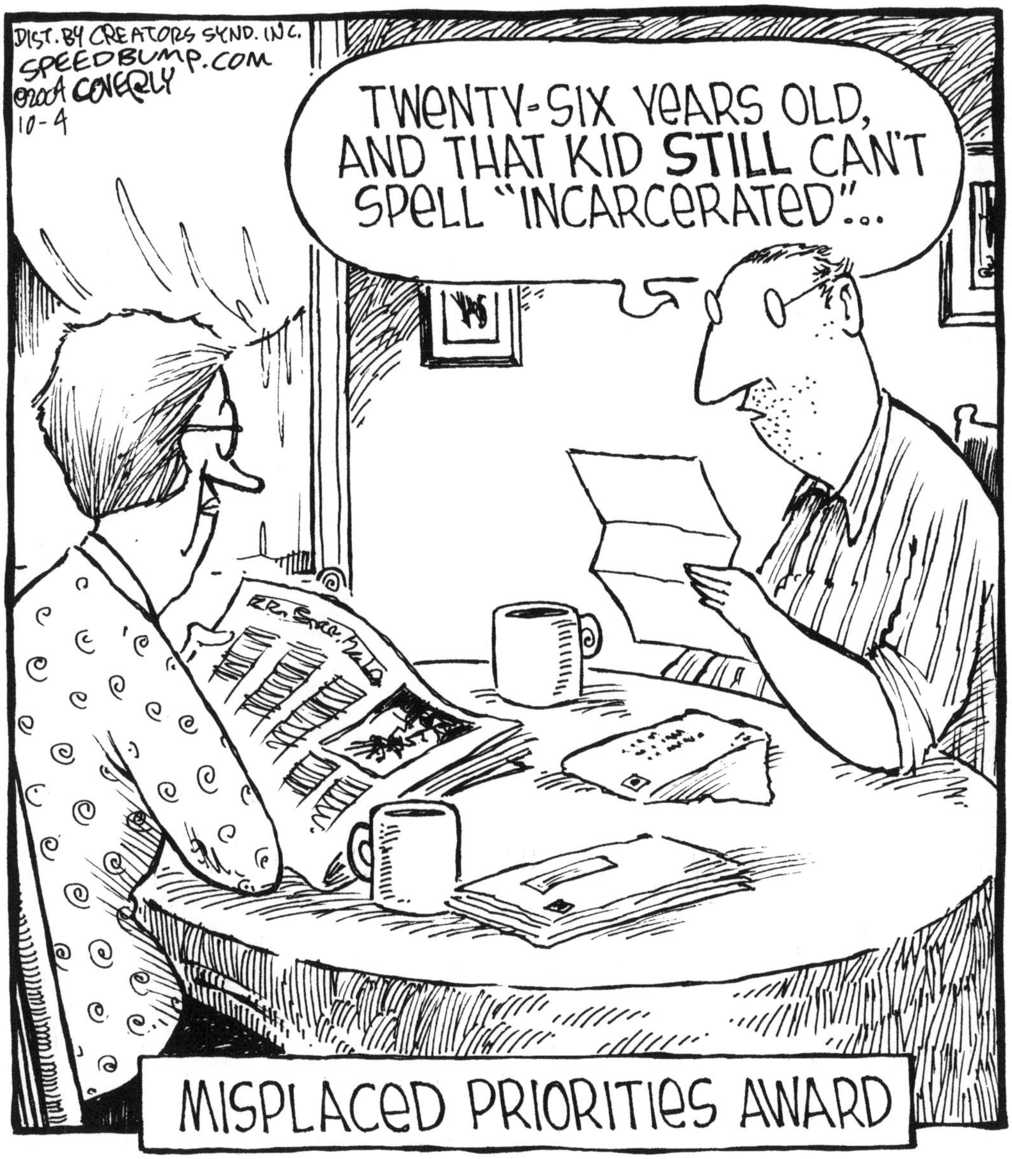
DIST. BY CREATORS SYND. INC.
SPEEDBUMP.COM
©2004 COVERLY
10-4
TWENTY-SIX YEARS OLD, AND THAT KID STILL CAN'T SPELL "INCARCERATED"...
MISPLACED PRIORITIES AWARD

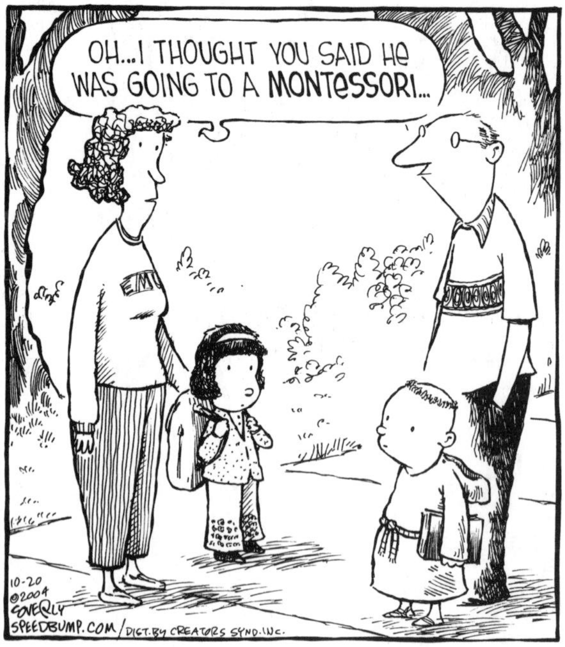
OH...I THOUGHT YOU SAID HE WAS GOING TO A MONTESSORI...
10-20 ©2004 COVERLY
SPEEDBUMP.COM / DIST. BY CREATORS SYND. INC.

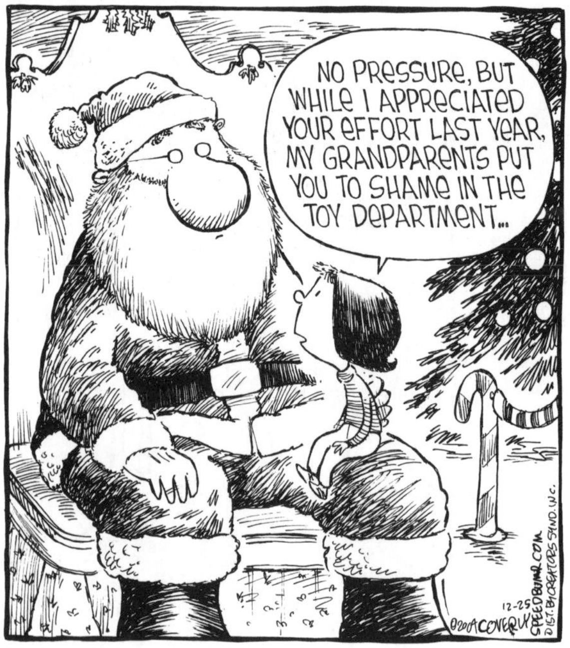
NO PRESSURE, BUT WHILE I APPRECIATED YOUR EFFORT LAST YEAR, MY GRANDPARENTS PUT YOU TO SHAME IN THE TOY DEPARTMENT...

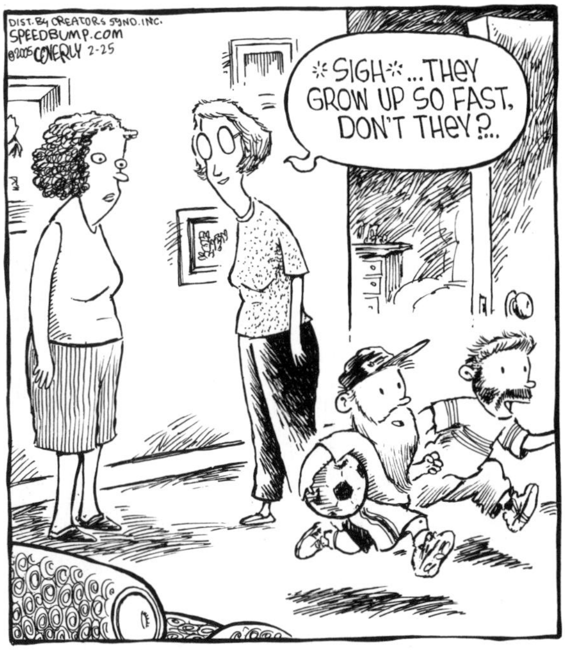
DIST. BY CREATORS SYND. INC.
SPEEDBUMP.COM
©2005 COVERLY 2-25
SIGH...THEY GROW UP SO FAST, DON'T THEY?...

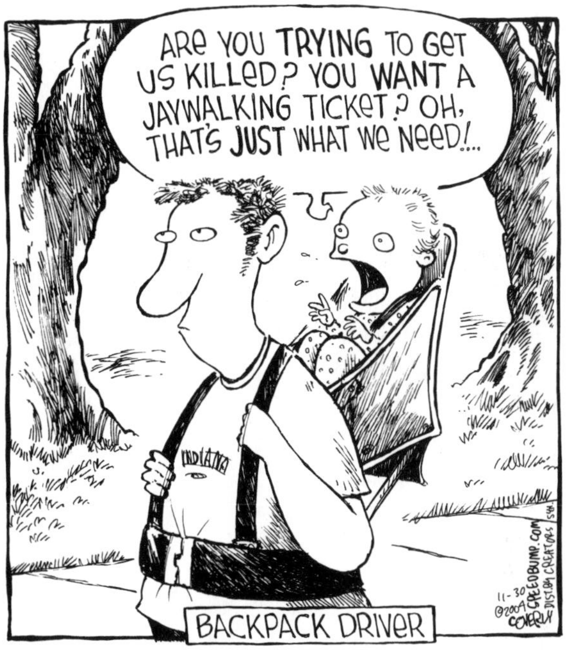
ARE YOU TRYING TO GET US KILLED? YOU WANT A JAYWALKING TICKET? OH, THAT'S JUST WHAT WE NEED!...
INDIANA
BACKPACK DRIVER
11-30
©2004 COVERLY
SPEEDBUMP.COM
DIST. BY CREATORS SYND.

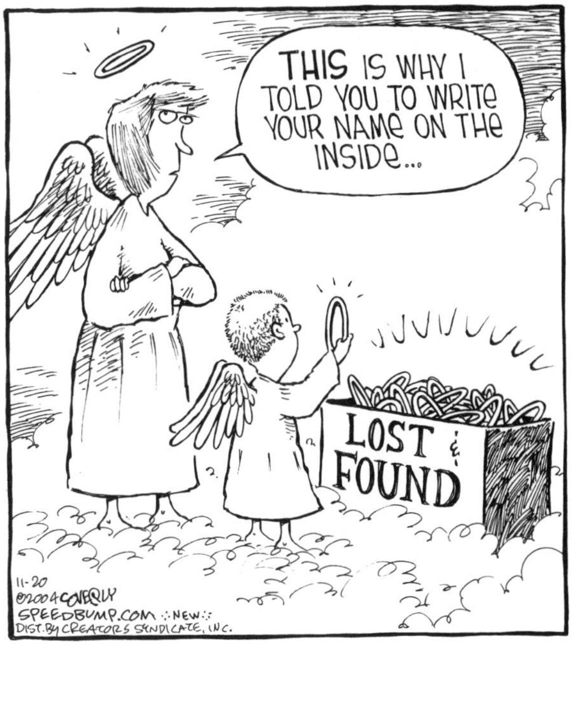
THIS IS WHY I TOLD YOU TO WRITE YOUR NAME ON THE INSIDE...
LOST & FOUND
11-20
©2004 COVERLY
SPEEDBUMP.COM NEW
DIST. BY CREATORS SYNDICATE, INC.

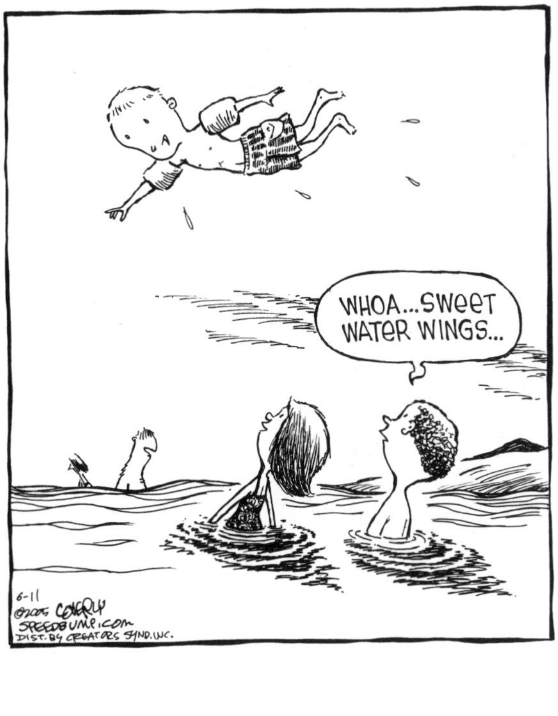
WHOA...SWEET WATER WINGS...
6-11
©2005 COVERLY
SPEEDBUMP.COM
DIST. BY CREATORS SYND. INC.

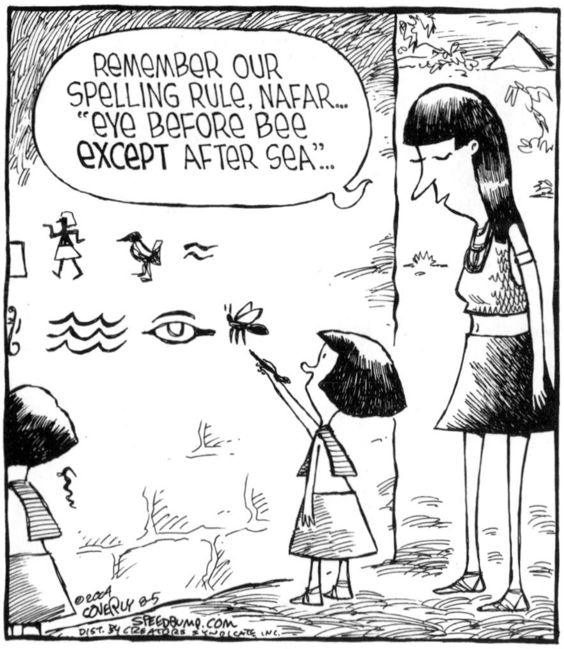
REMEMBER OUR SPELLING RULE, NAFAR... "EYE BEFORE BEE **EXCEPT** AFTER SEA"...
©2004 COVERLY 8-5
SPEEDBUMP.COM
DIST. BY CREATORS SYNDICATE INC.

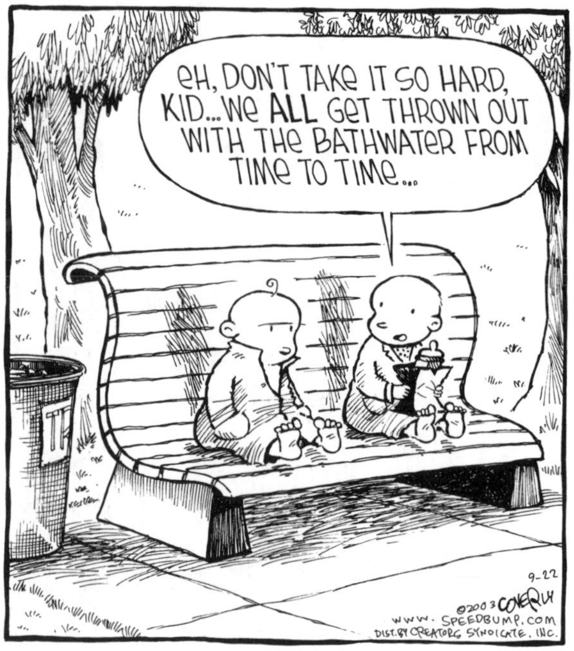
EH, DON'T TAKE IT SO HARD, KID...WE **ALL** GET THROWN OUT WITH THE BATHWATER FROM TIME TO TIME...
9-22
©2003 COVERLY
WWW. SPEEDBUMP.COM
DIST. BY CREATORS SYNDICATE, INC.

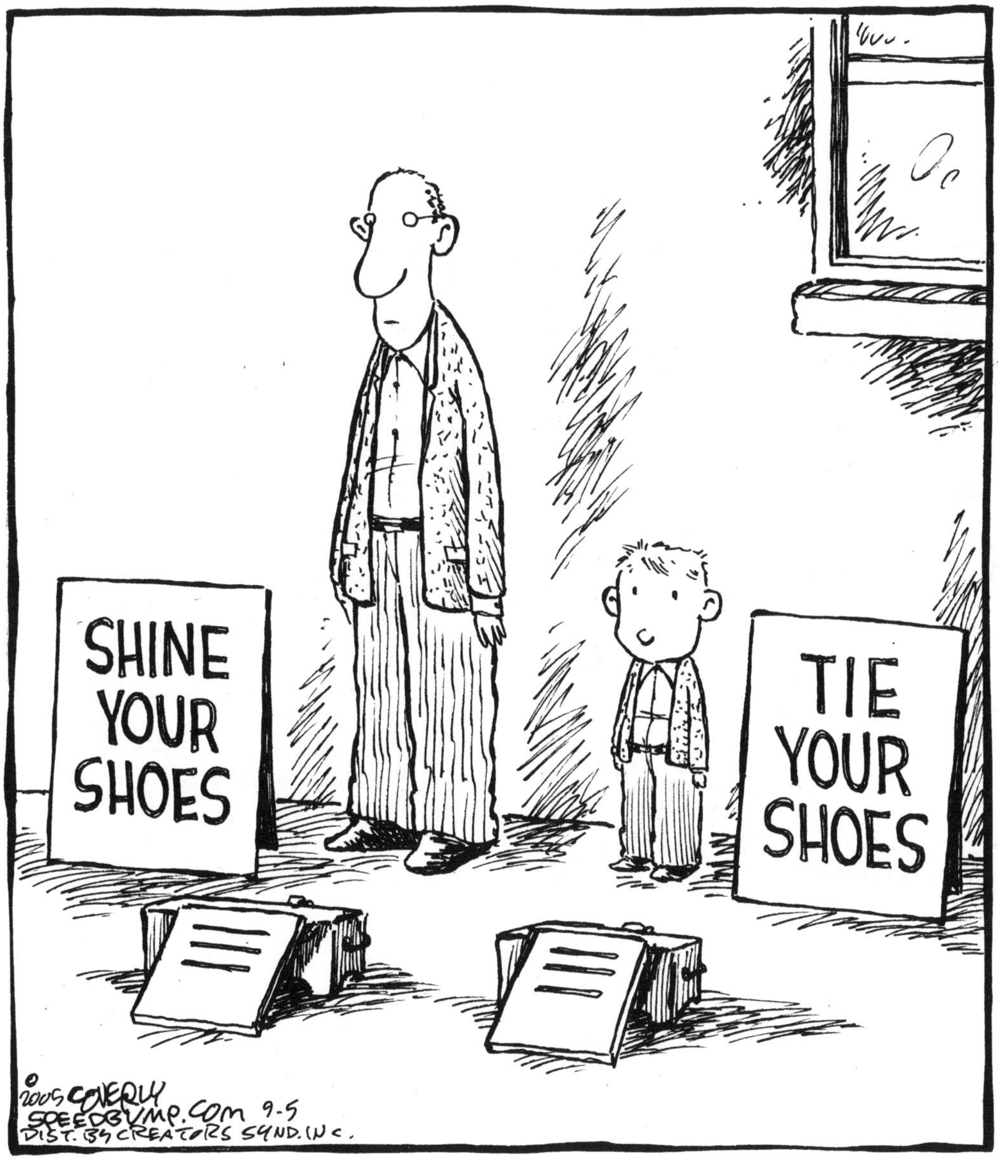
SHINE YOUR SHOES
TIE YOUR SHOES
© 2005 COVERLY
SPEEDBUMP.COM 9-5
DIST. BY CREATORS SYND. INC.

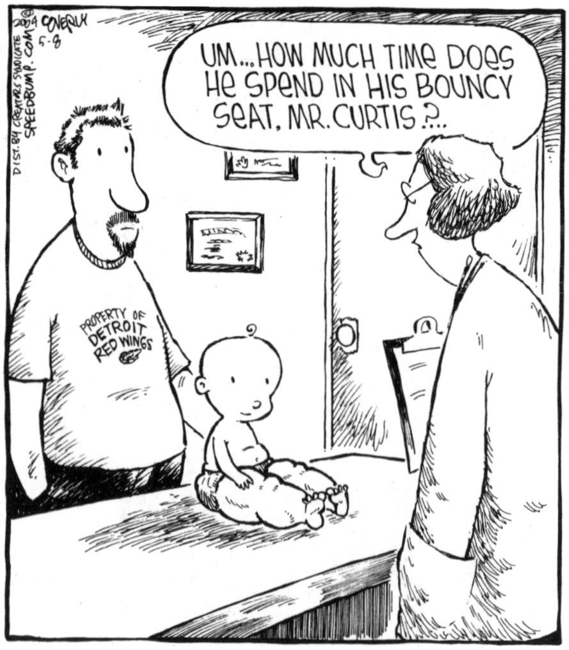
©2004 COVERLY 5-8
DIST. BY CREATORS SYNDICATE SPEEDBUMP.COM
UM...HOW MUCH TIME DOES HE SPEND IN HIS BOUNCY SEAT, MR. CURTIS?...
PROPERTY OF DETROIT RED WINGS

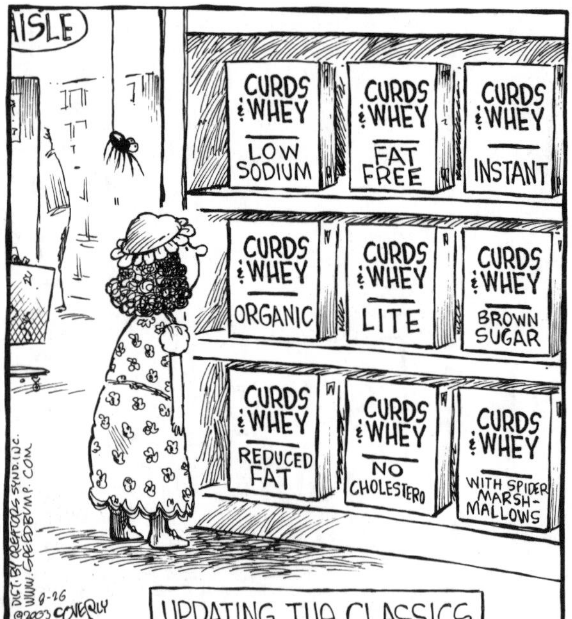
AISLE
CURDS & WHEY LOW SODIUM
CURDS & WHEY FAT FREE
CURDS & WHEY INSTANT
CURDS & WHEY ORGANIC
CURDS & WHEY LITE
CURDS & WHEY BROWN SUGAR
CURDS & WHEY REDUCED FAT
CURDS & WHEY NO CHOLESTERO
CURDS & WHEY WITH SPIDER MARSH-MALLOWS
DIST. BY CREATORS SYND. INC. WWW.SPEEDBUMP.COM
8-26 ©2003 COVERLY

UPDATING THE CLASSICS

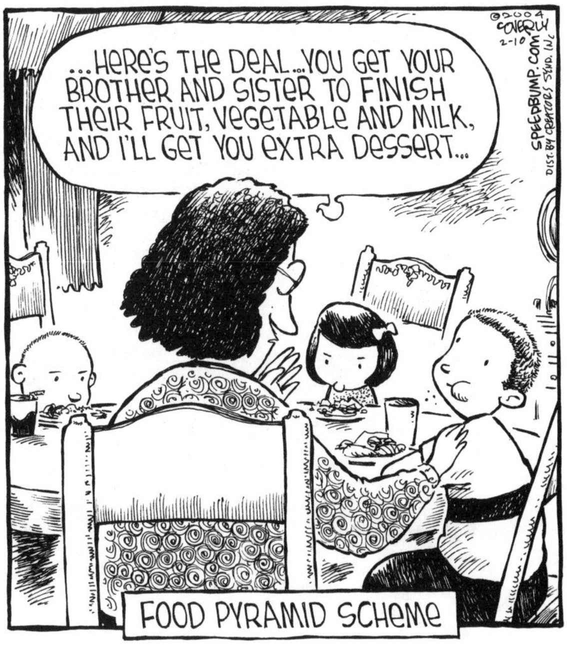
...HERE'S THE DEAL...YOU GET YOUR BROTHER AND SISTER TO FINISH THEIR FRUIT, VEGETABLE AND MILK, AND I'LL GET YOU EXTRA DESSERT...
©2004 COVERLY 2-10
SPEEDBUMP.COM
DIST. BY CREATORS SYND. INC.

FOOD PYRAMID SCHEME

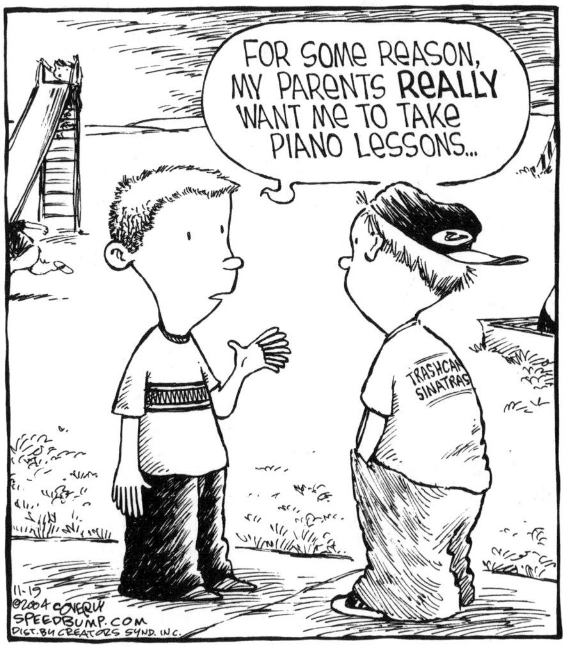
FOR SOME REASON, MY PARENTS **REALLY** WANT ME TO TAKE PIANO LESSONS...
TRASHCAN SINATRAS
11-19
©2004 COVERLY
SPEEDBUMP.COM
DIST. BY CREATORS SYND. INC.

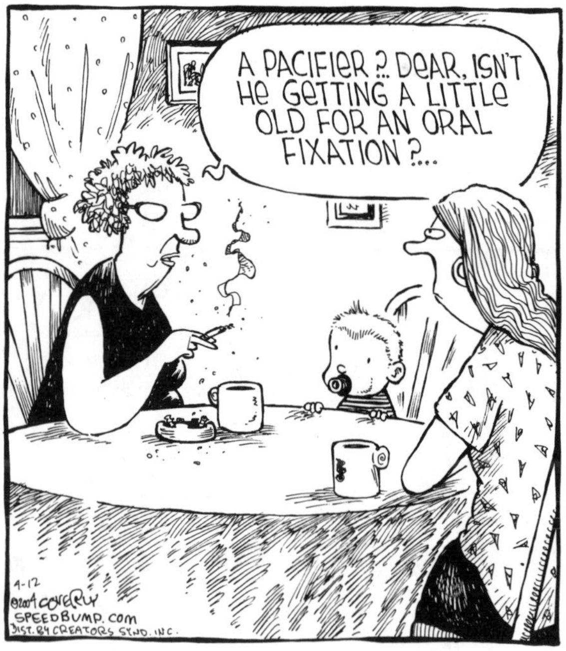
A PACIFIER ?? DEAR, ISN'T HE GETTING A LITTLE OLD FOR AN ORAL FIXATION ?...
4-12
©2004 COVERLY
SPEEDBUMP.COM
DIST. BY CREATORS SYND. INC.

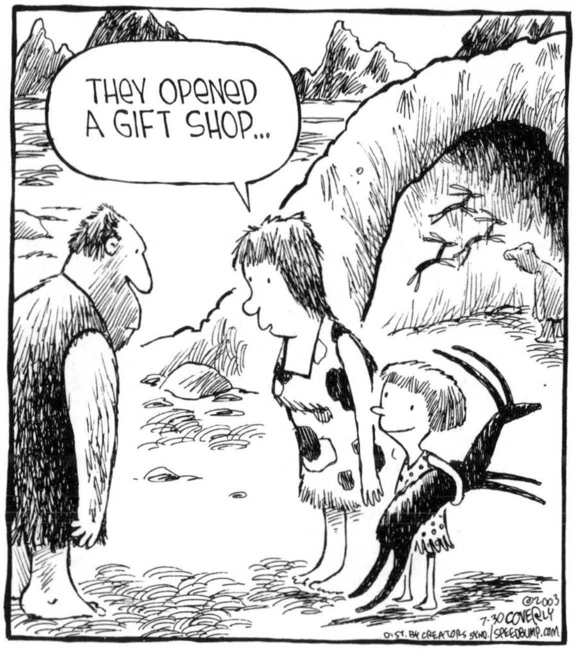
THEY OPENED A GIFT SHOP...
©2003
7-30 COVERLY
DIST. BY CREATORS SYND. SPEEDBUMP.COM

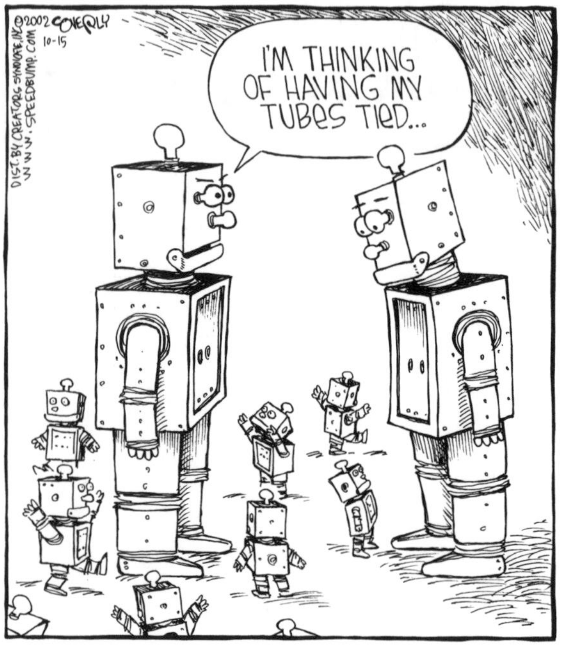
©2002 COVERLY
10-15
DIST. BY CREATORS SYNDICATE, INC.
WWW.SPEEDBUMP.COM
I'M THINKING OF HAVING MY TUBES TIED...

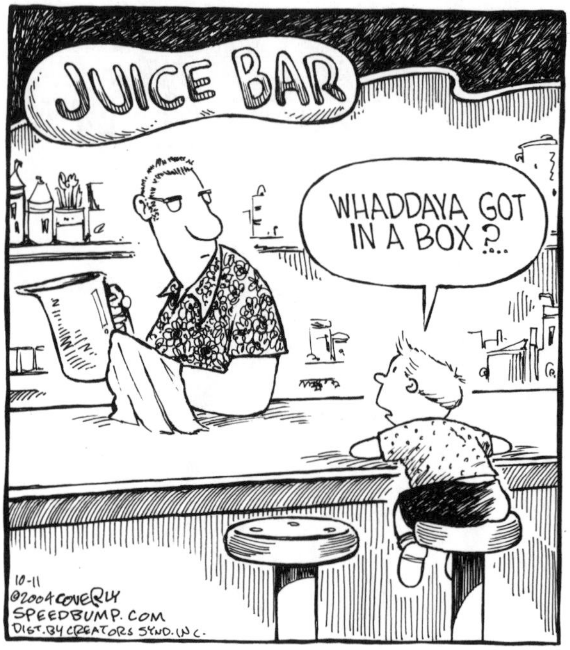
JUICE BAR
WHADDAYA GOT IN A BOX ?...
10-11
©2004 COVERLY
SPEEDBUMP.COM
DIST. BY CREATORS SYND. INC.

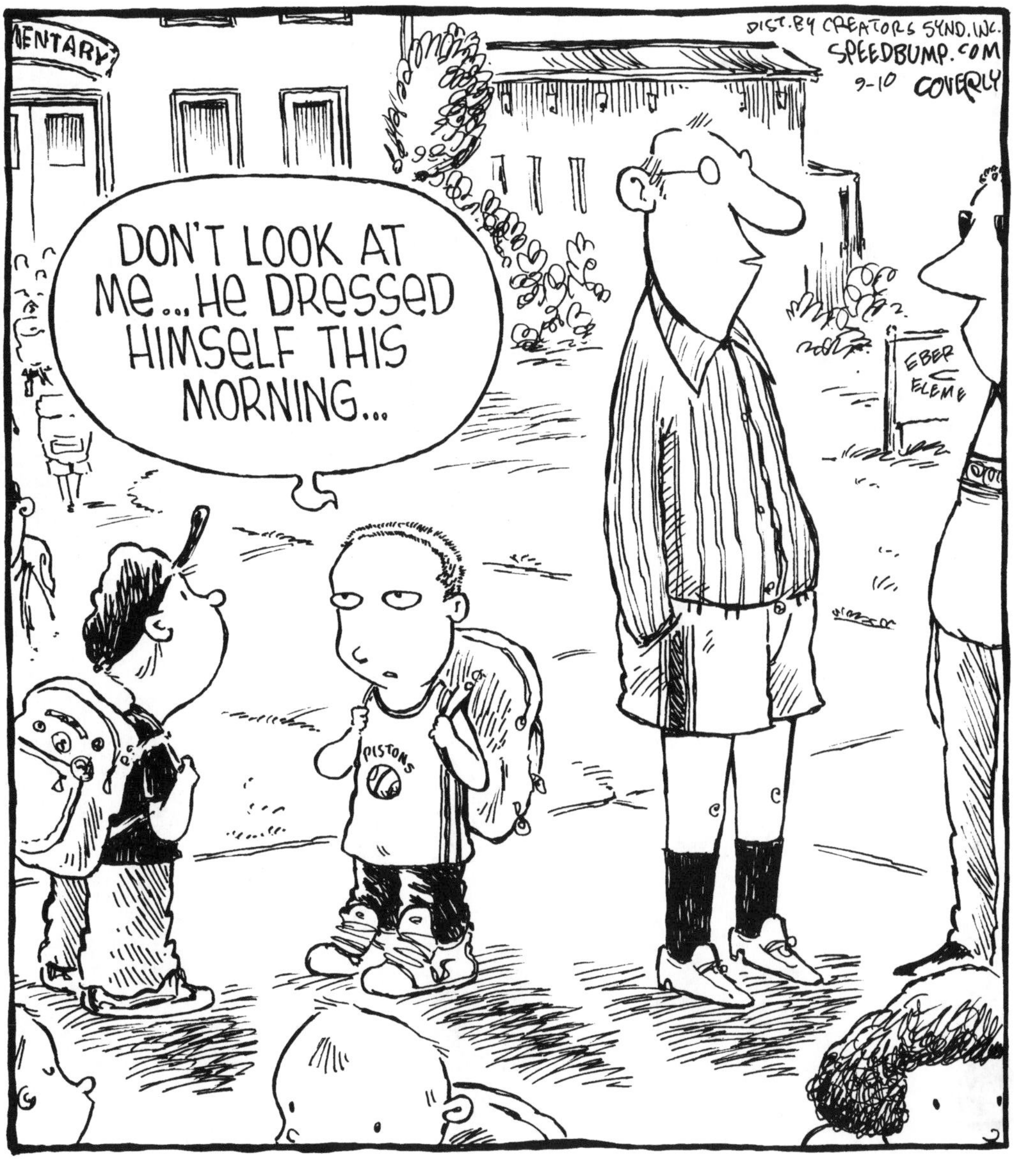
DIST. BY CREATORS SYND. INC.
SPEEDBUMP.COM
9-10 COVERLY
ENTARY
DON'T LOOK AT ME... HE DRESSED HIMSELF THIS MORNING...
PISTONS
EBER
ELEME

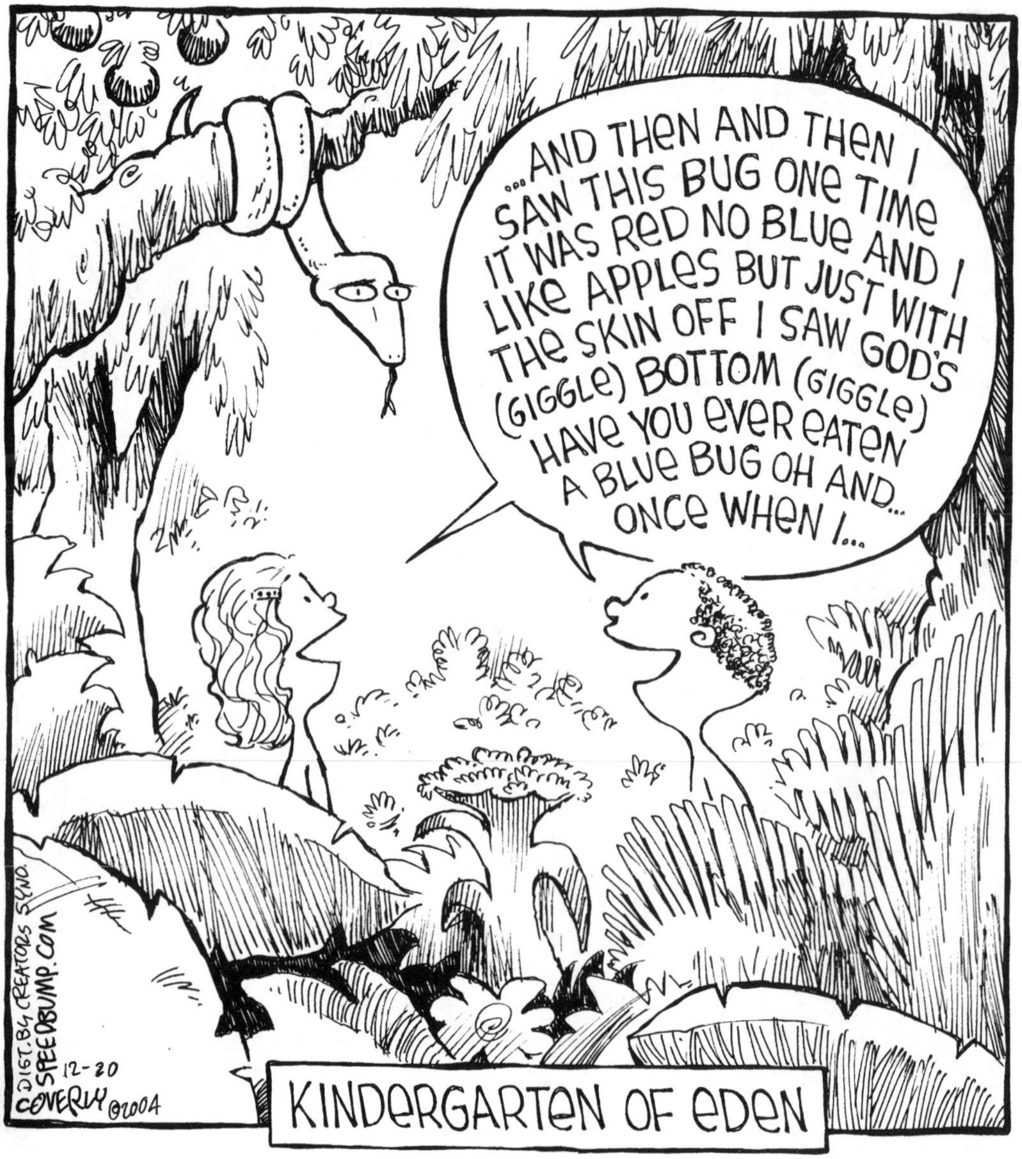
...AND THEN AND THEN I SAW THIS BUG ONE TIME IT WAS RED NO BLUE AND I LIKE APPLES BUT JUST WITH THE SKIN OFF I SAW GOD'S (GIGGLE) BOTTOM (GIGGLE) HAVE YOU EVER EATEN A BLUE BUG OH AND... ONCE WHEN I...
DIST. BY CREATORS SYND.
SPEEDBUMP.COM
12-20
COVERLY ©2004
KINDERGARTEN OF EDEN

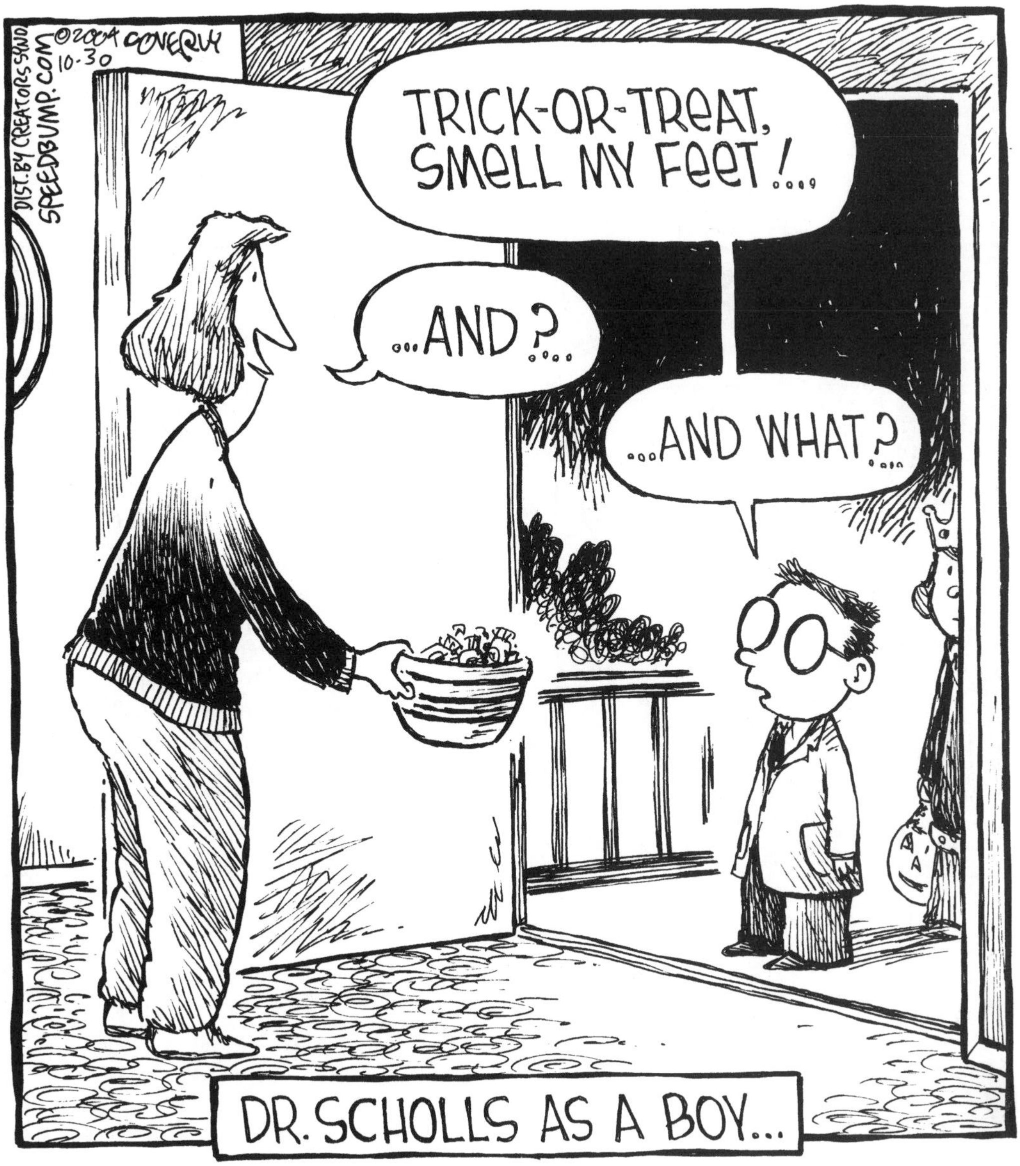
©2004 COVERLY
10-30
DIST. BY CREATORS SYND
SPEEDBUMP.COM
TRICK-OR-TREAT, SMELL MY FEET!...
...AND?...
...AND WHAT?...
DR. SCHOLLS AS A BOY...

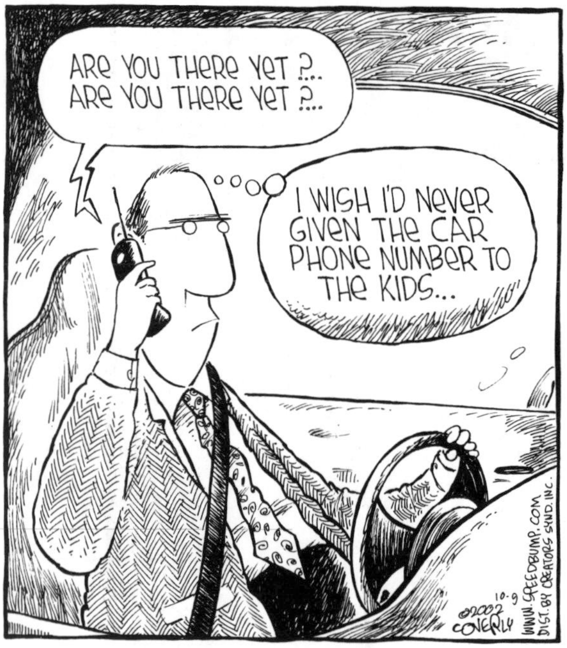
ARE YOU THERE YET ?...
ARE YOU THERE YET ?...
I WISH I'D NEVER GIVEN THE CAR PHONE NUMBER TO THE KIDS...
10-9 ©2002 COVERLY
WWW.SPEEDBUMP.COM
DIST. BY CREATORS SYND. INC.
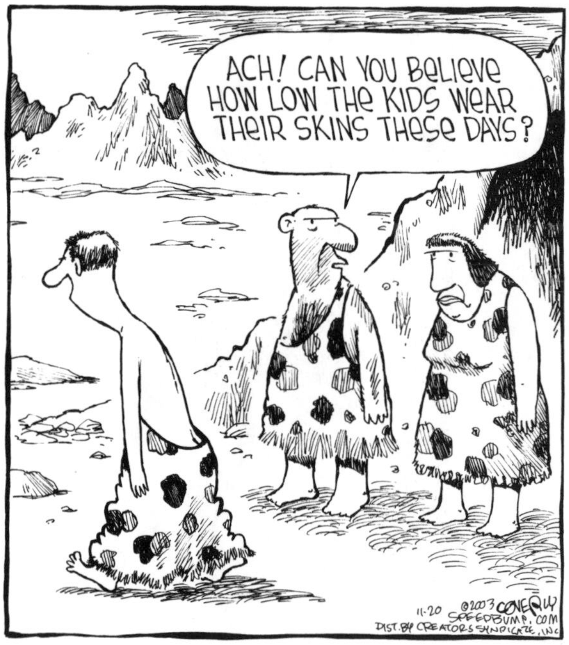
ACH! CAN YOU BELIEVE HOW LOW THE KIDS WEAR THEIR SKINS THESE DAYS?
11-20 ©2003 COVERLY
SPEEDBUMP.COM
DIST. BY CREATORS SYNDICATE, INC

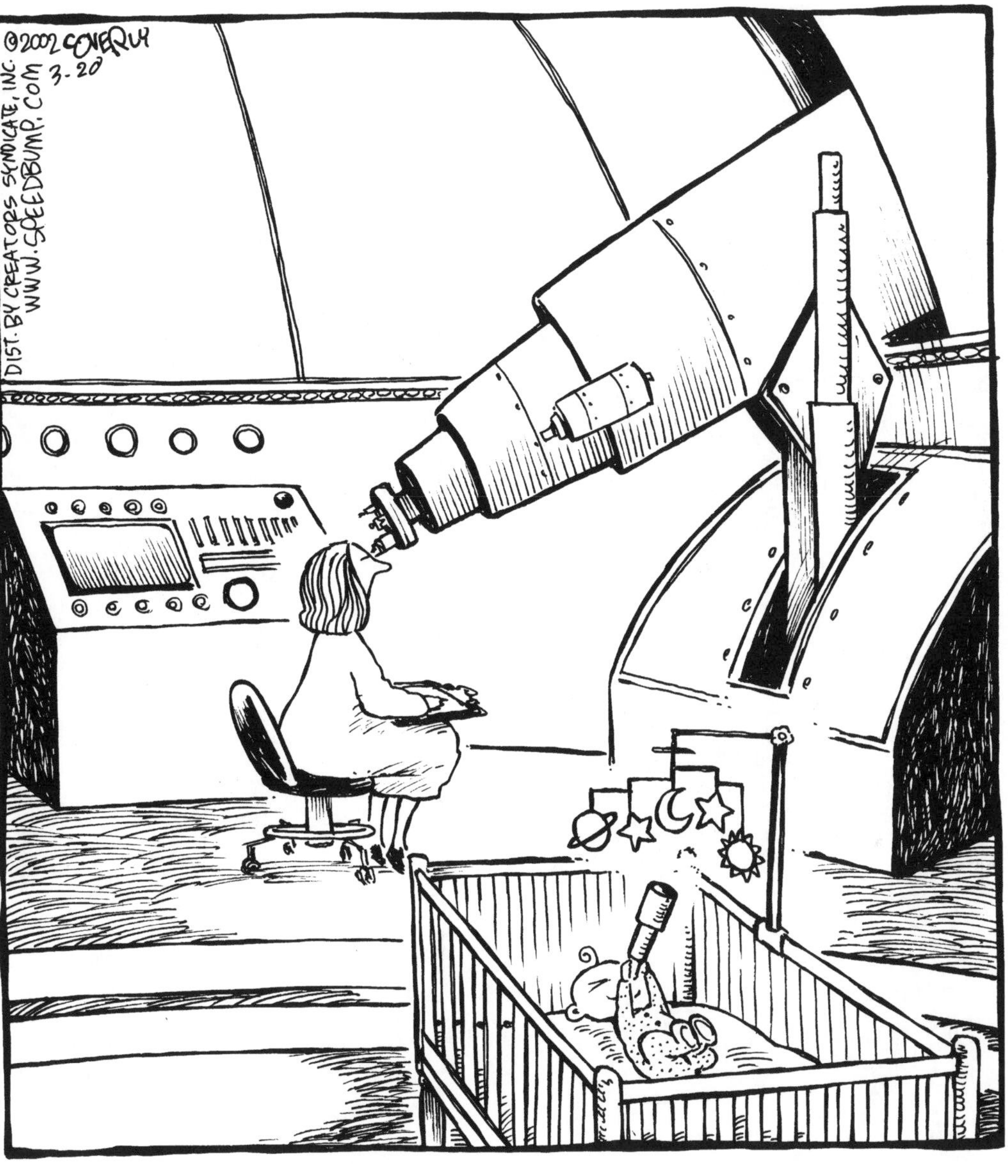
©2002 COVERLY
3-20
DIST. BY CREATORS SYNDICATE, INC.
WWW.SPEEDBUMP.COM

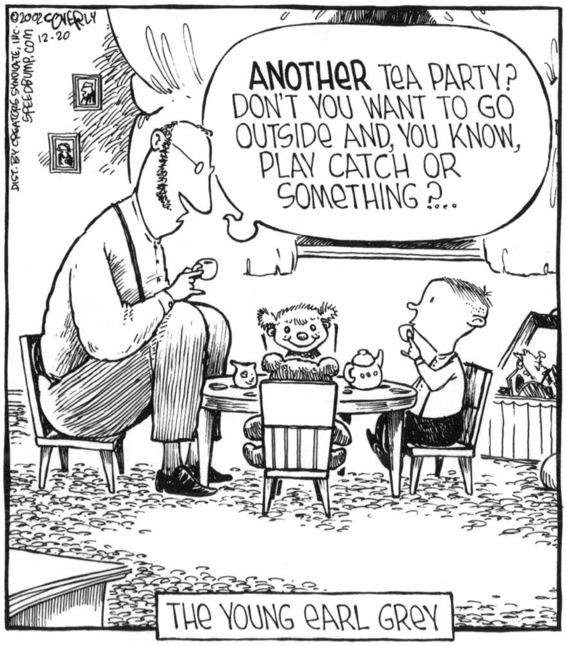
©2002 COVERLY 12-20
DIST. BY CREATORS SYNDICATE, INC. SPEEDBUMP.COM
ANOTHER TEA PARTY? DON'T YOU WANT TO GO OUTSIDE AND, YOU KNOW, PLAY CATCH OR SOMETHING ?...
THE YOUNG EARL GREY

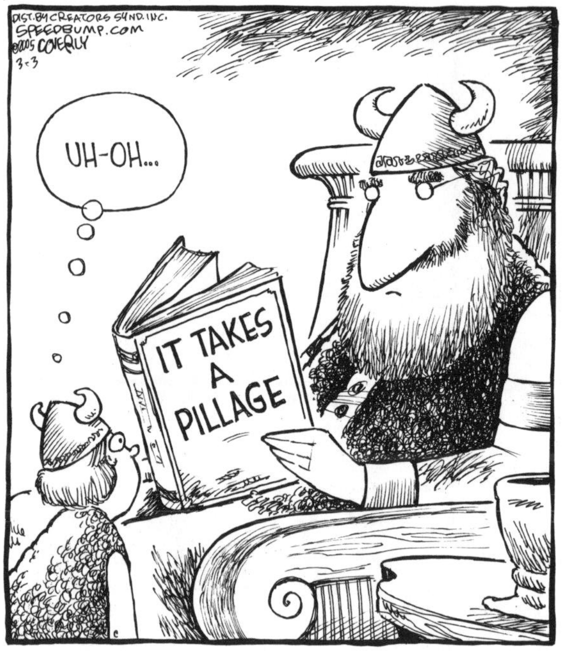
DIST. BY CREATORS SYND. INC.
SPEEDBUMP.COM
©2005 COVERLY
3-3
UH-OH...
IT TAKES A PILLAGE

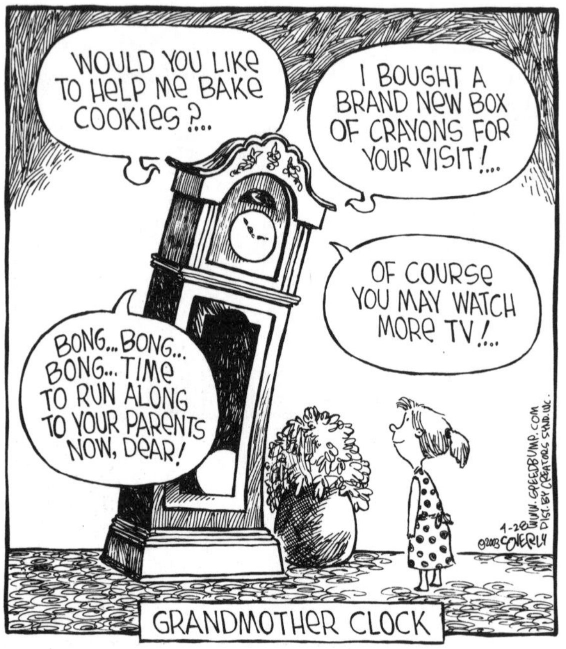
WOULD YOU LIKE TO HELP ME BAKE COOKIES ?...
I BOUGHT A BRAND NEW BOX OF CRAYONS FOR YOUR VISIT!...
OF COURSE YOU MAY WATCH MORE TV!...
BONG... BONG... BONG... TIME TO RUN ALONG TO YOUR PARENTS NOW, DEAR!
WWW.SPEEDBUMP.COM
DIST. BY CREATORS SYND. INC.
4-28
©2003 COVERLY
GRANDMOTHER CLOCK

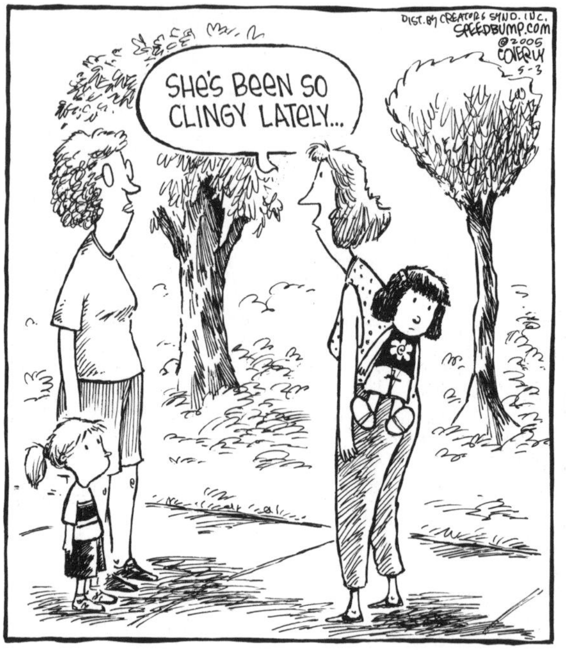
DIST. BY CREATORS SYND. INC.
SPEEDBUMP.COM
©2005
COVERLY
5-3
SHE'S BEEN SO CLINGY LATELY...

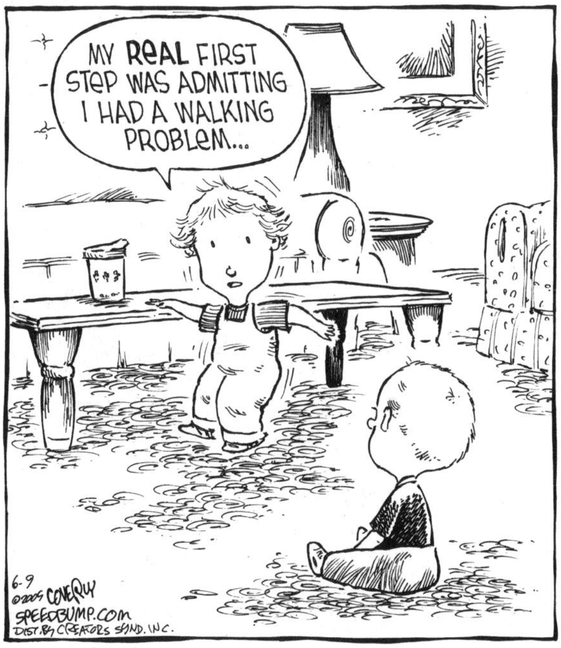
MY REAL FIRST STEP WAS ADMITTING I HAD A WALKING PROBLEM...
6-9 ©2005 COVERLY
SPEEDBUMP.COM
DIST. BY CREATORS SYND. INC.

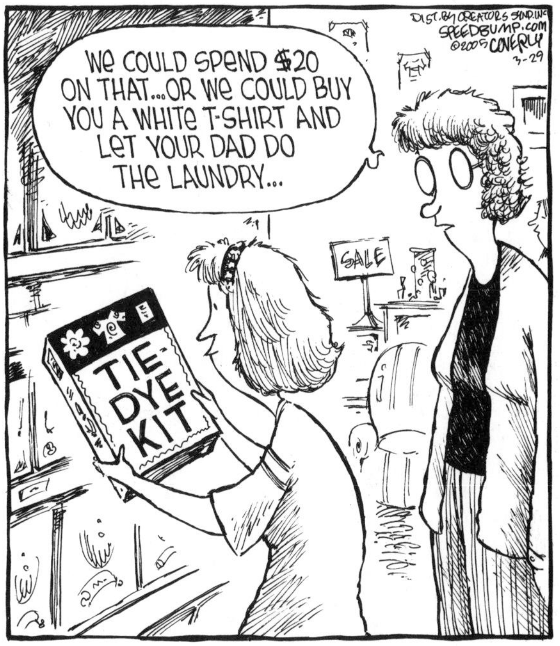
DIST. BY CREATORS SYND. INC.
SPEEDBUMP.COM
©2005 COVERLY
3-29
WE COULD SPEND $20 ON THAT...OR WE COULD BUY YOU A WHITE T-SHIRT AND LET YOUR DAD DO THE LAUNDRY...
SALE
TIE DYE KIT

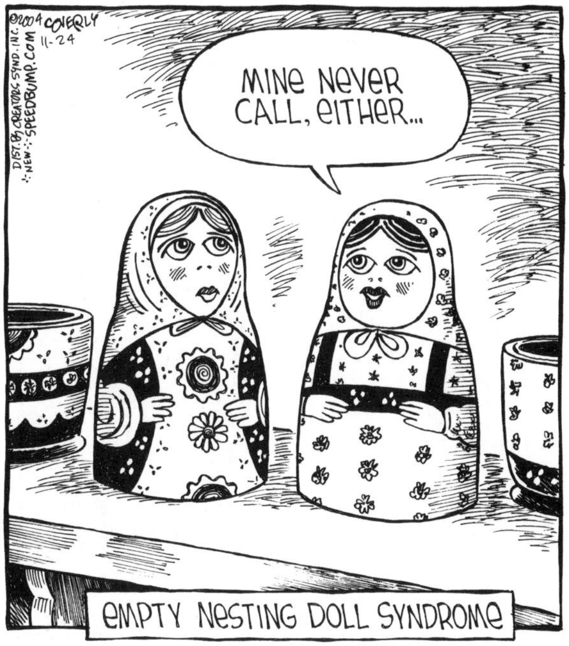
©2004 COVERLY
11-24
DIST. BY CREATORS SYND. INC.
NEW SPEEDBUMP.COM
MINE NEVER CALL, EITHER...
EMPTY NESTING DOLL SYNDROME

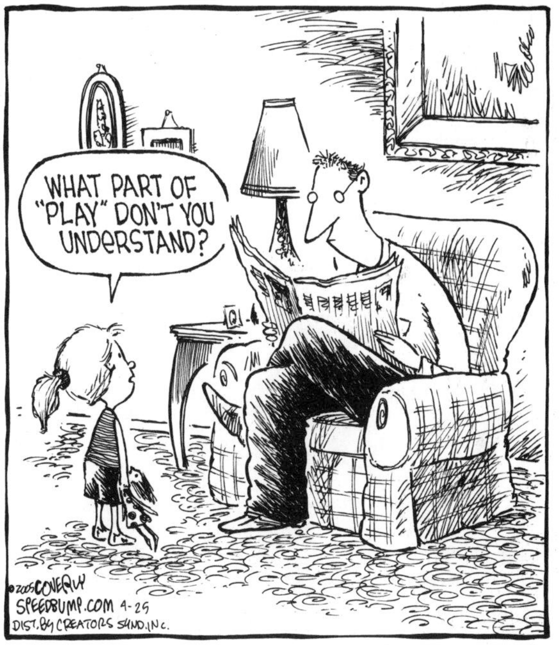
WHAT PART OF "PLAY" DON'T YOU UNDERSTAND?
©2005 COVERLY
SPEEDBUMP.COM 4-25
DIST. BY CREATORS SYND. INC.

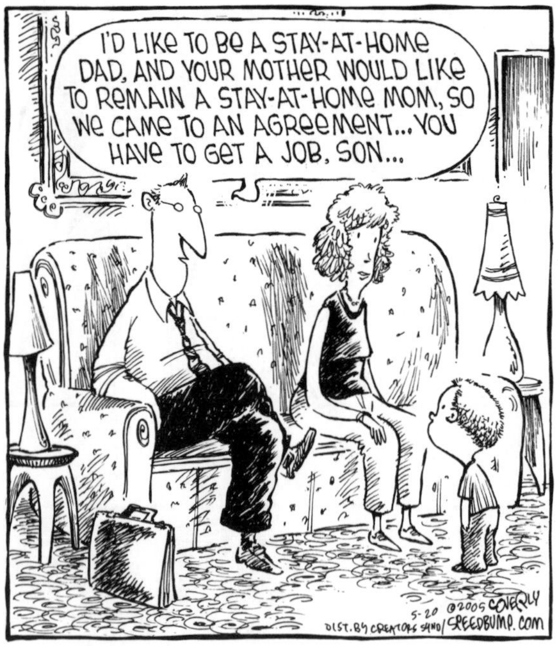
I'D LIKE TO BE A STAY-AT-HOME DAD, AND YOUR MOTHER WOULD LIKE TO REMAIN A STAY-AT-HOME MOM, SO WE CAME TO AN AGREEMENT... YOU HAVE TO GET A JOB, SON...
5-20 ©2005 COVERLY
DIST. BY CREATORS SYND/ SPEEDBUMP.COM

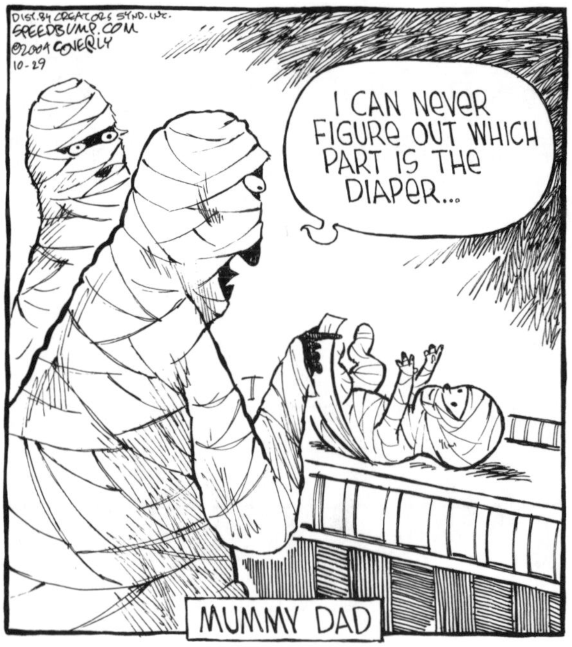
DIST. BY CREATORS SYND. INC.
SPEEDBUMP.COM
©2004 COVERLY
10-29
I CAN NEVER FIGURE OUT WHICH PART IS THE DIAPER...
MUMMY DAD

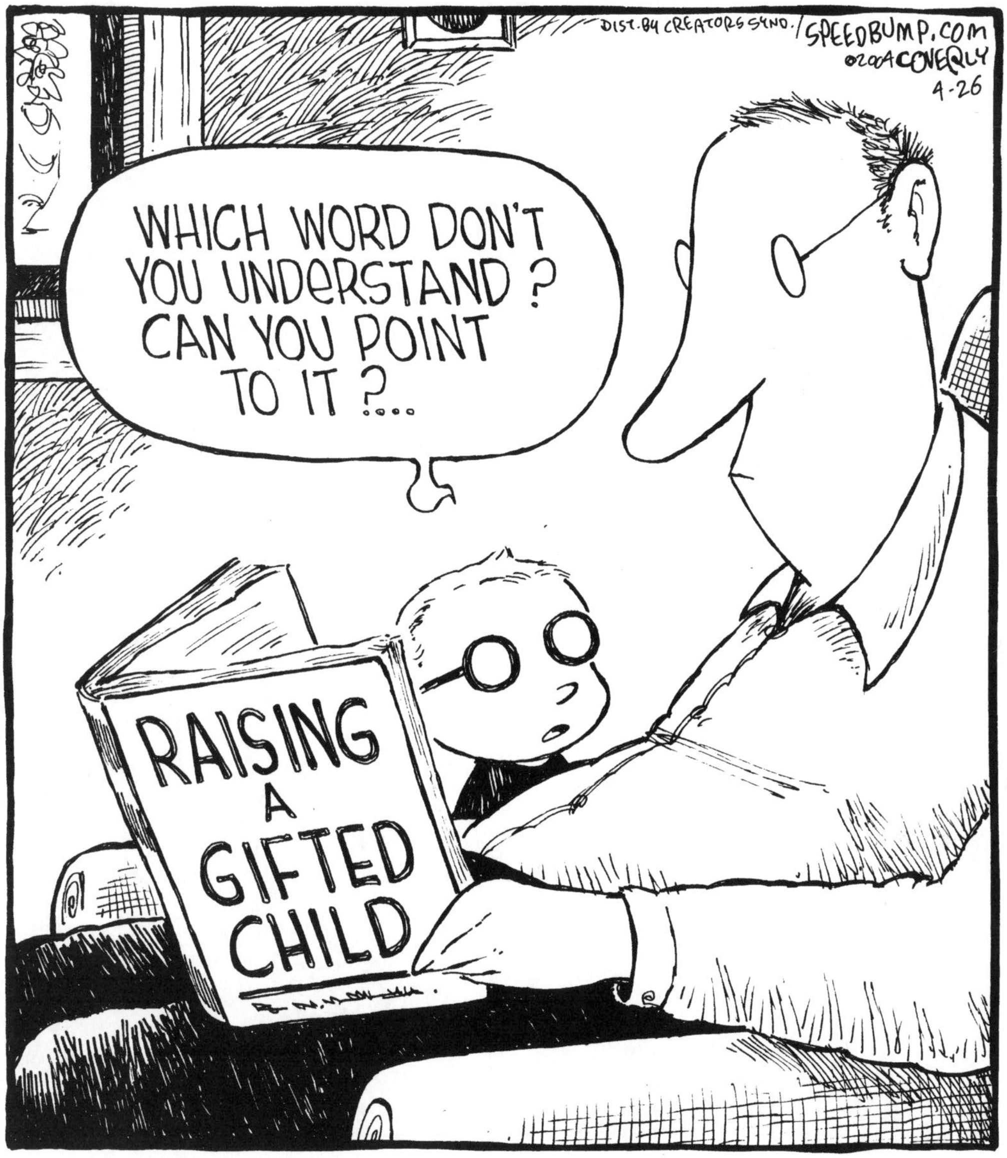
DIST. BY CREATORS SYND. / SPEEDBUMP.COM
©2004 COVERLY
4-26
WHICH WORD DON'T YOU UNDERSTAND? CAN YOU POINT TO IT?...
RAISING A GIFTED CHILD

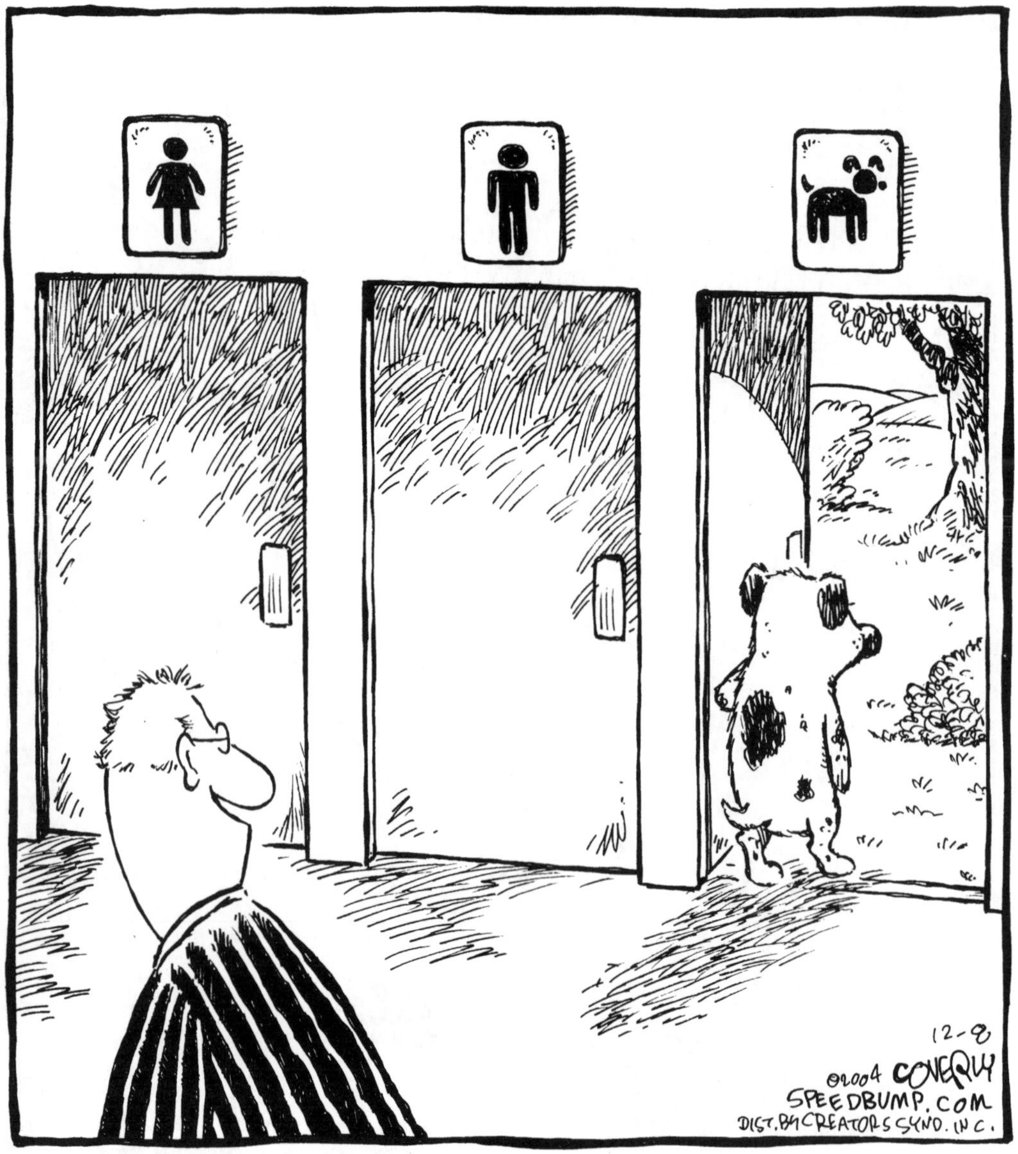
12-8
©2004 COVERLY
SPEEDBUMP.COM
DIST.BY CREATORS SYND. INC.

Beasts

Probably everyone who's ever had a pet has watched it in a moment of rest and wondered, "What is she thinking about right now?" Or, "If he could talk, what would he say to me?"

We all know that, chances are, the answer to both of these questions would likely be "Food" or "Play" or "STOP STARING AT ME!" But it's not much of a leap to impose all our quirks and neuroses on them and to imagine what else they could be thinking. I've done this since I was a kid, not just with pets but with all animals — conversations were imagined between ants on the sidewalk, birds at the feeder, or the bluegills in our lake. I attribute this condition to the fact that I've had three dogs in my life, and all of them have been goofballs with high doses of personality.

We got Shag when I was eight. My grandfather rescued him from the streets of Detroit, and he was small, blonde, and wild — the dog, that is, not my grandfather. Our convertible had punctures in the roof from his nails, because he slept on top of the car in the garage. We tried to keep him inside, but he was untrainable. Anything that looked or smelled like wood said to him, "urinal." And he was fast. When he would run in circles in our backyard, he would gather so much speed that his front legs would achieve a sort of lift-off, and then (and I'm not kidding) he would end up running on just his back legs.

We got a second dog, Tigger, a couple of years later. He was Shag's son, as Shag was a bit of a ladies man in the neighborhood. Then again, Tigger was the only blonde-spotted puppy in a litter of black-spotted puppies, so rumors were rife that the mom, Queenie, also got around a little bit. When Tigger was a puppy, I dropped him on his head, a fact that I was forever reminded of by my sister, since Tigger turned out to be good-natured but a bit of a dim bulb. He would do things you rarely see animals do, like trip or walk headfirst into a wall. If he'd been human, he'd have been the kid everyone liked but always got picked last for the playground baseball game.

Now we have Kenzi, who looks like a small border collie cut off at the knees. When we saw her at the dog shelter, we liked her immediately for her happy aura and the fact that she was so easygoing, you could actually carry her over your shoulder like a sack of flour. Once she moved in, though, she became territorial and surprised us with a hidden talent of yapping so loudly it causes the elderly to reach for heart medication. I've seen hearing aids smoke and spark when she barks. She's spent countless dog-hours in the backyard, barking at sights that humans cannot see, or yapping at objects that have yet to prove they're inanimate, like plastic bags floating in the wind or pine cones minding their own business on the sidewalk.

So these next cartoons were created under the influence of a lifetime spent with nutty dogs. Somewhere, somehow, I'm sure they're saying the same thing about me.

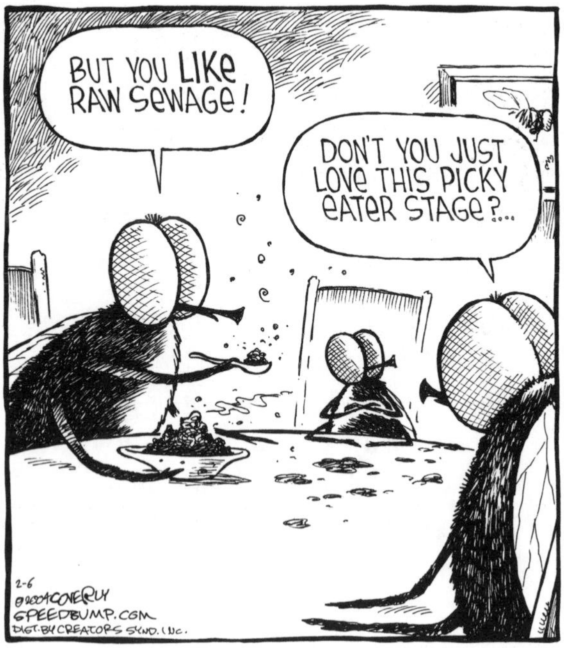
BUT YOU LIKE RAW SEWAGE!
DON'T YOU JUST LOVE THIS PICKY EATER STAGE?...
2-6 ©2004 COVERLY SPEEDBUMP.COM DIST. BY CREATORS SYND. INC.

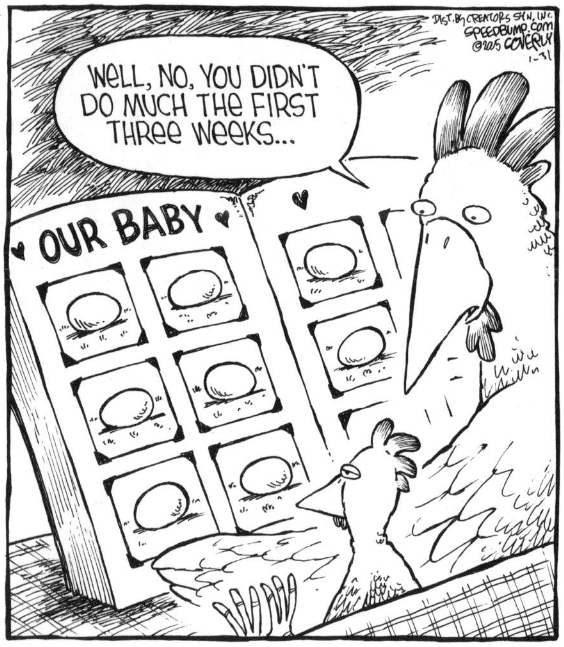
DIST. BY CREATORS SYN. INC. SPEEDBUMP.com ©2005 COVERLY 1-31
WELL, NO, YOU DIDN'T DO MUCH THE FIRST THREE WEEKS...
OUR BABY

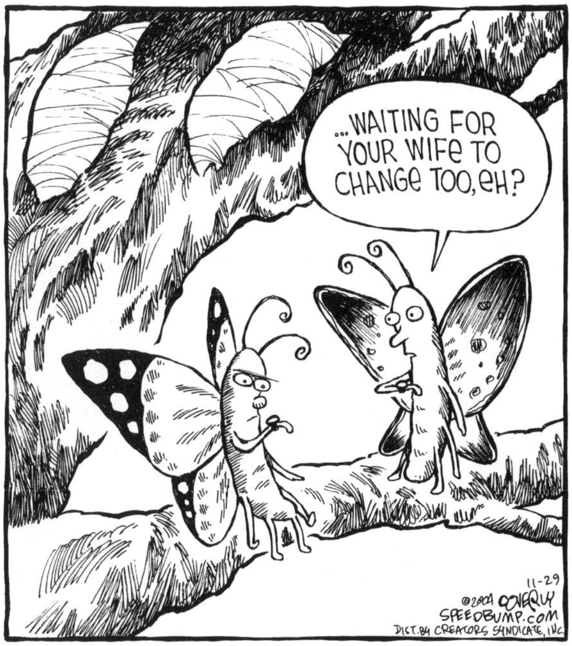
...WAITING FOR YOUR WIFE TO CHANGE TOO, EH?
11-29
©2004 COVERLY
SPEEDBUMP.COM
DIST. BY CREATORS SYNDICATE, INC.

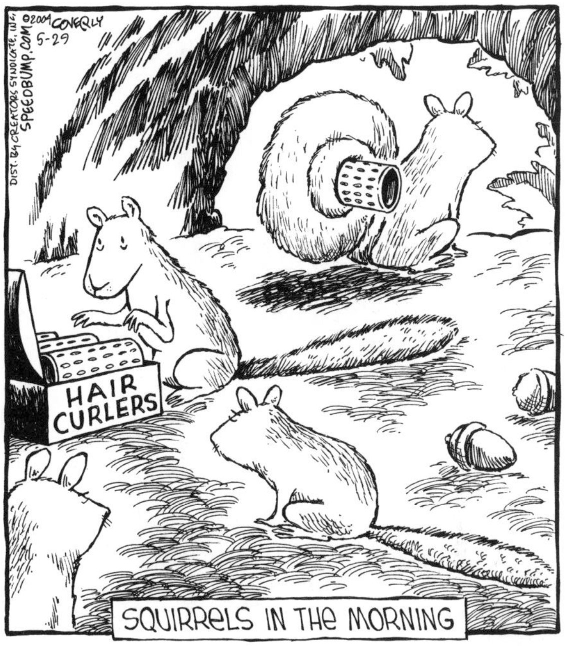
DIST. BY CREATORS SYNDICATE, INC.
SPEEDBUMP.COM
©2004 COVERLY
5-29
HAIR CURLERS
SQUIRRELS IN THE MORNING

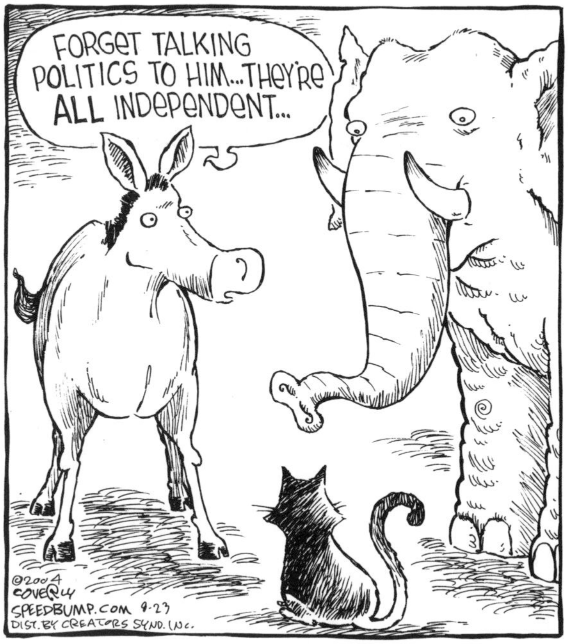
FORGET TALKING POLITICS TO HIM...THEY'RE ALL INDEPENDENT...
©2004
COVERLY
SPEEDBUMP.COM 8-23
DIST. BY CREATORS SYND. INC.

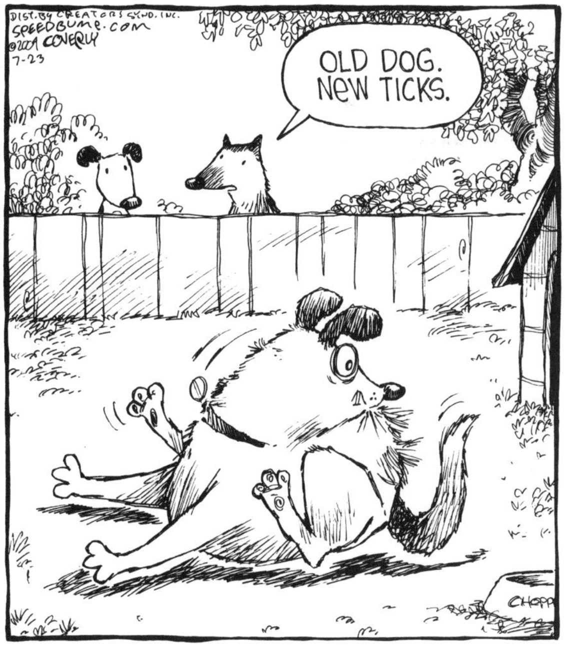
DIST. BY CREATORS SYND. INC.
SPEEDBUMP.COM
©2004 COVERLY
7-23
OLD DOG. NEW TICKS.

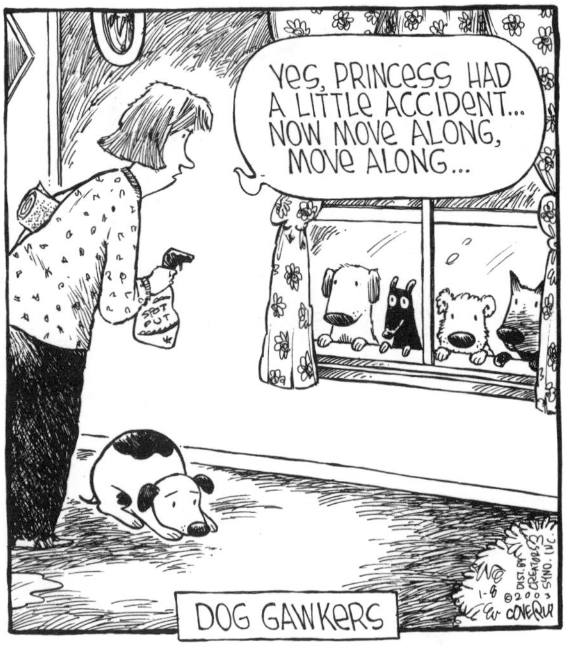
YES, PRINCESS HAD A LITTLE ACCIDENT... NOW MOVE ALONG, MOVE ALONG...
DOG GAWKERS

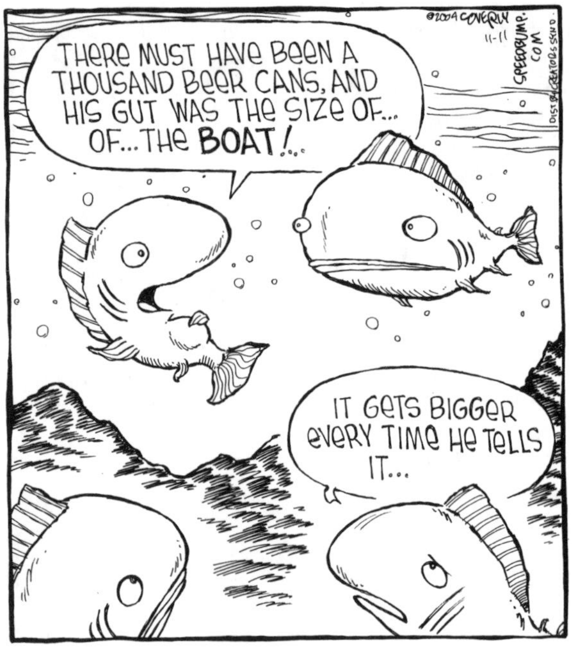
THERE MUST HAVE BEEN A THOUSAND BEER CANS, AND HIS GUT WAS THE SIZE OF... OF... THE **BOAT**!..
IT GETS BIGGER EVERY TIME HE TELLS IT...

I THINK BRUCE IS STARTING TO IDENTIFY WITH HIS CAPTORS...
4-2 ©2004 COVERLY
SPEEDBUMP.COM
DIST. BY CREATORS SYND. INC.

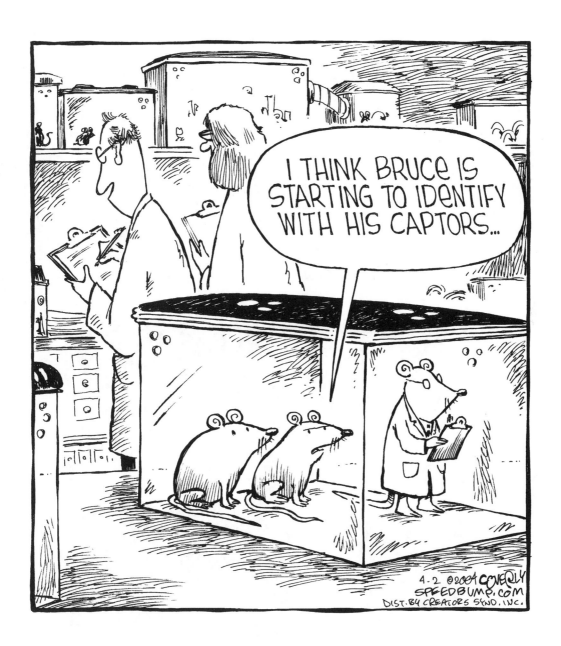

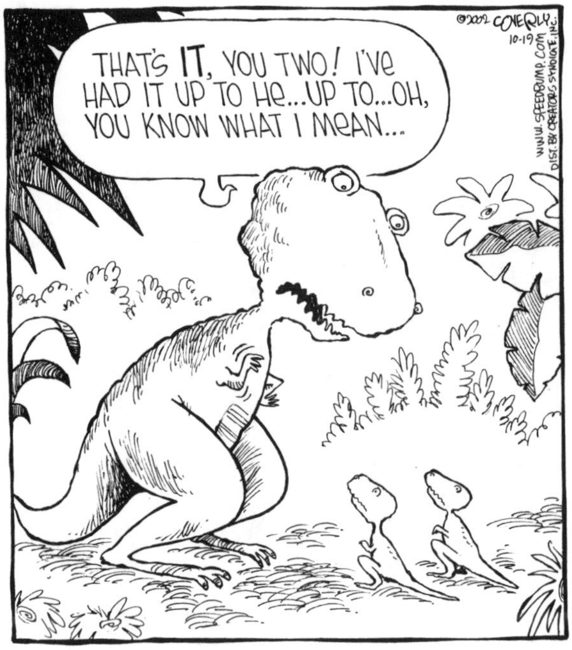
THAT'S IT, YOU TWO! I'VE HAD IT UP TO HE...UP TO...OH, YOU KNOW WHAT I MEAN...
©2002 COVERLY 10-19
WWW.SPEEDBUMP.COM
DIST. BY CREATORS SYNDICATE, INC.

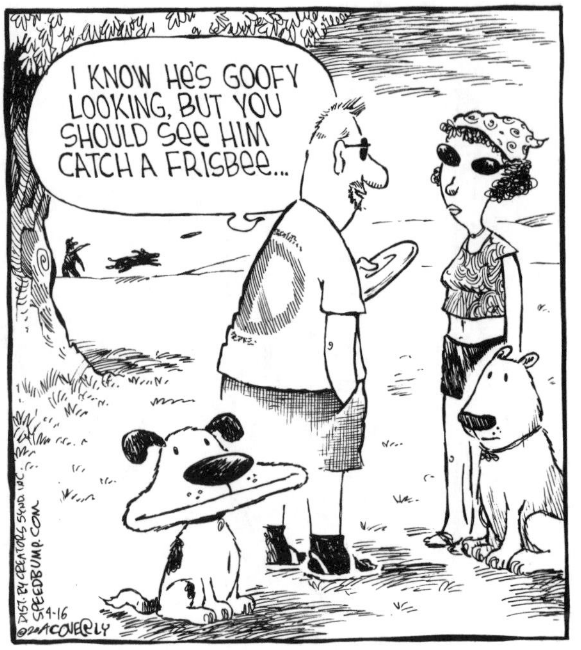
I KNOW HE'S GOOFY LOOKING, BUT YOU SHOULD SEE HIM CATCH A FRISBEE...
DIST. BY CREATORS SYND. INC.
SPEEDBUMP.COM
COVERLY

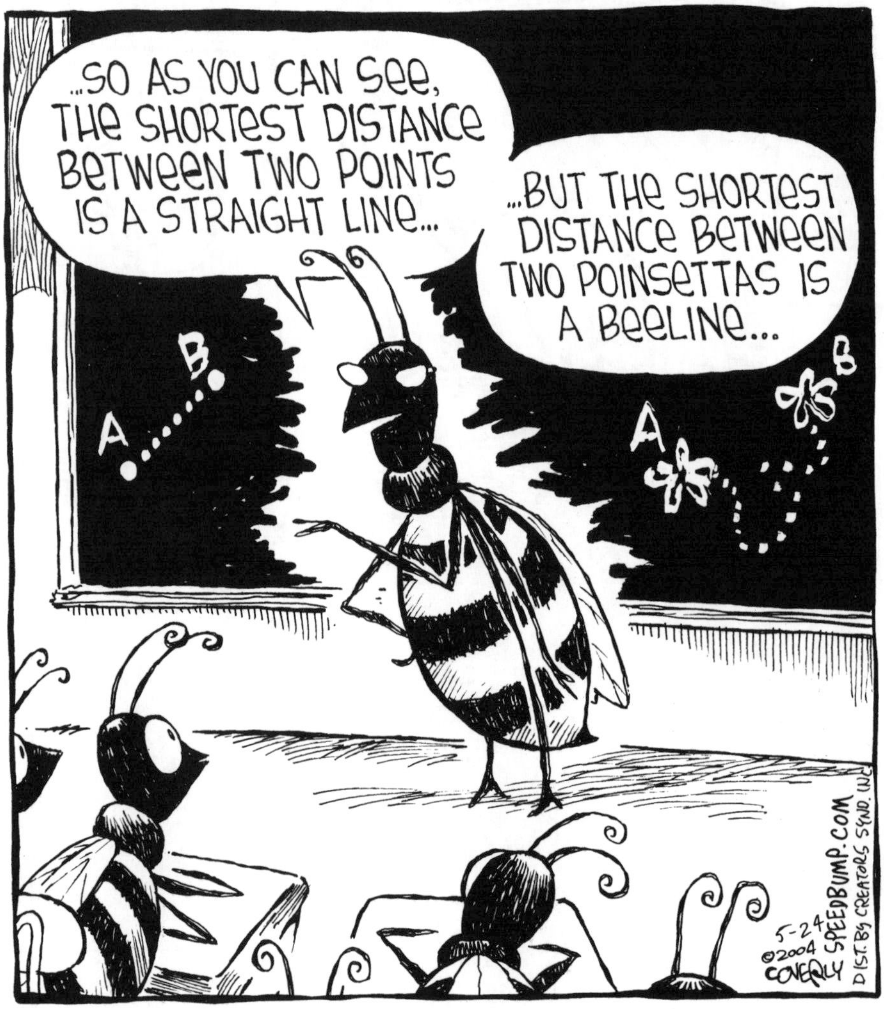
...SO AS YOU CAN SEE, THE SHORTEST DISTANCE BETWEEN TWO POINTS IS A STRAIGHT LINE...
...BUT THE SHORTEST DISTANCE BETWEEN TWO POINSETTAS IS A BEELINE...
A
B
A
B
5-24
©2004
COVERLY
SPEEDBUMP.COM
DIST. BY CREATORS SYND. INC.

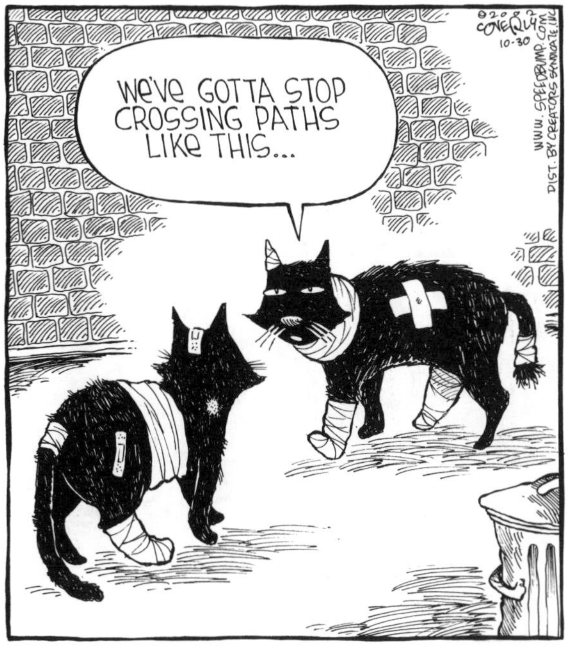
WE'VE GOTTA STOP CROSSING PATHS LIKE THIS...

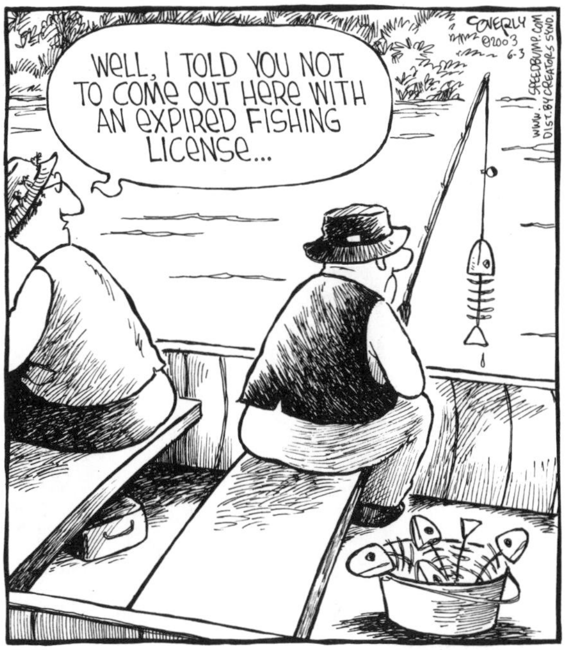
WELL, I TOLD YOU NOT TO COME OUT HERE WITH AN EXPIRED FISHING LICENSE...

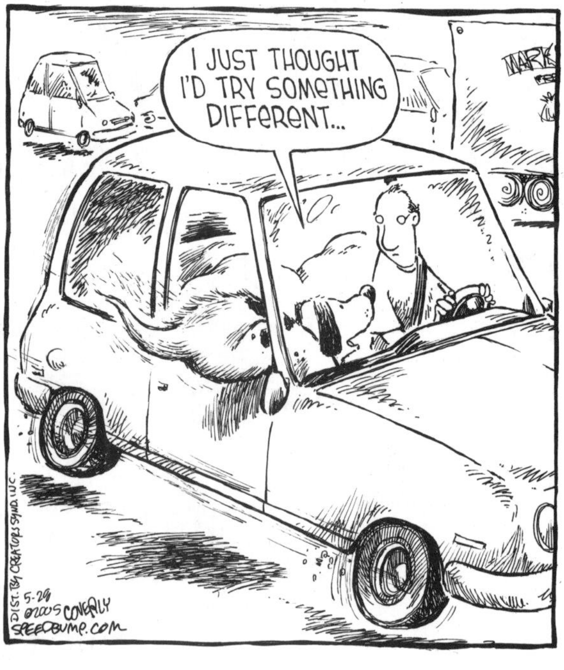
I JUST THOUGHT I'D TRY SOMETHING DIFFERENT...
DIST. BY CREATORS SYND. INC.
5-29
©2005 COVERLY
SPEEDBUMP.COM

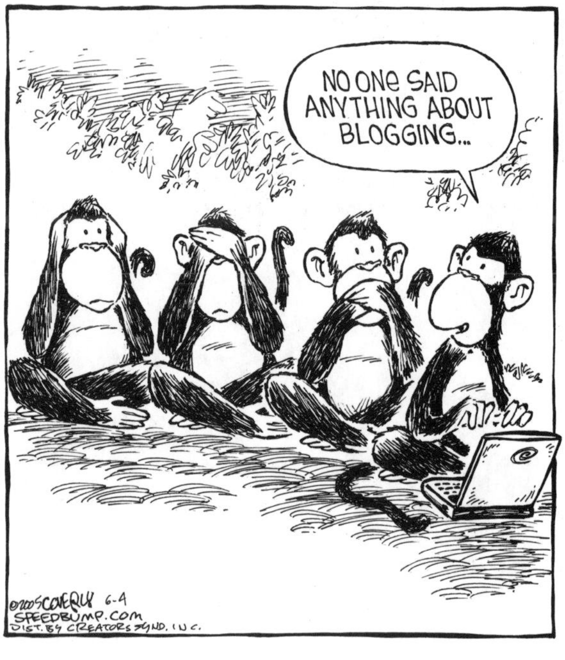
NO ONE SAID ANYTHING ABOUT BLOGGING...
©2005 COVERLY 6-4
SPEEDBUMP.COM
DIST. BY CREATORS SYND. INC.

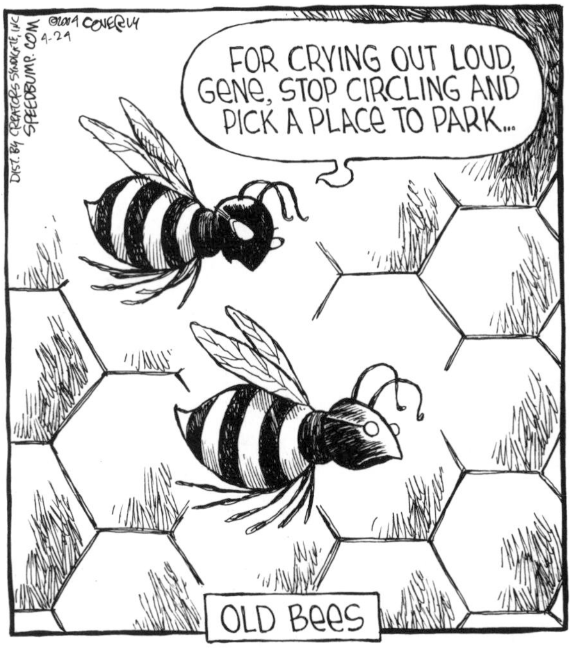
FOR CRYING OUT LOUD, GENE, STOP CIRCLING AND PICK A PLACE TO PARK...
OLD BEES

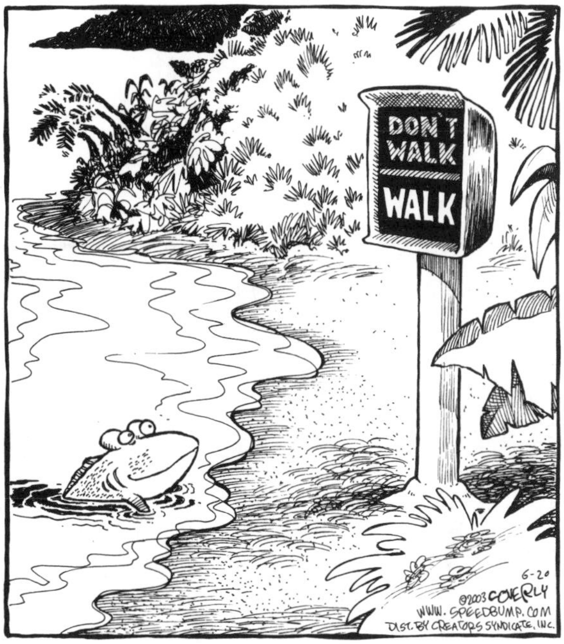
DON'T WALK
WALK

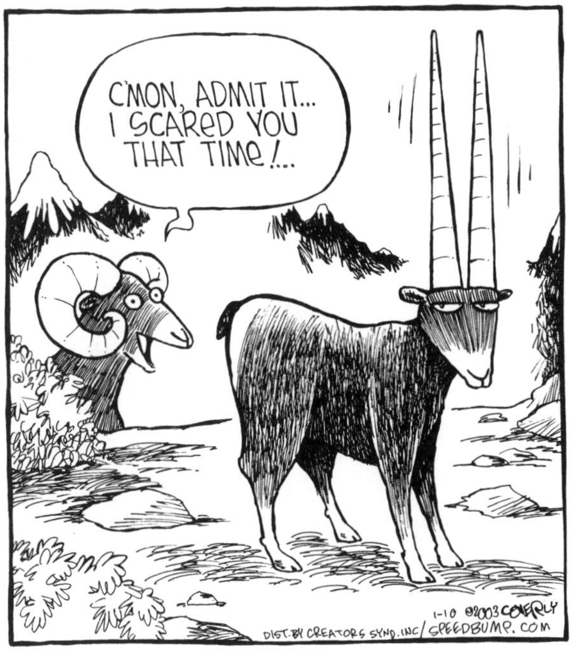
C'MON, ADMIT IT... I SCARED YOU THAT TIME!...

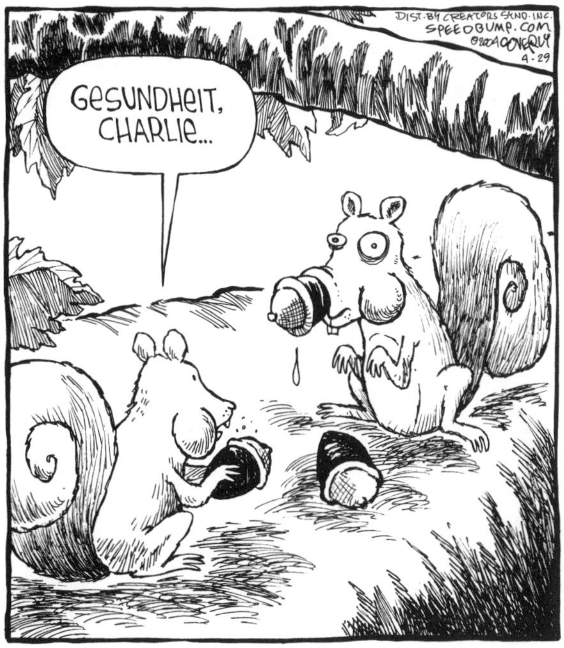
GESUNDHEIT, CHARLIE...

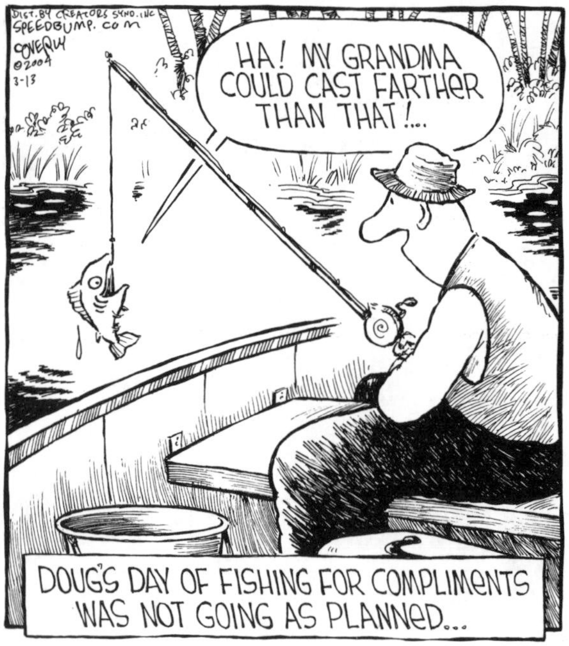
DIST. BY CREATORS SYND. INC
SPEEDBUMP.COM
COVERLY
©2004
3-13
HA! MY GRANDMA COULD CAST FARTHER THAN THAT!...
DOUG'S DAY OF FISHING FOR COMPLIMENTS WAS NOT GOING AS PLANNED...

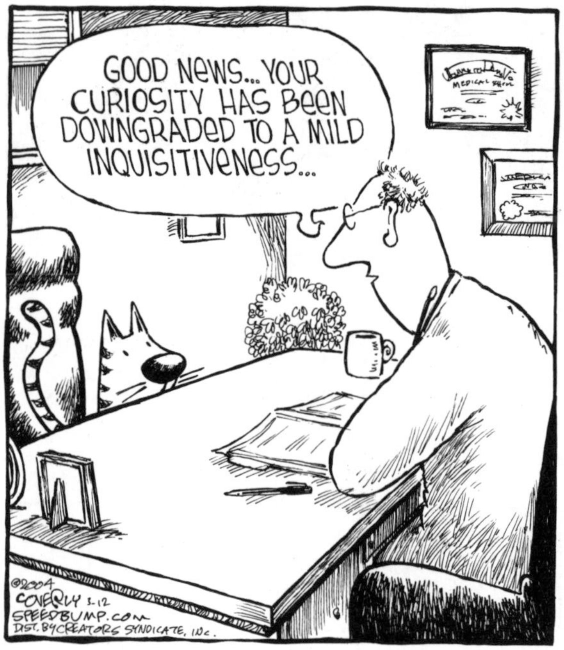
GOOD NEWS... YOUR CURIOSITY HAS BEEN DOWNGRADED TO A MILD INQUISITIVENESS...
©2004
COVERLY 3-12
SPEEDBUMP.COM
DIST. BY CREATORS SYNDICATE, INC.

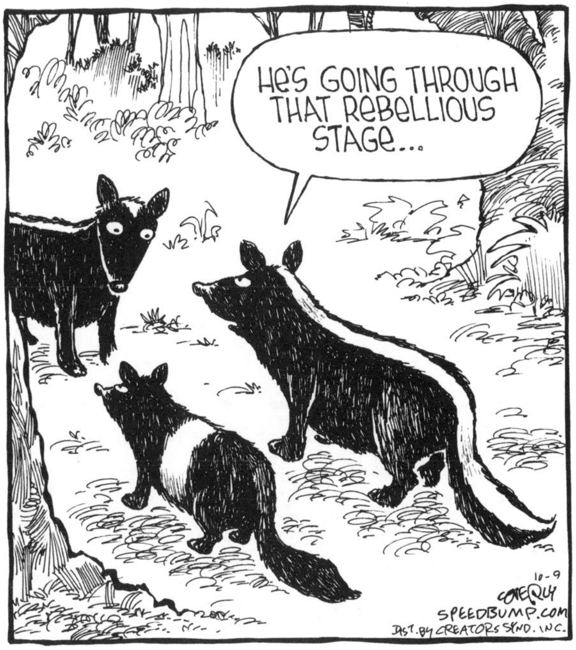
HE'S GOING THROUGH THAT REBELLIOUS STAGE...
10-9
COVERLY
SPEEDBUMP.COM
DIST. BY CREATORS SYND. INC.

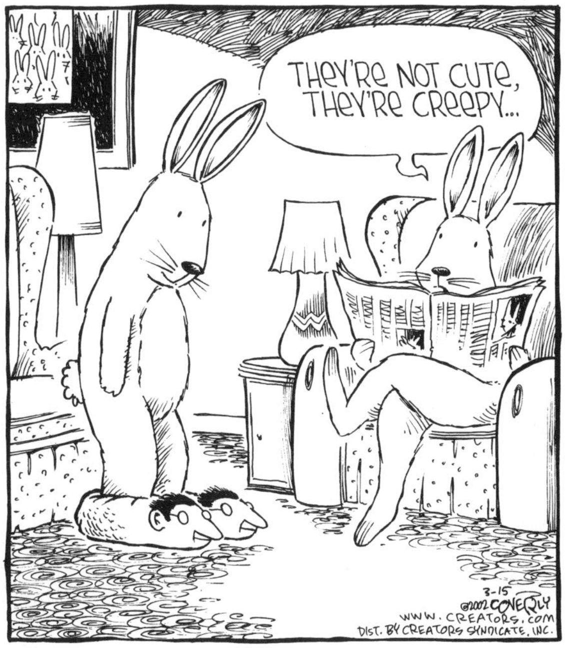
THEY'RE NOT CUTE, THEY'RE CREEPY...
3-15
©2002 COVERLY
WWW.CREATORS.COM
DIST. BY CREATORS SYNDICATE, INC.

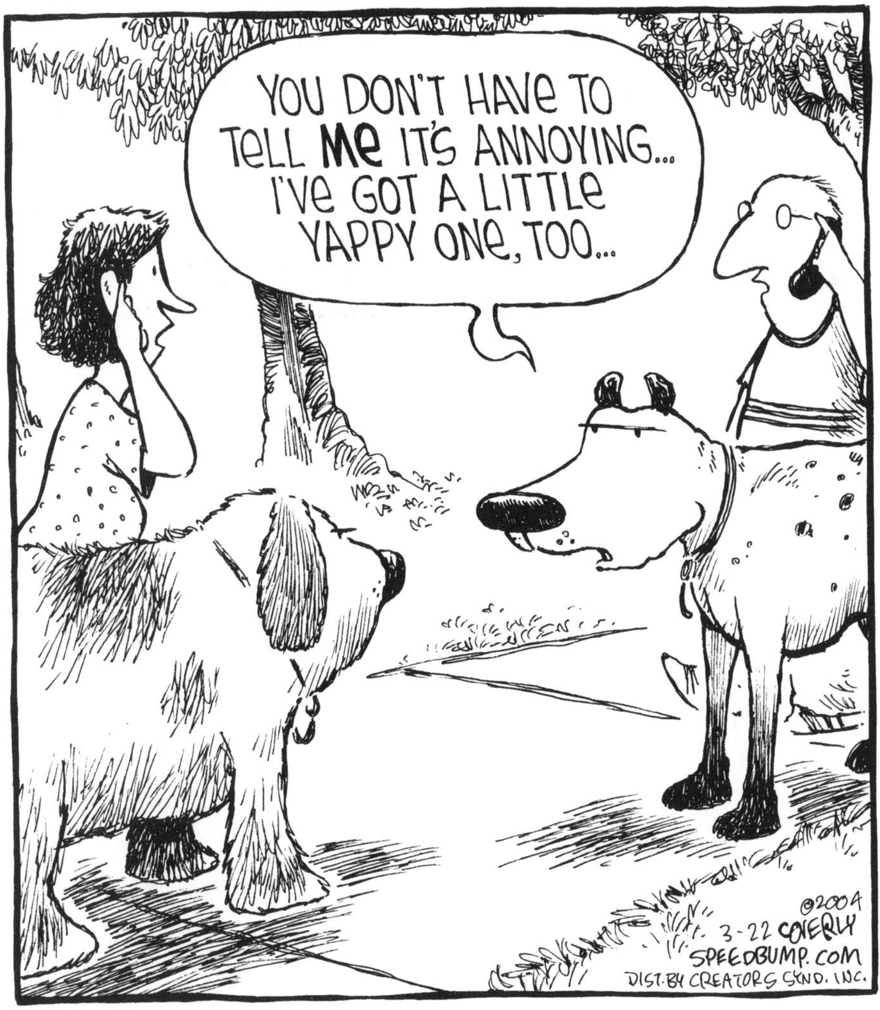
YOU DON'T HAVE TO TELL **ME** IT'S ANNOYING... I'VE GOT A LITTLE YAPPY ONE, TOO...
©2004
3-22 COVERLY
SPEEDBUMP.COM
DIST. BY CREATORS SYND. INC.

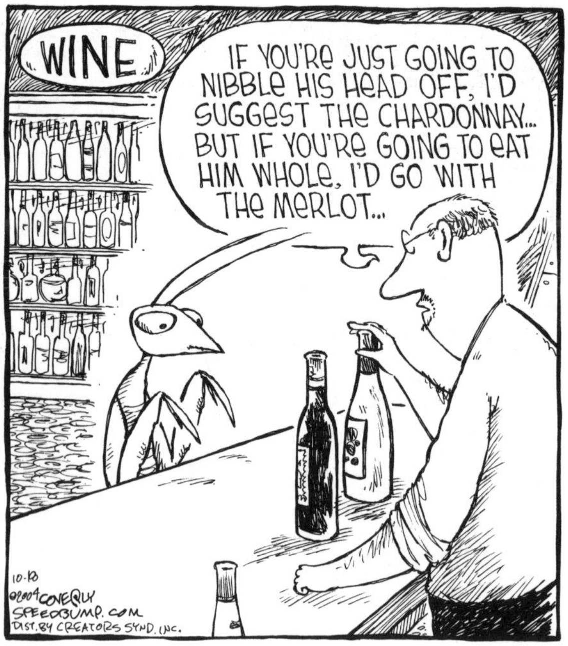
WINE
IF YOU'RE JUST GOING TO NIBBLE HIS HEAD OFF, I'D SUGGEST THE CHARDONNAY... BUT IF YOU'RE GOING TO EAT HIM WHOLE, I'D GO WITH THE MERLOT...
10-18
©2004 COVERLY
SPEEDBUMP.COM
DIST. BY CREATORS SYND. INC.

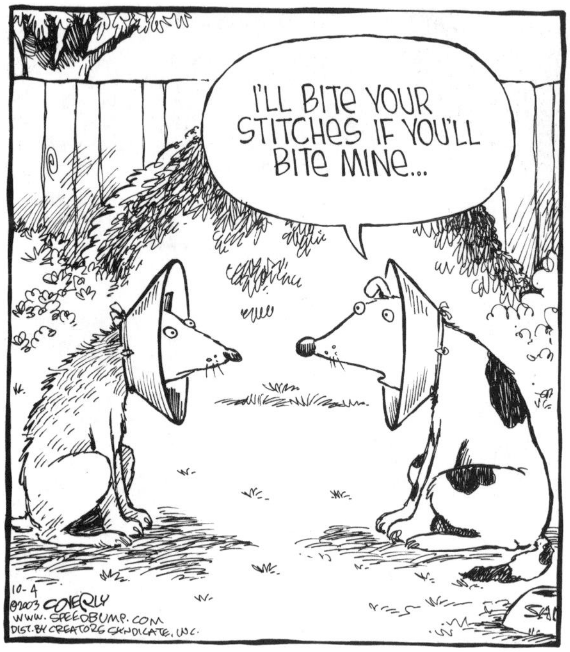
I'LL BITE YOUR STITCHES IF YOU'LL BITE MINE...
10-4
©2003 COVERLY
WWW.SPEEDBUMP.COM
DIST. BY CREATORS SYNDICATE, INC.

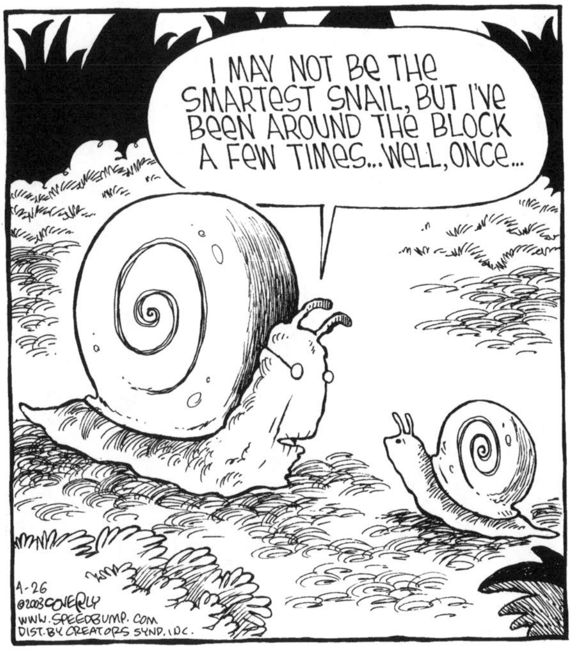
I MAY NOT BE THE SMARTEST SNAIL, BUT I'VE BEEN AROUND THE BLOCK A FEW TIMES...WELL, ONCE...
4-26 ©2003 COVERLY WWW.SPEEDBUMP.COM DIST. BY CREATORS SYND. INC.

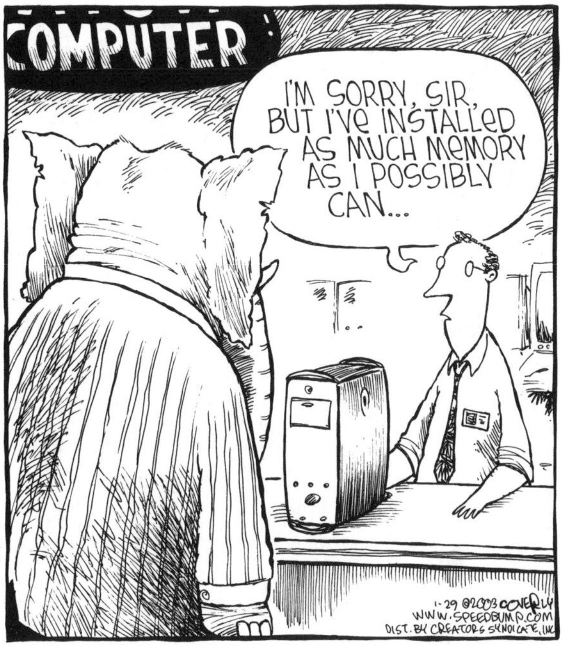
COMPUTER
I'M SORRY, SIR, BUT I'VE INSTALLED AS MUCH MEMORY AS I POSSIBLY CAN...
1-29 ©2003 COVERLY WWW.SPEEDBUMP.COM DIST. BY CREATORS SYNDICATE, INC

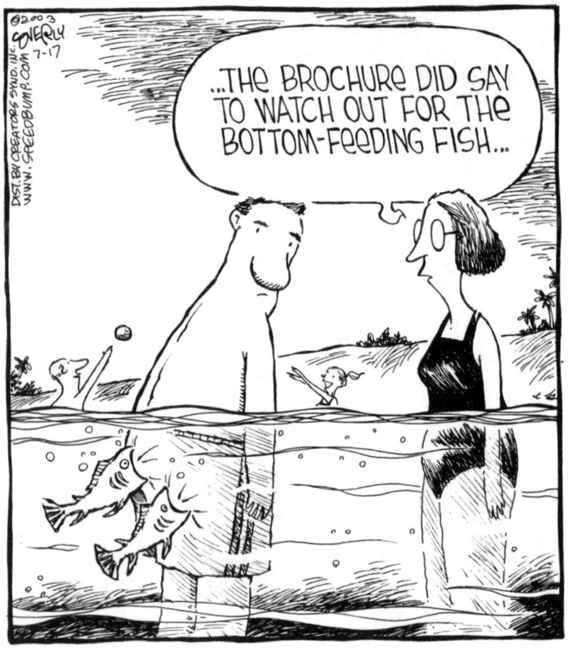
...THE BROCHURE DID SAY TO WATCH OUT FOR THE BOTTOM-FEEDING FISH...

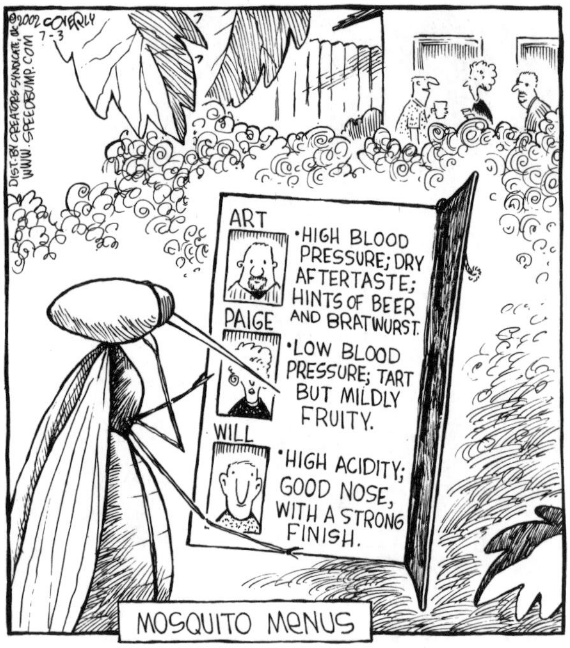
ART
•HIGH BLOOD PRESSURE; DRY AFTERTASTE; HINTS OF BEER AND BRATWURST.
PAIGE
•LOW BLOOD PRESSURE; TART BUT MILDLY FRUITY.
WILL
•HIGH ACIDITY; GOOD NOSE, WITH A STRONG FINISH.

MOSQUITO MENUS

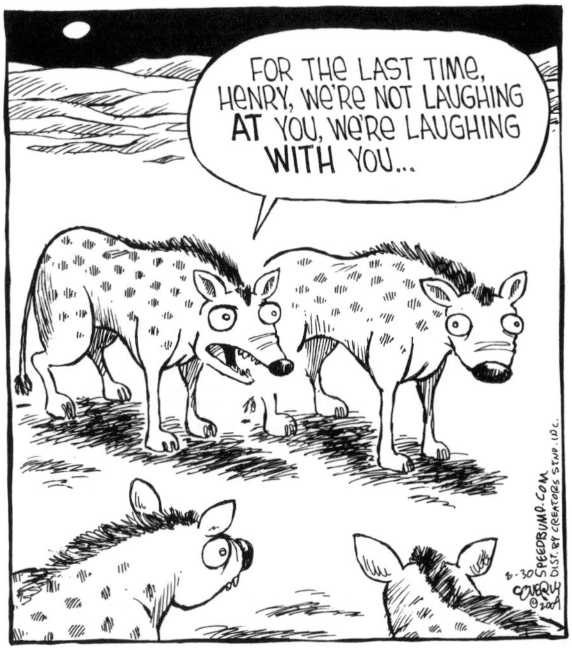
FOR THE LAST TIME, HENRY, WE'RE NOT LAUGHING **AT** YOU, WE'RE LAUGHING **WITH** YOU...

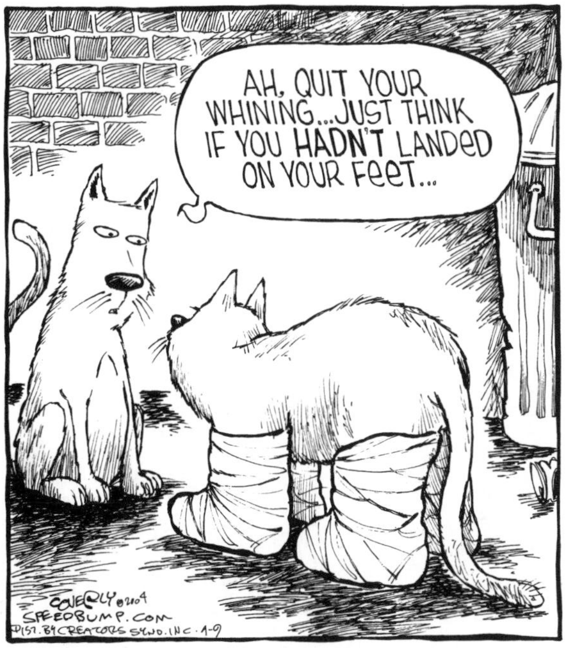
AH, QUIT YOUR WHINING...JUST THINK IF YOU **HADN'T** LANDED ON YOUR FEET...

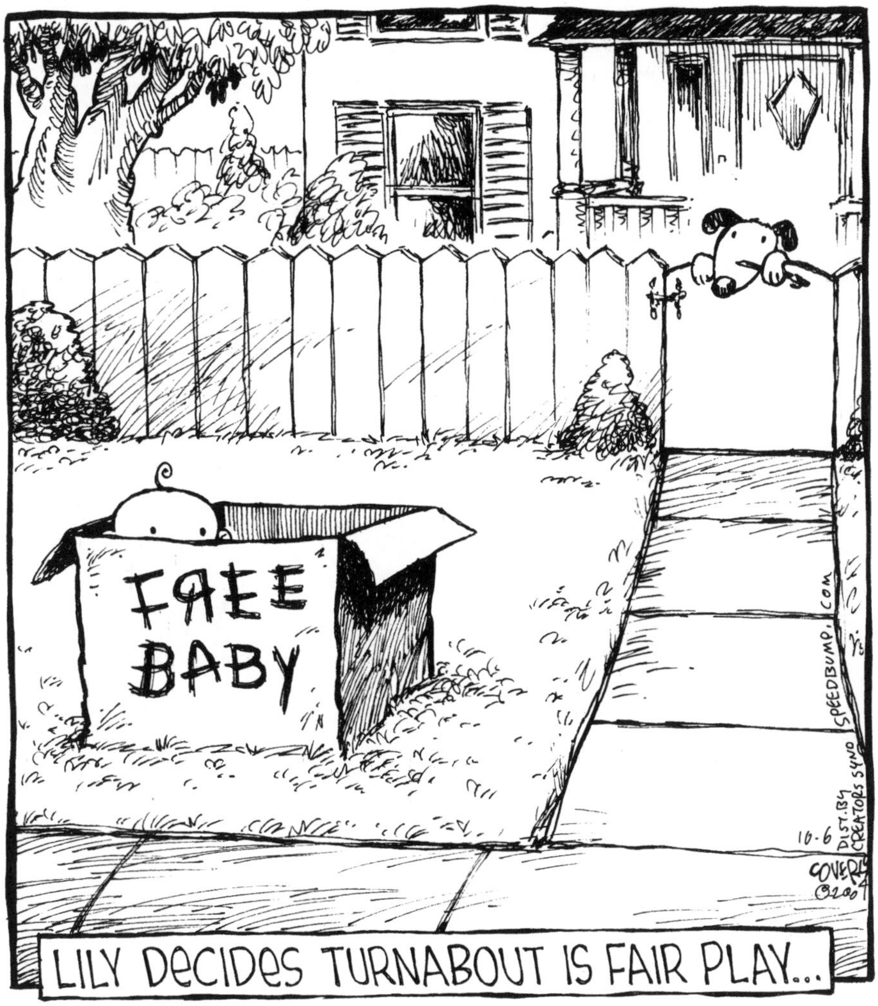
FREE BABY
LILY DECIDES TURNABOUT IS FAIR PLAY...

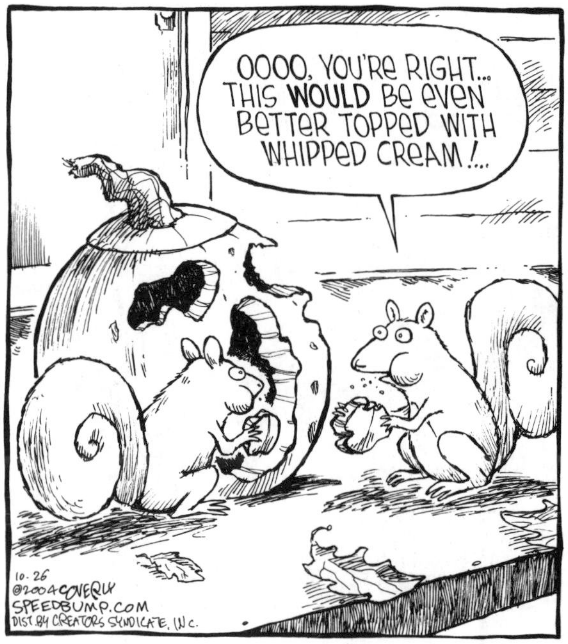
OOOO, YOU'RE RIGHT... THIS **WOULD** BE EVEN BETTER TOPPED WITH WHIPPED CREAM!...
10-26
©2004 COVERLY
SPEEDBUMP.COM
DIST. BY CREATORS SYNDICATE, INC.

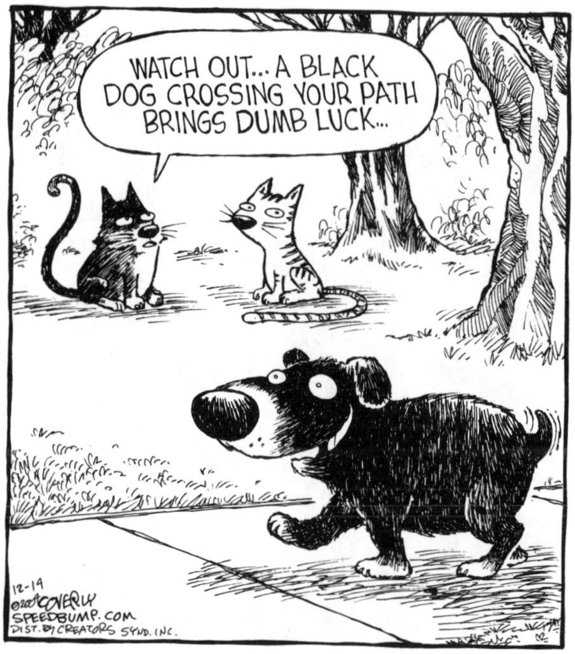
WATCH OUT... A BLACK DOG CROSSING YOUR PATH BRINGS **DUMB** LUCK...
12-14
©2004 COVERLY
SPEEDBUMP.COM
DIST. BY CREATORS SYND. INC.

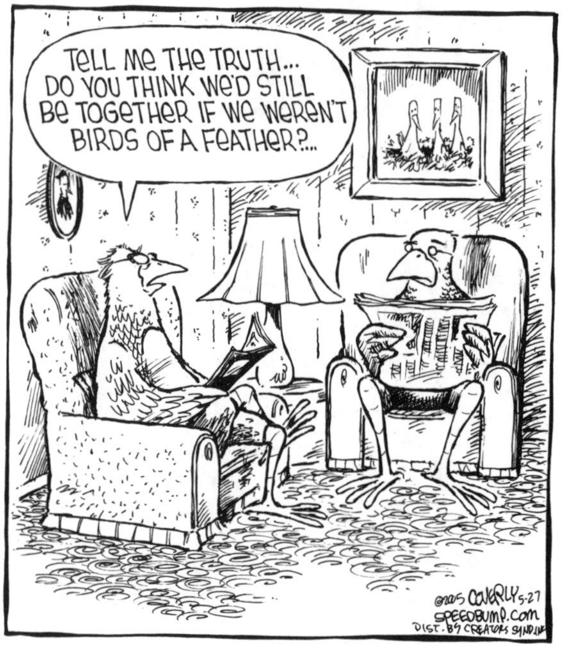
TELL ME THE TRUTH... DO YOU THINK WE'D STILL BE TOGETHER IF WE WEREN'T BIRDS OF A FEATHER?...
©2005 COVERLY 5-27
SPEEDBUMP.COM
DIST. BY CREATORS SYND. INC.

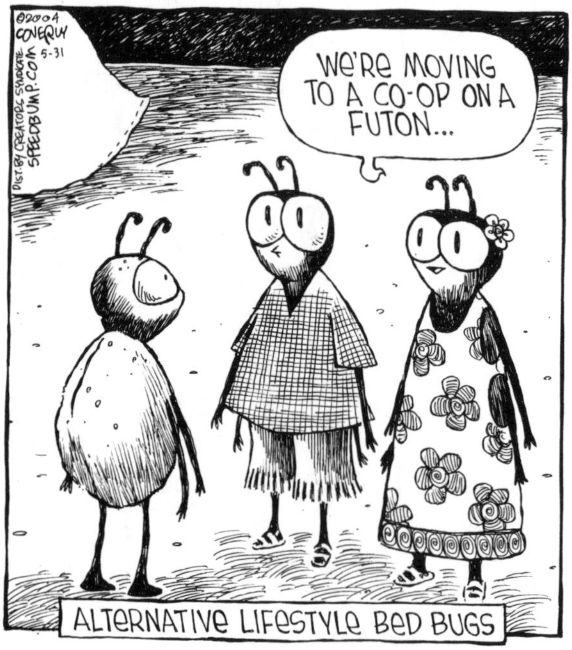
©2004
COVERLY
5-31
DIST. BY CREATORS SYNDICATE
SPEEDBUMP.COM
WE'RE MOVING TO A CO-OP ON A FUTON...
ALTERNATIVE LIFESTYLE BED BUGS

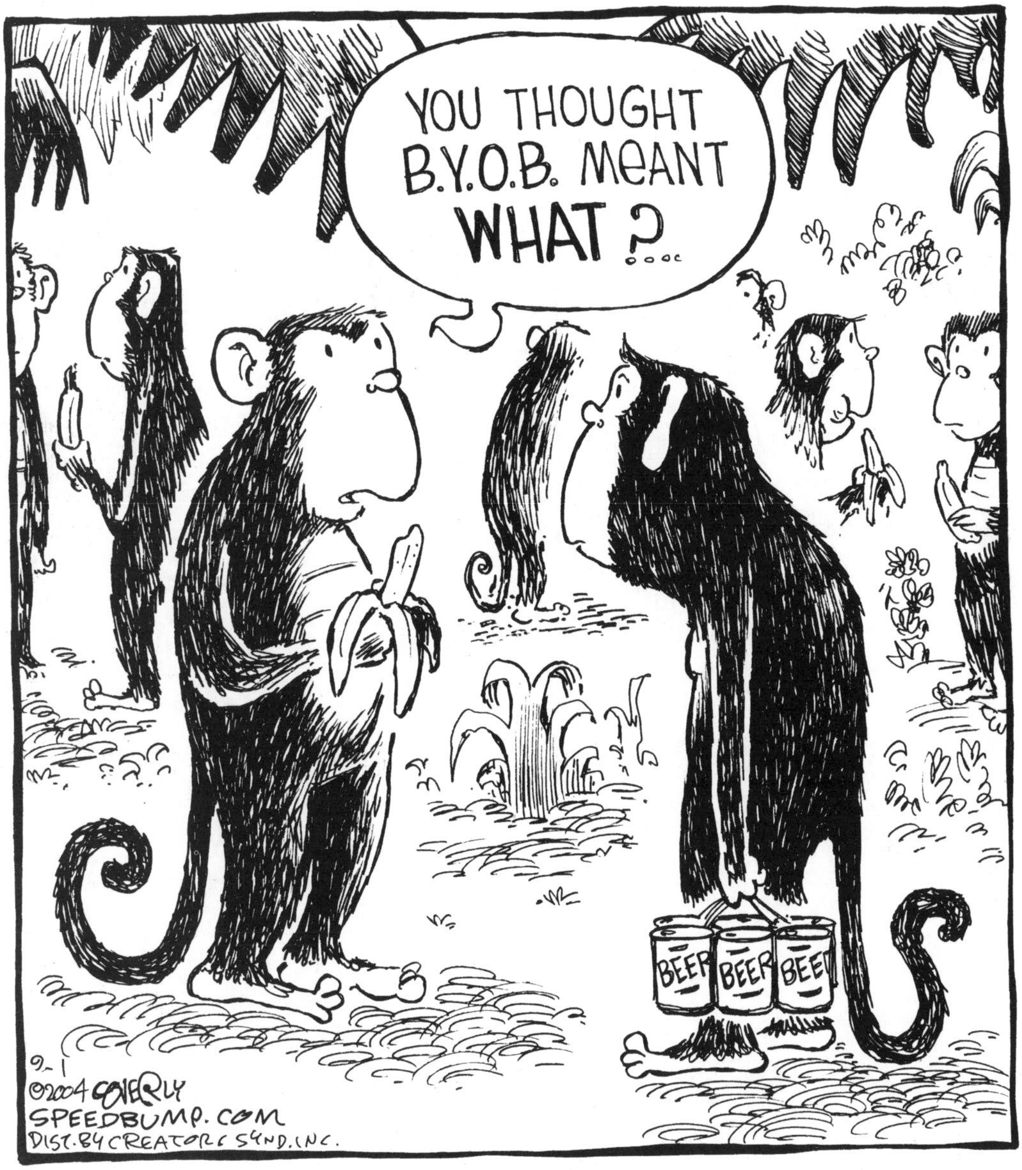
YOU THOUGHT B.Y.O.B. MEANT WHAT?...
BEER BEER BEER
9-1
©2004 COVERLY
SPEEDBUMP.COM
DIST. BY CREATORS SYND. INC.

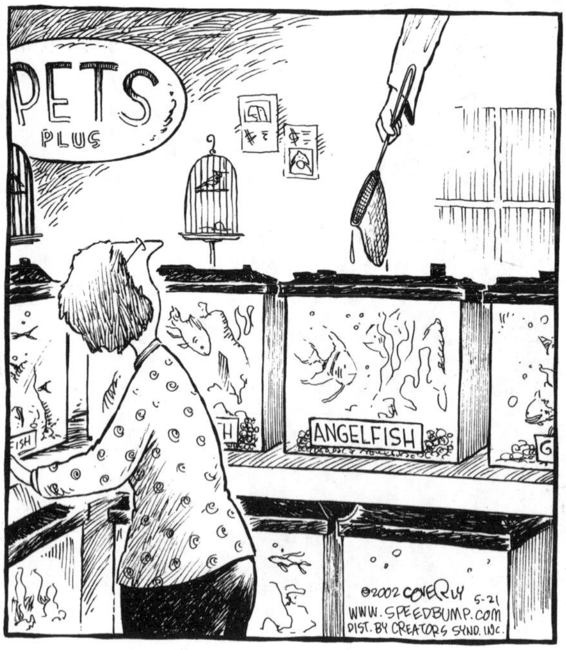
PETS
PLUS
ANGELFISH
©2002 COVERLY 5-21
WWW.SPEEDBUMP.COM
DIST. BY CREATORS SYND. INC.

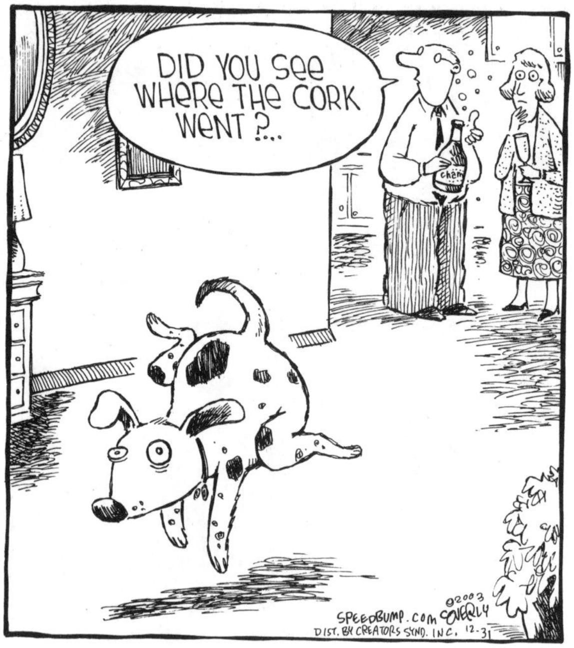
DID YOU SEE WHERE THE CORK WENT ?...
©2003
SPEEDBUMP.COM COVERLY
DIST. BY CREATORS SYND. INC. 12-31

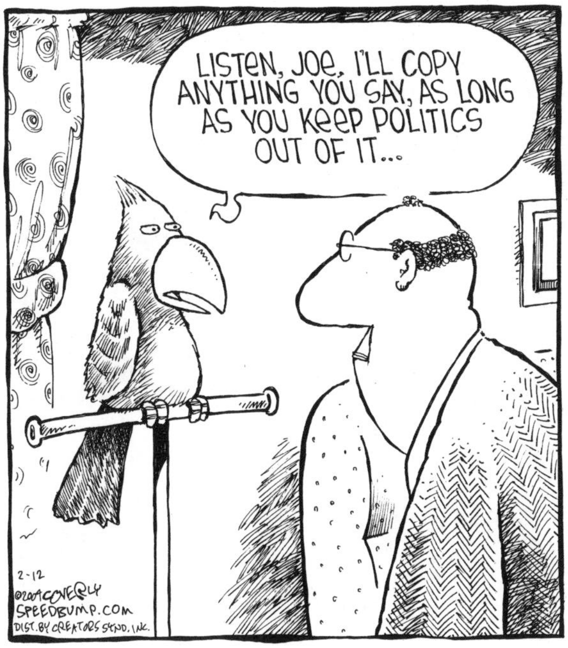
LISTEN, JOE. I'LL COPY ANYTHING YOU SAY, AS LONG AS YOU KEEP POLITICS OUT OF IT...

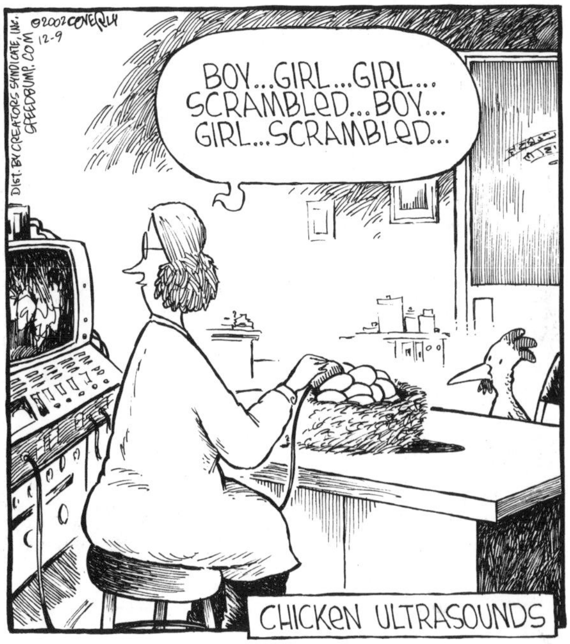
BOY...GIRL...GIRL... SCRAMBLED...BOY... GIRL...SCRAMBLED...
CHICKEN ULTRASOUNDS

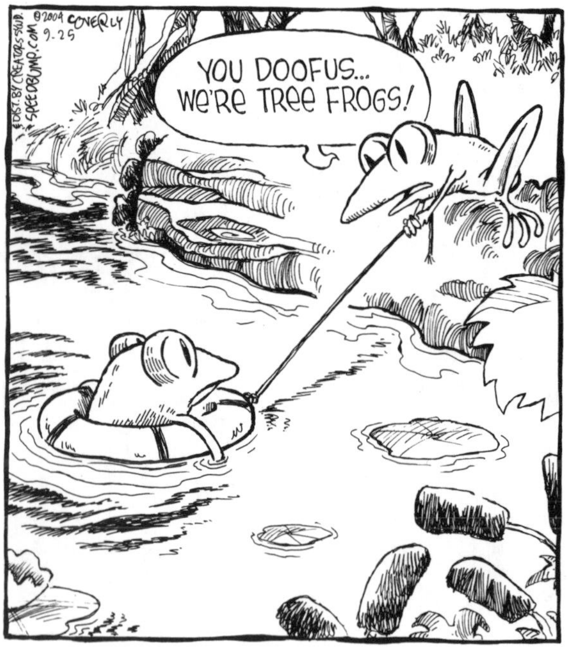
YOU DOOFUS... WE'RE TREE FROGS!
©2004 COVERLY
9-25
DIST. BY CREATORS SYND.
SPEEDBUMP.COM

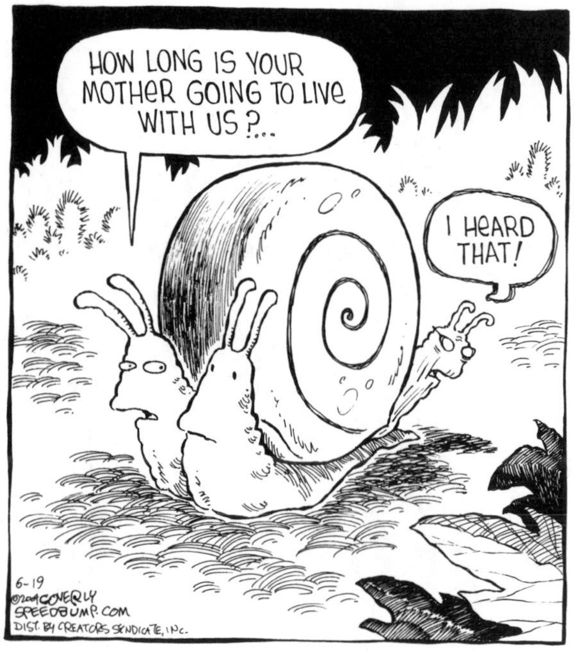
HOW LONG IS YOUR MOTHER GOING TO LIVE WITH US ?...
I HEARD THAT!
6-19
©2004 COVERLY
SPEEDBUMP.COM
DIST. BY CREATORS SYNDICATE, INC.

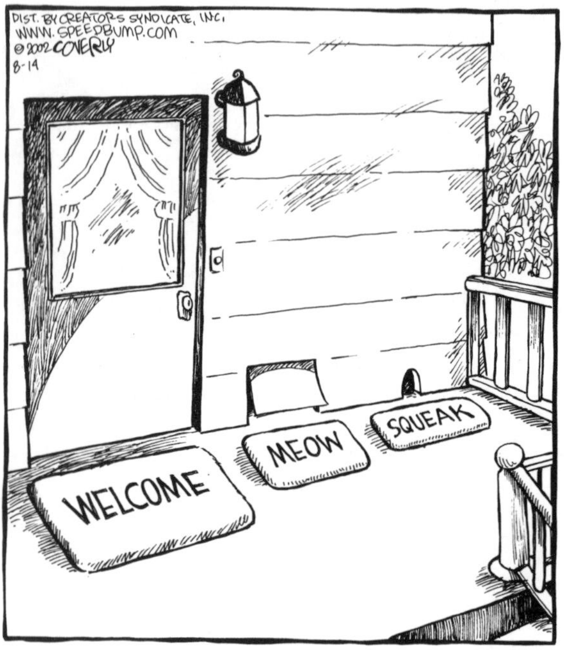
DIST. BY CREATORS SYNDICATE, INC.
WWW.SPEEDBUMP.COM
©2002 COVERLY
8-14
WELCOME
MEOW
SQUEAK

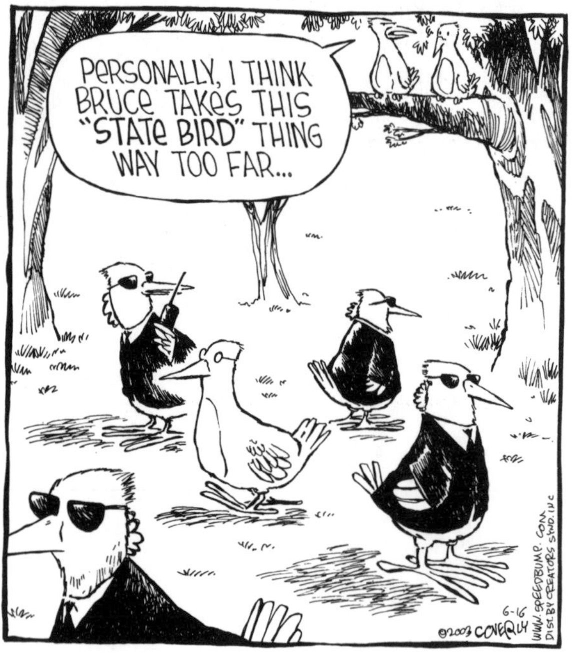
PERSONALLY, I THINK BRUCE TAKES THIS "STATE BIRD" THING WAY TOO FAR...
6-16
©2003 COVERLY
WWW.SPEEDBUMP.COM
DIST. BY CREATORS SYND. INC

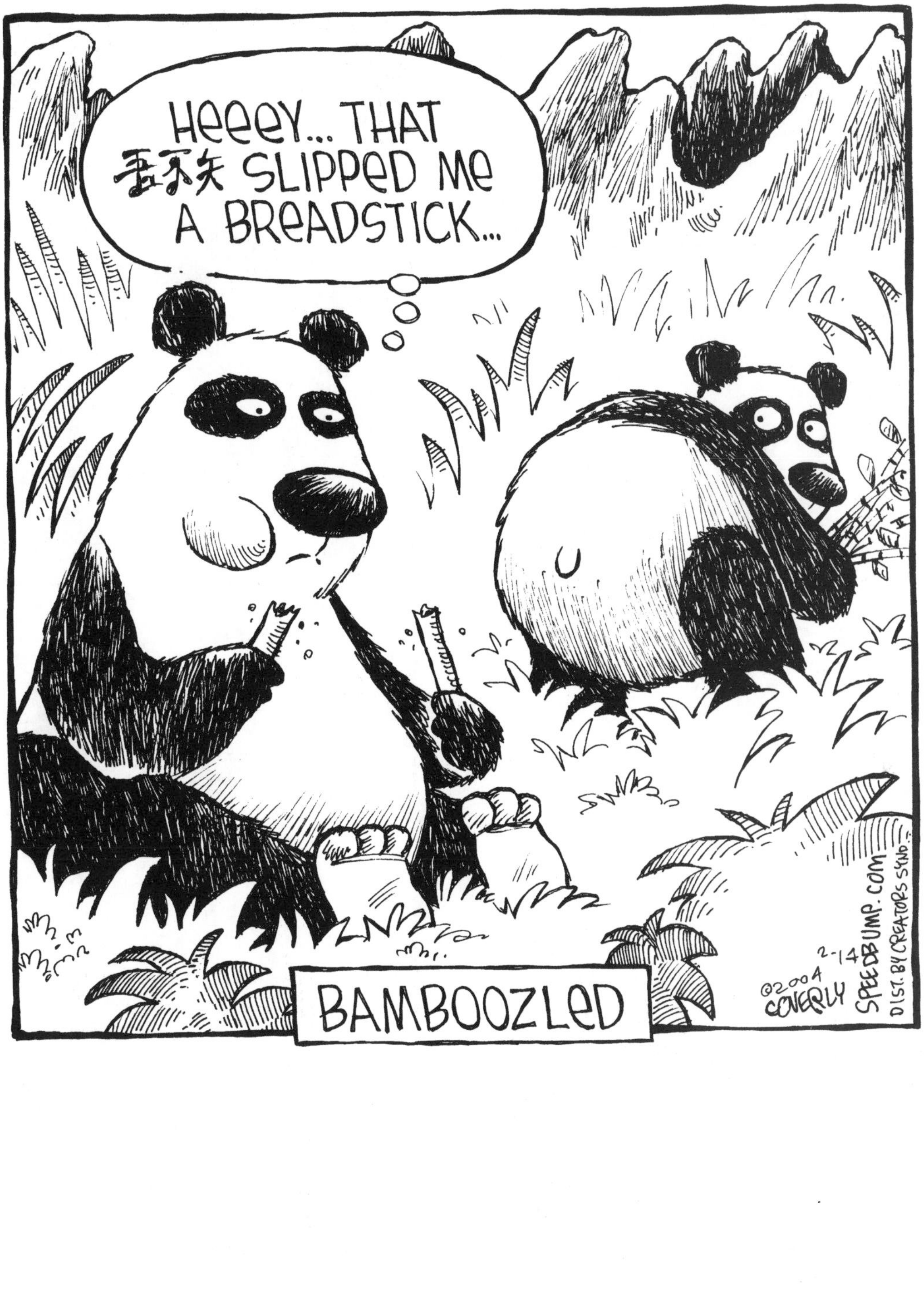
HEEEY... THAT SLIPPED ME A BREADSTICK...
©2004 COVERLY 2-14
SPEEDBUMP.COM
DIST. BY CREATORS SYND.
BAMBOOZLED

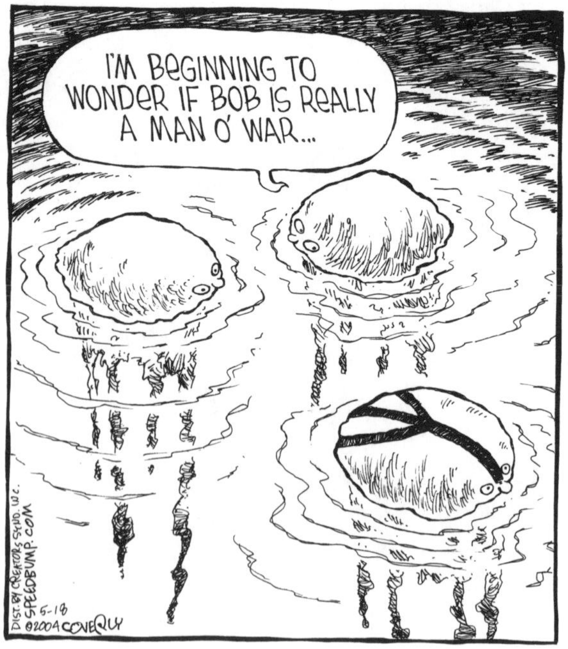
I'M BEGINNING TO WONDER IF BOB IS REALLY A MAN O' WAR...

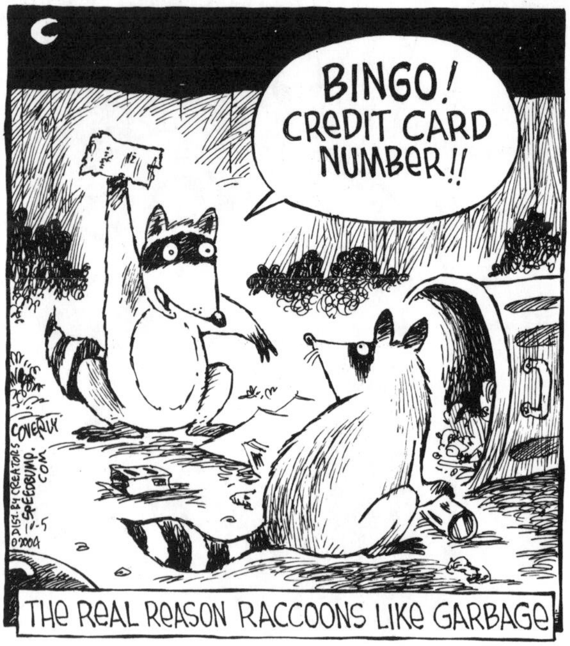
BINGO! CREDIT CARD NUMBER!!

THE REAL REASON RACCOONS LIKE GARBAGE

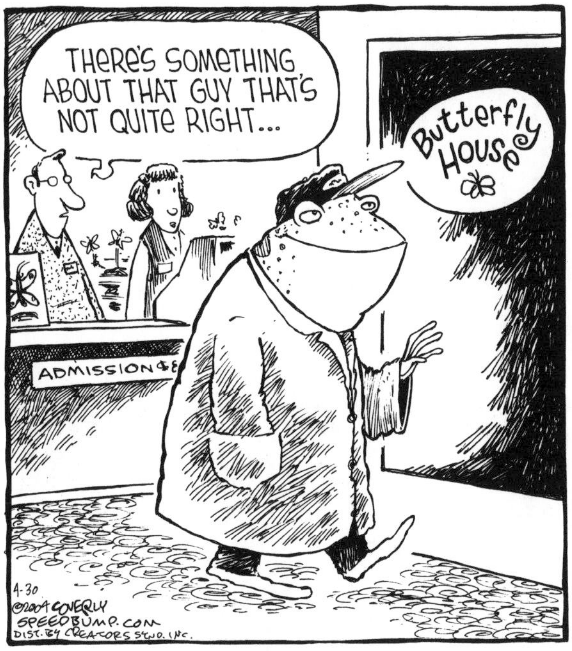
THERE'S SOMETHING ABOUT THAT GUY THAT'S NOT QUITE RIGHT...
Butterfly House
ADMISSION
4-30
©2004 COVERLY
SPEEDBUMP.COM
DIST. BY CREATORS SYND. INC.

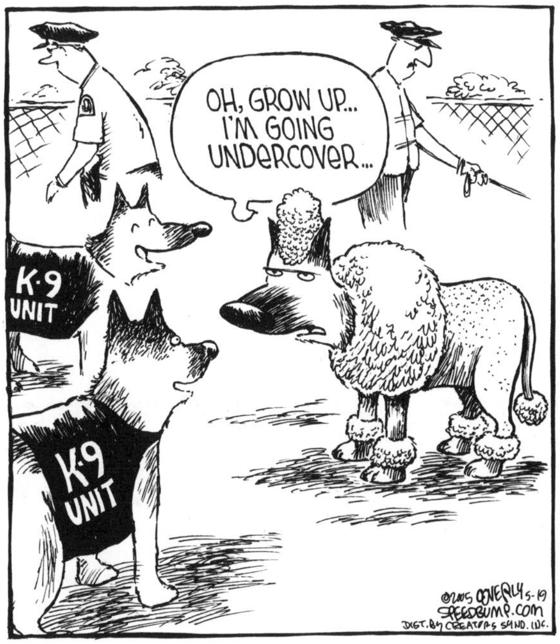
OH, GROW UP... I'M GOING UNDERCOVER...
K-9 UNIT
K-9 UNIT
©2005 COVERLY 5-19
SPEEDBUMP.COM
DIST. BY CREATORS SYND. INC.

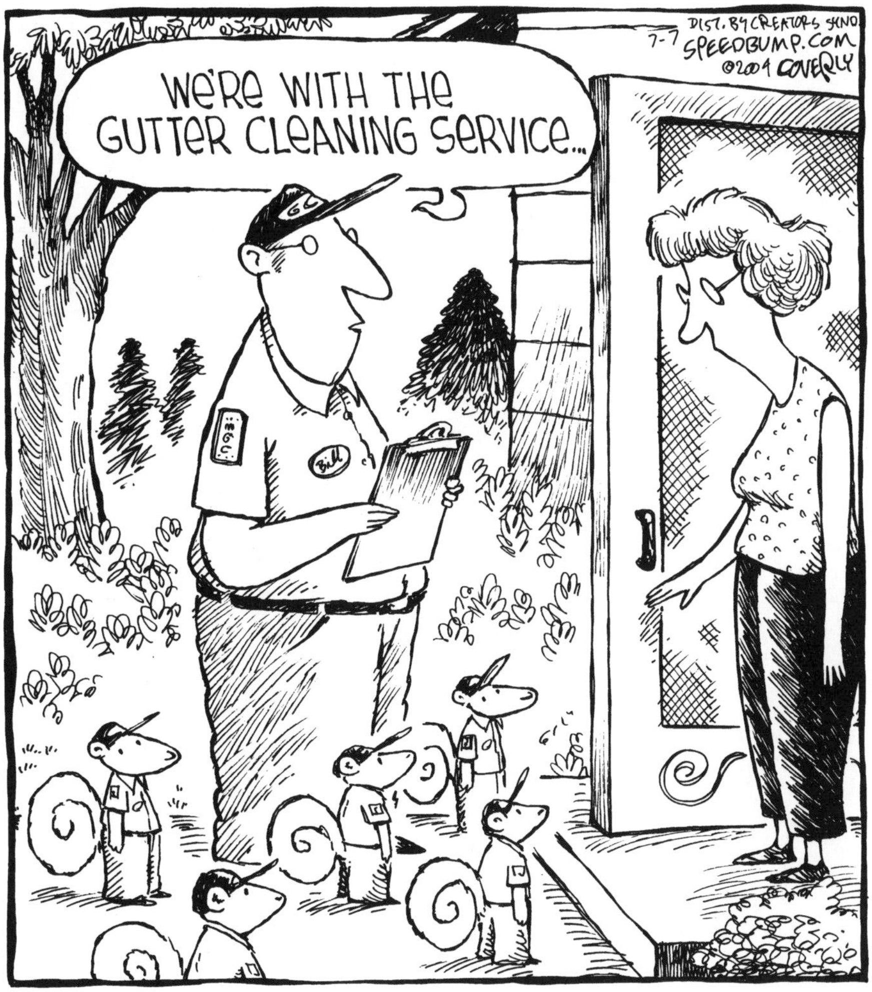
DIST. BY CREATORS SYND.
7-7
SPEEDBUMP.COM
©2004 COVERLY
WE'RE WITH THE GUTTER CLEANING SERVICE...
Bill

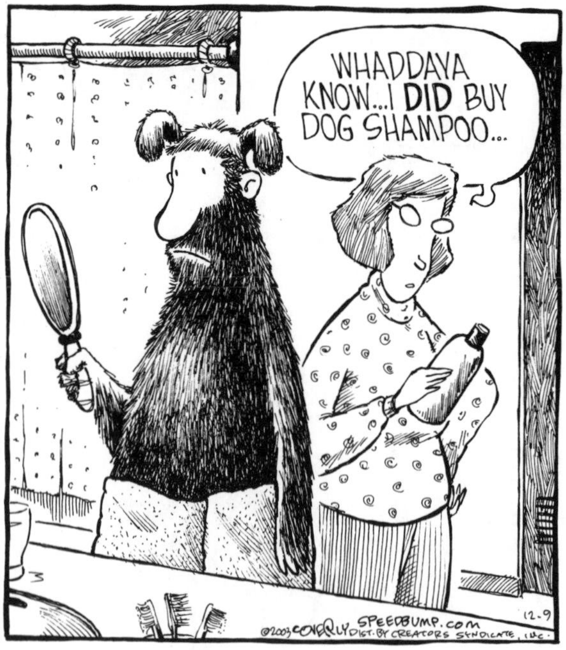
WHADDAYA KNOW...I **DID** BUY DOG SHAMPOO...
12-9
©2003 COVERLY SPEEDBUMP.COM DIST. BY CREATORS SYNDICATE, INC.

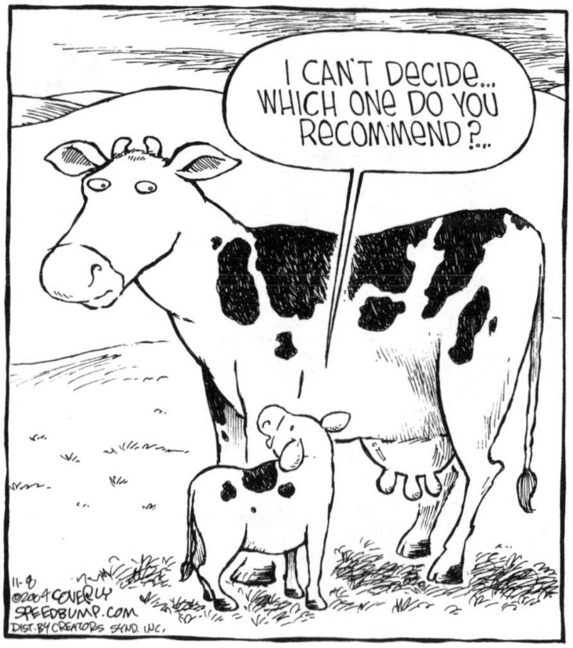
I CAN'T DECIDE... WHICH ONE DO YOU RECOMMEND?...
11-8
©2004 COVERLY
SPEEDBUMP.COM
DIST. BY CREATORS SYND. INC.

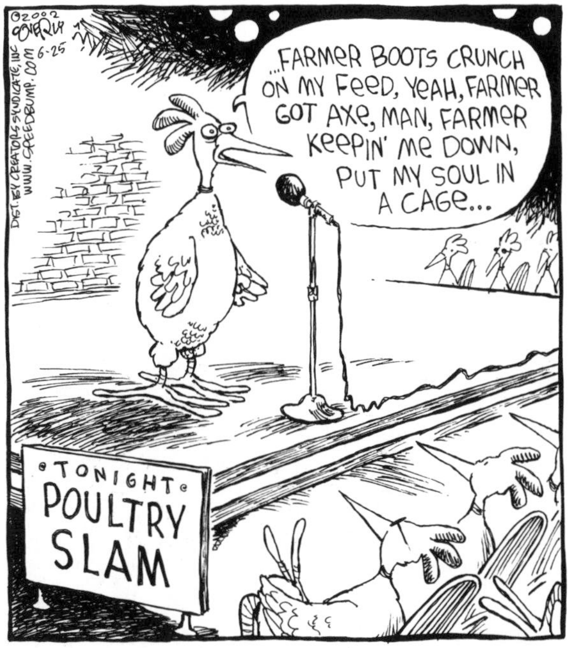
...FARMER BOOTS CRUNCH ON MY FEED, YEAH, FARMER GOT AXE, MAN, FARMER KEEPIN' ME DOWN, PUT MY SOUL IN A CAGE...
TONIGHT
POULTRY SLAM

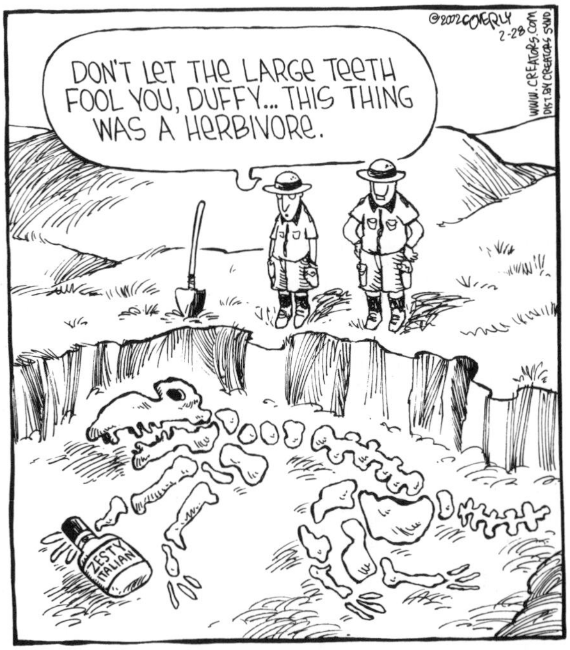
DON'T LET THE LARGE TEETH FOOL YOU, DUFFY... THIS THING WAS A HERBIVORE.
ZESTY ITALIAN

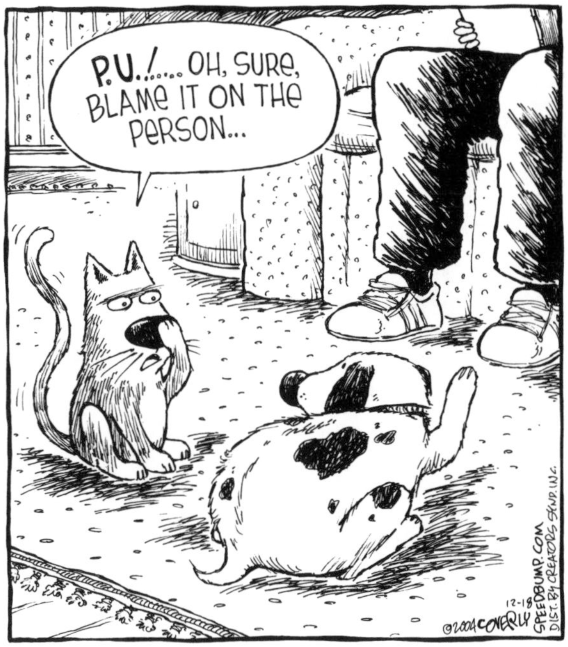
P.U.!... OH, SURE, BLAME IT ON THE PERSON...

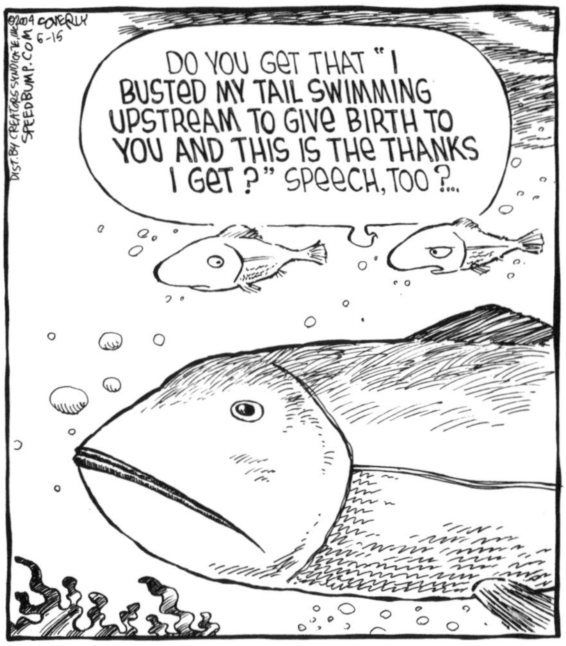
DO YOU GET THAT "I BUSTED MY TAIL SWIMMING UPSTREAM TO GIVE BIRTH TO YOU AND THIS IS THE THANKS I GET?" SPEECH, TOO?...

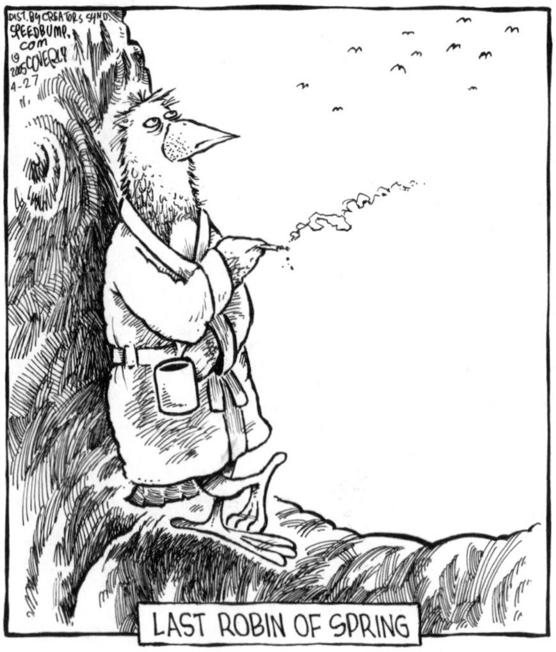
LAST ROBIN OF SPRING

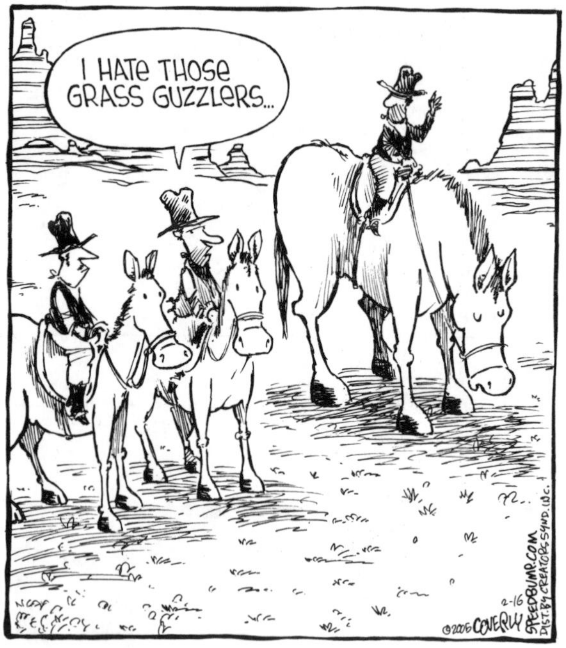
I HATE THOSE GRASS GUZZLERS...

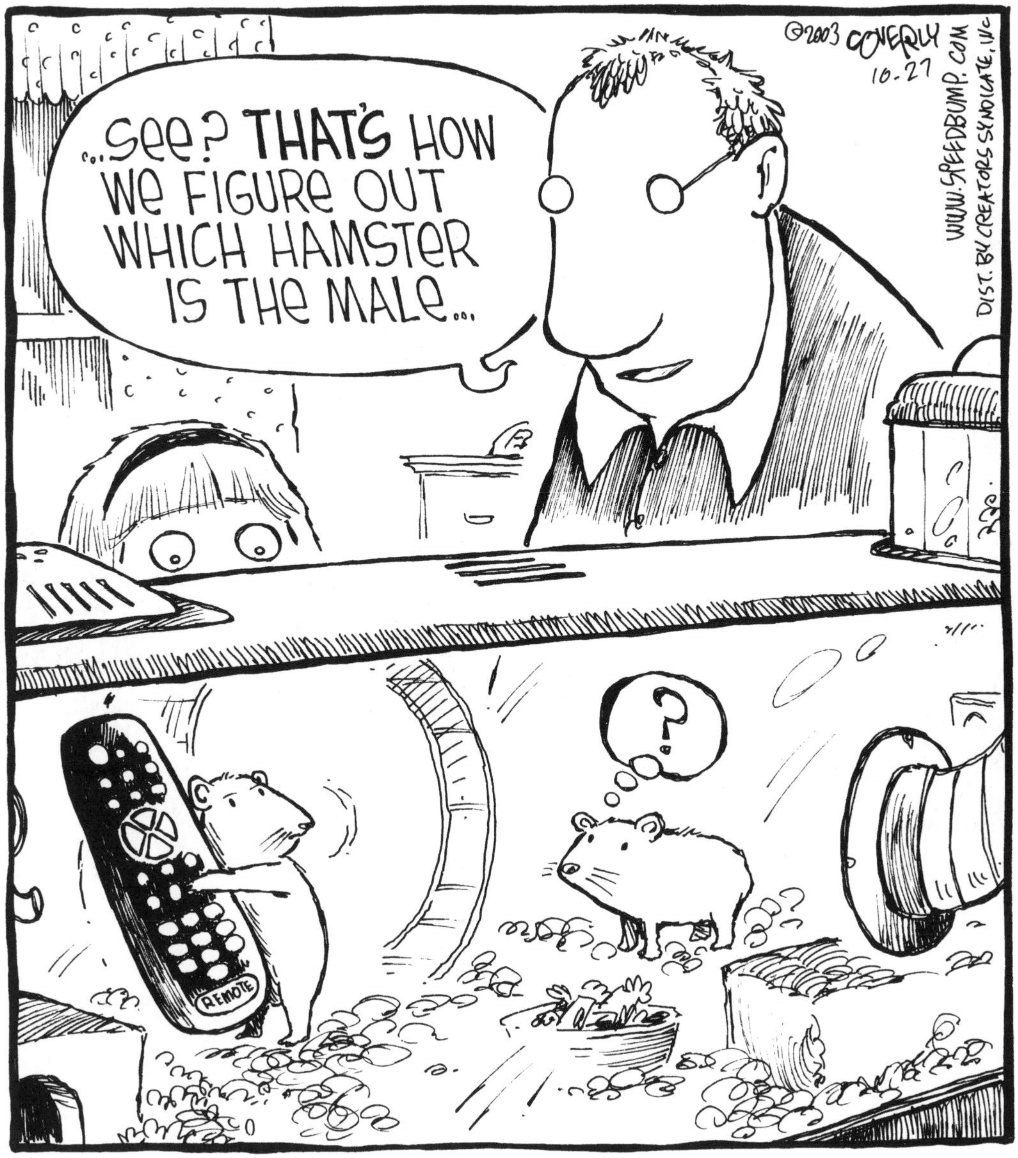
©2003 COVERLY 10-27
WWW.SPEEDBUMP.COM
DIST. BY CREATORS SYNDICATE, INC
...See? THAT'S HOW WE FIGURE OUT WHICH HAMSTER IS THE MALE...
?
REMOTE

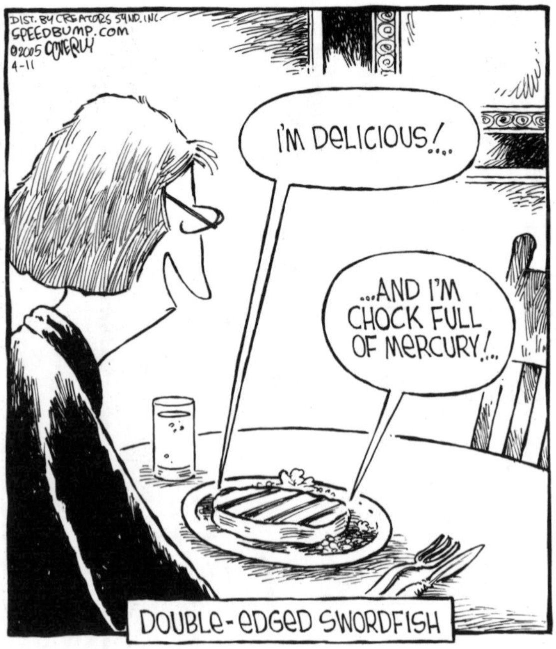
DIST. BY CREATORS SYND. INC.
SPEEDBUMP.COM
©2005 COVERLY
4-11
I'M DELICIOUS!...
...AND I'M CHOCK FULL OF MERCURY!...
DOUBLE-EDGED SWORDFISH

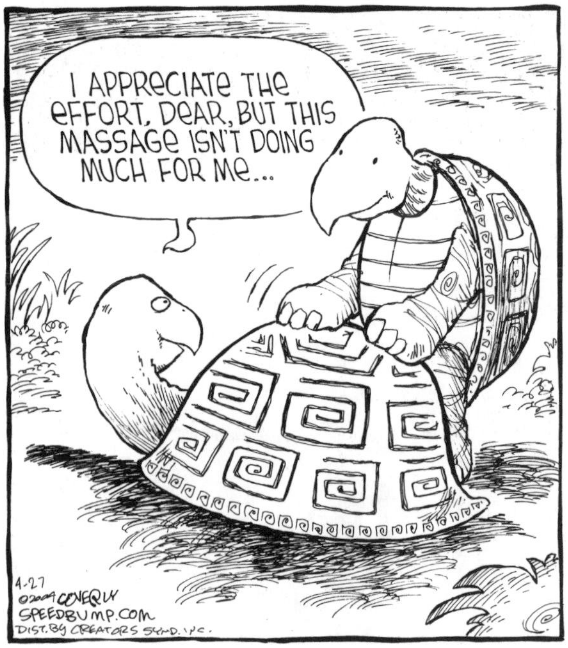
I APPRECIATE THE EFFORT, DEAR, BUT THIS MASSAGE ISN'T DOING MUCH FOR ME...
4-27
©2004 COVERLY
SPEEDBUMP.COM
DIST. BY CREATORS SYND. INC.

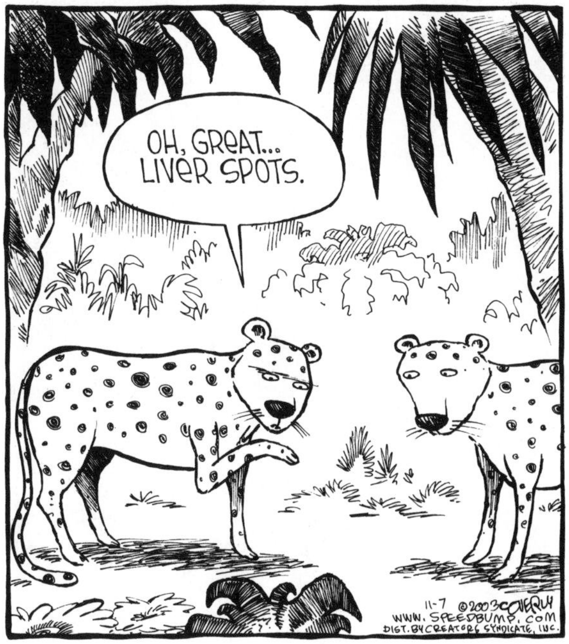
OH, GREAT... LIVER SPOTS.
11-7 ©2003 COVERLY
WWW.SPEEDBUMP.COM
DIST. BY CREATORS SYNDICATE, INC.

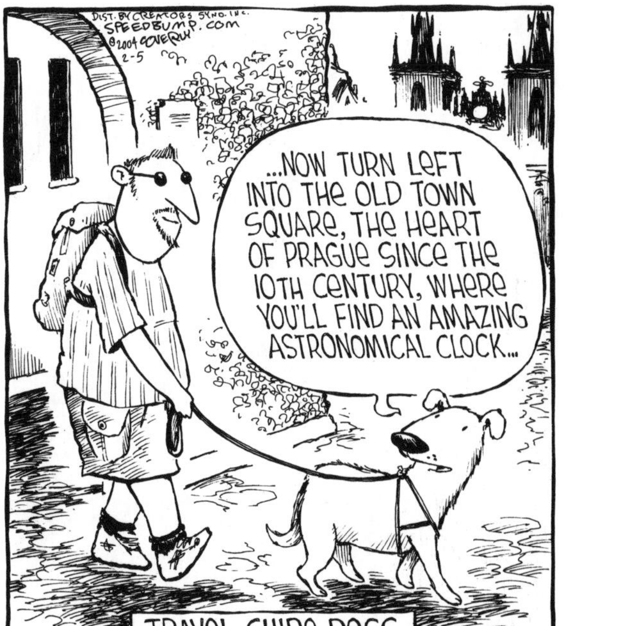
DIST. BY CREATORS SYND. INC.
SPEEDBUMP.COM
©2004 COVERLY
2-5
...NOW TURN LEFT INTO THE OLD TOWN SQUARE, THE HEART OF PRAGUE SINCE THE 10TH CENTURY, WHERE YOU'LL FIND AN AMAZING ASTRONOMICAL CLOCK...
TRAVEL GUIDE DOGS

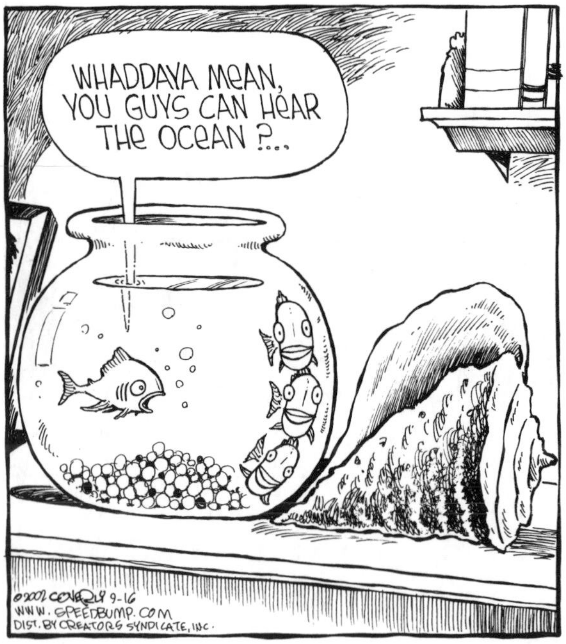
WHADDAYA MEAN, YOU GUYS CAN HEAR THE OCEAN ?...
©2002 COVERLY 9-16
WWW.SPEEDBUMP.COM
DIST. BY CREATORS SYNDICATE, INC.

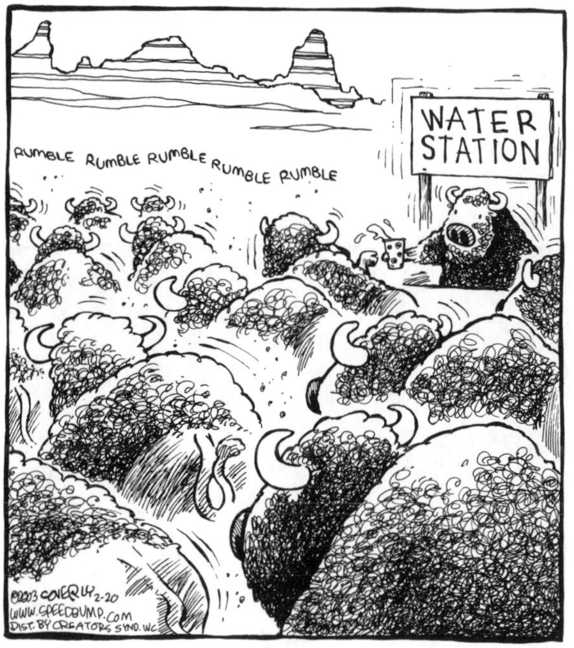
WATER STATION
RUMBLE RUMBLE RUMBLE RUMBLE RUMBLE
©2003 COVERLY 2-20
WWW.SPEEDBUMP.COM
DIST. BY CREATORS SYND. INC.

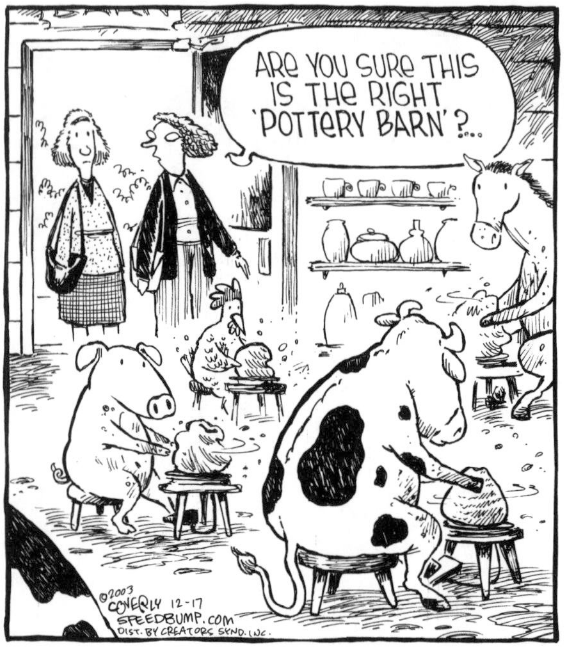
ARE YOU SURE THIS IS THE RIGHT 'POTTERY BARN' ?...
©2003 COVERLY 12-17
SPEEDBUMP.COM
DIST. BY CREATORS SYND. INC.

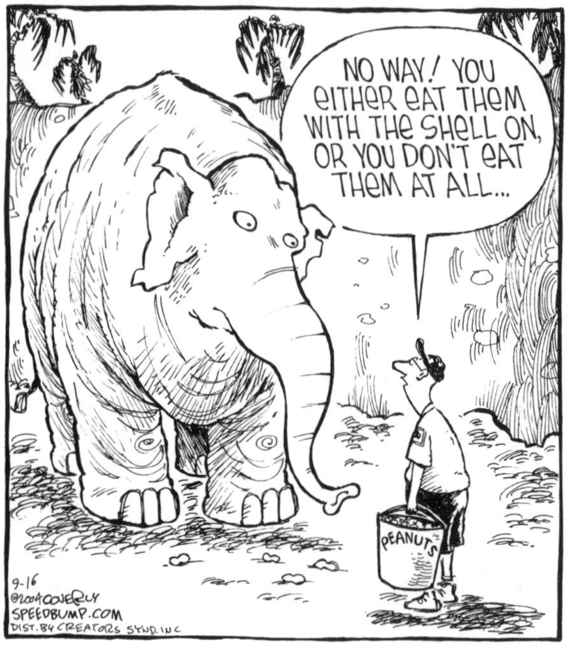
NO WAY! YOU EITHER EAT THEM WITH THE SHELL ON, OR YOU DON'T EAT THEM AT ALL...
PEANUTS
9-16
©2004 COVERLY
SPEEDBUMP.COM
DIST. BY CREATORS SYND. INC.

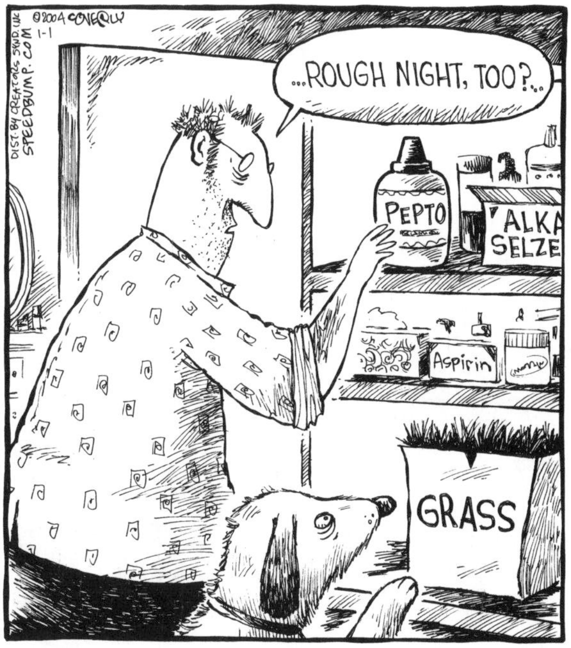
...ROUGH NIGHT, TOO?...
PEPTO
ALKA SELZE
Aspirin
GRASS
©2004 COVERLY 1-1
SPEEDBUMP.COM
DIST. BY CREATORS SYND. INC.

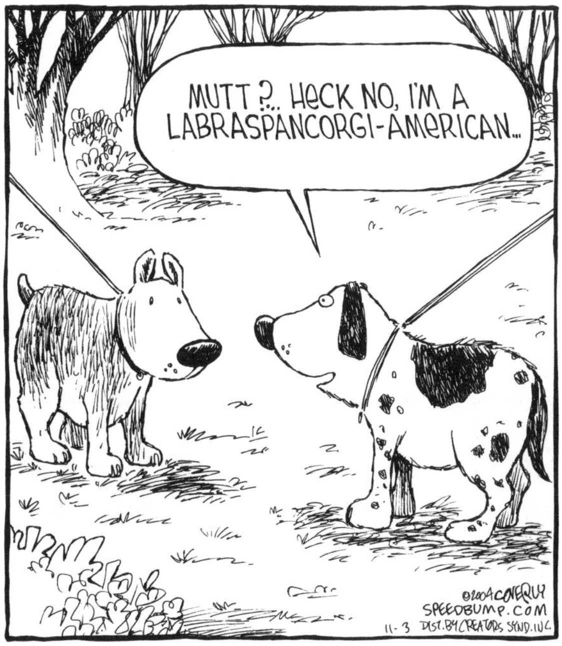
MUTT?.. HECK NO, I'M A LABRASPANCORGI-AMERICAN...
©2004 COVERLY
SPEEDBUMP.COM
11-3 DIST. BY CREATORS SYND. INC.

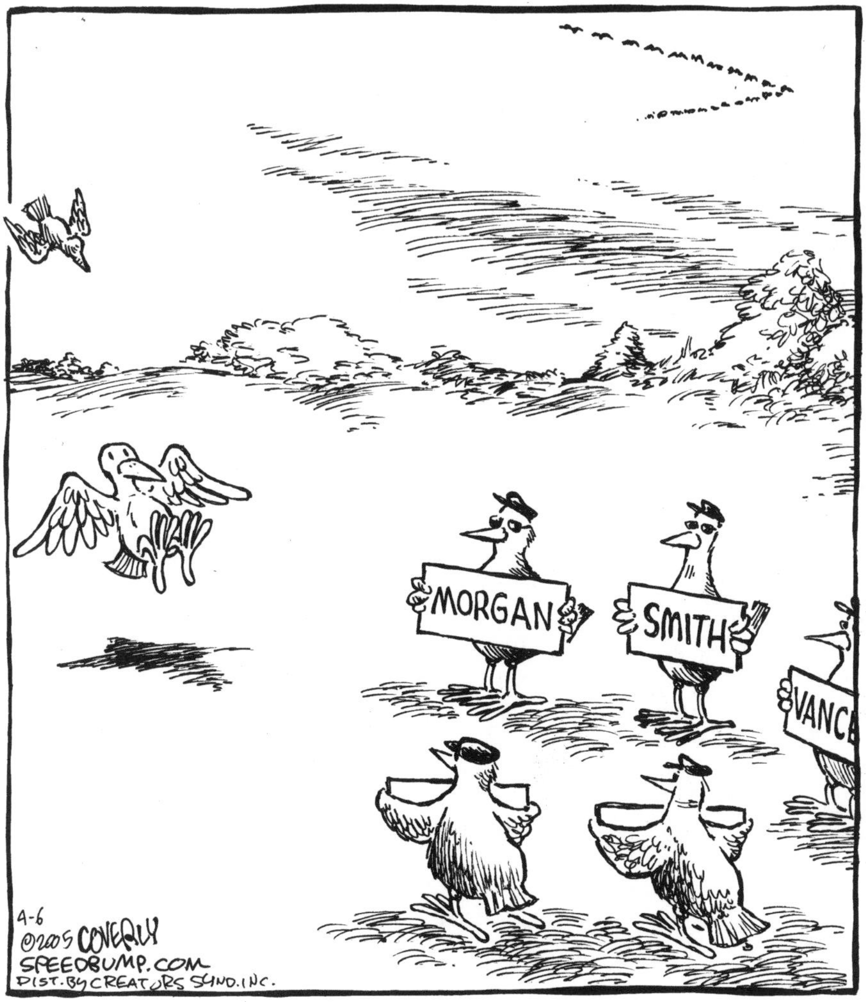
MORGAN
SMITH
VANC
4-6
©2005 COVERLY
SPEEDBUMP.COM
DIST. BY CREATORS SYND. INC.

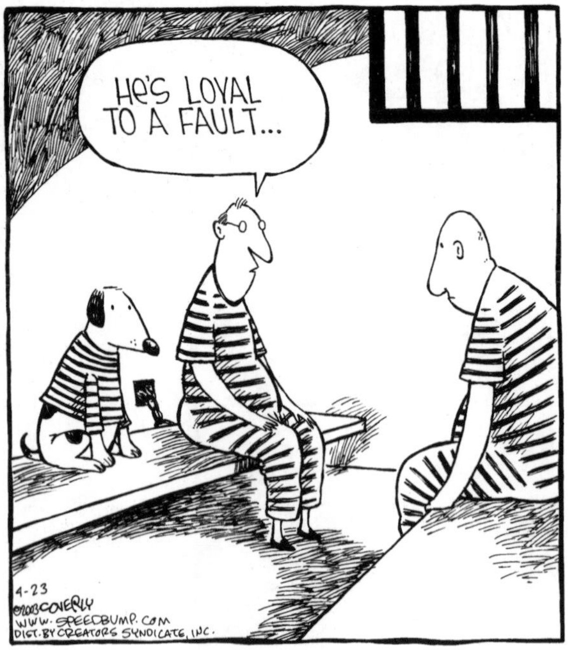
HE'S LOYAL TO A FAULT...
4-23
©2003 COVERLY
WWW.SPEEDBUMP.COM
DIST. BY CREATORS SYNDICATE, INC.

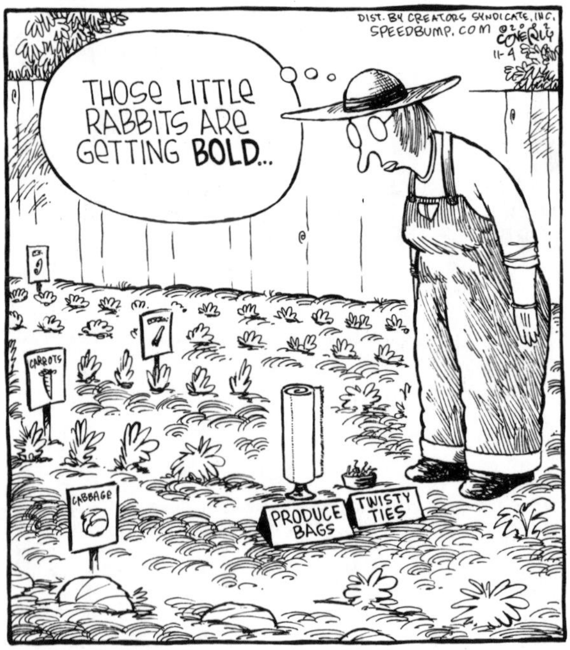
DIST. BY CREATORS SYNDICATE, INC.
SPEEDBUMP.COM ©2002 COVERLY
11-4
THOSE LITTLE RABBITS ARE GETTING **BOLD**...
CARROTS
CABBAGE
PRODUCE BAGS
TWISTY TIES

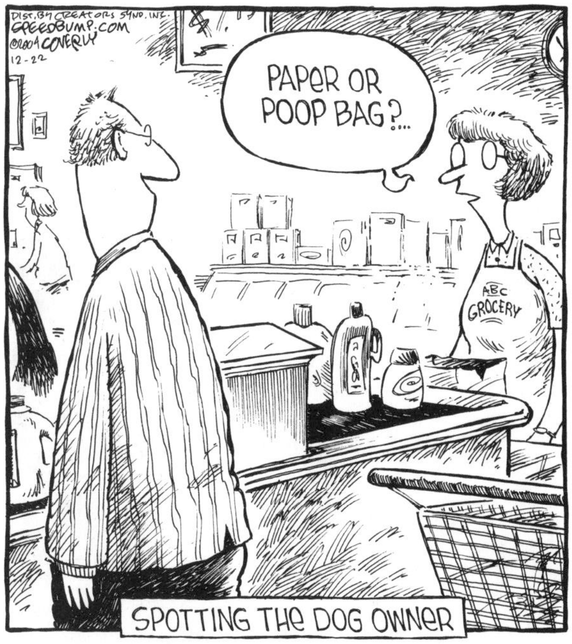
DIST. BY CREATORS SYND. INC.
SPEEDBUMP.COM
©2004 COVERLY
12-22
PAPER OR POOP BAG?...
ABC GROCERY
SPOTTING THE DOG OWNER

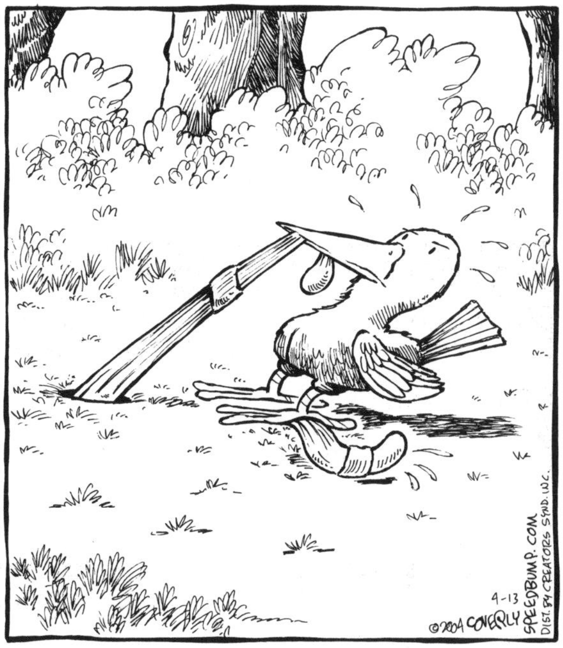
4-13
©2004 COVERLY
SPEEDBUMP.COM
DIST. BY CREATORS SYND. INC.

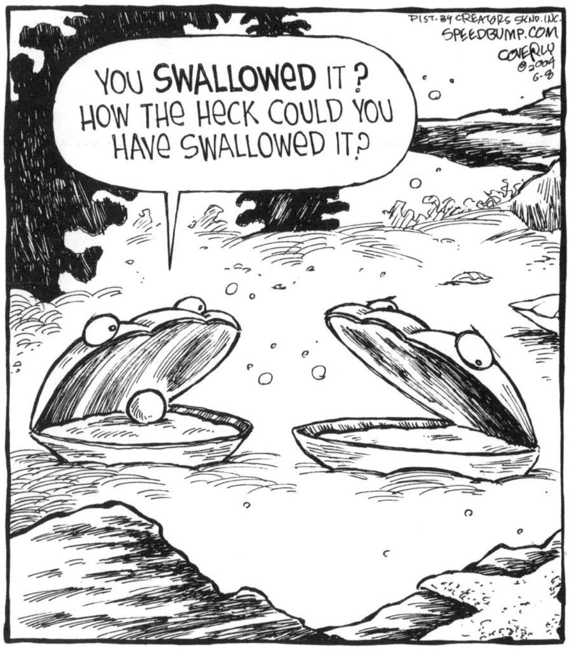
DIST. BY CREATORS SYND. INC.
SPEEDBUMP.COM
COVERLY ©2004 6-8
YOU **SWALLOWED** IT? HOW THE HECK COULD YOU HAVE SWALLOWED IT?

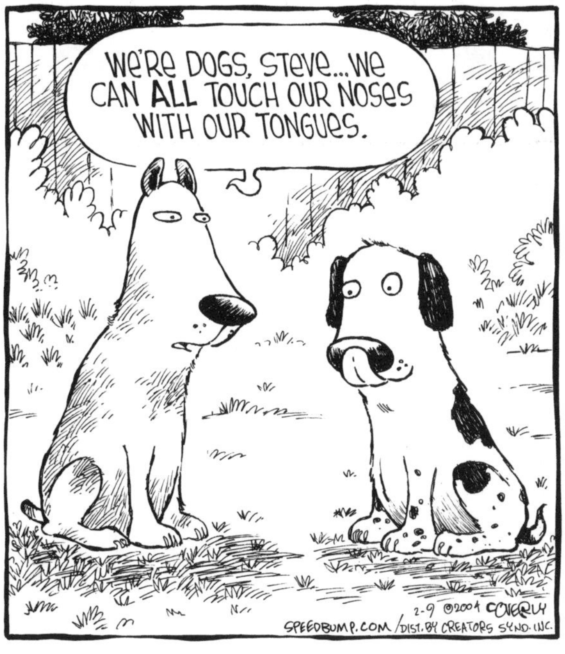
WE'RE DOGS, STEVE...WE CAN **ALL** TOUCH OUR NOSES WITH OUR TONGUES.
2-9 ©2004 COVERLY
SPEEDBUMP.COM / DIST. BY CREATORS SYND. INC.

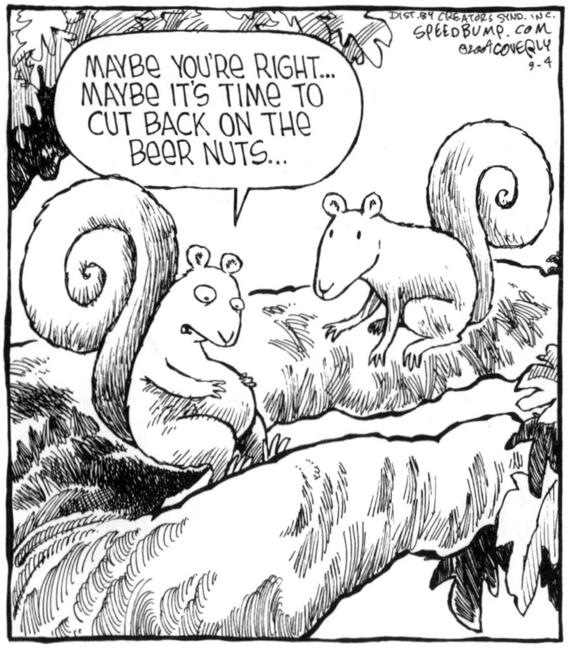
DIST. BY CREATORS SYND. INC.
SPEEDBUMP.COM
©2004 COVERLY
9-4
MAYBE YOU'RE RIGHT... MAYBE IT'S TIME TO CUT BACK ON THE BEER NUTS...

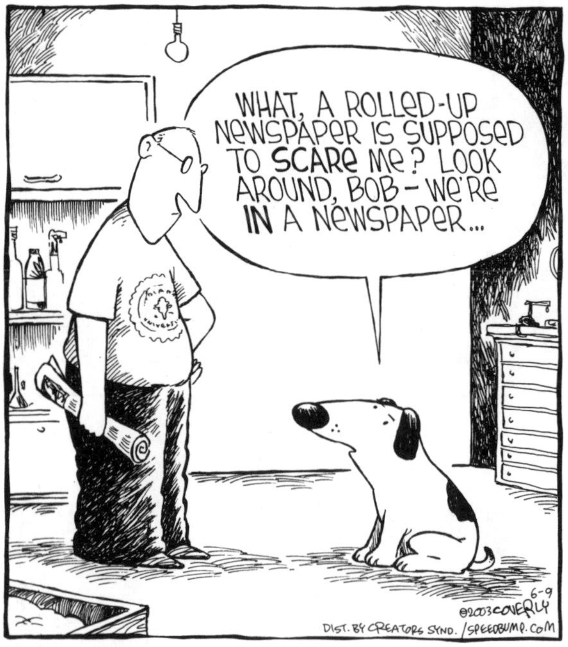
WHAT, A ROLLED-UP NEWSPAPER IS SUPPOSED TO SCARE ME? LOOK AROUND, BOB – WE'RE IN A NEWSPAPER...
6-9
©2003 COVERLY
DIST. BY CREATORS SYND. / SPEEDBUMP.COM

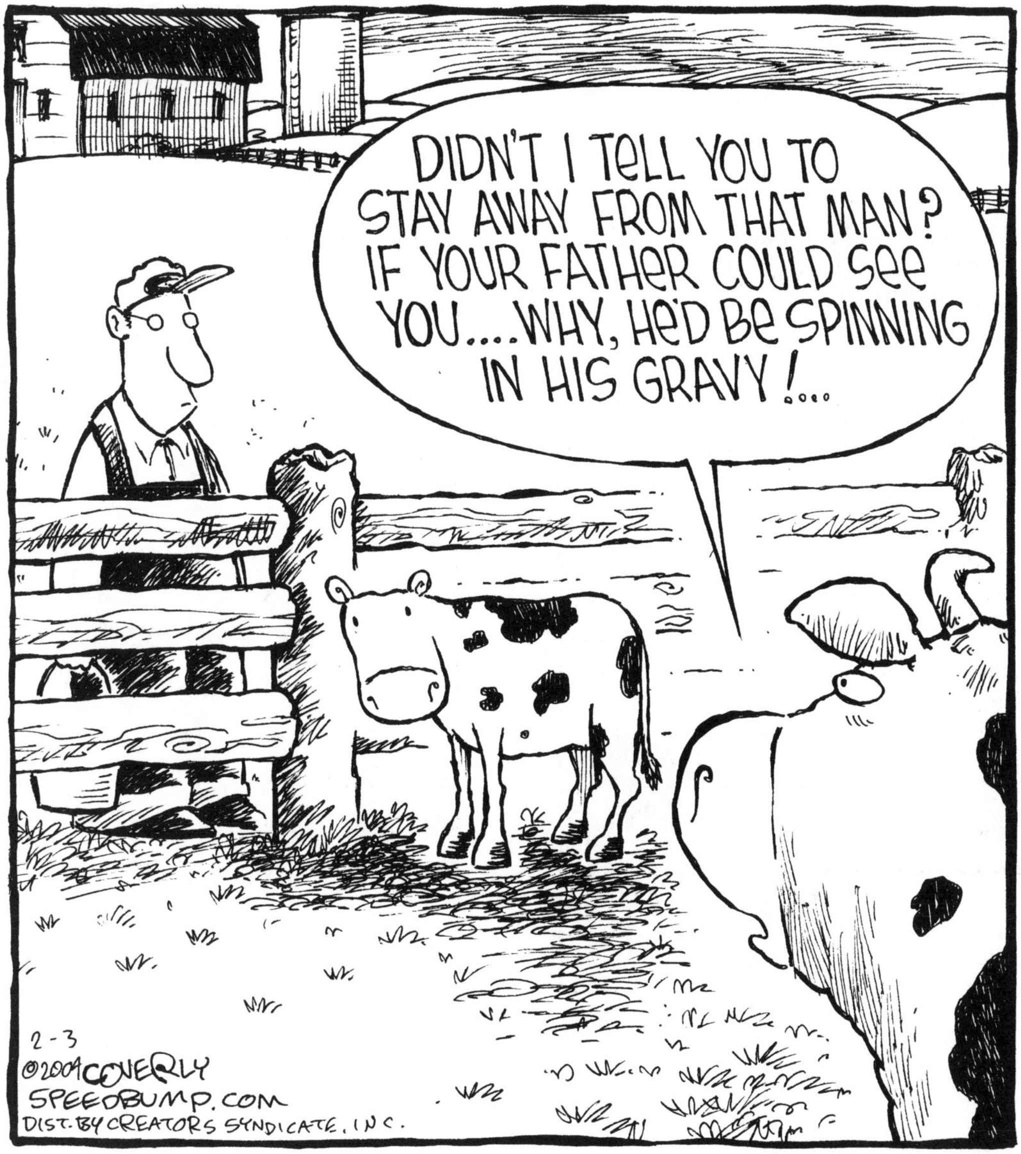
DIDN'T I TELL YOU TO STAY AWAY FROM THAT MAN? IF YOUR FATHER COULD SEE YOU....WHY, HE'D BE SPINNING IN HIS GRAVY!...
2-3
©2004 COVERLY
SPEEDBUMP.COM
DIST. BY CREATORS SYNDICATE, INC.

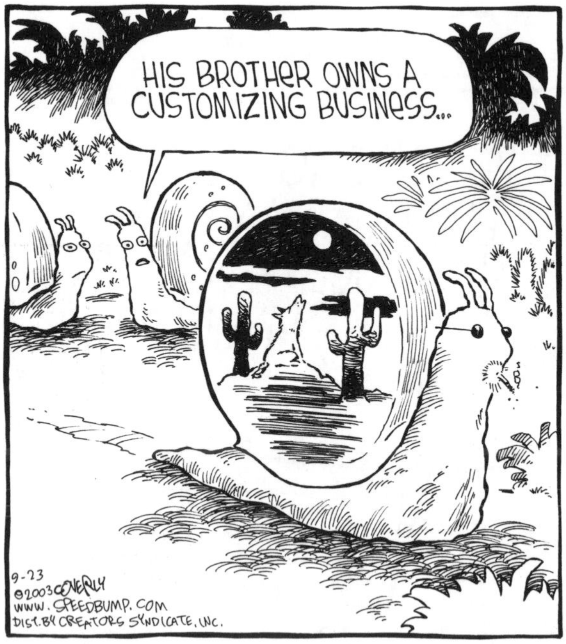
HIS BROTHER OWNS A CUSTOMIZING BUSINESS...
9-23
©2003 COVERLY
WWW.SPEEDBUMP.COM
DIST. BY CREATORS SYNDICATE, INC.

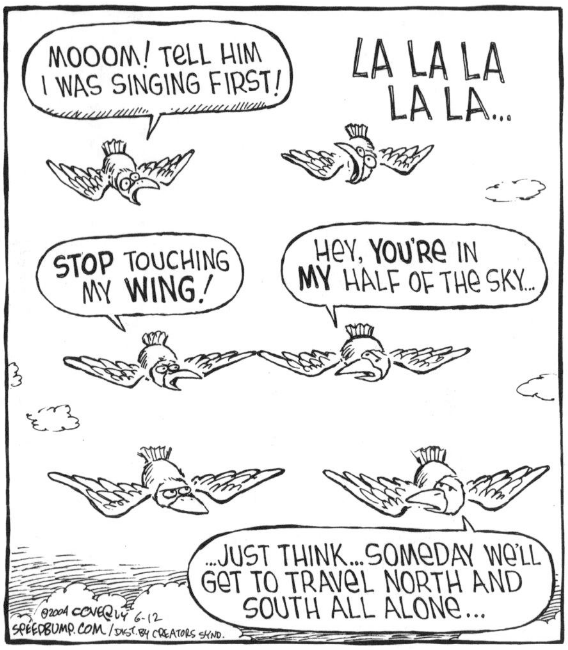
MOOOM! TELL HIM I WAS SINGING FIRST!
LA LA LA LA LA...
STOP TOUCHING MY WING!
HEY, YOU'RE IN MY HALF OF THE SKY...
...JUST THINK...SOMEDAY WE'LL GET TO TRAVEL NORTH AND SOUTH ALL ALONE...
©2004 COVERLY 6-12
SPEEDBUMP.COM / DIST. BY CREATORS SYND.

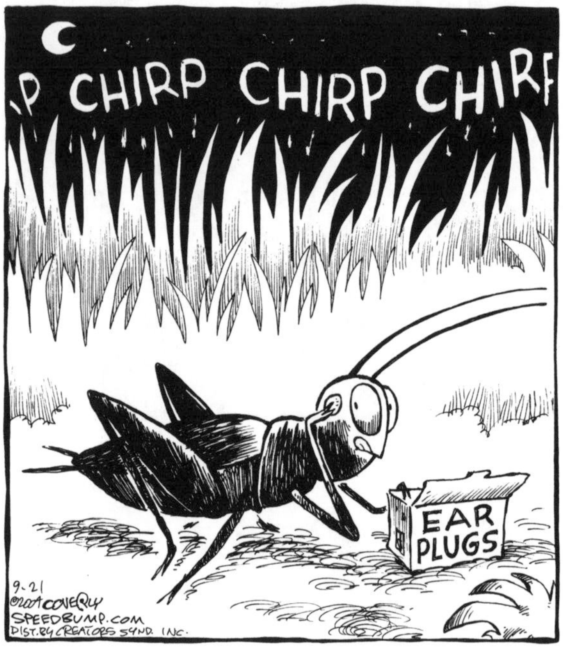
CHIRP CHIRP
EAR PLUGS
9-21
©2004 COVERLY
SPEEDBUMP.COM
DIST. BY CREATORS SYND. INC.

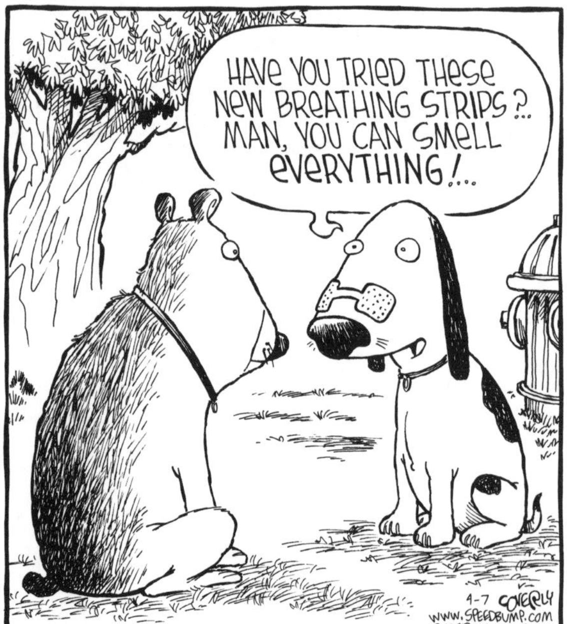
HAVE YOU TRIED THESE NEW BREATHING STRIPS?.. MAN, YOU CAN SMELL EVERYTHING!...
4-7 COVERLY
WWW.SPEEDBUMP.COM
DIST. BY CREATORS SYNDICATE, INC.

DIST. BY CREATORS SYNDICATE, INC
SPEEDBUMP.COM
©2004 COVERLY
11-17
BAD NEWS, MRS. HALPERN... YOU HAVE A CO-SPAY...
HMO'S FOR PETS

...I TOLD YOU MY WIFE WORSHIPS THAT DOG...
11-15
©2004 COVERLY
SPEEDBUMP.COM
DIST. BY CREATORS SYNDICATE, INC.

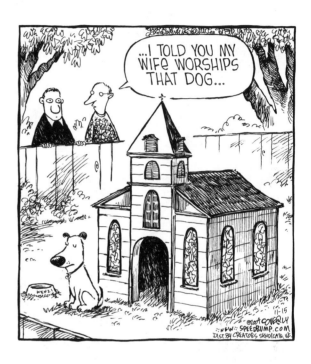

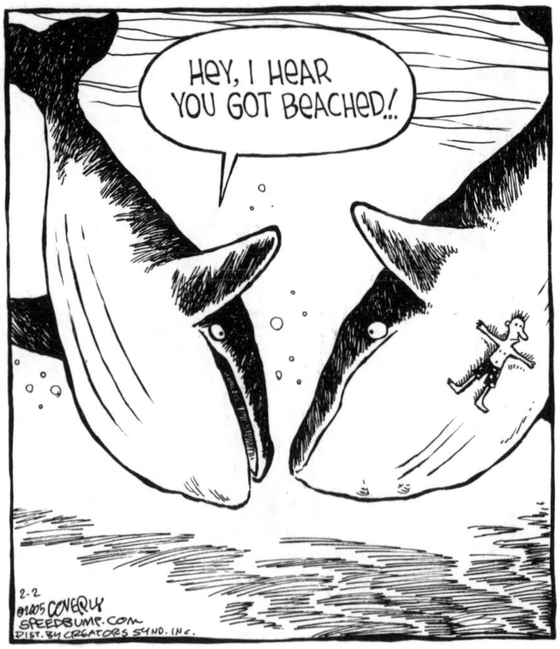
HEY, I HEAR YOU GOT BEACHED!.
2-2
©2005 COVERLY
SPEEDBUMP.COM
DIST. BY CREATORS SYND. INC.

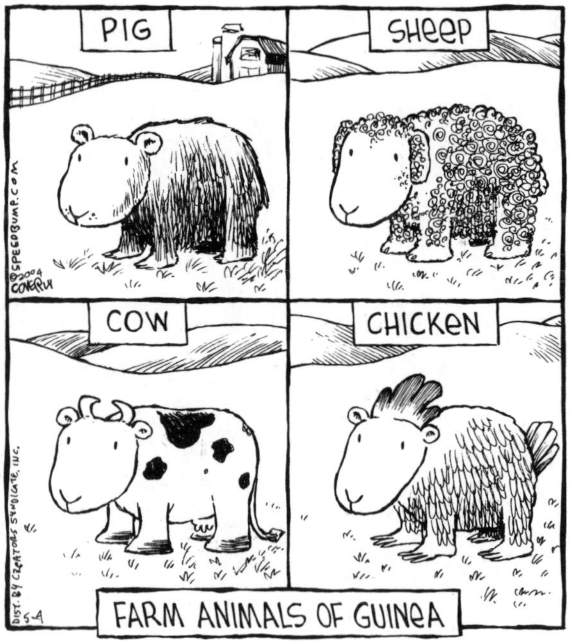
PIG
SHEEP
COW
CHICKEN
SPEEDBUMP.COM
©2004 COVERLY
DIST. BY CREATORS SYNDICATE, INC.
5-4
FARM ANIMALS OF GUINEA

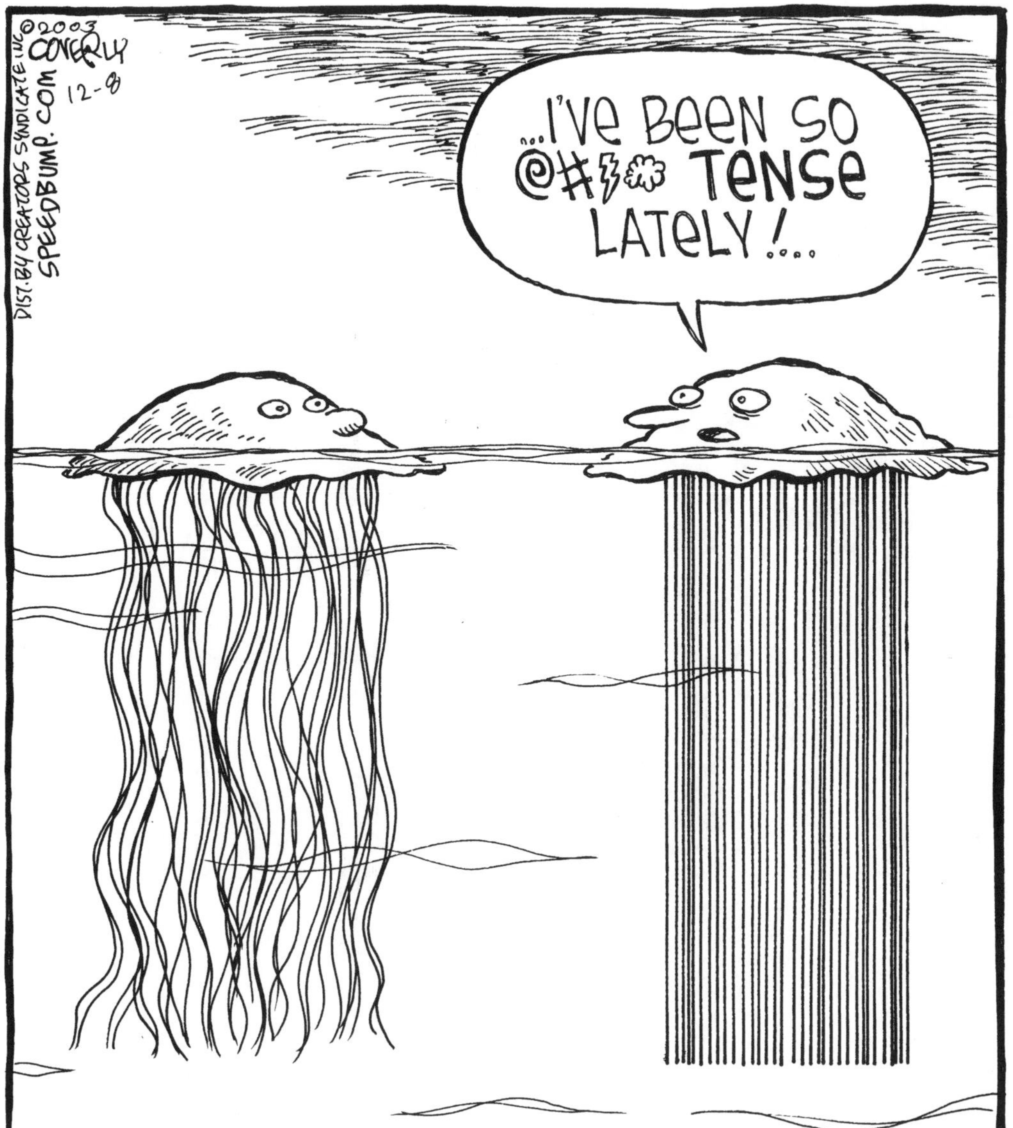
©2003 COVERLY 12-8
DIST. BY CREATORS SYNDICATE INC.
SPEEDBUMP.COM
...I've BEEN SO @#$* TENSE LATELY!...

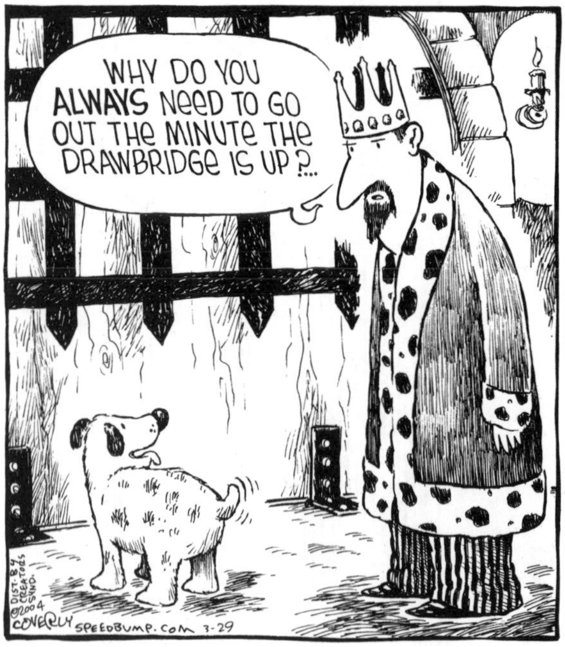
WHY DO YOU **ALWAYS** NEED TO GO OUT THE MINUTE THE DRAWBRIDGE IS UP?...
DIST. BY CREATORS SYND. ©2004
COVERLY SPEEDBUMP.COM 3-29

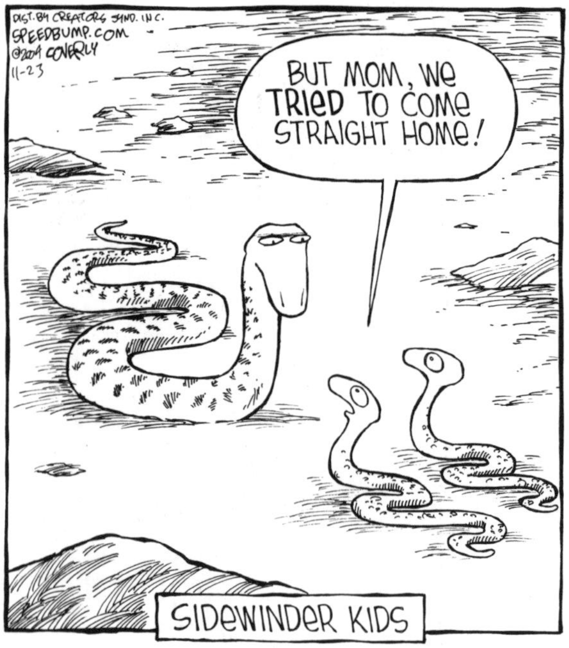
DIST. BY CREATORS SYND. INC.
SPEEDBUMP.COM
©2004 COVERLY
11-23
BUT MOM, WE **TRIED** TO COME STRAIGHT HOME!
SIDEWINDER KIDS

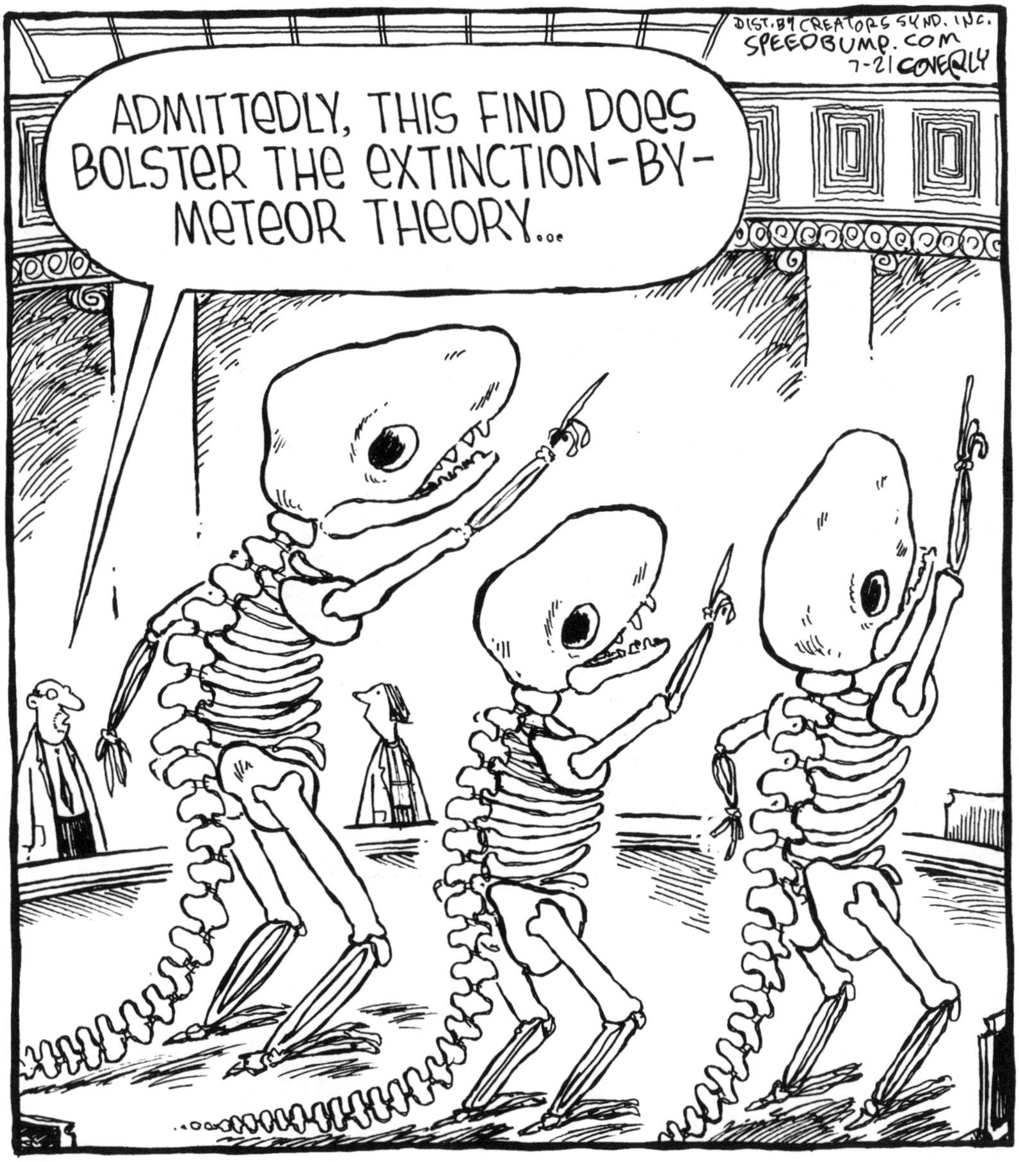
DIST. BY CREATORS SYND. INC.
SPEEDBUMP.COM
7-21 COVERLY
ADMITTEDLY, THIS FIND DOES BOLSTER THE EXTINCTION-BY-METEOR THEORY...

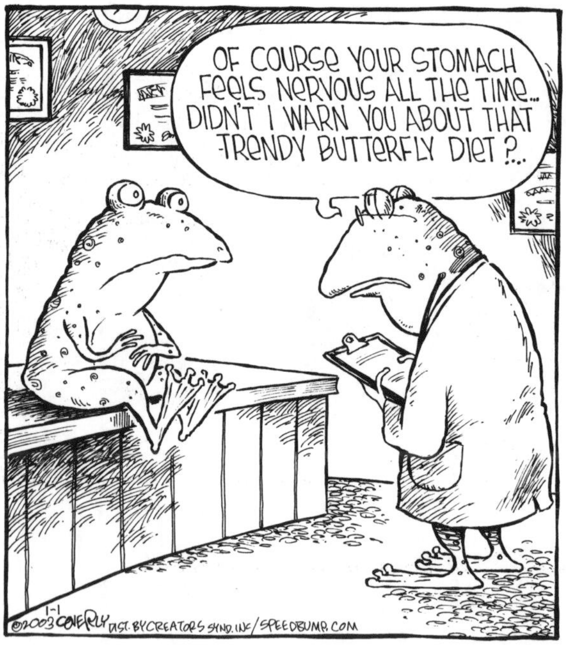
OF COURSE YOUR STOMACH FEELS NERVOUS ALL THE TIME... DIDN'T I WARN YOU ABOUT THAT TRENDY BUTTERFLY DIET ?...
1-1 ©2003 COVERLY DIST. BY CREATORS SYND. INC/SPEEDBUMP.COM

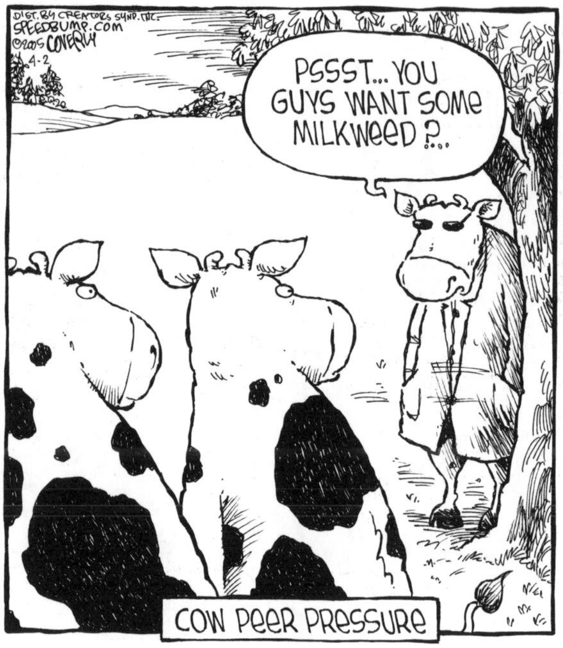
DIST. BY CREATORS SYND. INC. SPEEDBUMP.COM ©2005 COVERLY 4-2
PSSST... YOU GUYS WANT SOME MILKWEED ?...
COW PEER PRESSURE

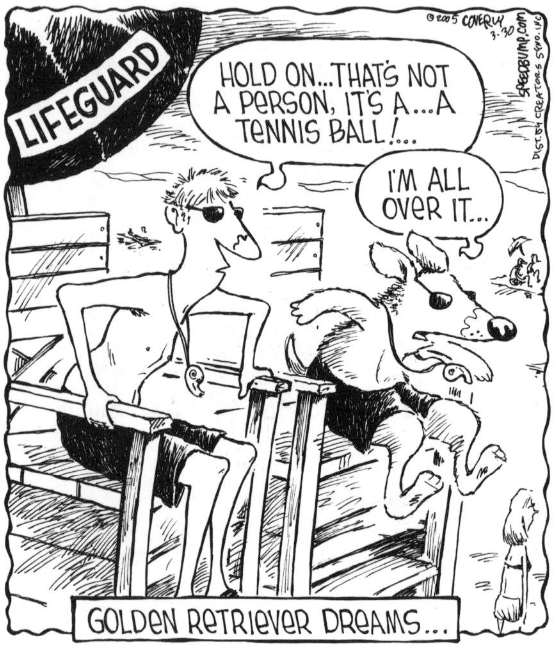
©2005 COVERLY 3-30 SPEEDBUMP.COM DIST. BY CREATORS SYND. INC.
LIFEGUARD
HOLD ON...THAT'S NOT A PERSON, IT'S A...A TENNIS BALL!...
I'M ALL OVER IT...
GOLDEN RETRIEVER DREAMS...

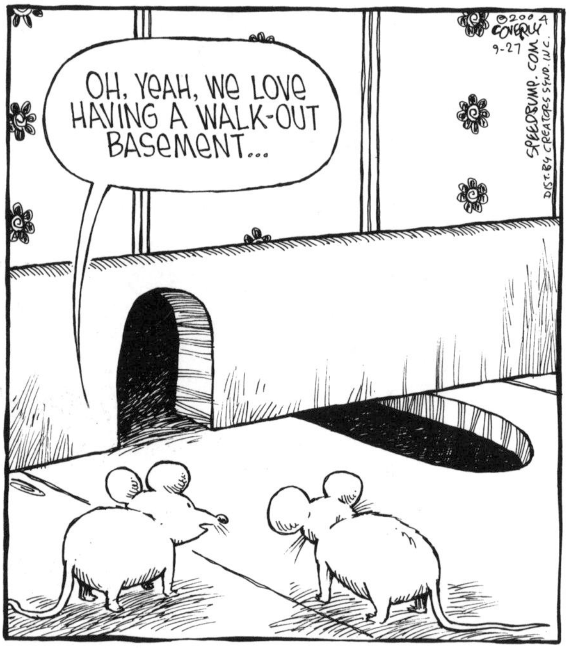
©2004 COVERLY 9-27 SPEEDBUMP.COM DIST. BY CREATORS SYND. INC.
OH, YEAH, WE LOVE HAVING A WALK-OUT BASEMENT...

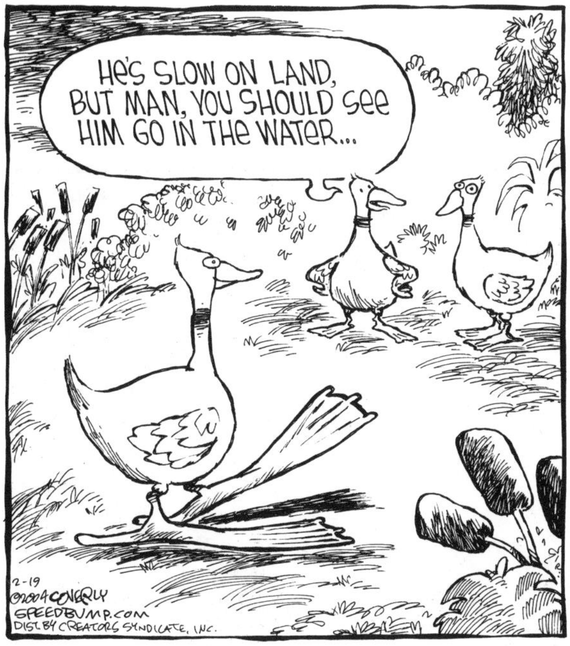
HE'S SLOW ON LAND, BUT MAN, YOU SHOULD SEE HIM GO IN THE WATER...
2-19
©2004 COVERLY
SPEEDBUMP.COM
DIST. BY CREATORS SYNDICATE, INC.

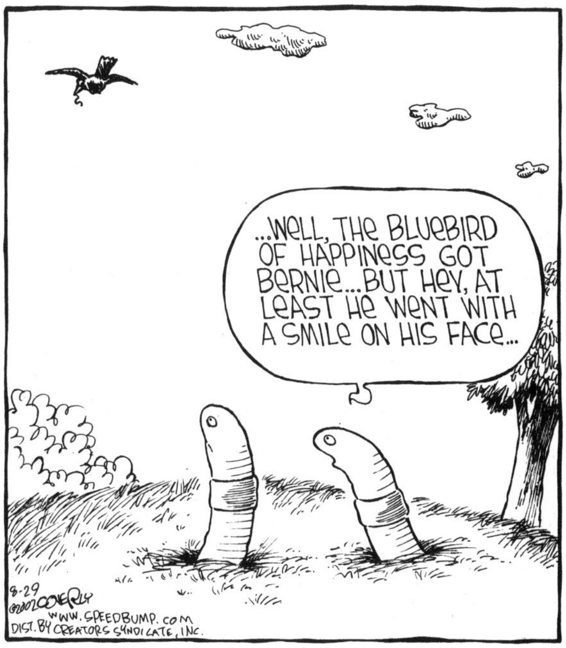
...WELL, THE BLUEBIRD OF HAPPINESS GOT BERNIE... BUT HEY, AT LEAST HE WENT WITH A SMILE ON HIS FACE...
8-29
©2002 COVERLY
WWW.SPEEDBUMP.COM
DIST. BY CREATORS SYNDICATE, INC.

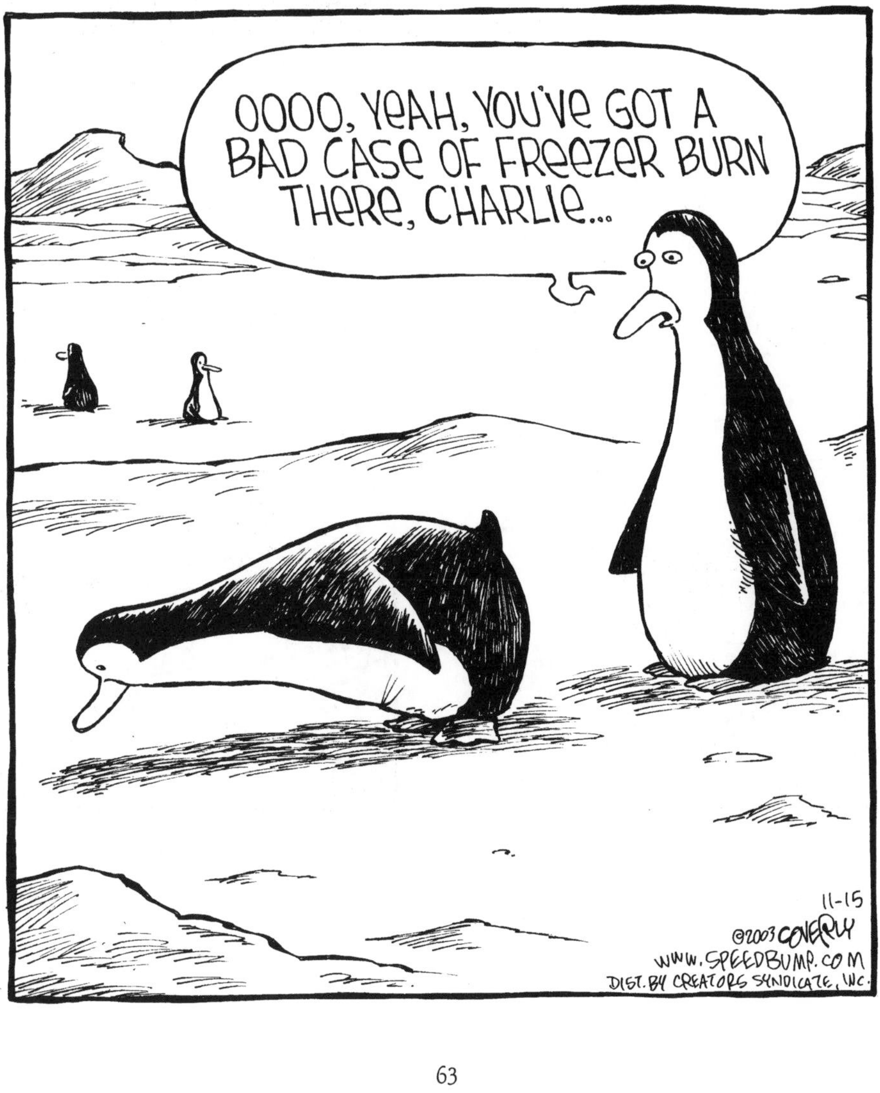
OOOO, YEAH, YOU'VE GOT A BAD CASE OF FREEZER BURN THERE, CHARLIE...
11-15
©2003 COVERLY
WWW.SPEEDBUMP.COM
DIST. BY CREATORS SYNDICATE, INC.

©2003 COVERLY 9-3
DIST. BY CREATORS SYND. INC.
SPEEDBUMP.COM
...NOT AGAIN!... WHAT DID I TELL YOU TWO ABOUT ARM WRESTLING?

BABECO
FERTILITY RESEARCH
REMEMBER WHEN WE JUST DELIVERED THE BABIES?...
9-15
©2004 COVERLY
SPEEDBUMP.COM
DIST. BY CREATORS SYND. INC.

©2004 COVERLY 6-23
DIST. BY CREATORS SYND.
SPEEDBUMP.COM
WELL, SOME HOUSES HAVE DOG DOORS...SOME HOUSES HAVE CAT DOORS...

©2005 COVERLY 2-1
SPEEDBUMP.COM
DIST. BY CREATORS SYND. INC.
KREST
YELLOW STRIPS

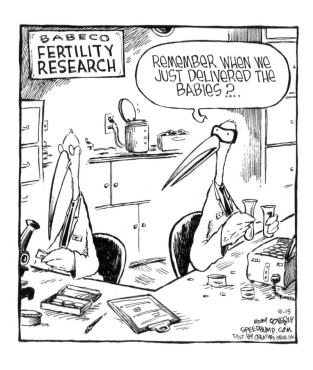

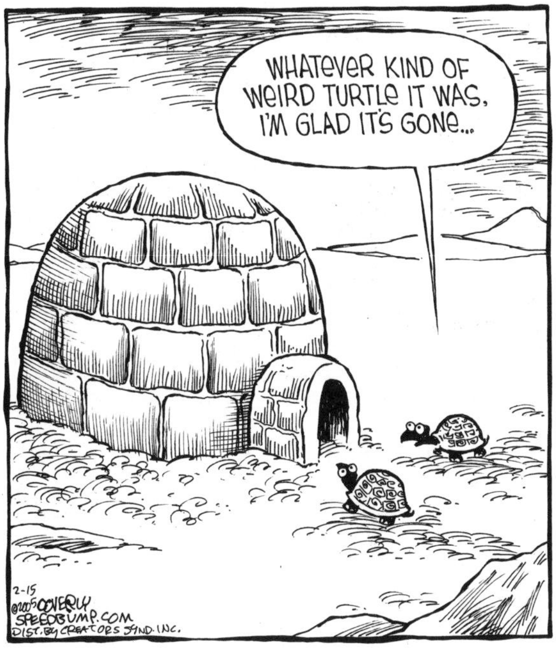
WHATEVER KIND OF WEIRD TURTLE IT WAS, I'M GLAD IT'S GONE...
2-15
©2005 COVERLY
SPEEDBUMP.COM
DIST. BY CREATORS SYND. INC.

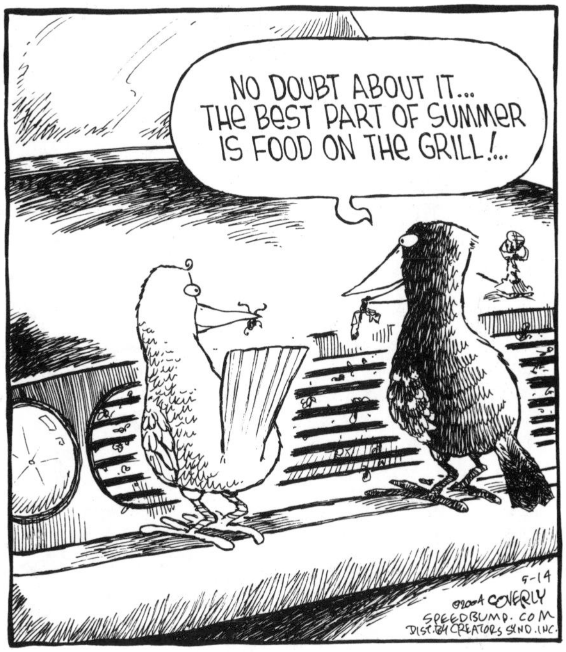
NO DOUBT ABOUT IT... THE BEST PART OF SUMMER IS FOOD ON THE GRILL!...
5-14
©2004 COVERLY
SPEEDBUMP.COM
DIST. BY CREATORS SYND. INC.

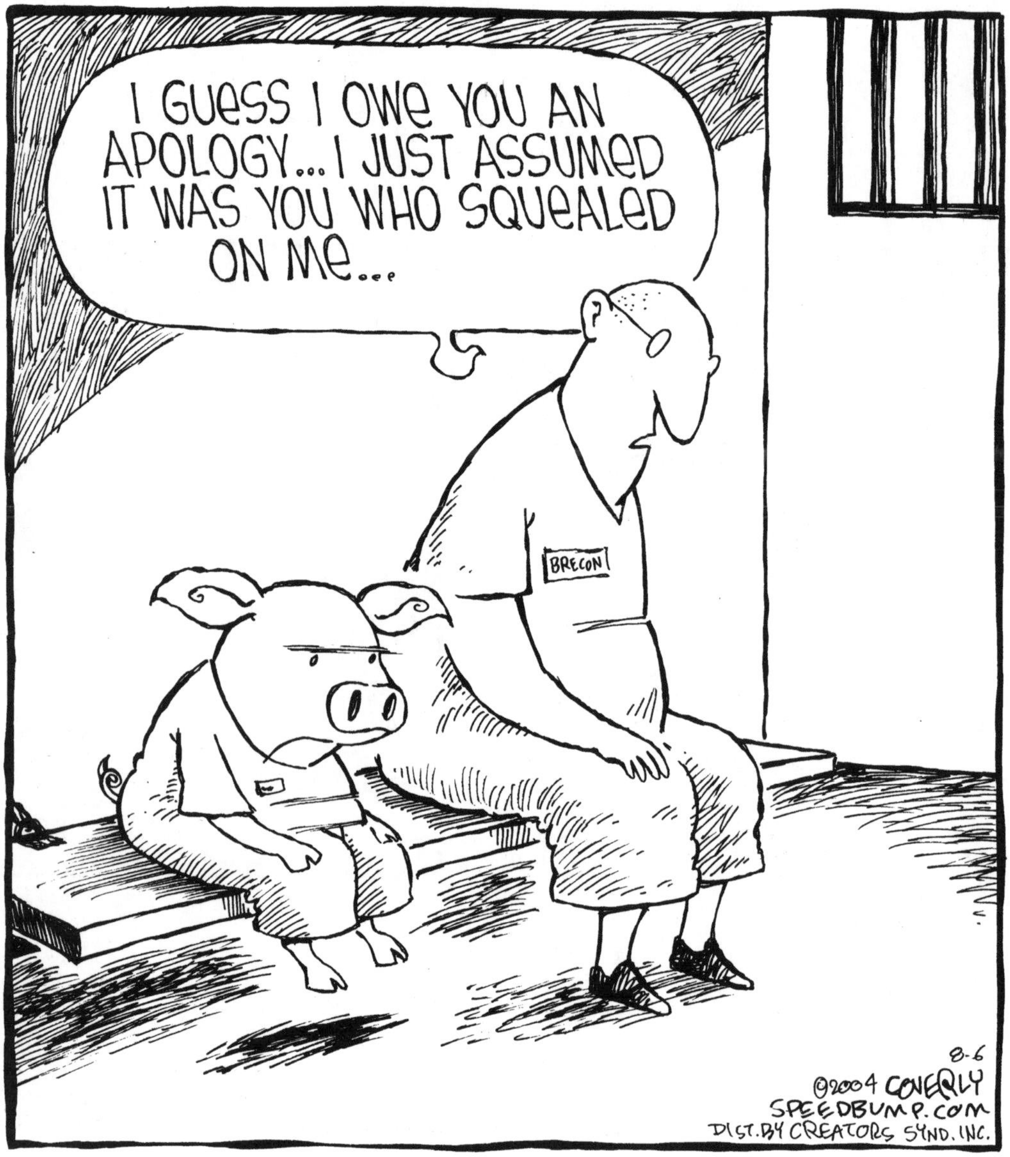
I GUESS I OWE YOU AN APOLOGY... I JUST ASSUMED IT WAS YOU WHO SQUEALED ON ME...
BRECON
8-6
©2004 COVERLY
SPEEDBUMP.COM
DIST. BY CREATORS SYND. INC.

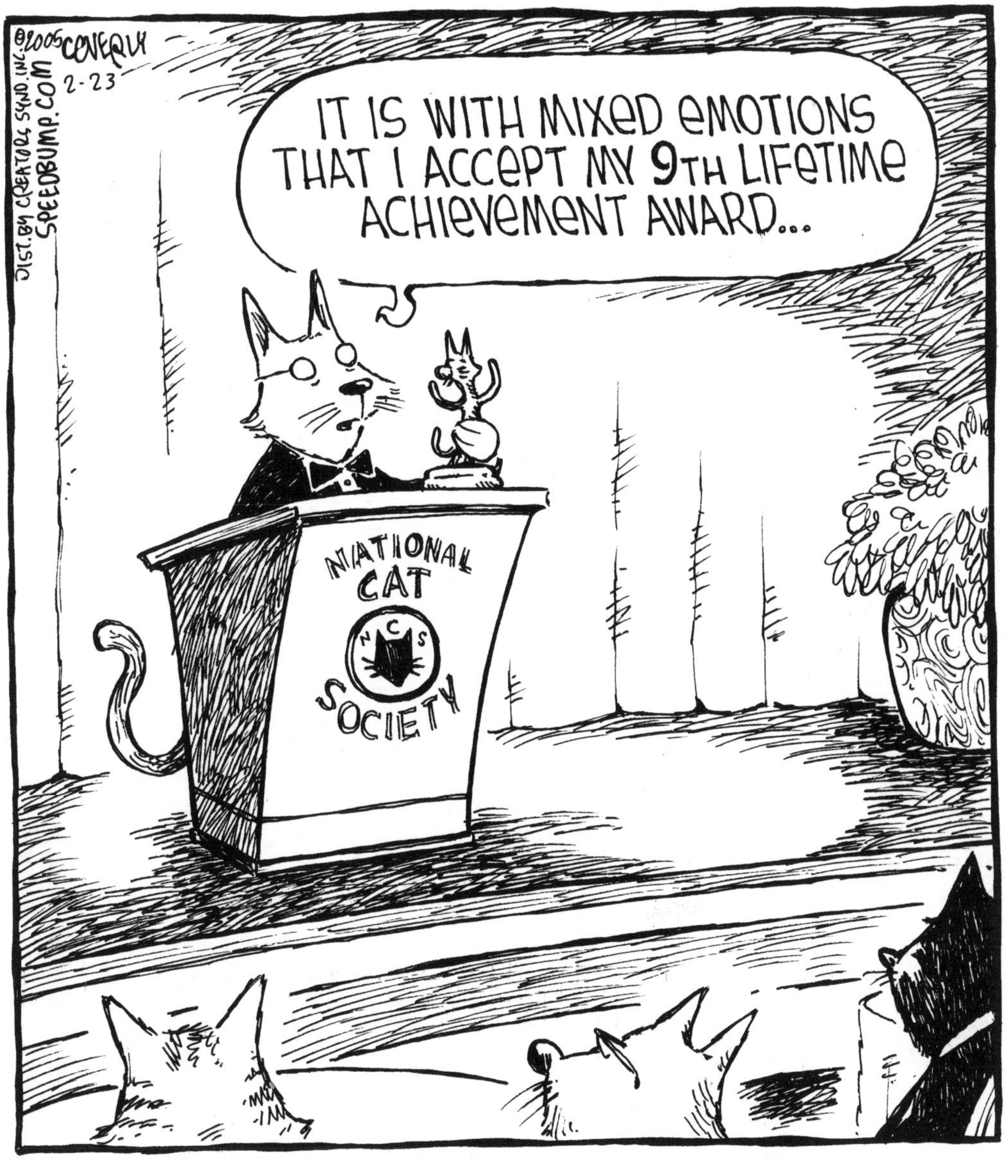
©2005 COVERLY
2-23
DIST. BY CREATORS SYND. INC.
SPEEDBUMP.COM
IT IS WITH MIXED EMOTIONS THAT I ACCEPT MY 9TH LIFETIME ACHIEVEMENT AWARD...
NATIONAL CAT SOCIETY
NCS

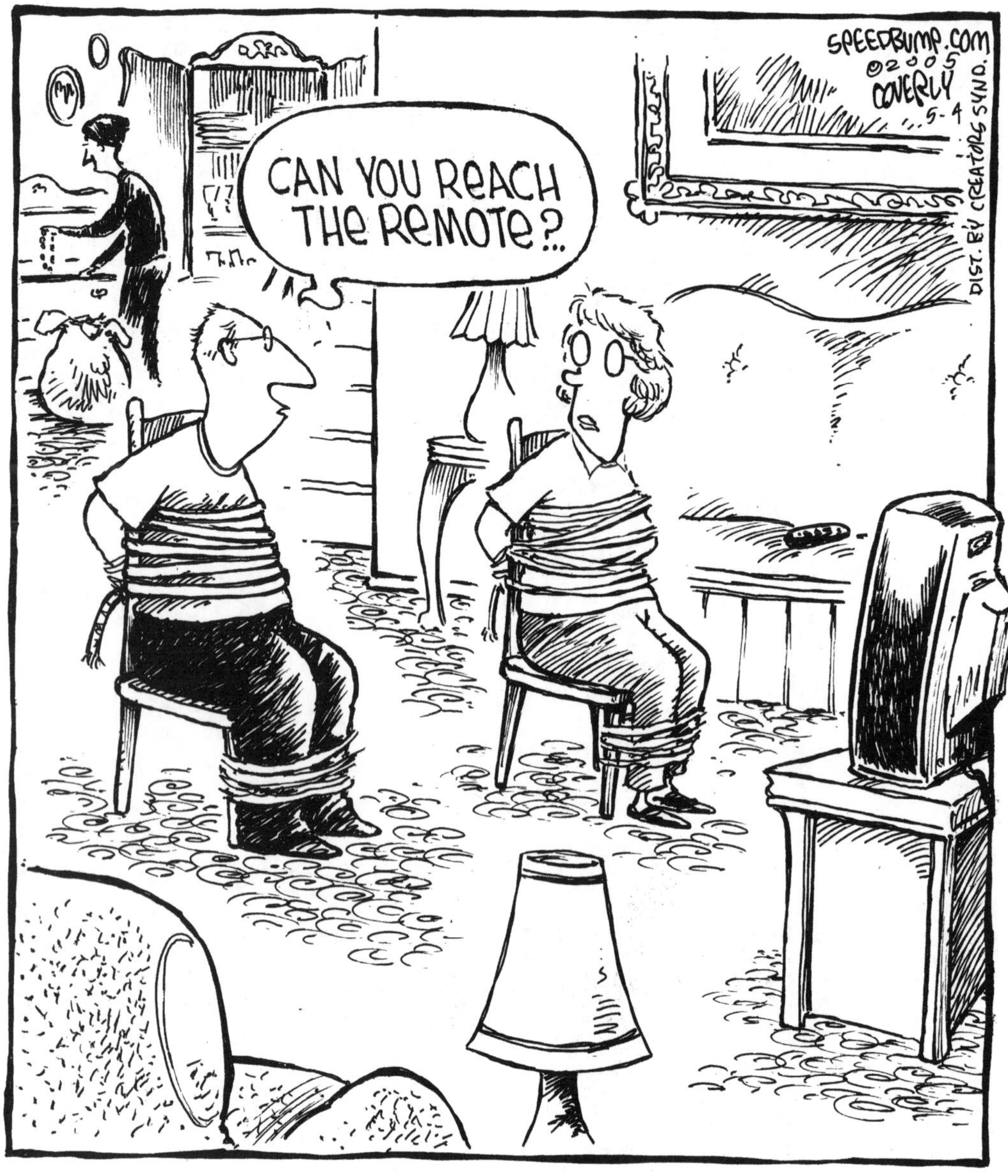
CAN YOU REACH THE REMOTE?..
SPEEDBUMP.COM ©2005 COVERLY 5-4
DIST. BY CREATORS SYND.

XX vs. XY

If men are from Mars and women are from Venus, as they say, then it's too bad relationships don't come with frequent flyer miles attached. What is it that draws us together and keeps (some) of us together, when it's pretty clear we've got different hard wiring? When my oldest daughter was a toddler in daycare, I watched a ball roll next to a group of kids. One girl looked at it and eventually sort of reached out to grab it. Then the two boys saw it. One started punching on it; the other tried to bite it.

Fortunately, opposites do attract, right down to our chromosomes. The trick is to find the humor in that kind of tension.

Right, dear? Hello?

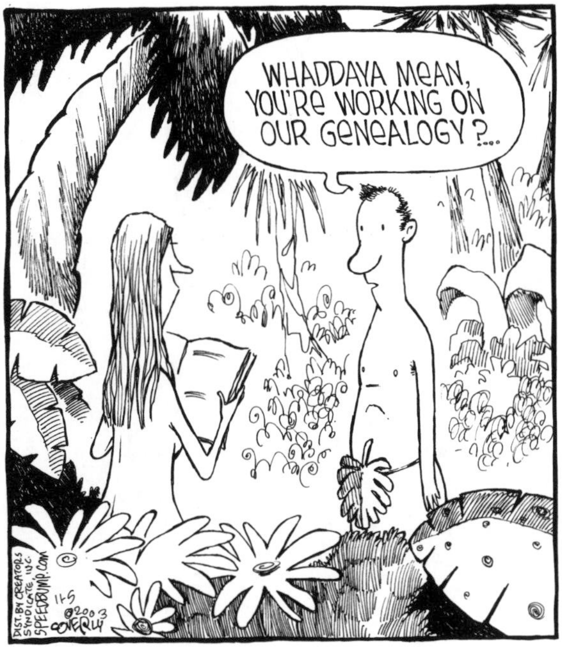
WHADDAYA MEAN, YOU'RE WORKING ON OUR GENEALOGY ?...

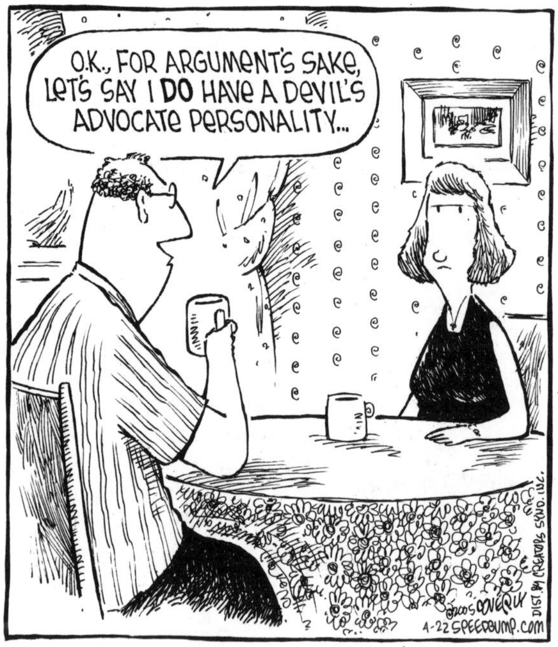
O.K., FOR ARGUMENT'S SAKE, LET'S SAY I DO HAVE A DEVIL'S ADVOCATE PERSONALITY...
DIST. BY CREATORS SYND. INC.
4-22 SPEEDBUMP.COM

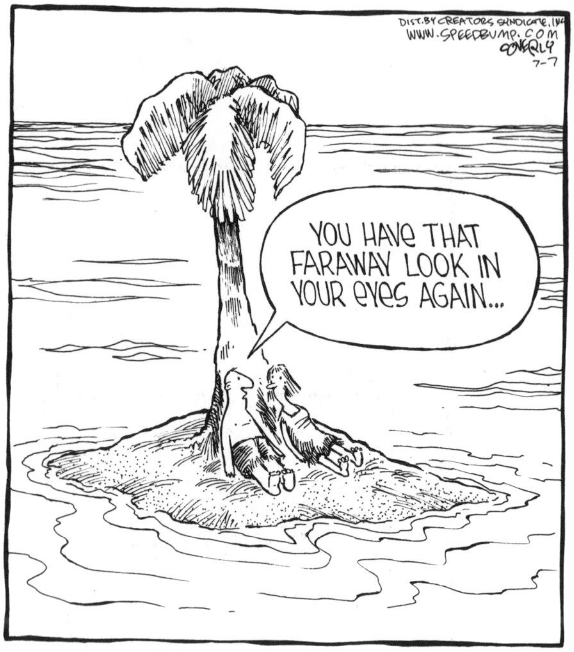
DIST. BY CREATORS SYNDICATE, INC
WWW.SPEEDBUMP.COM
7-7
YOU HAVE THAT FARAWAY LOOK IN YOUR EYES AGAIN...

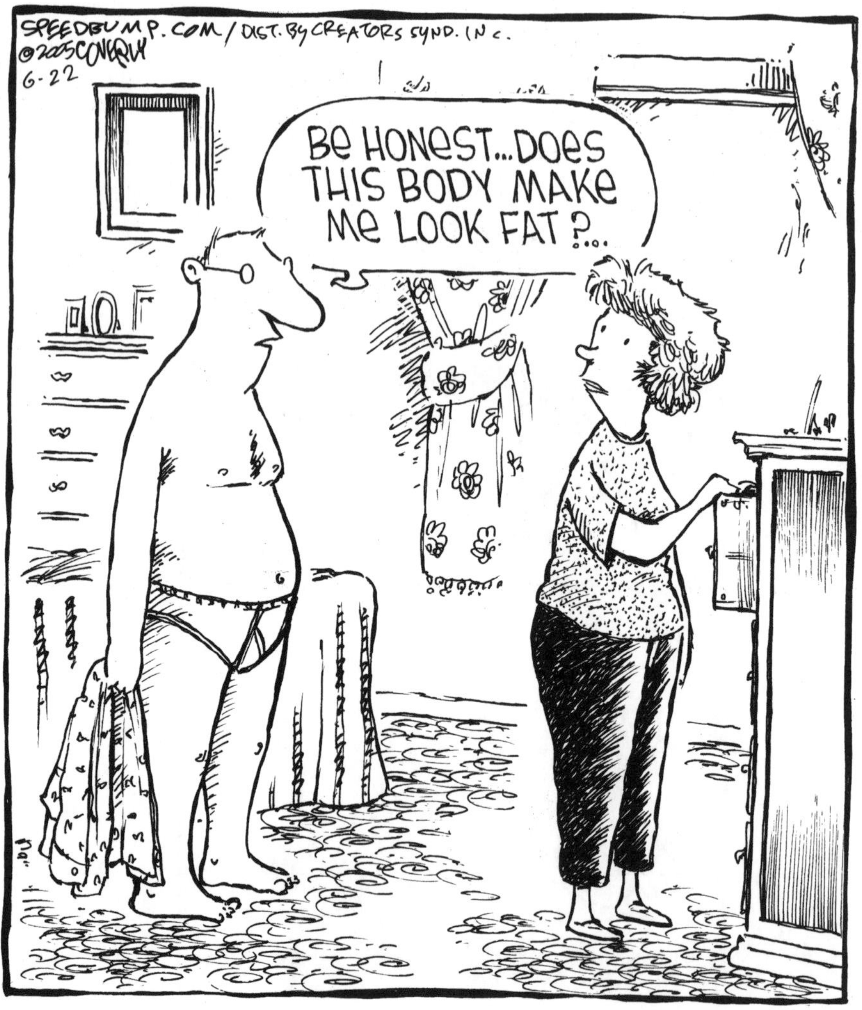
SPEEDBUMP.COM / DIST. BY CREATORS SYND. INC.
6-22
BE HONEST...DOES THIS BODY MAKE ME LOOK FAT?...

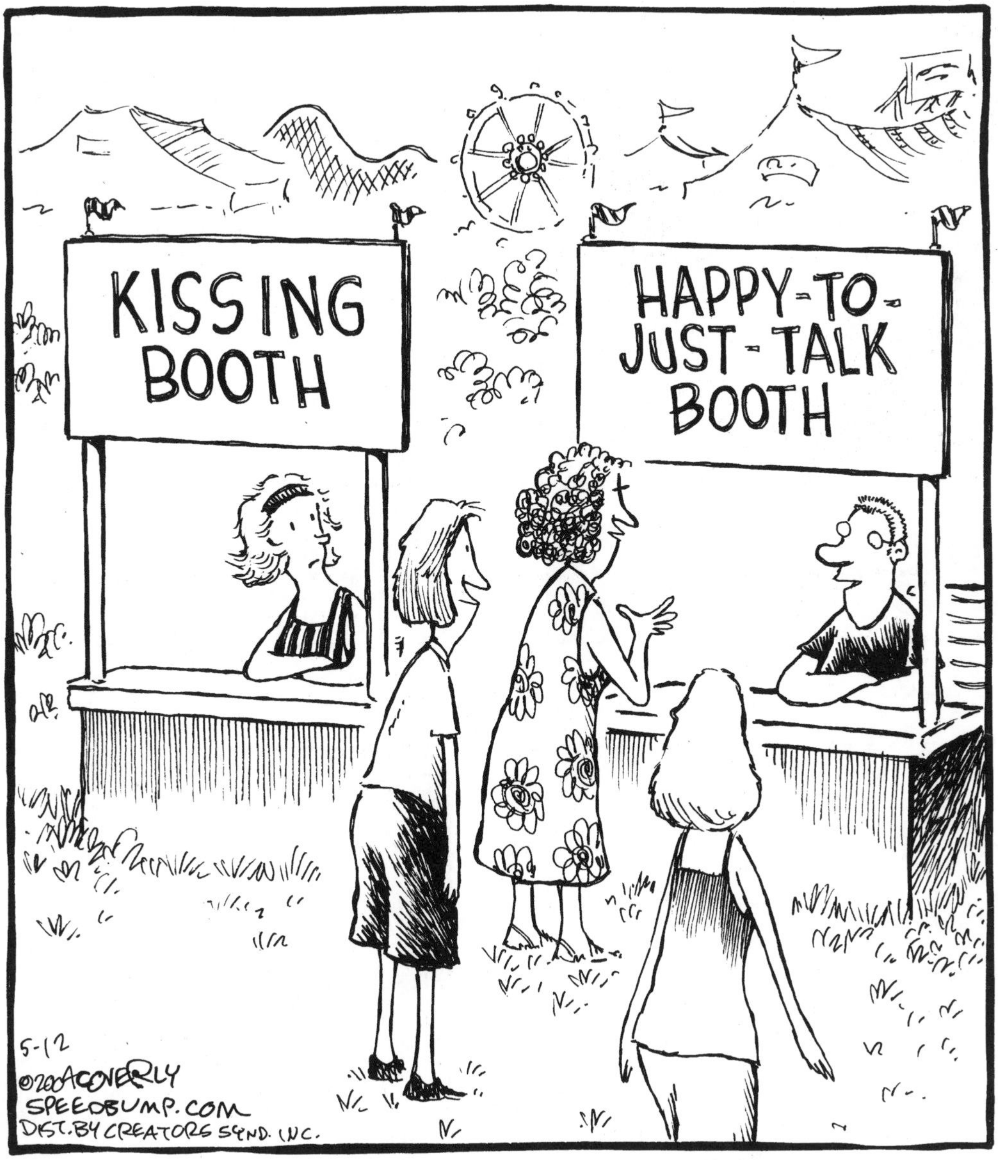
KISSING BOOTH
HAPPY-TO-JUST-TALK BOOTH
5-12
©2004 COVERLY
SPEEDBUMP.COM
DIST. BY CREATORS SYND. INC.

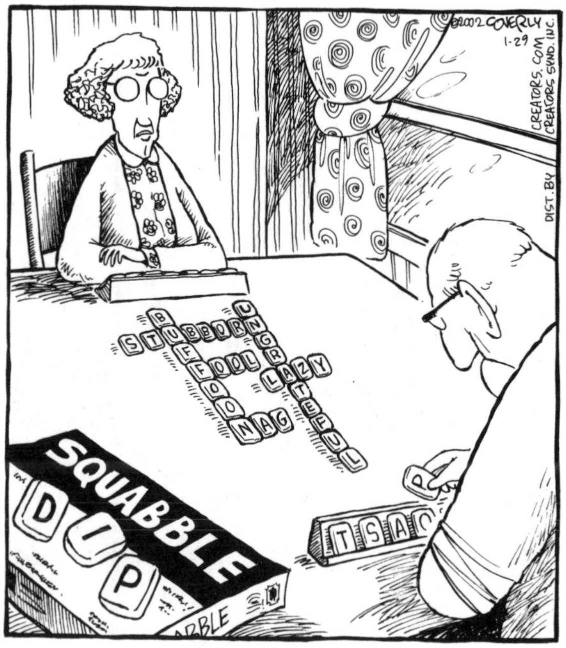
©2002 COVERLY 1-29
DIST. BY CREATORS.COM CREATORS SYND. INC.
SQUABBLE
STUBBORN
BUFFOON
UNGRATEFUL
FOOL
LAZY
NAG

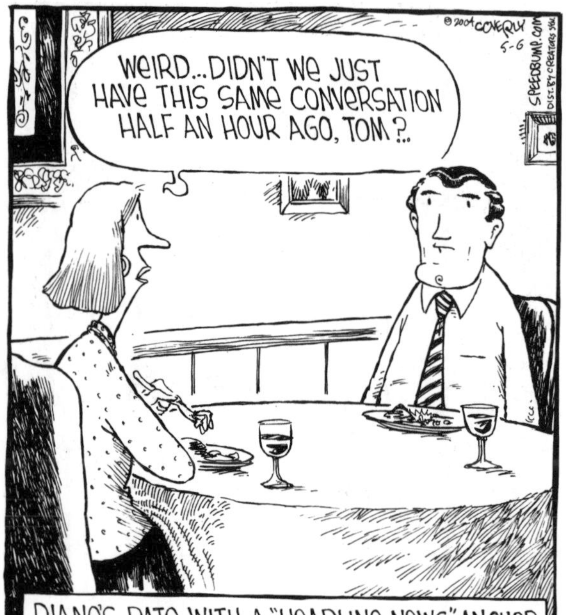
©2004 COVERLY 5-6
SPEEDBUMP.COM DIST. BY CREATORS SYND.
WEIRD...DIDN'T WE JUST HAVE THIS SAME CONVERSATION HALF AN HOUR AGO, TOM?..
DIANE'S DATE WITH A "HEADLINE NEWS" ANCHOR

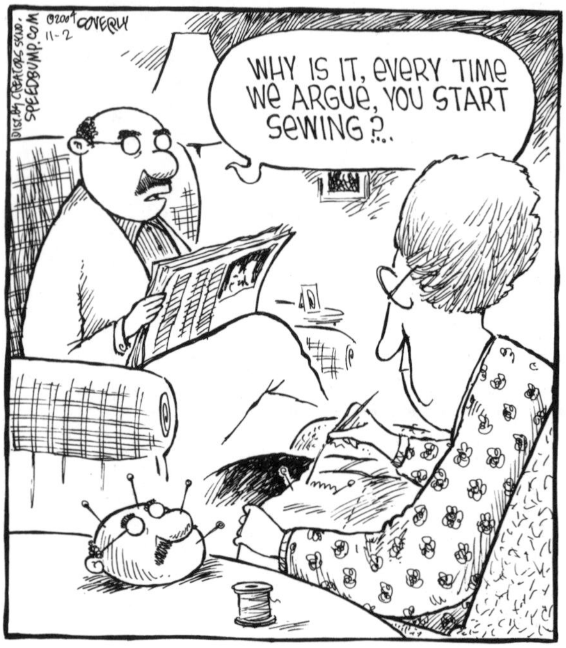
©2004 COVERLY 11-2
DIST. BY CREATORS SYND. SPEEDBUMP.COM
WHY IS IT, EVERY TIME WE ARGUE, YOU START SEWING?..

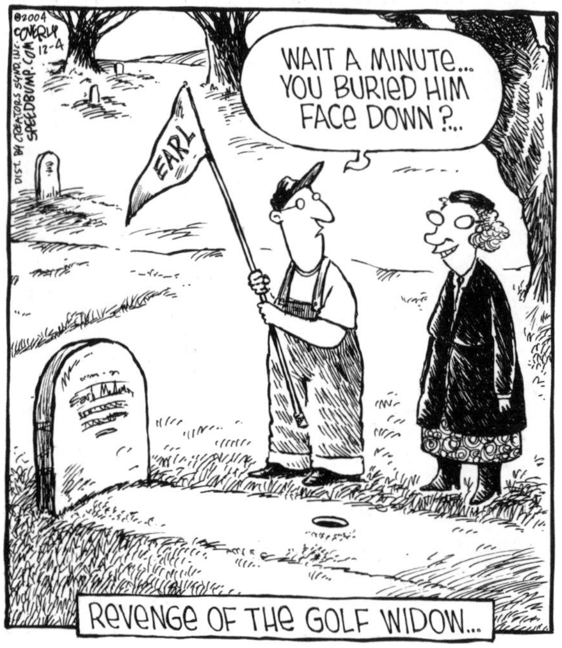
©2004 COVERLY 12-4
DIST. BY CREATORS SYND. INC. SPEEDBUMP.COM
EARL
WAIT A MINUTE... YOU BURIED HIM FACE DOWN?..
REVENGE OF THE GOLF WIDOW...

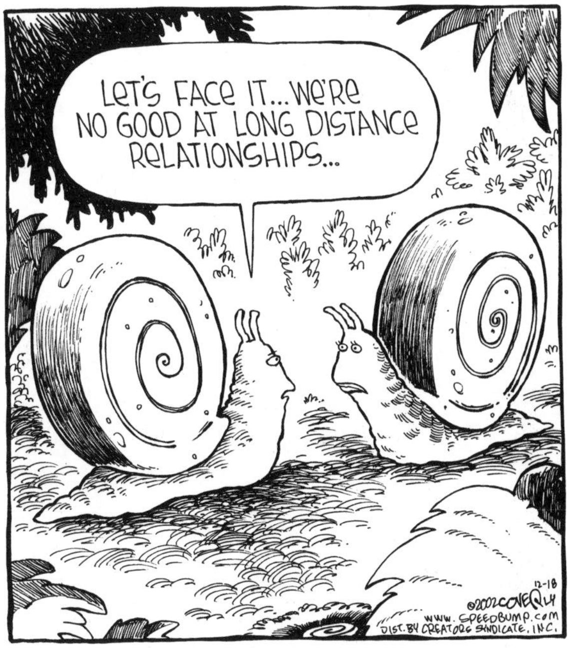
LET'S FACE IT... WE'RE NO GOOD AT LONG DISTANCE RELATIONSHIPS...
©2002 COVERLY
WWW.SPEEDBUMP.COM
DIST. BY CREATORS SYNDICATE, INC.

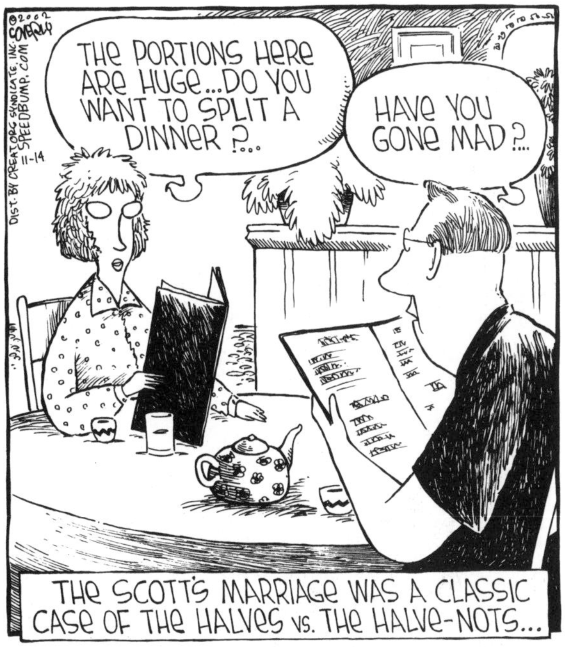
THE PORTIONS HERE ARE HUGE... DO YOU WANT TO SPLIT A DINNER ?...
HAVE YOU GONE MAD ?...
©2002 COVERLY
DIST. BY CREATORS SYNDICATE, INC.
SPEEDBUMP.COM
THE SCOTT'S MARRIAGE WAS A CLASSIC CASE OF THE HALVES vs. THE HALVE-NOTS...

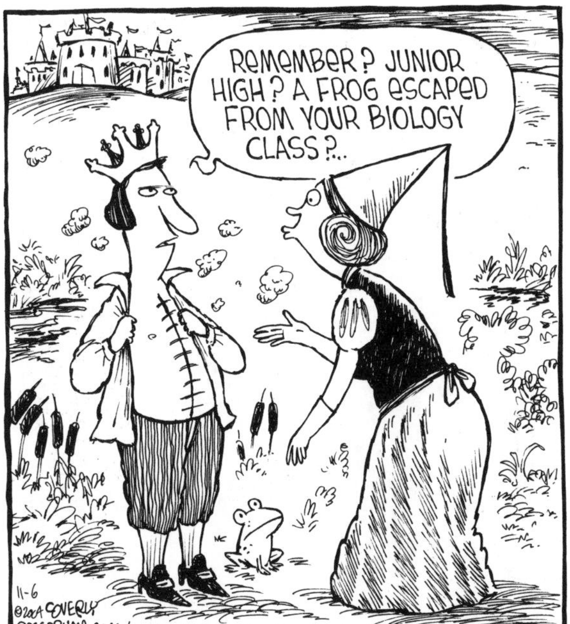
REMEMBER ? JUNIOR HIGH ? A FROG ESCAPED FROM YOUR BIOLOGY CLASS ?...
©2004 COVERLY
SPEEDBUMP.COM / DIST. BY CREATORS SYND. INC.

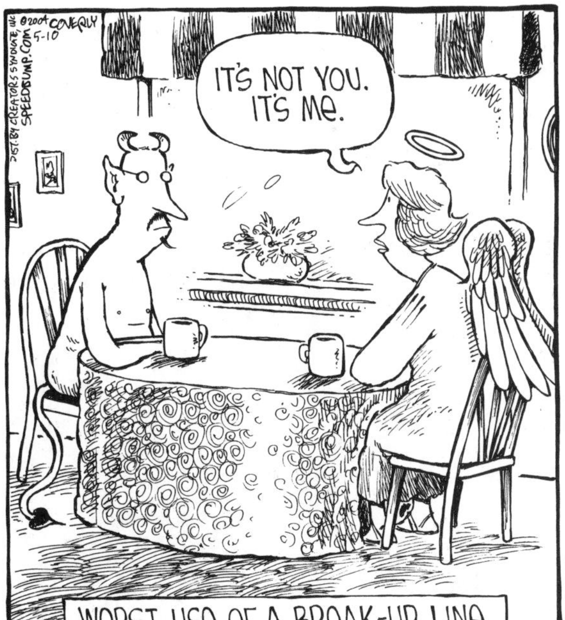
IT'S NOT YOU. IT'S ME.
©2004 COVERLY
DIST. BY CREATORS SYNDICATE, INC.
SPEEDBUMP.COM
WORST USE OF A BREAK-UP LINE...

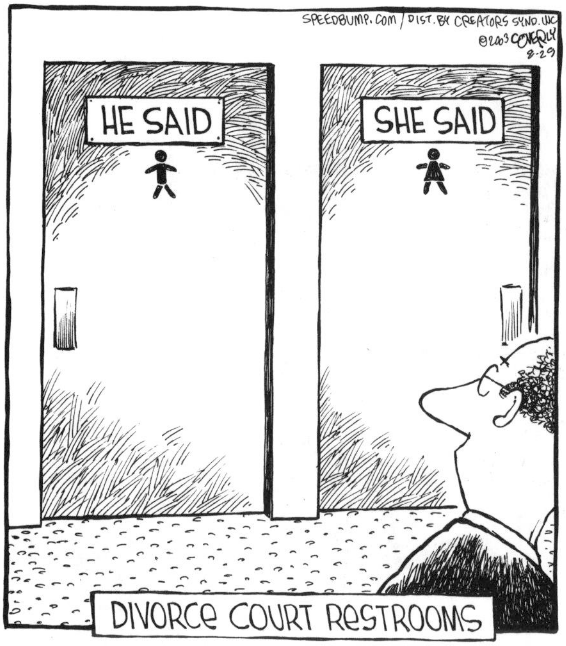
SPEEDBUMP.COM / DIST. BY CREATORS SYND. INC.
©2003 COVERLY 8-29
HE SAID
SHE SAID
DIVORCE COURT RESTROOMS

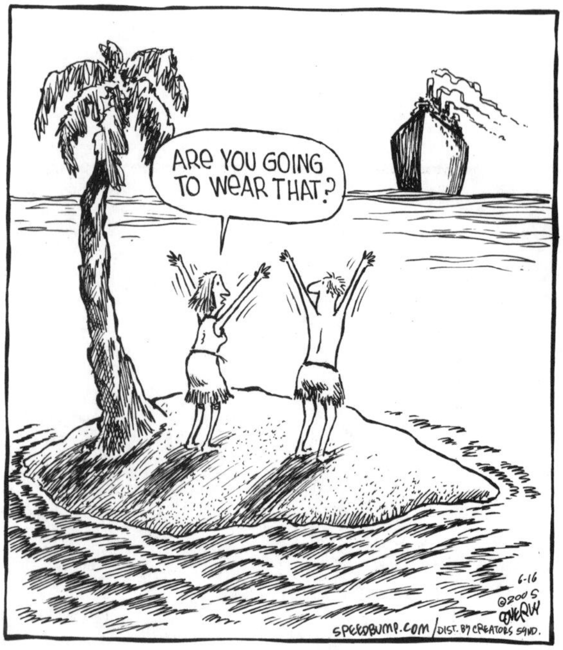
ARE YOU GOING TO WEAR THAT?
6-16 ©2005 COVERLY
SPEEDBUMP.COM / DIST. BY CREATORS SYND.

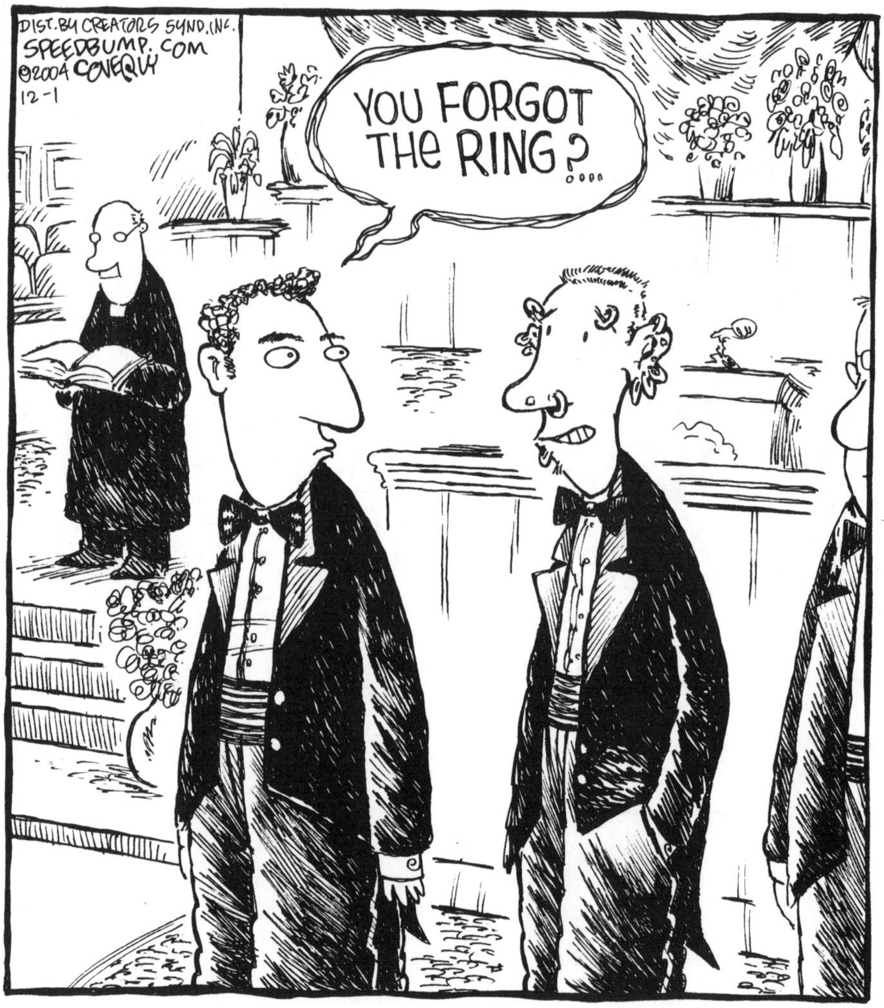
DIST. BY CREATORS SYND. INC.
SPEEDBUMP.COM
©2004 COVERLY
12-1
YOU FORGOT THE RING?...

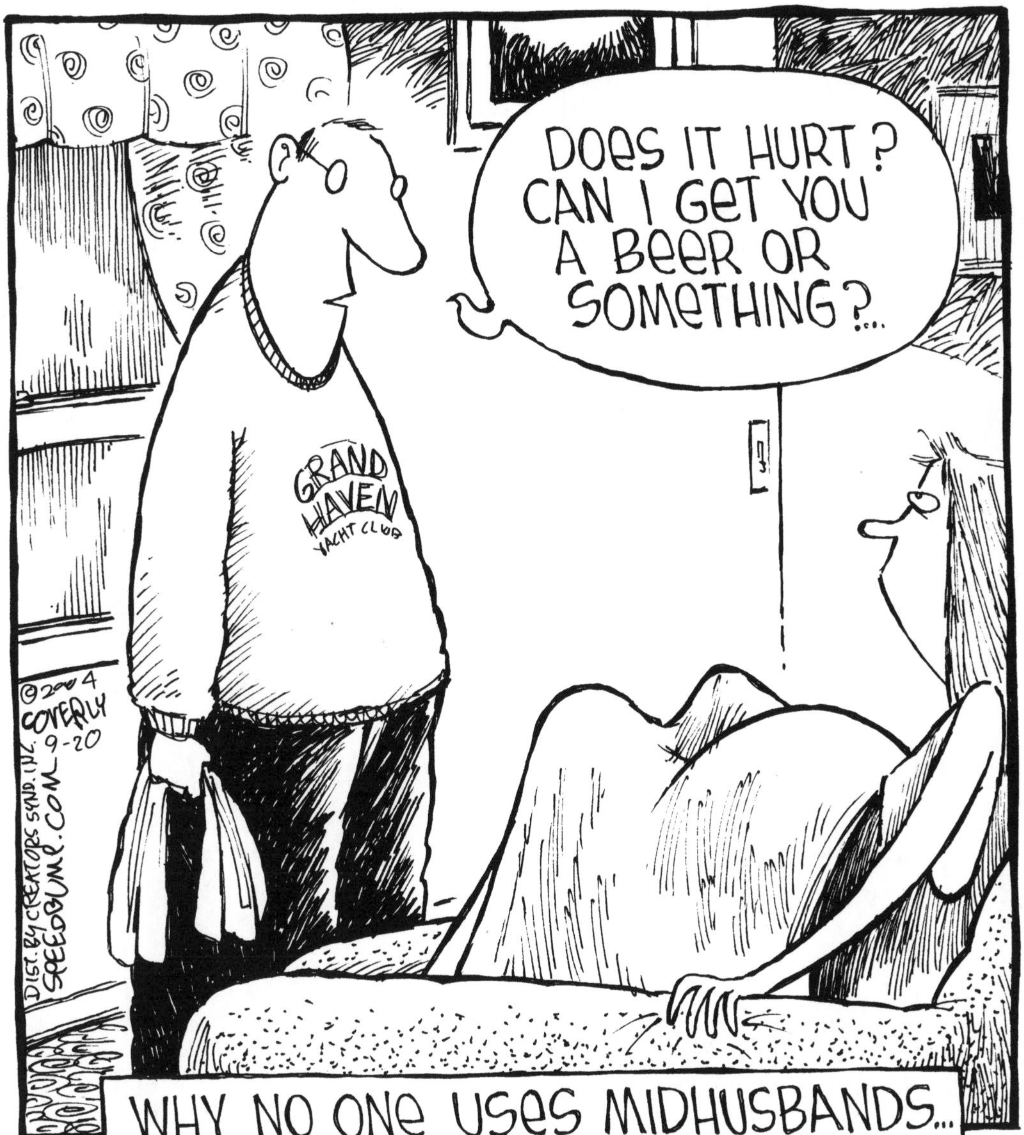
DOES IT HURT? CAN I GET YOU A BEER OR SOMETHING?...
GRAND HAVEN YACHT CLUB
©2004 COVERLY 9-20
DIST. BY CREATORS SYND. INC.
SPEEDBUMP.COM
WHY NO ONE USES MIDHUSBANDS...

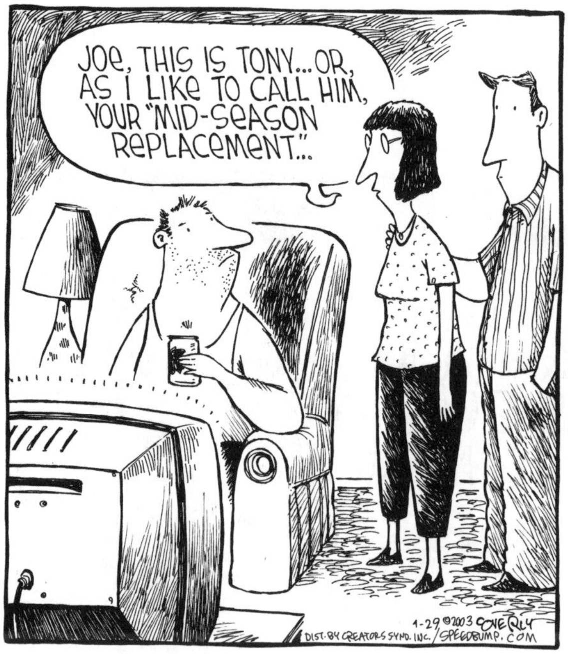
JOE, THIS IS TONY...OR, AS I LIKE TO CALL HIM, YOUR "MID-SEASON REPLACEMENT."...
1-29 ©2003 COVERLY
DIST. BY CREATORS SYND. INC. SPEEDBUMP.COM

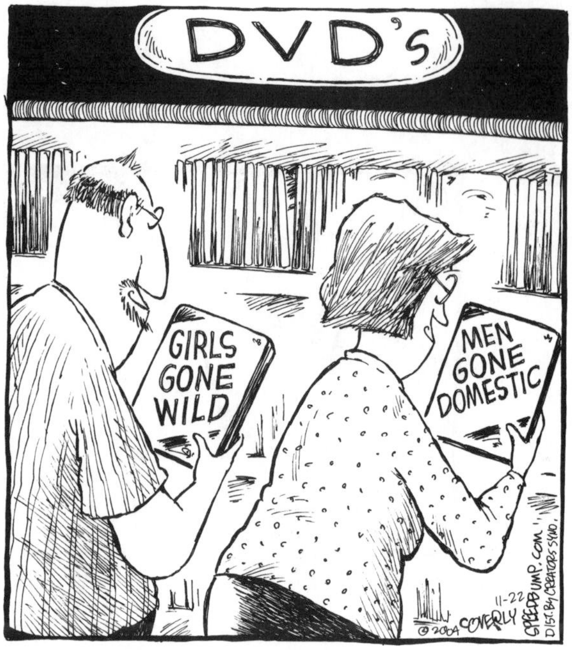
DVD's
GIRLS GONE WILD
MEN GONE DOMESTIC
11-22 ©2004 COVERLY
SPEEDBUMP.COM
DIST. BY CREATORS SYND.

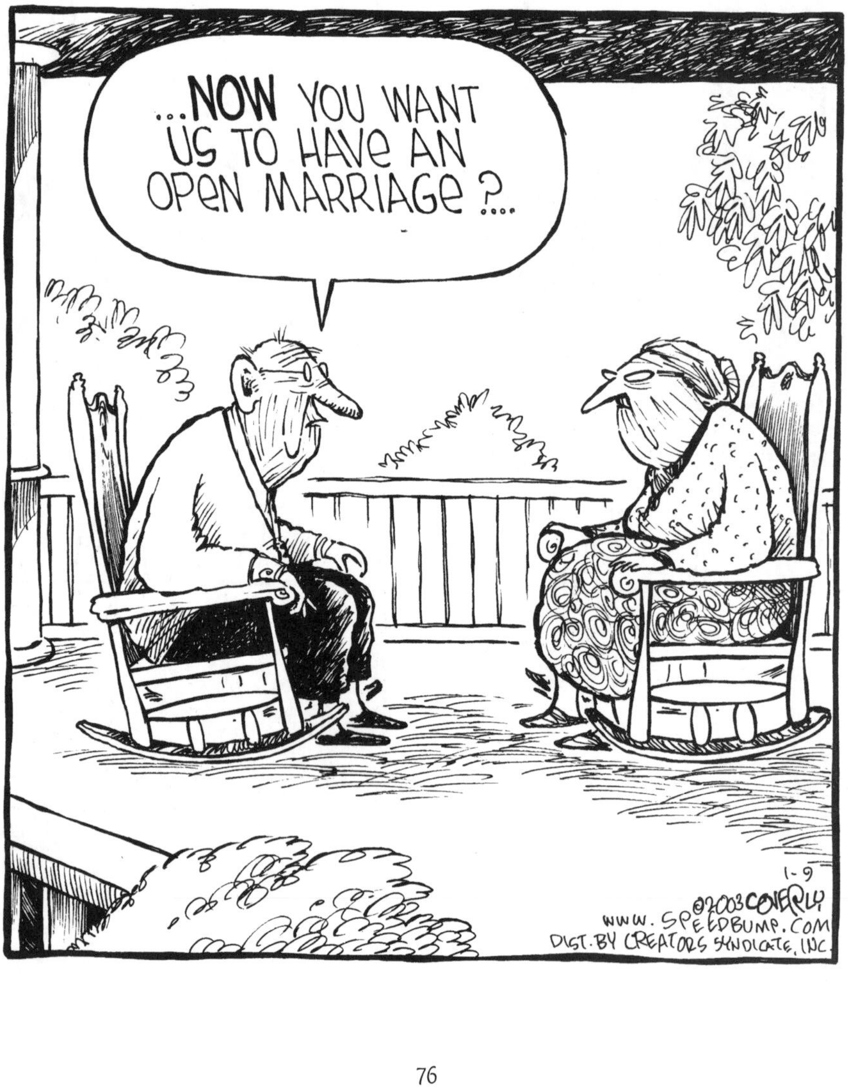
...NOW YOU WANT US TO HAVE AN OPEN MARRIAGE ?...
1-9 ©2003 COVERLY
www.SPEEDBUMP.COM
DIST. BY CREATORS SYNDICATE, INC.

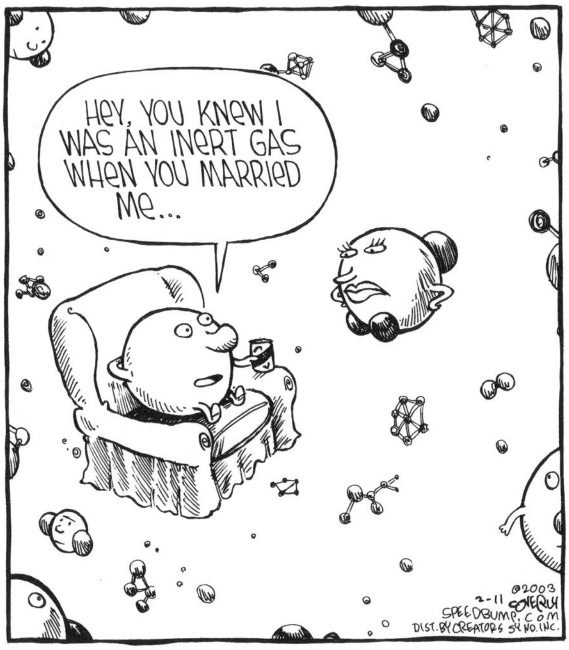
HEY, YOU KNEW I WAS AN INERT GAS WHEN YOU MARRIED ME...
©2003 2-11 COVERLY
SPEEDBUMP.COM
DIST. BY CREATORS SYND. INC.

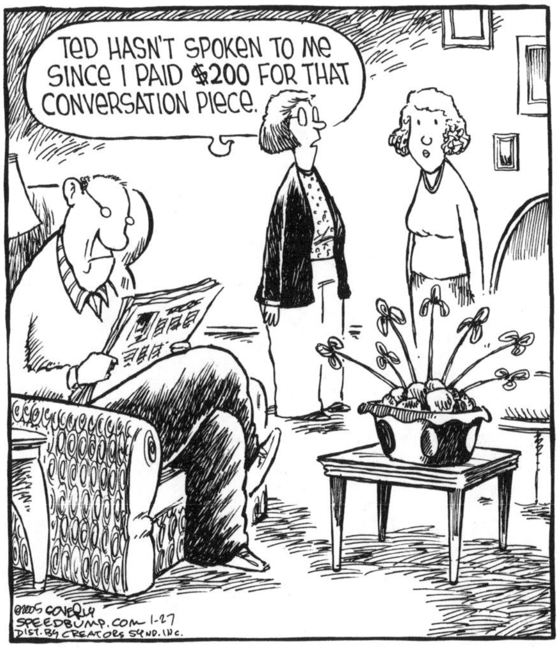
TED HASN'T SPOKEN TO ME SINCE I PAID $200 FOR THAT CONVERSATION PIECE.
©2005 COVERLY
SPEEDBUMP.COM 1-27
DIST. BY CREATORS SYND. INC.

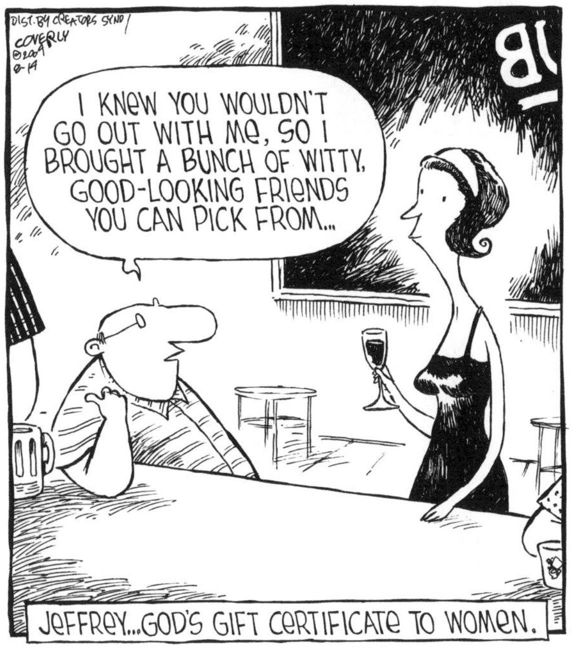
DIST. BY CREATORS SYND.
COVERLY
I KNEW YOU WOULDN'T GO OUT WITH ME, SO I BROUGHT A BUNCH OF WITTY, GOOD-LOOKING FRIENDS YOU CAN PICK FROM...
JEFFREY...GOD'S GIFT CERTIFICATE TO WOMEN.

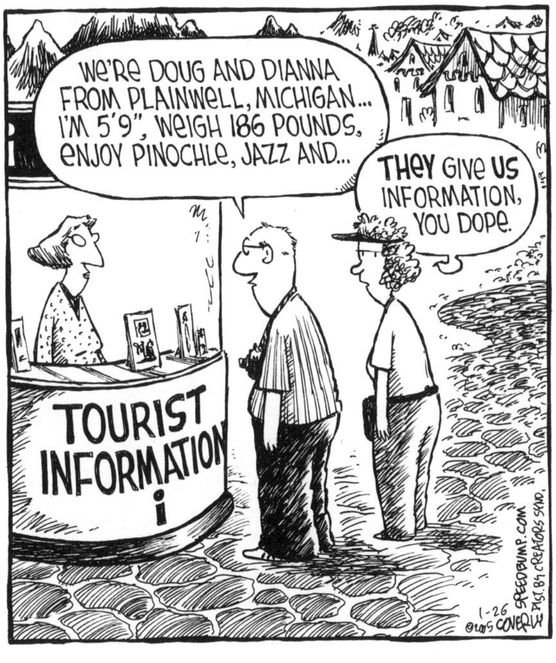
WE'RE DOUG AND DIANNA FROM PLAINWELL, MICHIGAN... I'M 5'9", WEIGH 186 POUNDS, ENJOY PINOCHLE, JAZZ AND...
THEY GIVE US INFORMATION, YOU DOPE.
TOURIST INFORMATION
i
SPEEDBUMP.COM
DIST. BY CREATORS SYND.
1-26
©2005 COVERLY

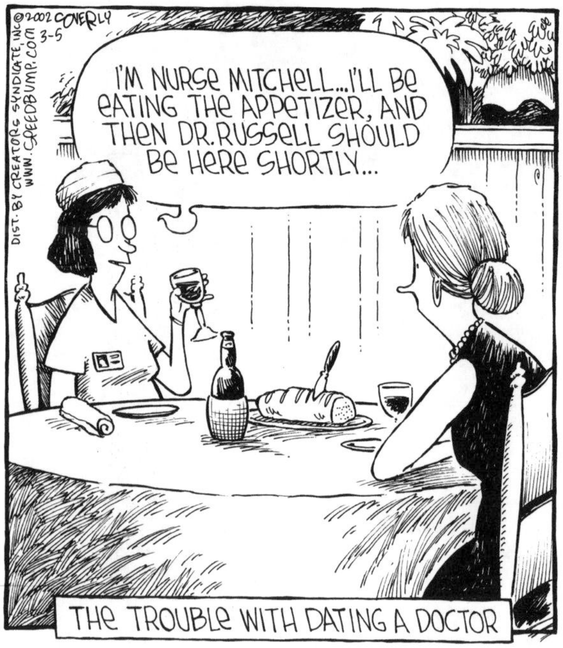
I'M NURSE MITCHELL...I'LL BE EATING THE APPETIZER, AND THEN DR. RUSSELL SHOULD BE HERE SHORTLY...
©2002 COVERLY 3-5
DIST. BY CREATORS SYNDICATE, INC. WWW.SPEEDBUMP.COM

THE TROUBLE WITH DATING A DOCTOR

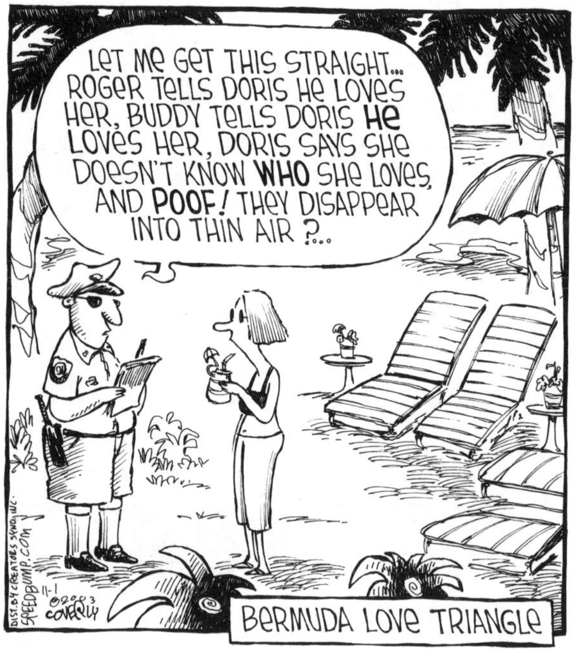
LET ME GET THIS STRAIGHT... ROGER TELLS DORIS HE LOVES HER, BUDDY TELLS DORIS **HE** LOVES HER, DORIS SAYS SHE DOESN'T KNOW **WHO** SHE LOVES, AND **POOF!** THEY DISAPPEAR INTO THIN AIR ?...
DIST. BY CREATORS SYND. INC. SPEEDBUMP.COM 11-1 ©2003 COVERLY

BERMUDA LOVE TRIANGLE

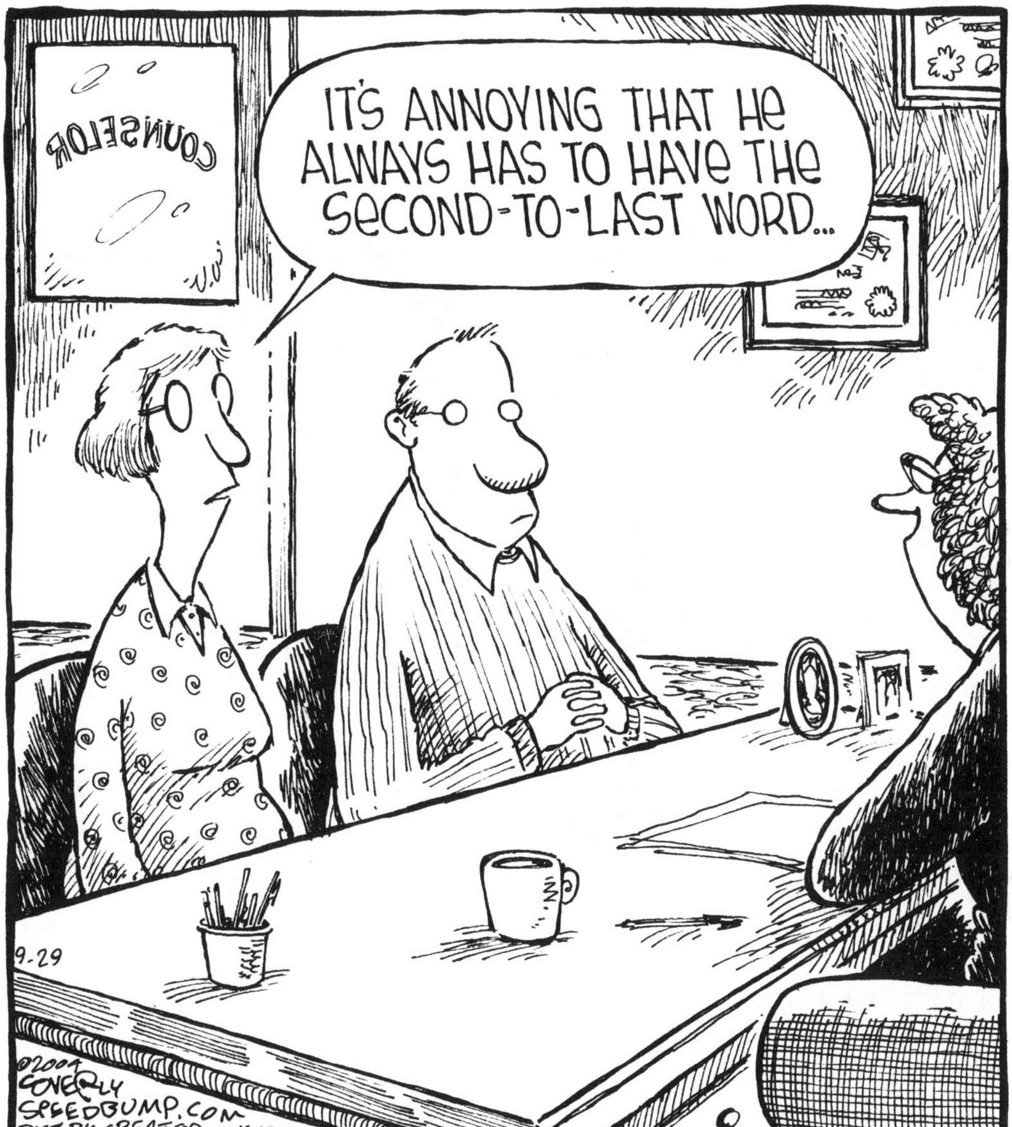
IT'S ANNOYING THAT HE ALWAYS HAS TO HAVE THE SECOND-TO-LAST WORD...
9-29
©2004 COVERLY
SPEEDBUMP.COM
DIST. BY CREATORS SYND, INC

Work, Work, Work

People ask me all the time: What's your work day like? Do you sit around in your ill-fitting boxers, eating taco chips and staring out the window? Do you spend your day watching Australian Rules football while the elves up in the belfry hammer out cartoon product? What gives?

Well, no, it's not like that. Or that. Let me tell you about a cartoonist's day.

The alarm goes off at 4:37 a.m. After a quick shower, I throw on my royal blue jumpsuit with the name patch on the left breast (it reads "Speed Bump"), grab my yellow and black hard hat and the lunch pail I packed the night before (peanut butter and pickle sandwich, small pretzel twists, tangerine, and a thermos of coffee), and walk under the street lights to the bus stop near Bill Amend's ("Fox Trot" name patch) house. He's usually running late and I have to hold up the bus for him. Unless they're on vacation, we're joined by Dan Piraro ("Bizarro"), Hilary Price ("Rhymes With Orange"), Glenn McCoy ("The Duplex"), and Jef Mallett ("Frazz"). It's become a pretty hip neighborhood, and I'm thankful every day I bought my house early, otherwise I doubt they'd let me even rent a place here now.

On the bus, some of us chat, others sleep or do crosswords. Most days we'll be passed by two or three limos as we skirt the gated communities where Mort Walker, Scott Adams, Lynn Johnston, and others live. They don't wear name patches anymore . . . and who can blame them?

It's about a 45-minute drive to the Factory. If we're early, we'll often sit for a spell in the lunchroom, going through newspapers and offering each other constructive criticism. Some days we're late, depending on traffic or if we have to pick up a newbie, and the Thinking Whistle will have already blown. That means it's time to scramble to our assigned chairs at the assembly line, put our heads down, and wait for the machine to spit out pencil and paper. Sometimes the pencils are spit out too hard, which is why the hard hats are required. We have three hours to fill three pages with ideas, with only one ten-minute break. There are editors watching; we can't see them, but we know they're up there on the level above us, looking down through the reflective glass.

During lunch we don't talk. We eat, silent, our brains squeezed dry like sponges under a heavy boot. Occasionally someone will moan softly or drop a fork. Usually it's Greg Evans ("Luann"), but he has other issues as well. Rick Stromoski ("Soup to Nutz") is the quiet one. He's scary.

The whistle blows again. Chairs scrape against the floor and wrists are stretched in preparation for the manual labor portion of our day. Back at the assembly line, the conveyor belt shudders to life and begins to inch from right to left, almost imperceptibly, at a pace that allows the strip artists exactly one hour to finish one piece of work. For those few of us who ignorantly decided on a career path creating panels, we need to lean far to our right as we begin, gradually shifting our weight from right elbow to

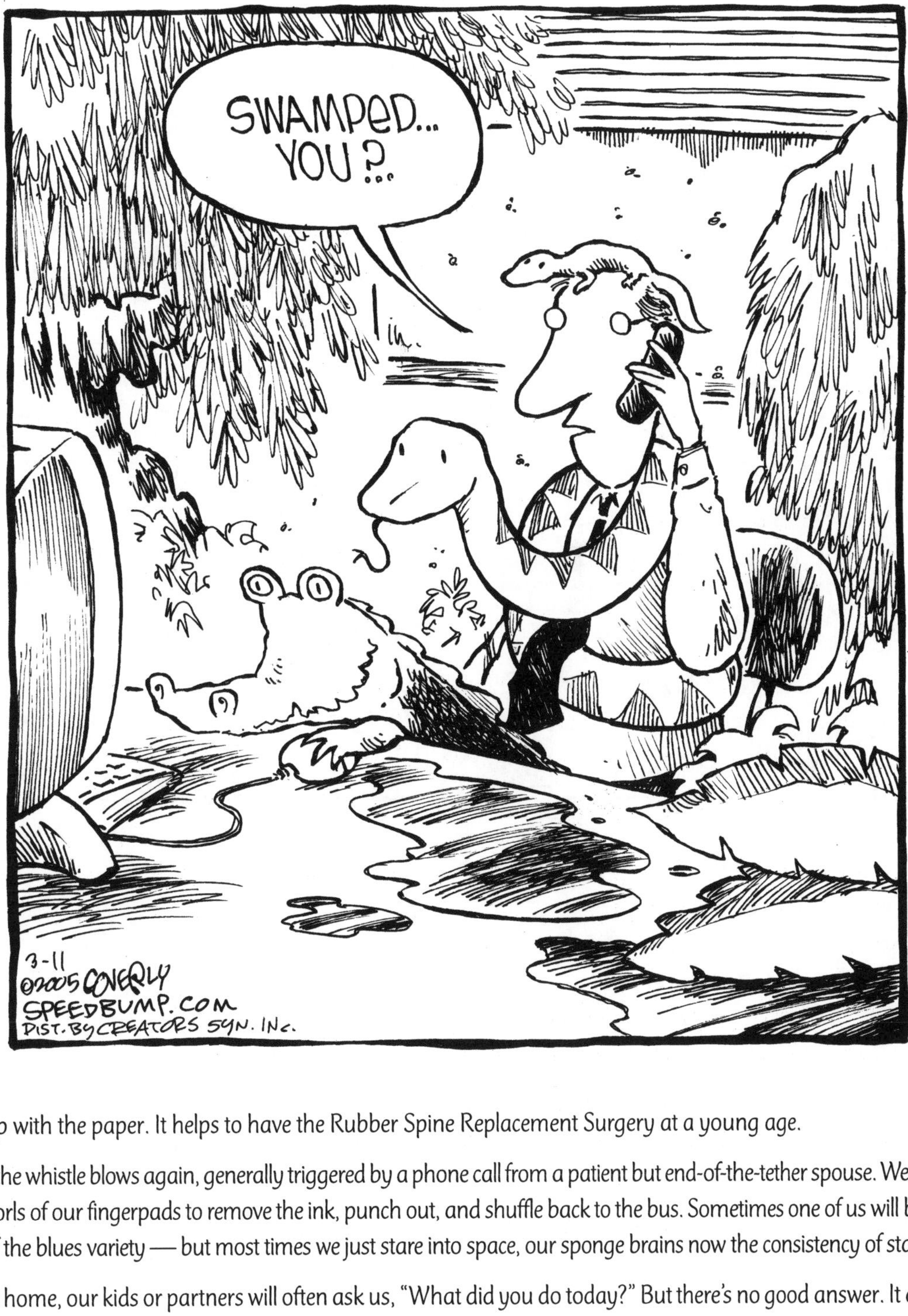
SWAMPED... YOU?...
3-11
©2005 COVERLY
SPEEDBUMP.COM
DIST. BY CREATORS SYN. INC.

left to keep up with the paper. It helps to have the Rubber Spine Replacement Surgery at a young age.

At 6:28 p.m., the whistle blows again, generally triggered by a phone call from a patient but end-of-the-tether spouse. We drop our pens, scrub the whorls of our fingerpads to remove the ink, punch out, and shuffle back to the bus. Sometimes one of us will break into song — usually of the blues variety — but most times we just stare into space, our sponge brains now the consistency of stale melba toast.

When we get home, our kids or partners will often ask us, "What did you do today?" But there's no good answer. It always sounds stupid when you say it out loud, you know? Then the blue jumpsuit goes in the hamper, and another one comes off the hanger, because tomorrow you'll do it all over again.

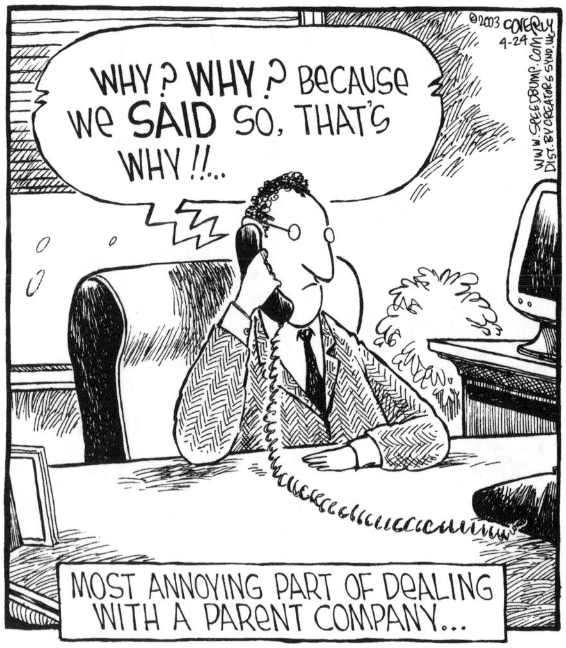
WHY? WHY? BECAUSE WE SAID SO, THAT'S WHY!!...
©2003 COVERLY 4-24
MOST ANNOYING PART OF DEALING WITH A PARENT COMPANY...

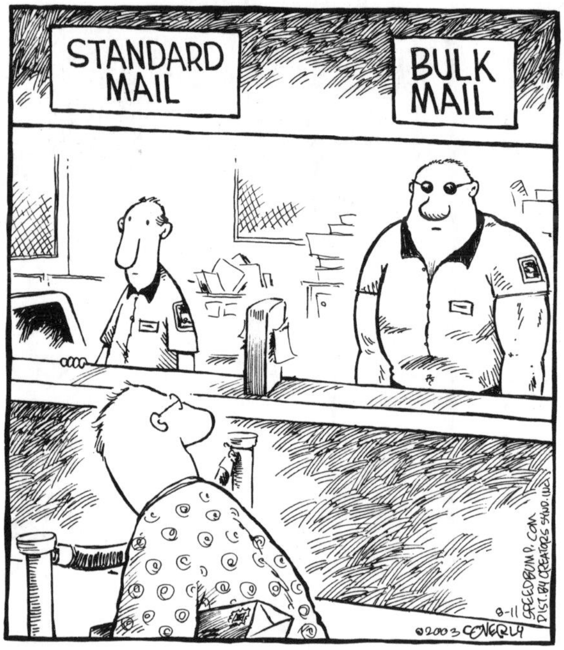
STANDARD MAIL
BULK MAIL
©2003 COVERLY

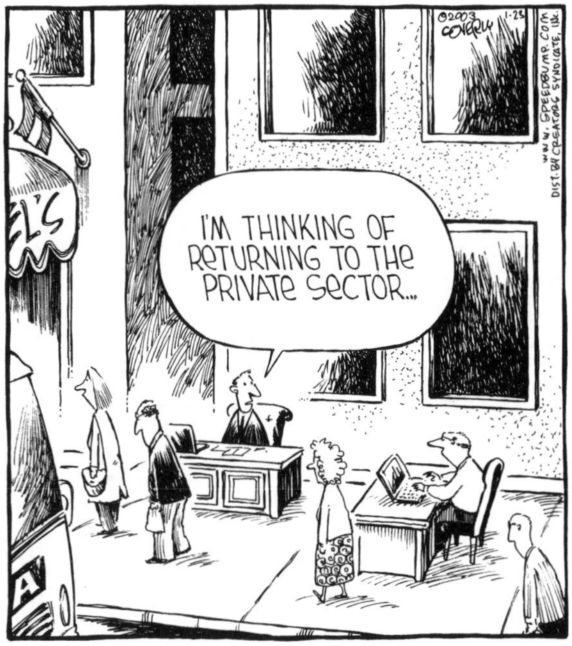
I'M THINKING OF RETURNING TO THE PRIVATE SECTOR...

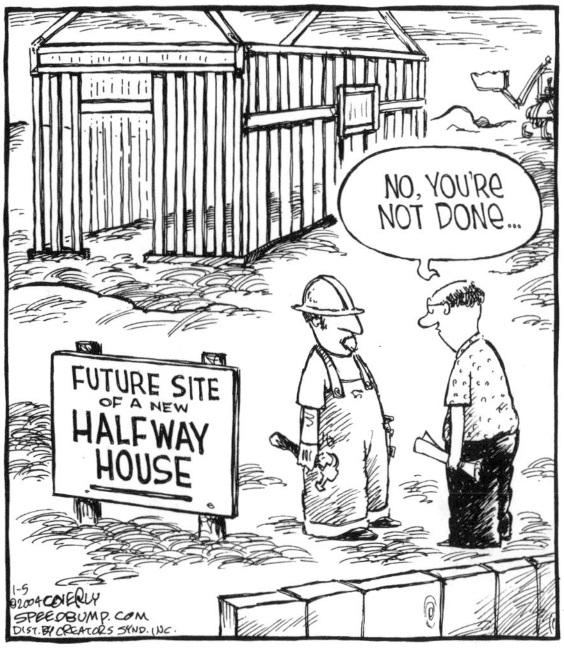
NO, YOU'RE NOT DONE...
FUTURE SITE OF A NEW HALFWAY HOUSE

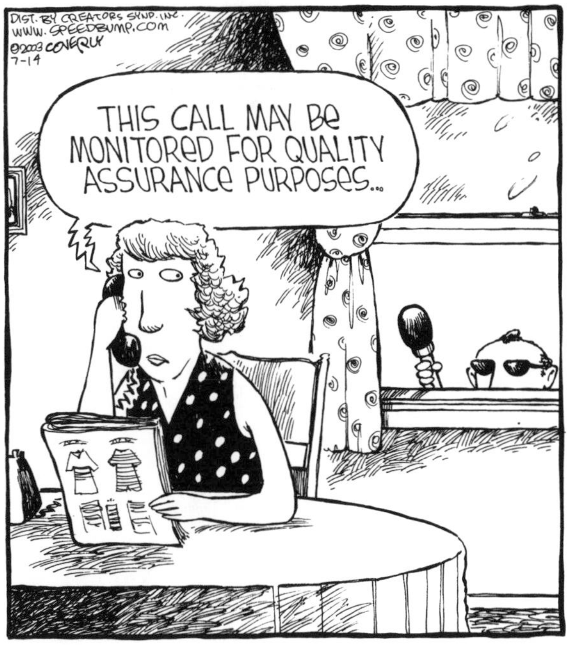
THIS CALL MAY BE MONITORED FOR QUALITY ASSURANCE PURPOSES...

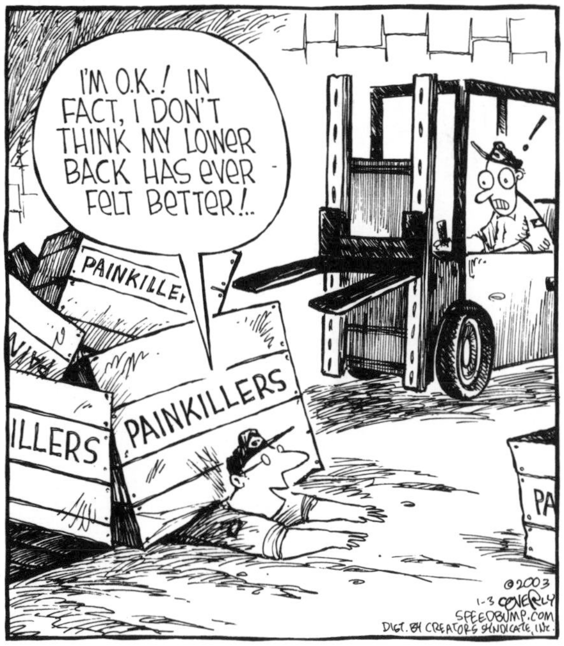
I'M O.K.! IN FACT, I DON'T THINK MY LOWER BACK HAS EVER FELT BETTER!..
PAINKILLERS

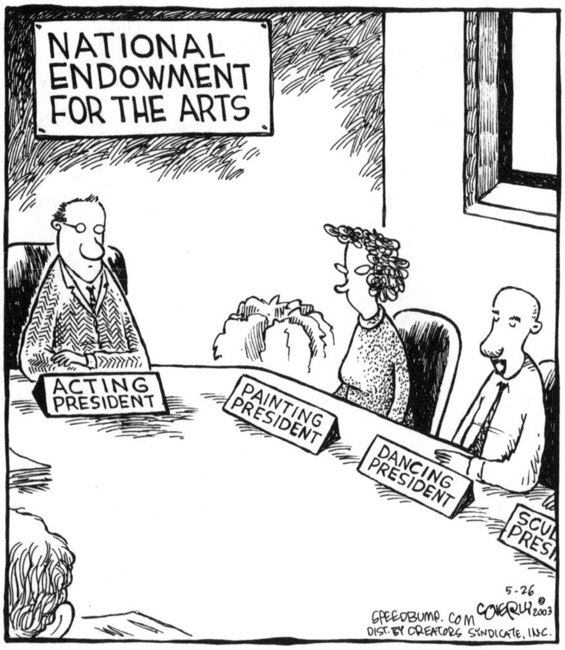
NATIONAL ENDOWMENT FOR THE ARTS
ACTING PRESIDENT
PAINTING PRESIDENT
DANCING PRESIDENT
5-26
SPEEDBUMP.COM COVERLY ©2003
DIST. BY CREATORS SYNDICATE, INC.

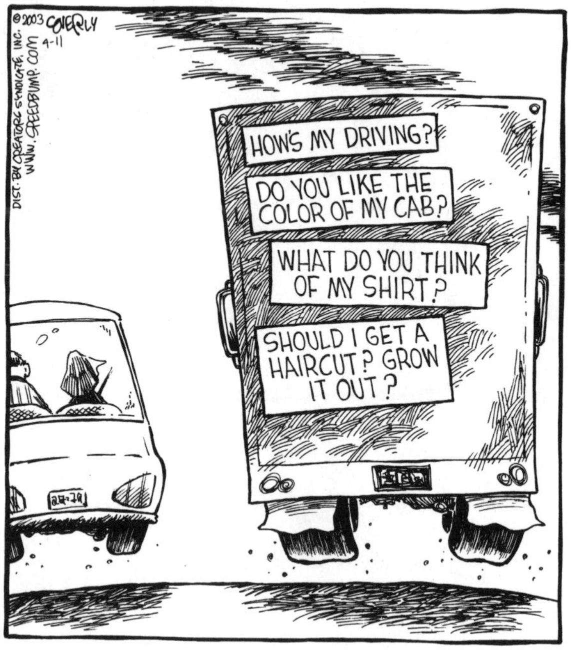
©2003 COVERLY 4-11
DIST. BY CREATORS SYNDICATE, INC.
WWW.SPEEDBUMP.COM
HOW'S MY DRIVING?
DO YOU LIKE THE COLOR OF MY CAB?
WHAT DO YOU THINK OF MY SHIRT?
SHOULD I GET A HAIRCUT? GROW IT OUT?

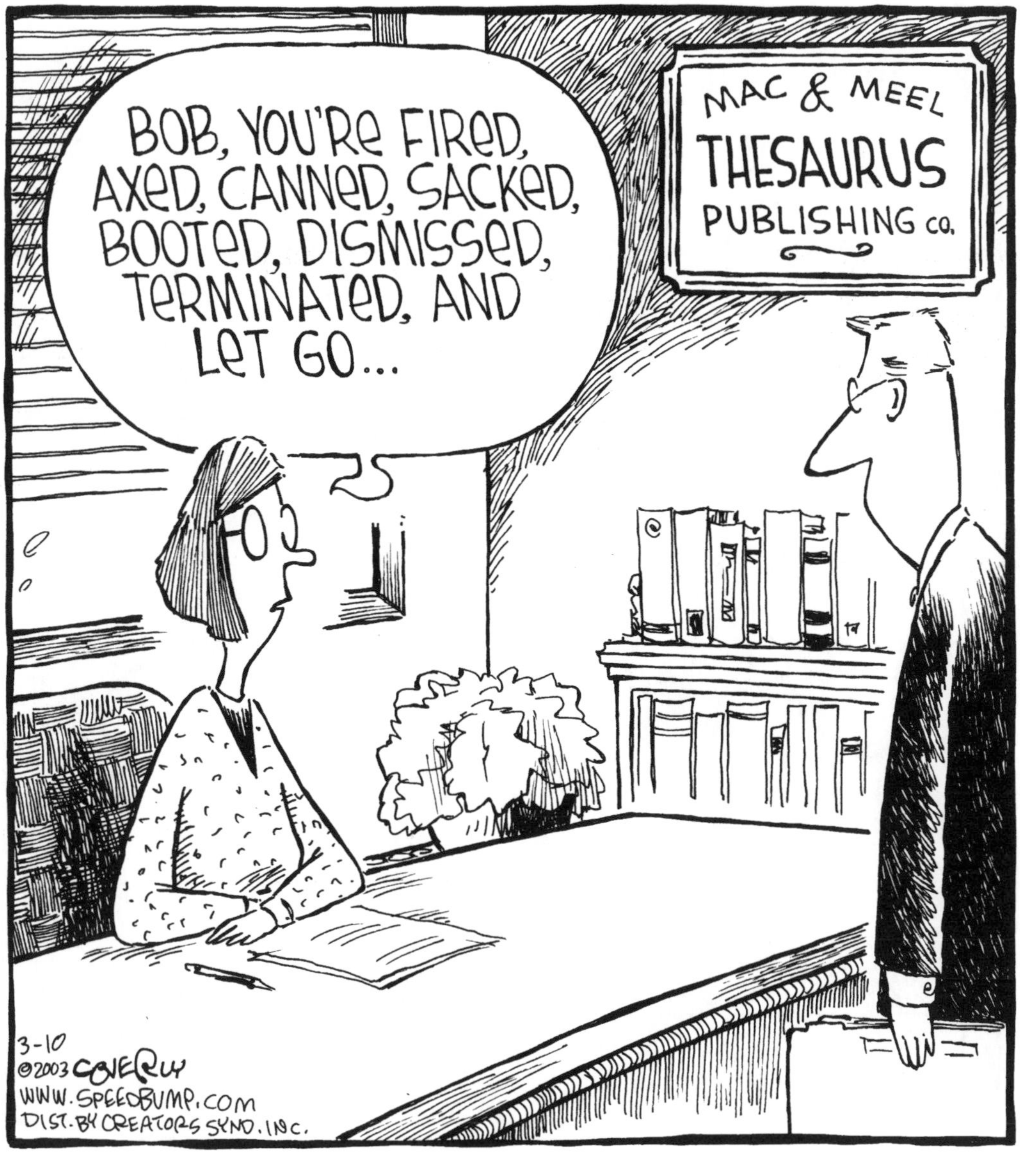
BOB, YOU'RE FIRED, AXED, CANNED, SACKED, BOOTED, DISMISSED, TERMINATED, AND LET GO...
MAC & MEEL THESAURUS PUBLISHING CO.
3-10 ©2003 COVERLY WWW.SPEEDBUMP.COM DIST. BY CREATORS SYND. INC.

©2004 COVERLY 9-8
DIST. BY CREATORS SYND. SPEEDBUMP.COM
BEANS, BEANS, THE MAGICAL FRUIT, THE MORE YOU EAT, THE MORE YOU TOOT, THE MORE YOU TOOT, THE BETTER YOU FEEL, SO EAT SOME BEANS AT EVERY MEAL.
IF DOCTORS LISTENED TO THE FARM LOBBY INSTEAD OF THE DRUG LOBBY...

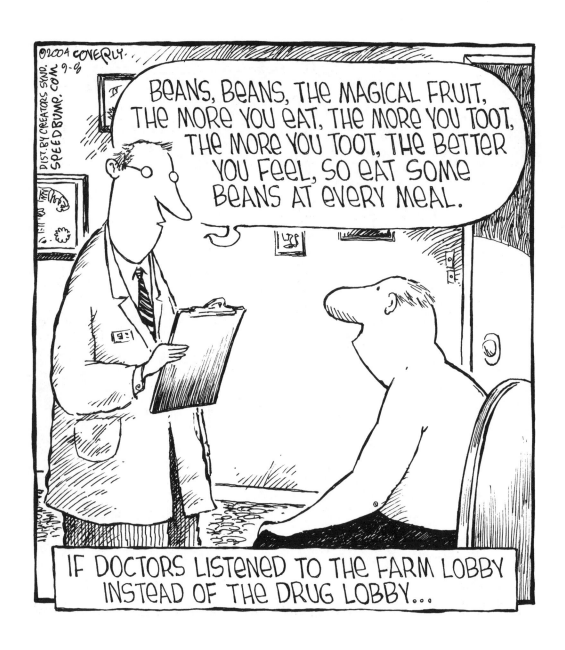

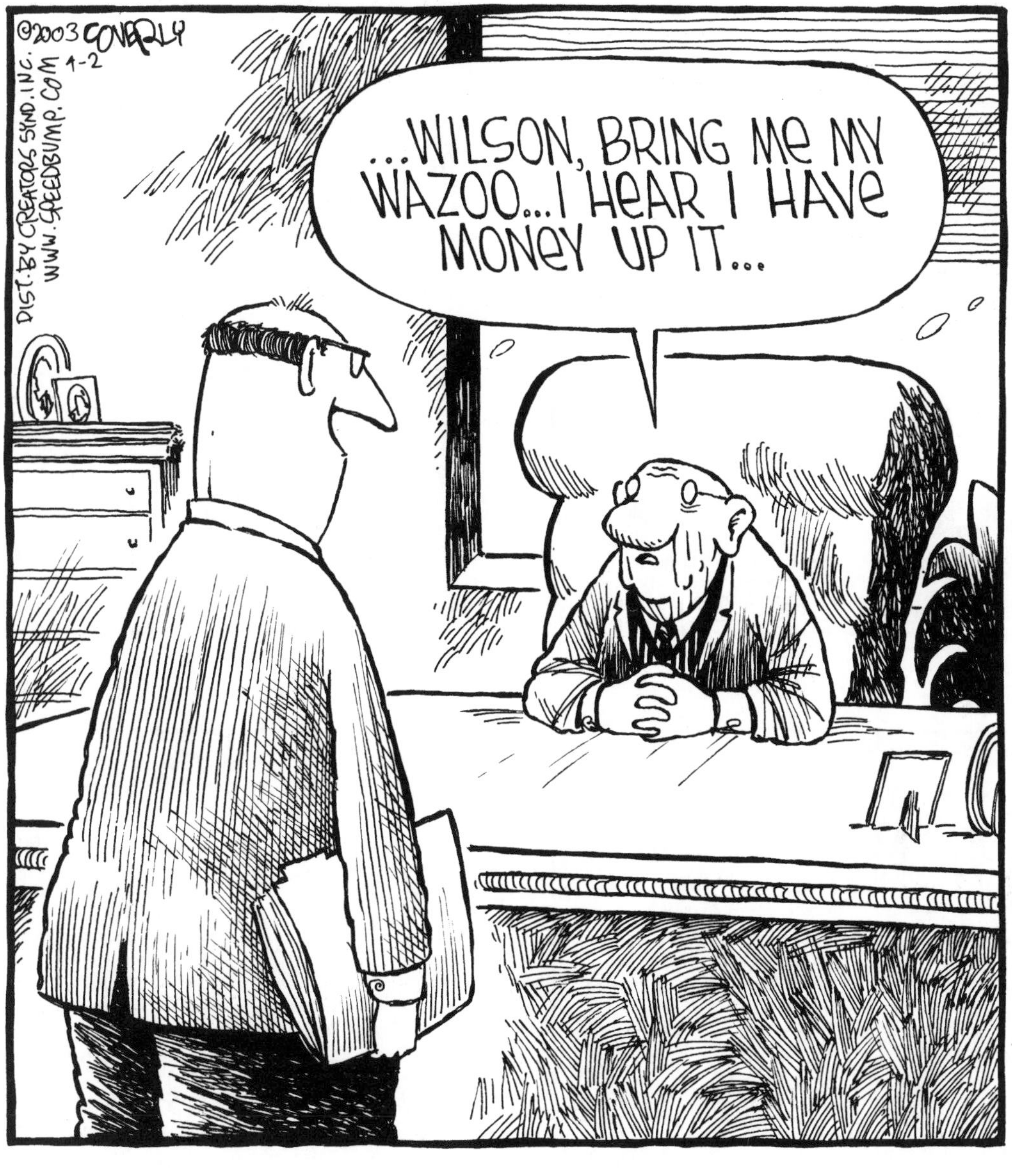
©2003 COVERLY
1-2
DIST. BY CREATORS SYND. INC.
WWW.SPEEDBUMP.COM
...WILSON, BRING ME MY WAZOO...I HEAR I HAVE MONEY UP IT...

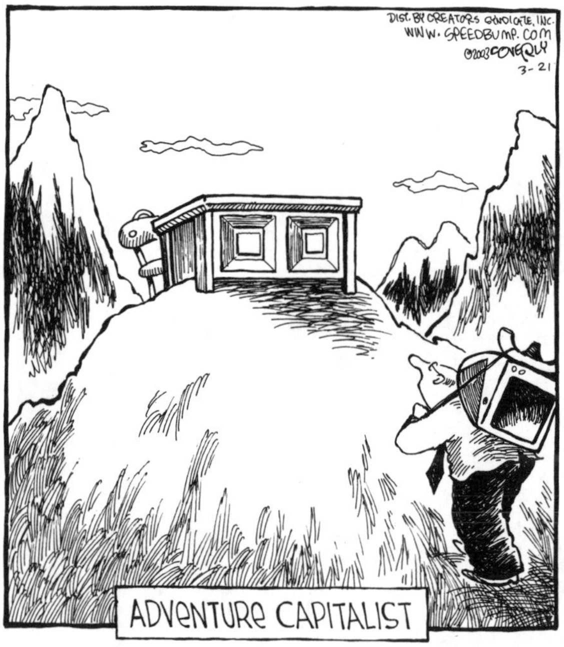
ADVENTURE CAPITALIST

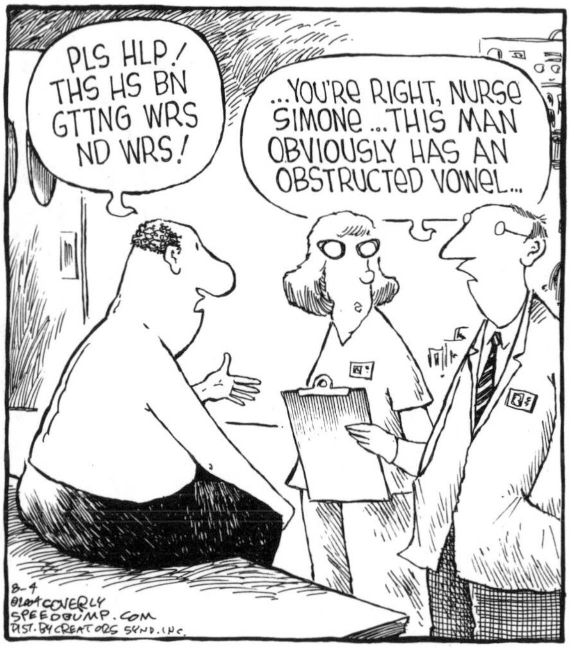
PLS HLP! THS HS BN GTTNG WRS ND WRS!
...YOU'RE RIGHT, NURSE SIMONE ...THIS MAN OBVIOUSLY HAS AN OBSTRUCTED VOWEL...

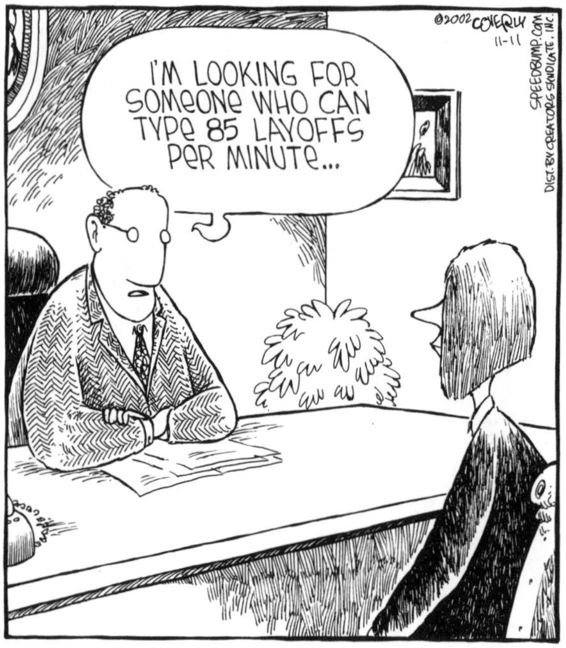
I'M LOOKING FOR SOMEONE WHO CAN TYPE 85 LAYOFFS PER MINUTE...

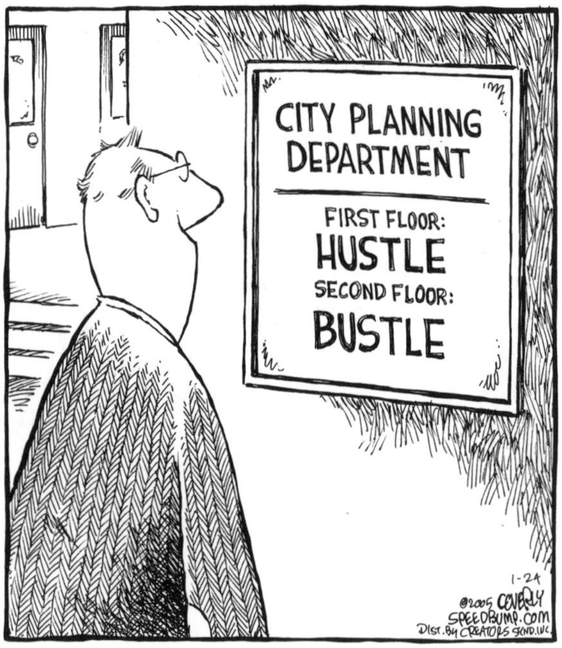
CITY PLANNING DEPARTMENT
FIRST FLOOR:
HUSTLE
SECOND FLOOR:
BUSTLE

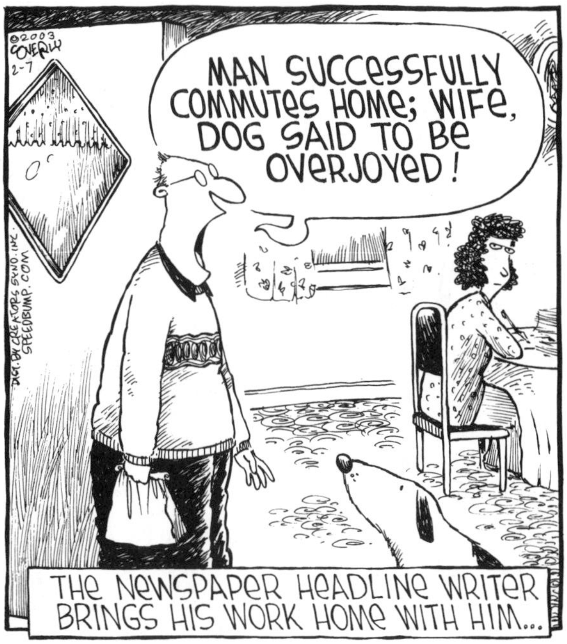
©2003 Coverly 2-7
Dist. by Creators Synd. Inc. speedbump.com
MAN SUCCESSFULLY COMMUTES HOME; WIFE, DOG SAID TO BE OVERJOYED!
THE NEWSPAPER HEADLINE WRITER BRINGS HIS WORK HOME WITH HIM...

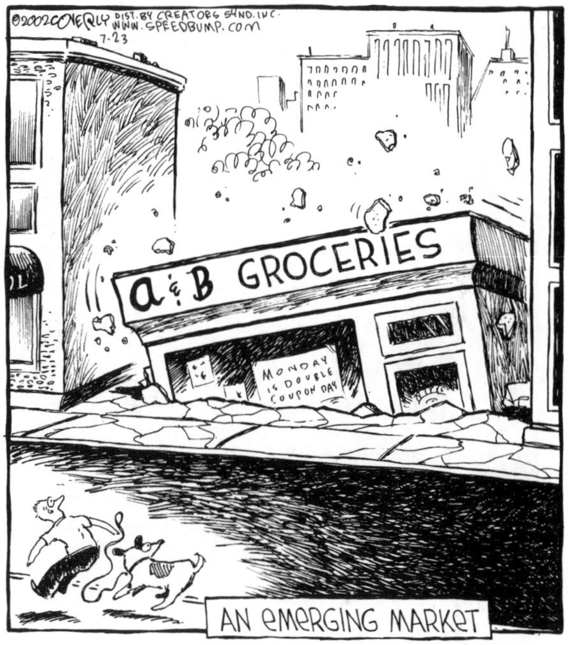
©2002 Coverly Dist. by Creators Synd. Inc. www.speedbump.com 7-23
A & B GROCERIES
MONDAY IS DOUBLE COUPON DAY
AN EMERGING MARKET

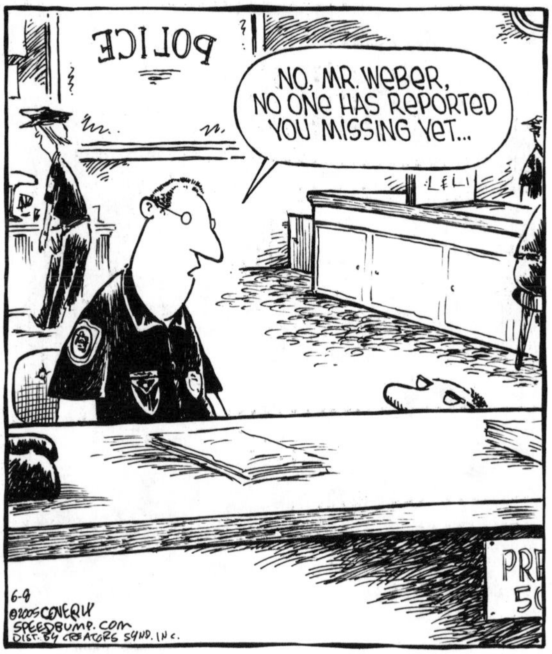
POLICE
NO, MR. WEBER, NO ONE HAS REPORTED YOU MISSING YET...
6-8
©2005 COVERLY
SPEEDBUMP.COM
DIST. BY CREATORS SYND. INC.

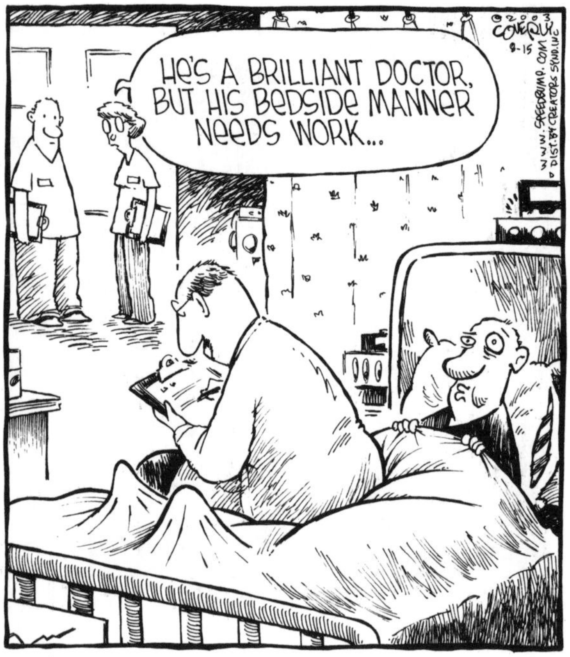
HE'S A BRILLIANT DOCTOR, BUT HIS BEDSIDE MANNER NEEDS WORK...
©2003 COVERLY
8-15
WWW.SPEEDBUMP.COM
©DIST. BY CREATORS SYND. INC

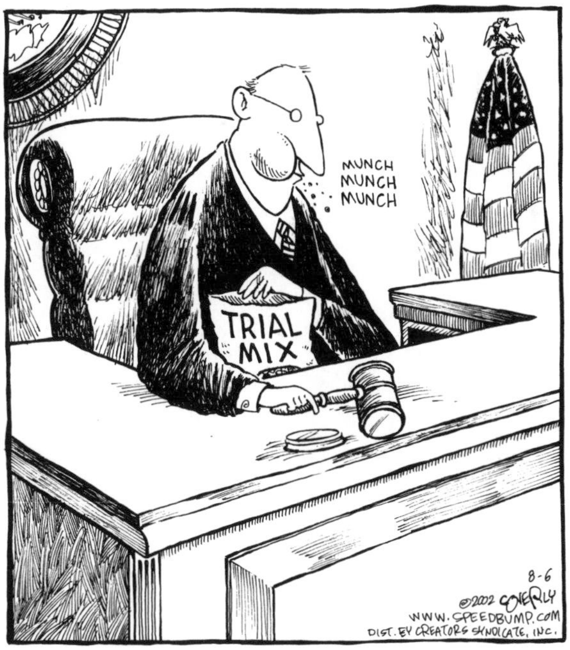
MUNCH
MUNCH
MUNCH
TRIAL MIX
8-6
©2002 COVERLY
WWW.SPEEDBUMP.COM
DIST. BY CREATORS SYNDICATE, INC.

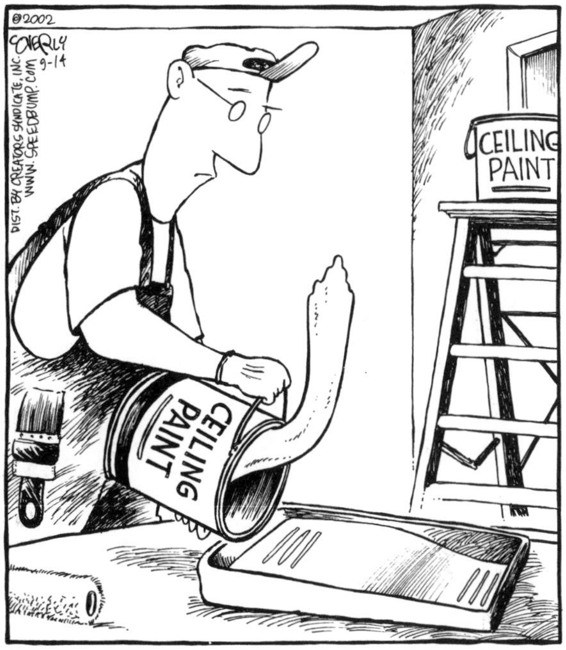
©2002
COVERLY
9-14
DIST. BY CREATORS SYNDICATE, INC.
WWW.SPEEDBUMP.COM
CEILING PAINT
CEILING PAINT

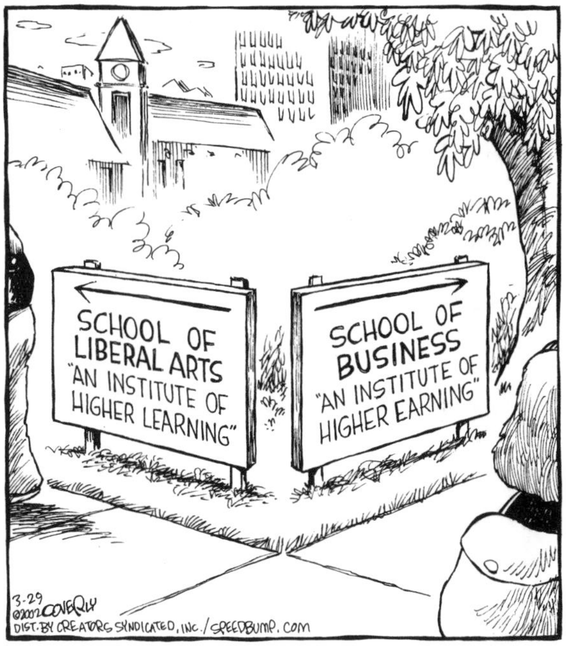
SCHOOL OF LIBERAL ARTS
"AN INSTITUTE OF HIGHER LEARNING"
SCHOOL OF BUSINESS
"AN INSTITUTE OF HIGHER EARNING"
3-29
©2002 COVERLY
DIST. BY CREATORS SYNDICATED, INC./SPEEDBUMP.COM

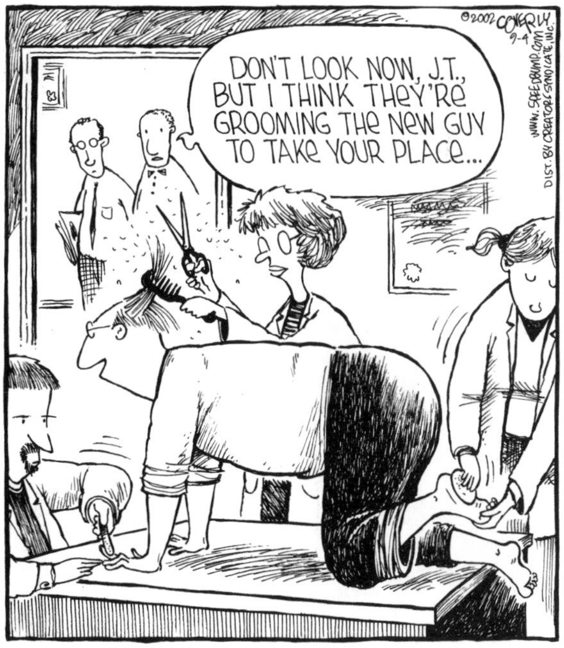
©2002 COVERLY
9-4
WWW.SPEEDBUMP.COM
DIST. BY CREATORS SYNDICATE, INC.
DON'T LOOK NOW, J.T., BUT I THINK THEY'RE GROOMING THE NEW GUY TO TAKE YOUR PLACE...

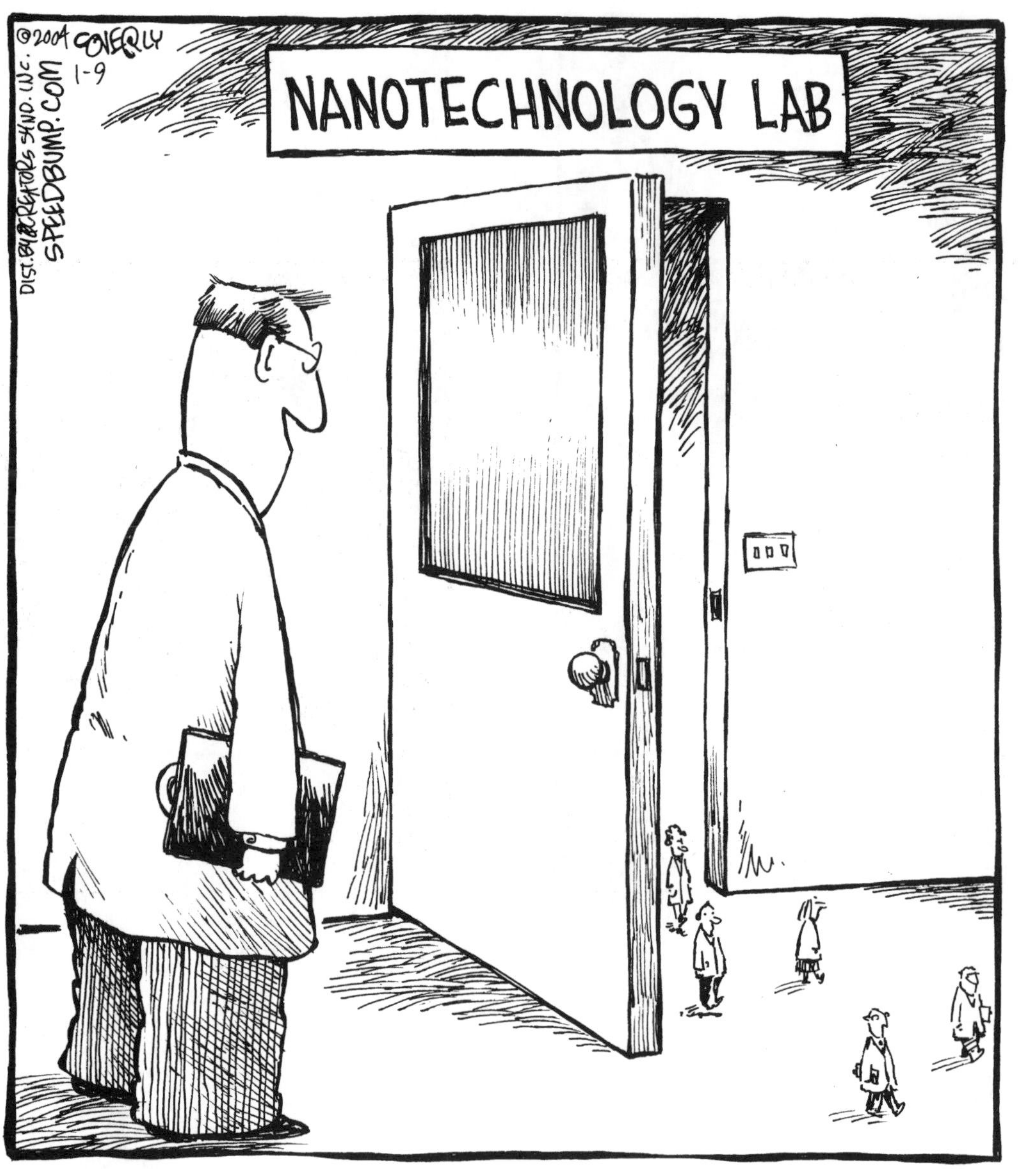
NANOTECHNOLOGY LAB
©2004 COVERLY 1-9
DIST. BY CREATORS SYND. INC.
SPEEDBUMP.COM

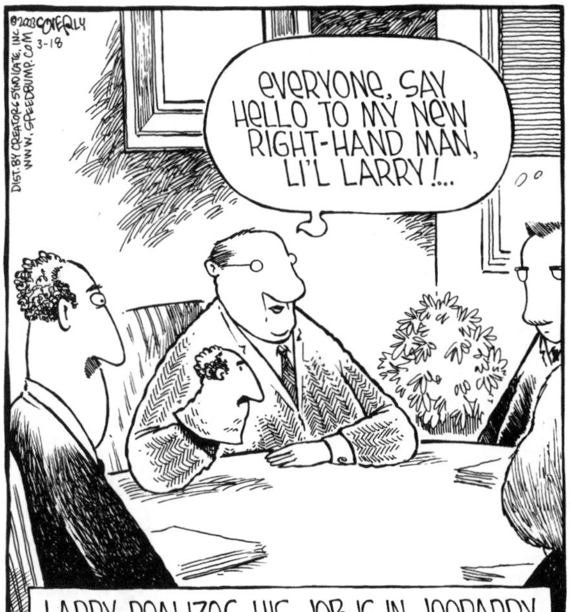
EVERYONE, SAY HELLO TO MY NEW RIGHT-HAND MAN, LI'L LARRY!...
LARRY REALIZES HIS JOB IS IN JEOPARDY...

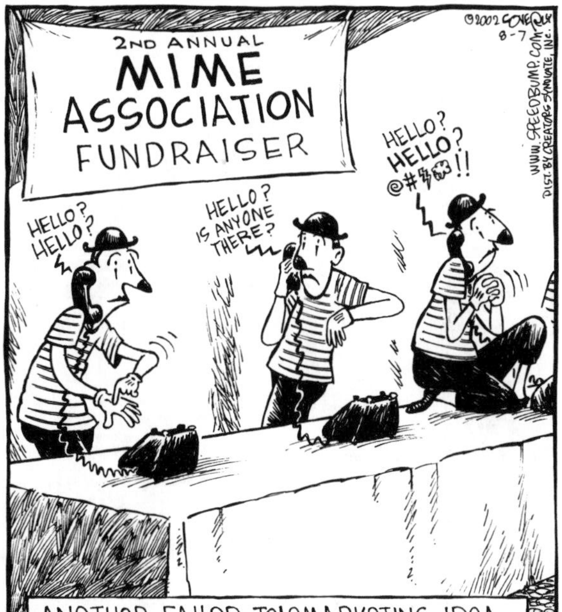
2ND ANNUAL
MIME
ASSOCIATION
FUNDRAISER
HELLO? HELLO?
HELLO? IS ANYONE THERE?
HELLO? HELLO?
ANOTHER FAILED TELEMARKETING IDEA...

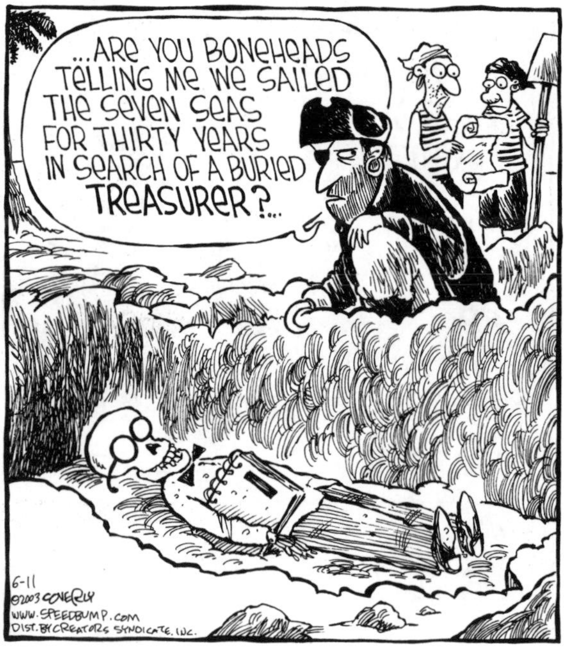
...ARE YOU BONEHEADS TELLING ME WE SAILED THE SEVEN SEAS FOR THIRTY YEARS IN SEARCH OF A BURIED **TREASURER**?...
6-11 ©2003 COVERLY WWW.SPEEDBUMP.COM DIST. BY CREATORS SYNDICATE, INC.

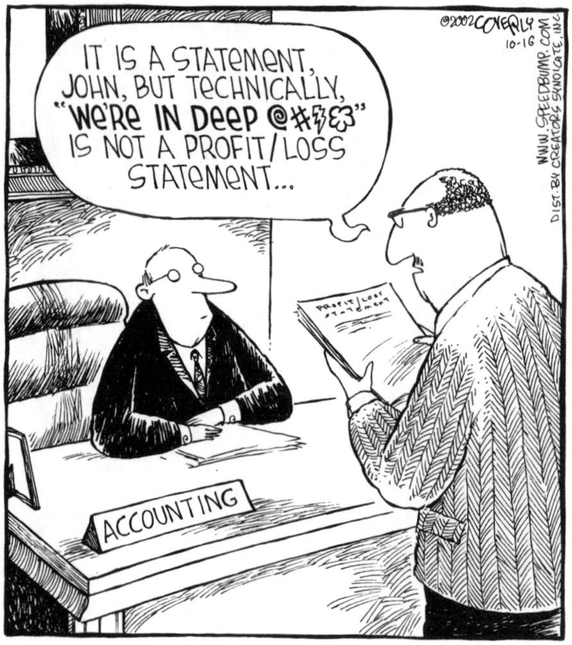
©2002 COVERLY 10-16
WWW.SPEEDBUMP.COM DIST. BY CREATORS SYNDICATE, INC.
IT IS A STATEMENT, JOHN, BUT TECHNICALLY, "**WE'RE IN DEEP @#$%**" IS NOT A PROFIT/LOSS STATEMENT...
ACCOUNTING

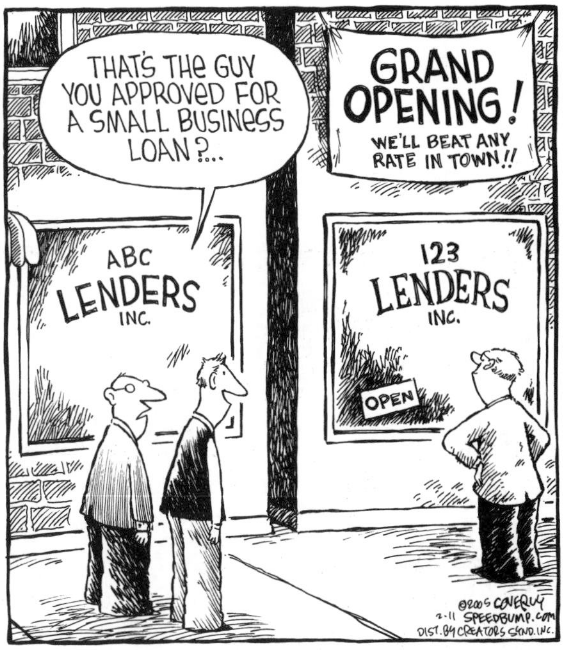
THAT'S THE GUY YOU APPROVED FOR A SMALL BUSINESS LOAN?...
GRAND OPENING!
WE'LL BEAT ANY RATE IN TOWN!!
ABC LENDERS INC.
123 LENDERS INC.
OPEN
©2005 COVERLY 2-11 SPEEDBUMP.COM DIST. BY CREATORS SYND. INC.

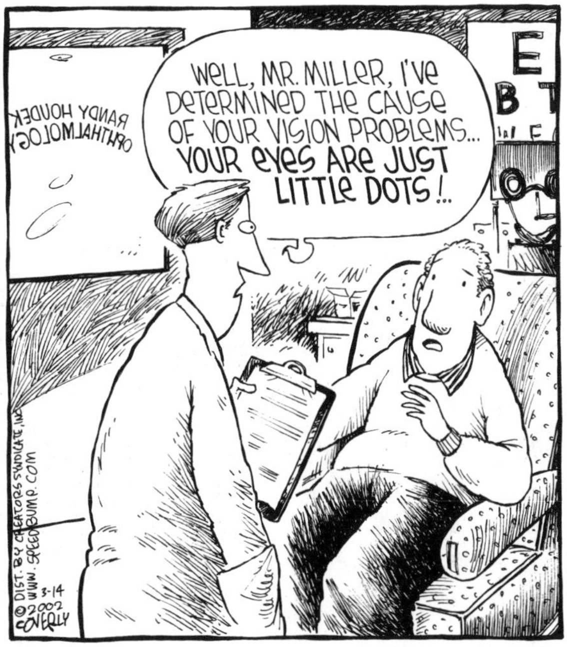
WELL, MR. MILLER, I've DETERMINED THE CAUSE OF YOUR VISION PROBLEMS... YOUR EYES ARE JUST LITTLE DOTS!..
RANDY HOUDEK OPHTHALMOLOGY
E
B T
DIST. BY CREATORS SYNDICATE, INC. WWW.SPEEDBUMP.COM
3-14 ©2002 COVERLY

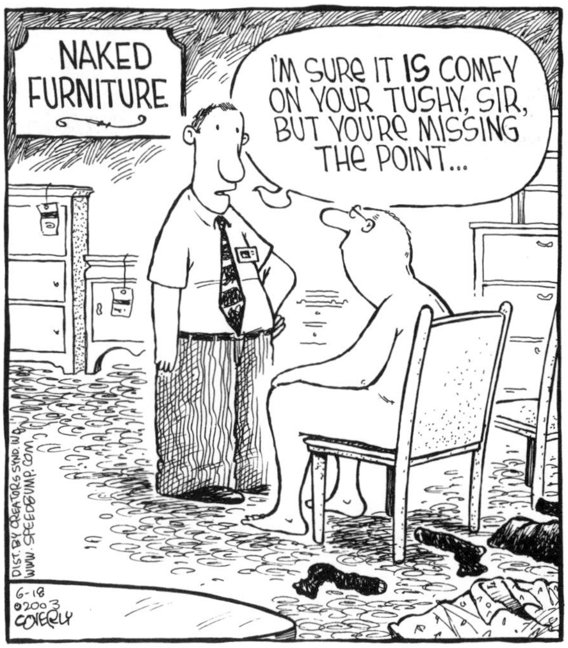
NAKED FURNITURE
I'M SURE IT IS COMFY ON YOUR TUSHY, SIR, BUT YOU'RE MISSING THE POINT...
DIST. BY CREATORS SYND. INC. WWW.SPEEDBUMP.COM
6-18 ©2003 COVERLY

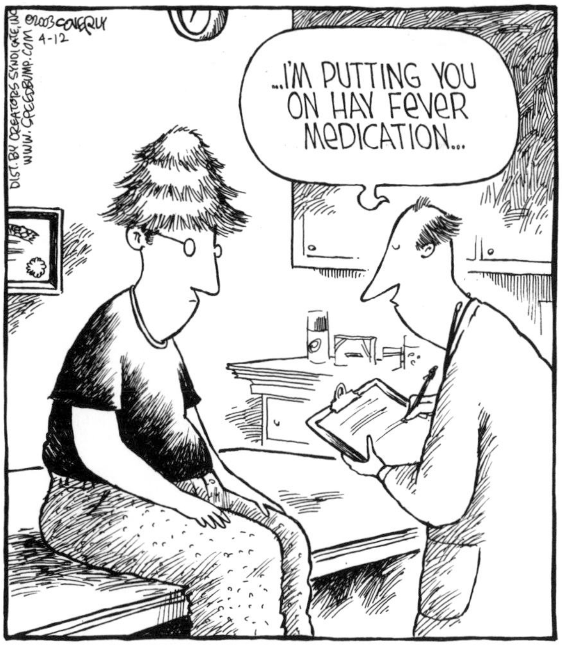
©2003 COVERLY 4-12
DIST. BY CREATORS SYNDICATE, INC WWW.SPEEDBUMP.COM
...I'M PUTTING YOU ON HAY FEVER MEDICATION...

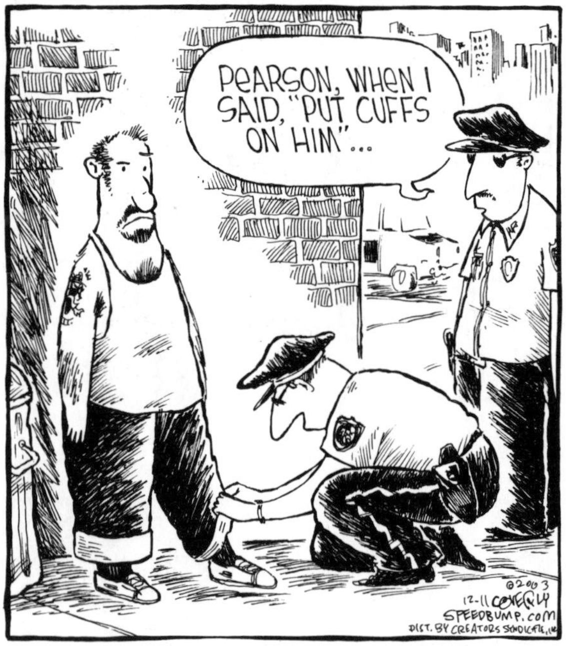
PEARSON, WHEN I SAID, "PUT CUFFS ON HIM"...
SPEEDBUMP.COM

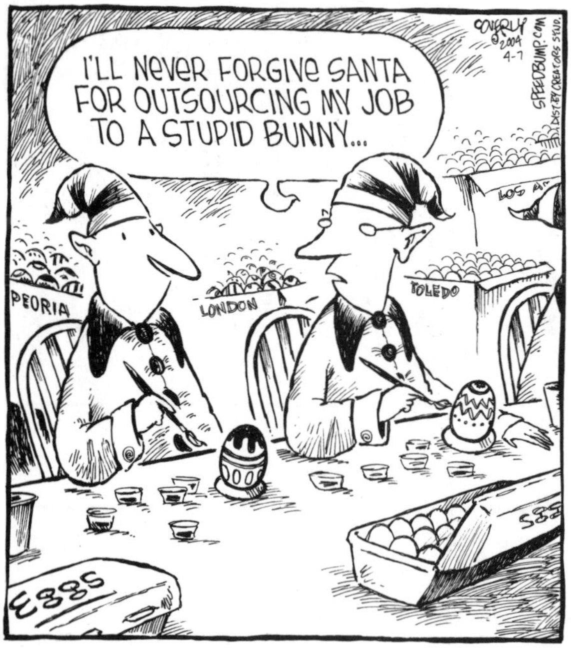
I'LL NEVER FORGIVE SANTA FOR OUTSOURCING MY JOB TO A STUPID BUNNY...
PEORIA
LONDON
TOLEDO
SPEEDBUMP.COM

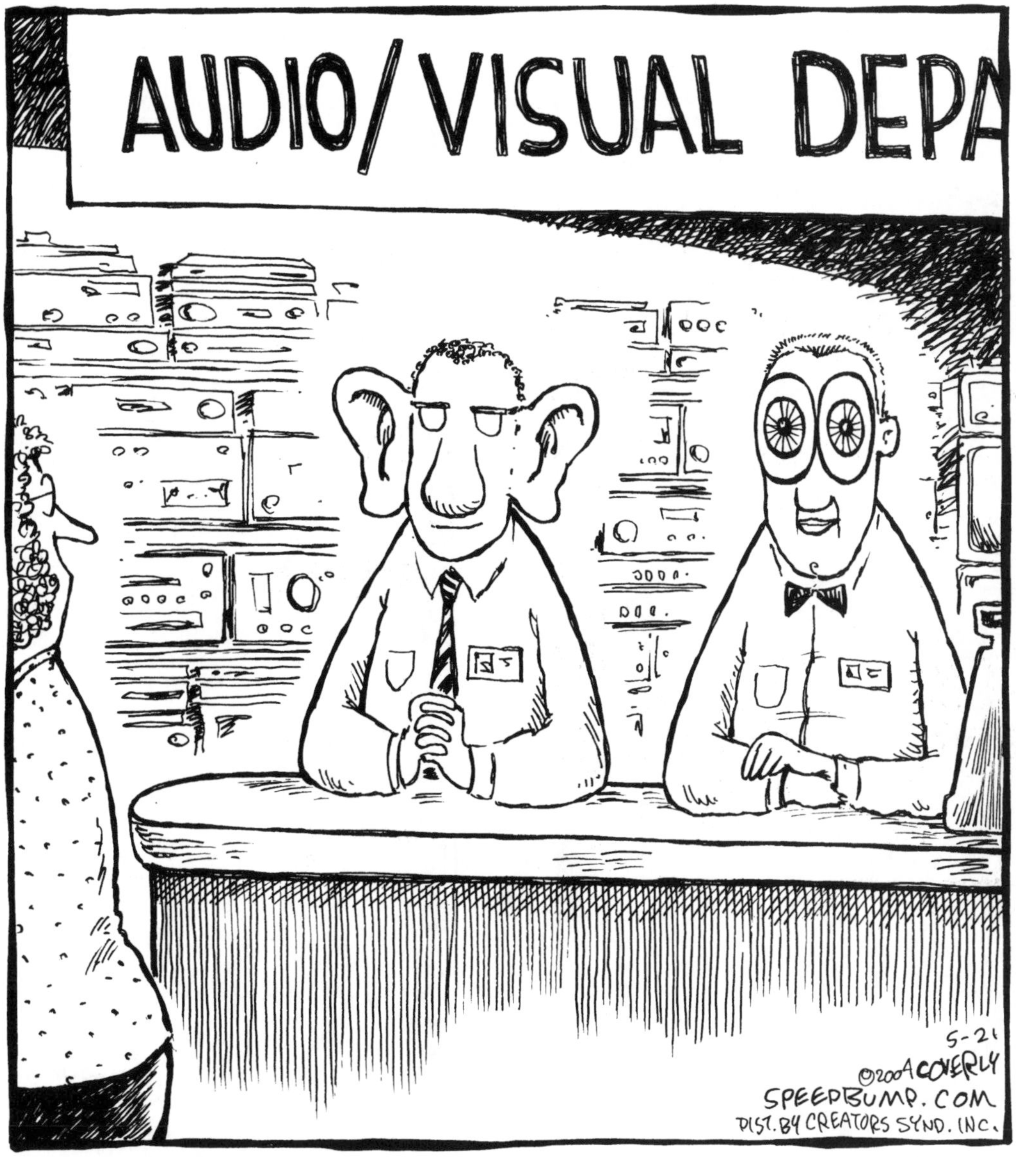
AUDIO/VISUAL DEPA
5-21
©2004 COVERLY
SPEEDBUMP.COM
DIST. BY CREATORS SYND. INC.

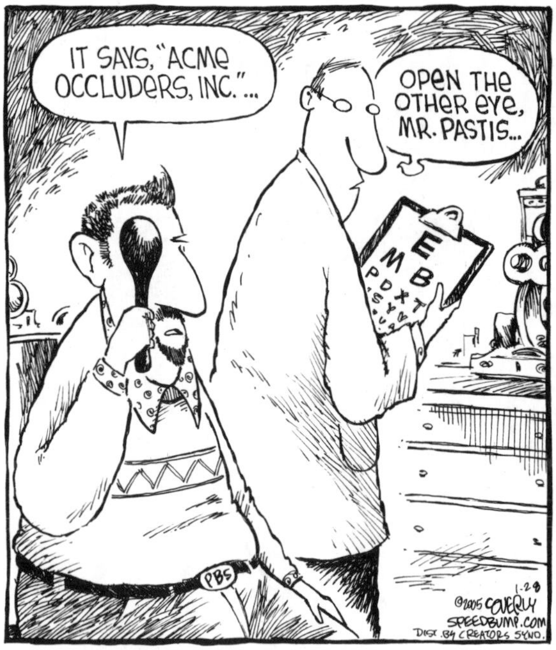
IT SAYS, "ACME OCCLUDERS, INC."...
OPEN THE OTHER EYE, MR. PASTIS...
PBS
1-28 ©2005 COVERLY SPEEDBUMP.COM DIST. BY CREATORS SYND.

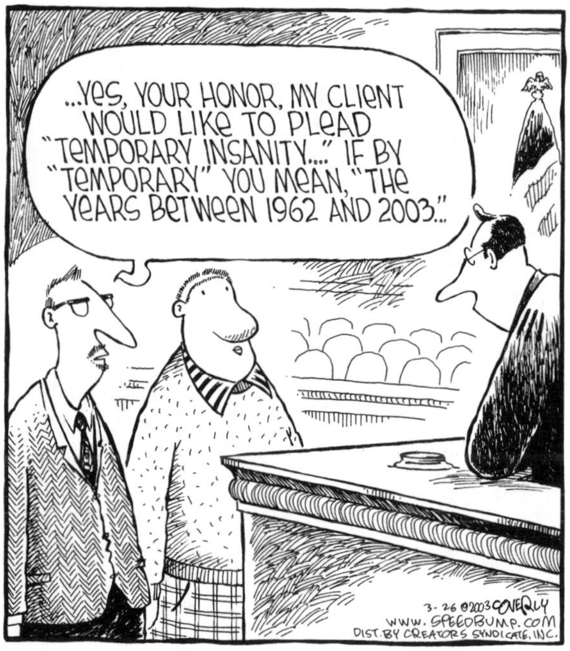
...YES, YOUR HONOR, MY CLIENT WOULD LIKE TO PLEAD "TEMPORARY INSANITY..." IF BY "TEMPORARY" YOU MEAN, "THE YEARS BETWEEN 1962 AND 2003."
3-26 ©2003 COVERLY WWW.SPEEDBUMP.COM DIST. BY CREATORS SYNDICATE, INC.

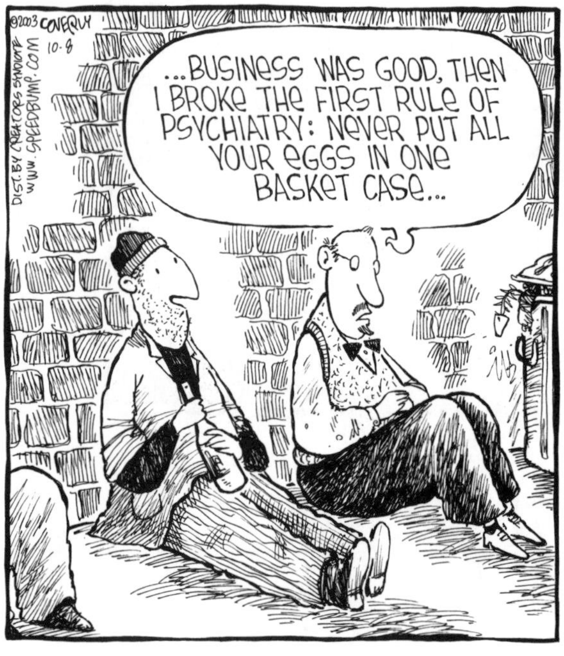
...BUSINESS WAS GOOD, THEN I BROKE THE FIRST RULE OF PSYCHIATRY: NEVER PUT ALL YOUR EGGS IN ONE BASKET CASE...
©2003 COVERLY 10-8
DIST. BY CREATORS SYNDICATE WWW.SPEEDBUMP.COM

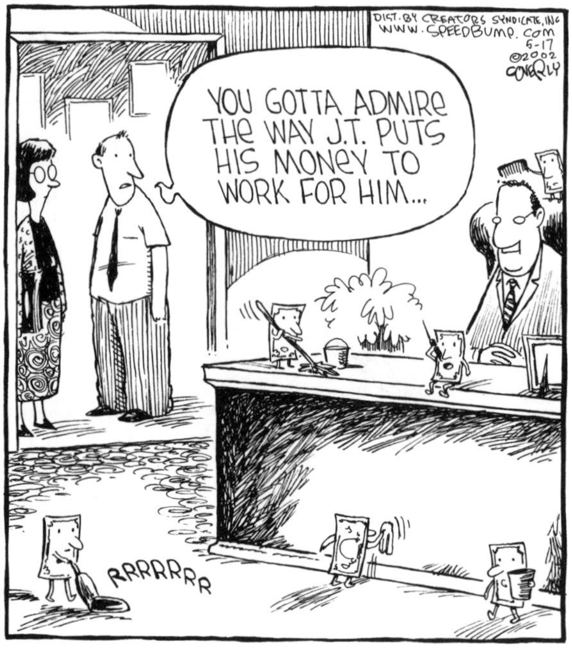
DIST. BY CREATORS SYNDICATE, INC WWW.SPEEDBUMP.COM 5-17 ©2002 COVERLY
YOU GOTTA ADMIRE THE WAY J.T. PUTS HIS MONEY TO WORK FOR HIM...
RRRRRRR

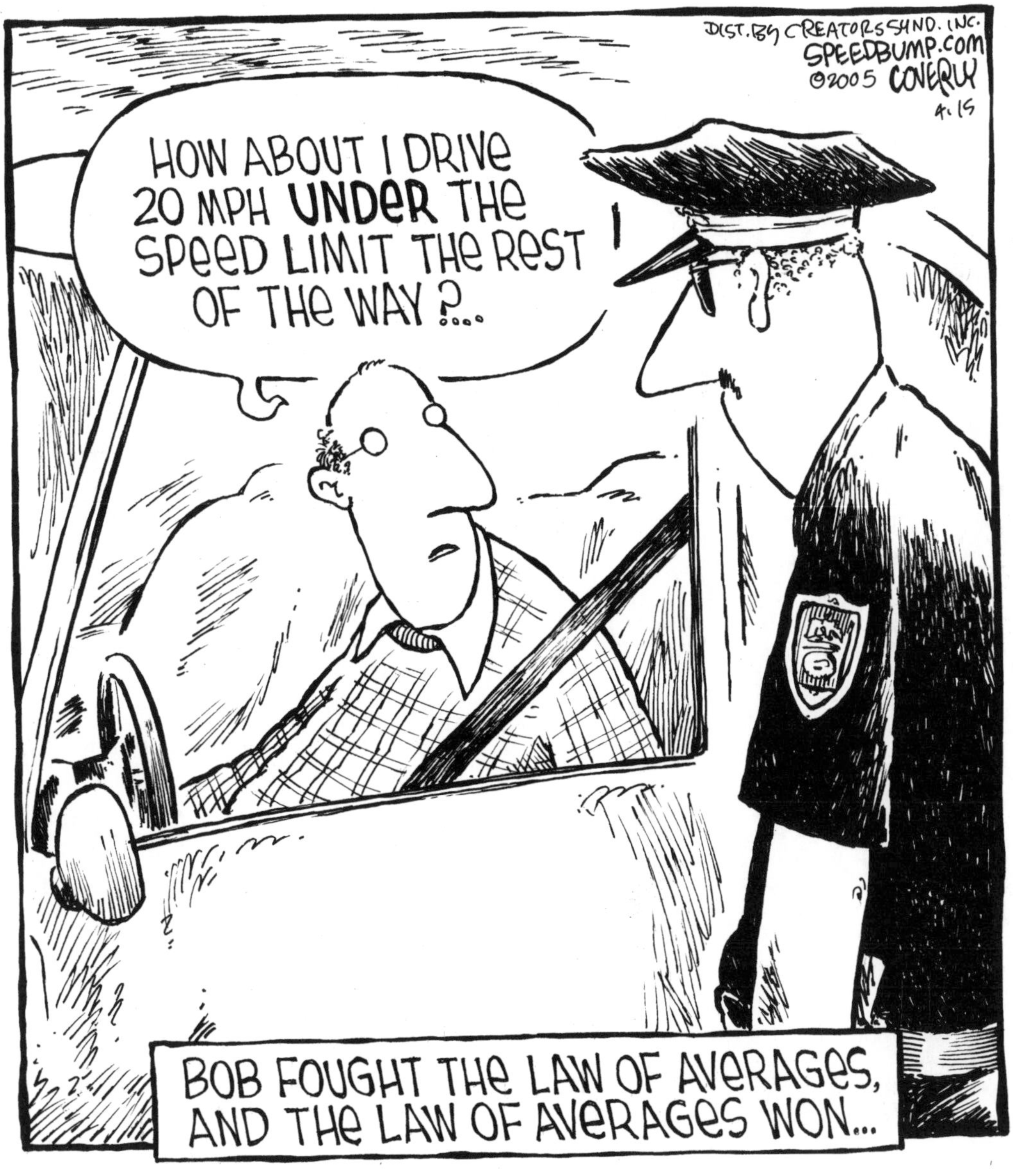
DIST. BY CREATORS SYND. INC.
SPEEDBUMP.COM
©2005 COVERLY
4.15
HOW ABOUT I DRIVE 20 MPH **UNDER** THE SPEED LIMIT THE REST OF THE WAY?...
BOB FOUGHT THE LAW OF AVERAGES, AND THE LAW OF AVERAGES WON...

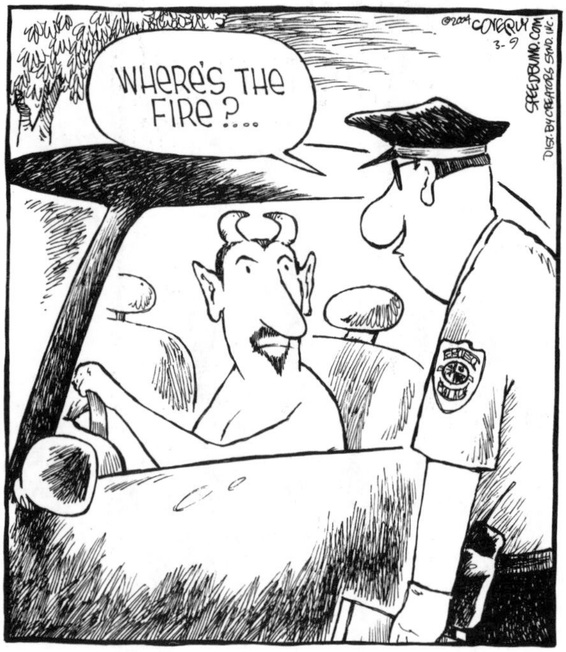
WHERE'S THE FIRE ?...
©2004 COVERLY 3-9
SPEEDBUMP.COM
DIST. BY CREATORS SYND. INC.

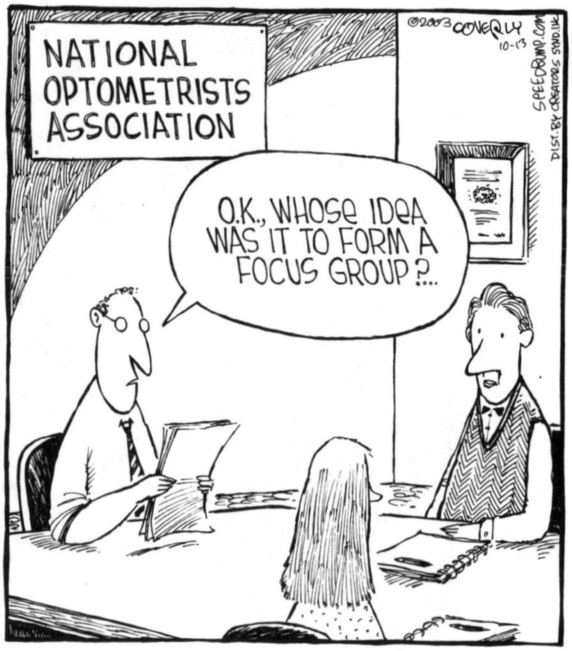
NATIONAL OPTOMETRISTS ASSOCIATION
O.K., WHOSE IDEA WAS IT TO FORM A FOCUS GROUP ?...
©2003 COVERLY 10-13
SPEEDBUMP.COM
DIST. BY CREATORS SYND. INC.

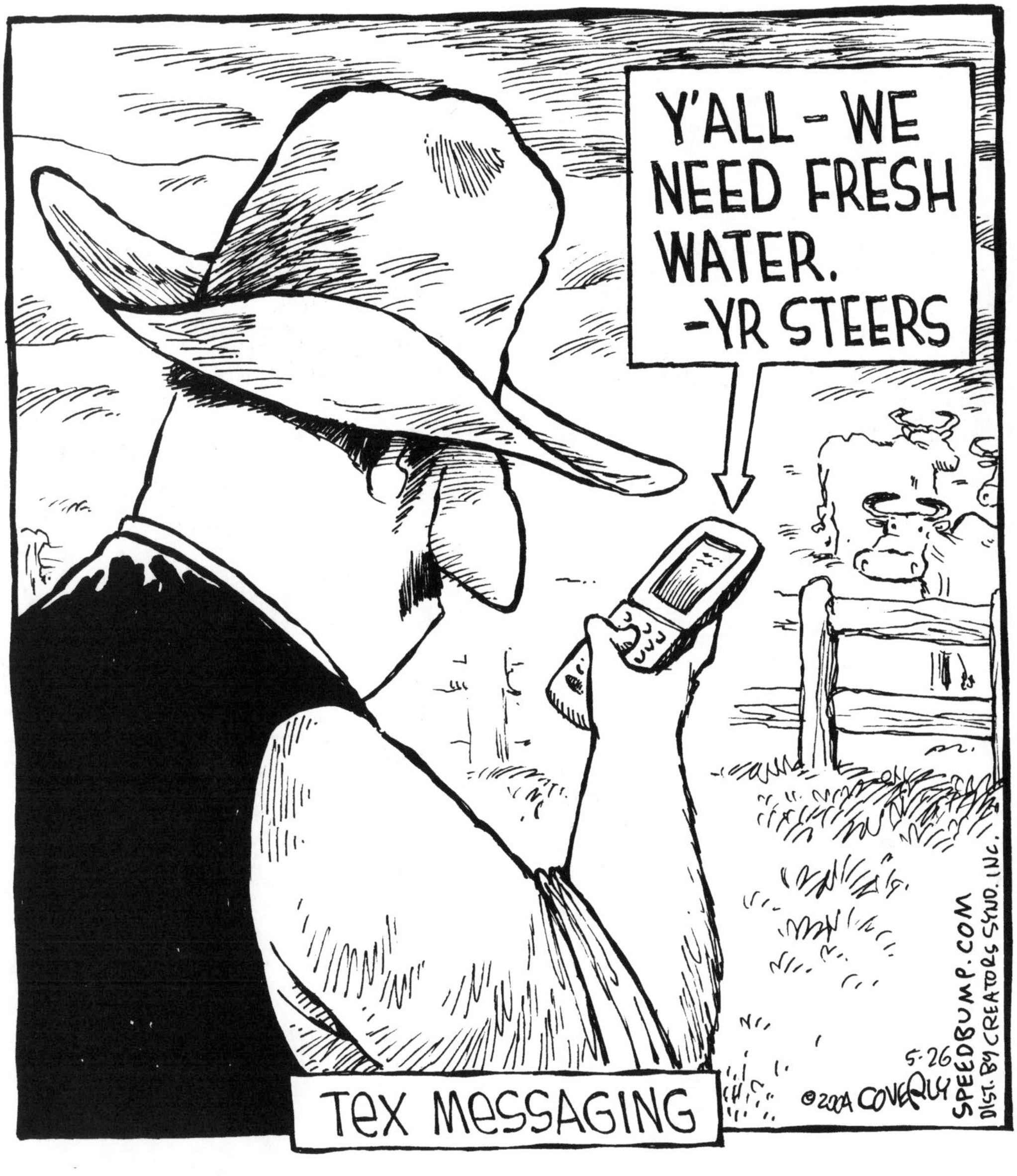
Y'ALL - WE NEED FRESH WATER. -YR STEERS
TEX MESSAGING
©2004 COVERLY 5.26
SPEEDBUMP.COM
DIST. BY CREATORS SYND. INC.

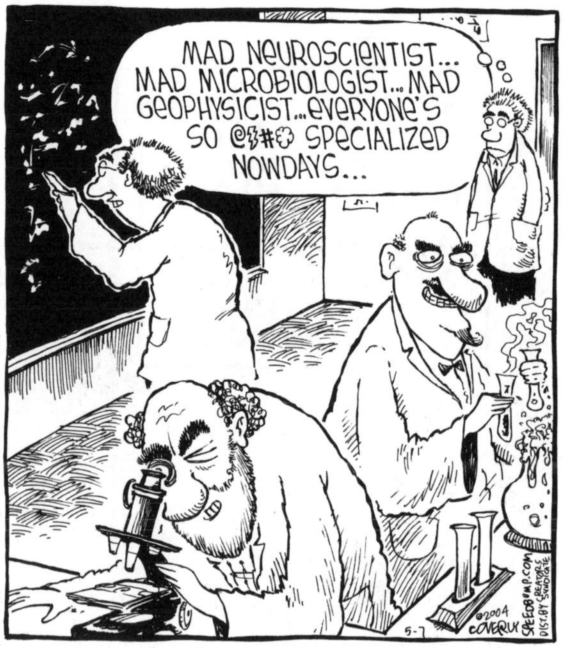
MAD NEUROSCIENTIST... MAD MICROBIOLOGIST... MAD GEOPHYSICIST... EVERYONE'S SO @#% SPECIALIZED NOWDAYS...

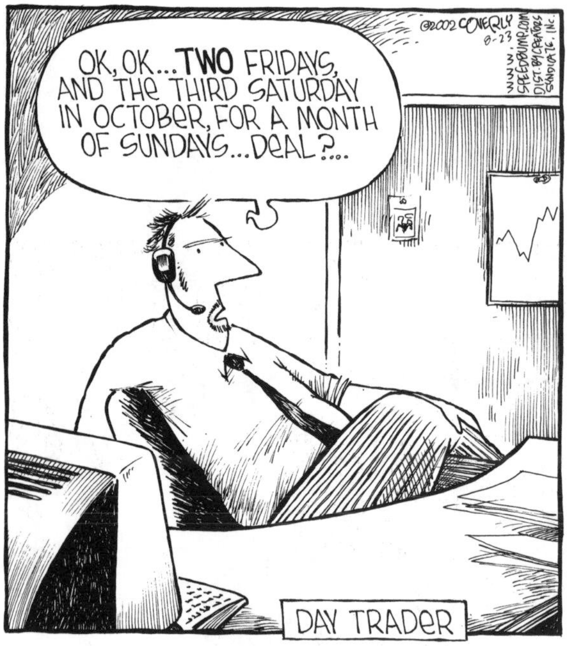
OK, OK... **TWO** FRIDAYS, AND THE THIRD SATURDAY IN OCTOBER, FOR A MONTH OF SUNDAYS... DEAL?...
DAY TRADER

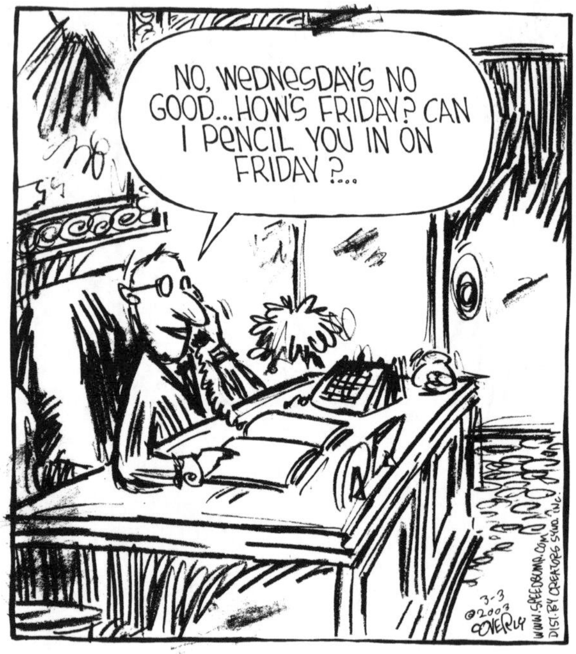
NO, WEDNESDAY'S NO GOOD... HOW'S FRIDAY? CAN I PENCIL YOU IN ON FRIDAY?...

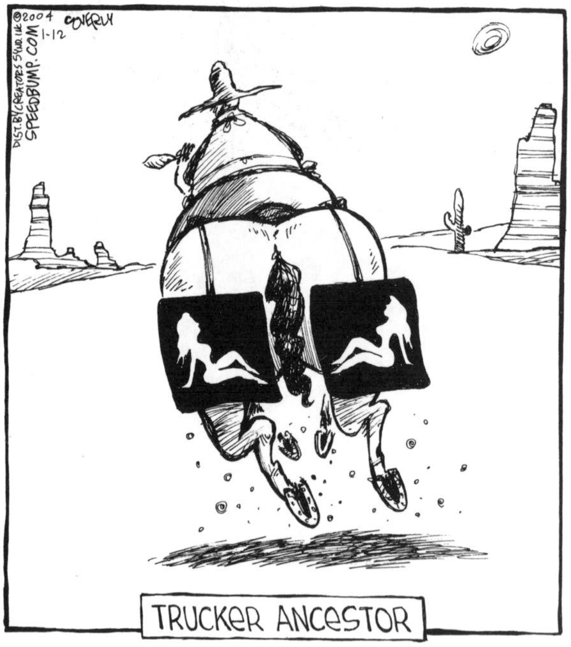
TRUCKER ANCESTOR

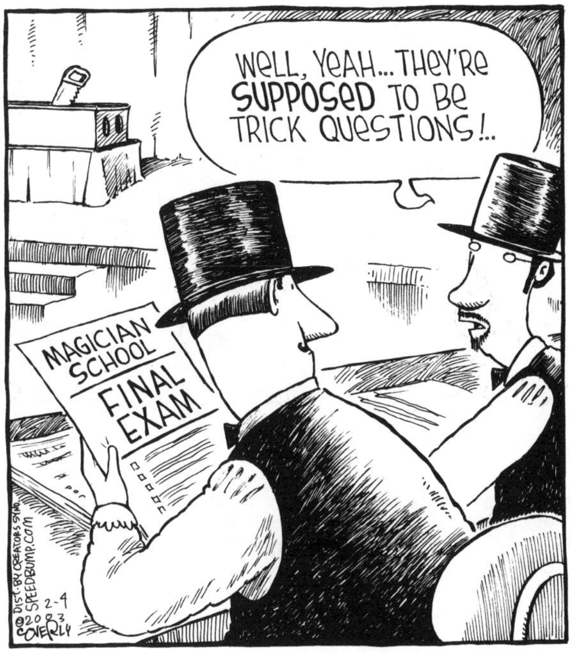
WELL, YEAH...THEY'RE **SUPPOSED** TO BE TRICK QUESTIONS!..
MAGICIAN SCHOOL
FINAL EXAM
DIST. BY CREATORS SYND. SPEEDBUMP.COM 2-4 ©2003 COVERLY

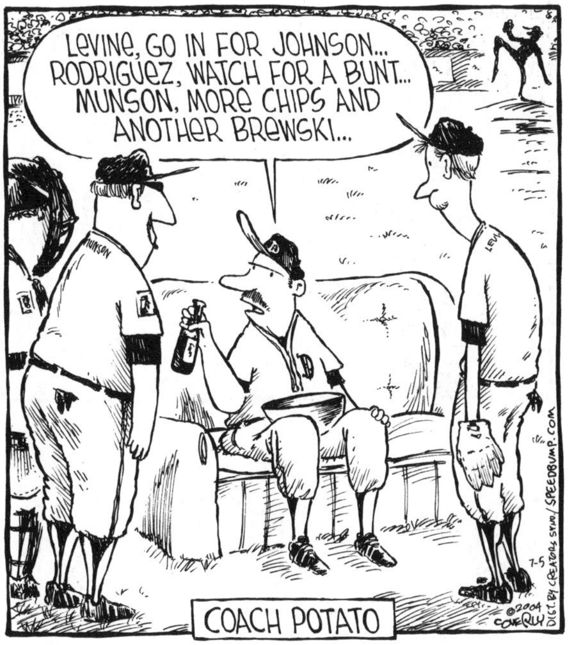
LEVINE, GO IN FOR JOHNSON... RODRIGUEZ, WATCH FOR A BUNT... MUNSON, MORE CHIPS AND ANOTHER BREWSKI...
7-5 ©2004 COVERLY DIST. BY CREATORS SYND. / SPEEDBUMP.COM

COACH POTATO

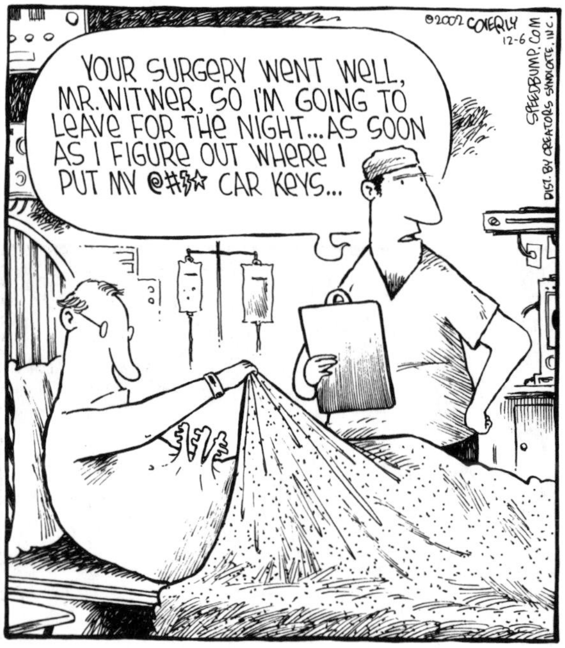
YOUR SURGERY WENT WELL, MR. WITWER, SO I'M GOING TO LEAVE FOR THE NIGHT... AS SOON AS I FIGURE OUT WHERE I PUT MY @#$☆ CAR KEYS...
©2002 COVERLY 12-6
SPEEDBUMP.COM
DIST. BY CREATORS SYNDICATE, INC.

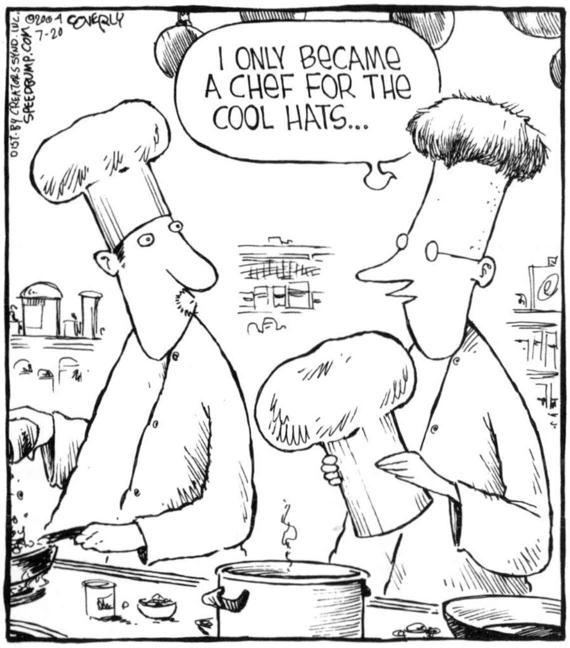
©2004 COVERLY 7-20
DIST. BY CREATORS SYND. INC.
SPEEDBUMP.COM
I ONLY BECAME A CHEF FOR THE COOL HATS...

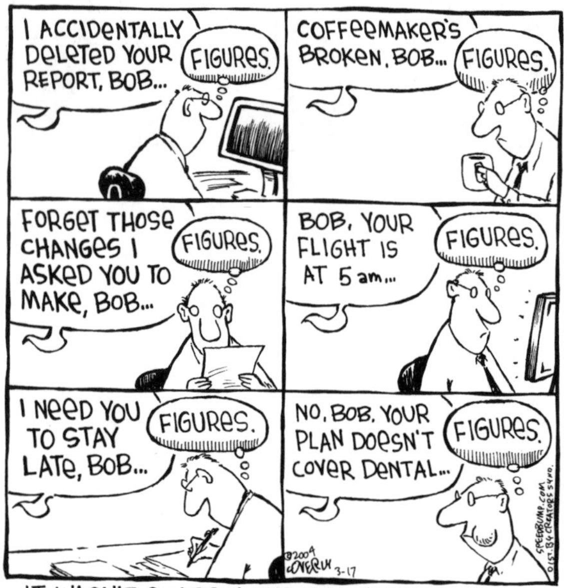
I ACCIDENTALLY DELETED YOUR REPORT, BOB...
FIGURES.
COFFEEMAKER'S BROKEN, BOB...
FIGURES.
FORGET THOSE CHANGES I ASKED YOU TO MAKE, BOB...
FIGURES.
BOB, YOUR FLIGHT IS AT 5 am...
FIGURES.
I NEED YOU TO STAY LATE, BOB...
FIGURES.
NO, BOB, YOUR PLAN DOESN'T COVER DENTAL...
FIGURES.
©2004 COVERLY 3-17
SPEEDBUMP.COM
DIST. BY CREATORS SYND.

IT WASN'T EXACTLY THE SIX-FIGURES JOB THAT BOB HAD HOPED FOR...

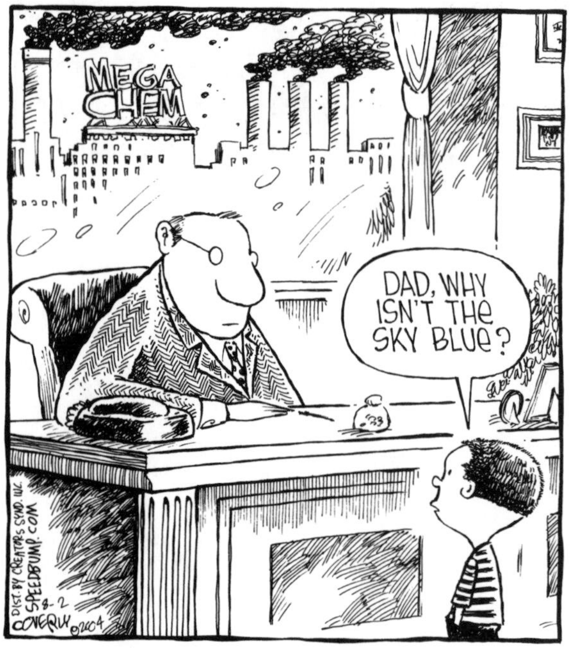
MEGA CHEM
DAD, WHY ISN'T THE SKY BLUE?
DIST. BY CREATORS SYND. INC.
SPEEDBUMP.COM
8-2
COVERLY ©2004

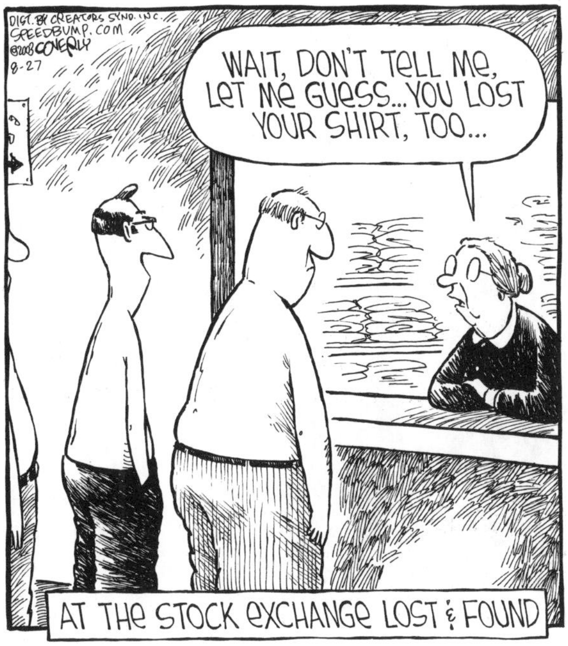
DIST. BY CREATORS SYND. INC.
SPEEDBUMP.COM
©2008 COVERLY
8-27
WAIT, DON'T TELL ME, LET ME GUESS... YOU LOST YOUR SHIRT, TOO...
AT THE STOCK EXCHANGE LOST & FOUND

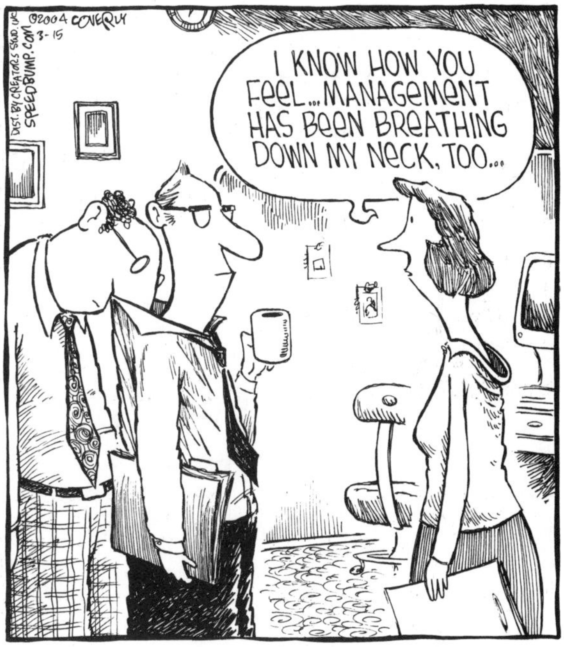
©2004 COVERLY
3-15
DIST. BY CREATORS SYND. INC.
SPEEDBUMP.COM
I KNOW HOW YOU FEEL... MANAGEMENT HAS BEEN BREATHING DOWN MY NECK, TOO...

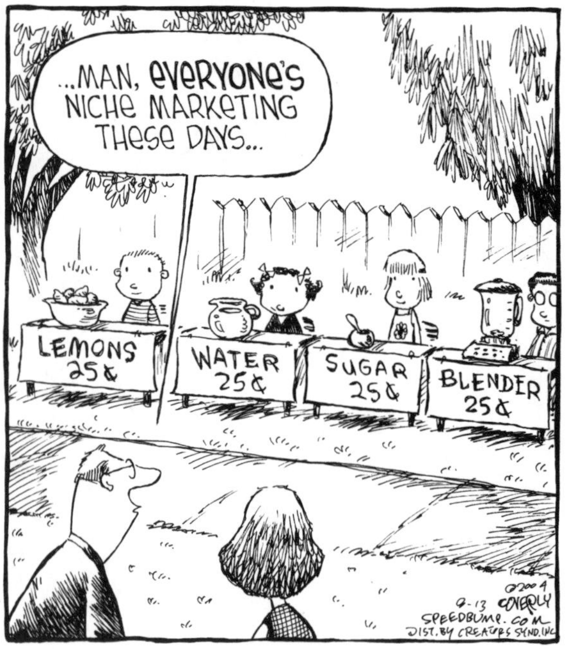
...MAN, EVERYONE'S NICHE MARKETING THESE DAYS...
LEMONS 25¢
WATER 25¢
SUGAR 25¢
BLENDER 25¢
©2004 COVERLY
6-13
SPEEDBUMP.COM
DIST. BY CREATORS SYND. INC

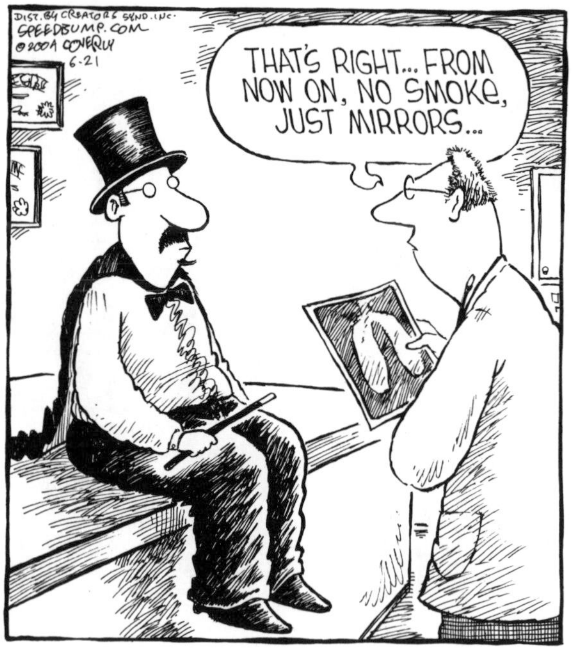
DIST. BY CREATORS SYND. INC.
SPEEDBUMP.COM
©2004 COVERLY
6-21
THAT'S RIGHT... FROM NOW ON, NO SMOKE, JUST MIRRORS...

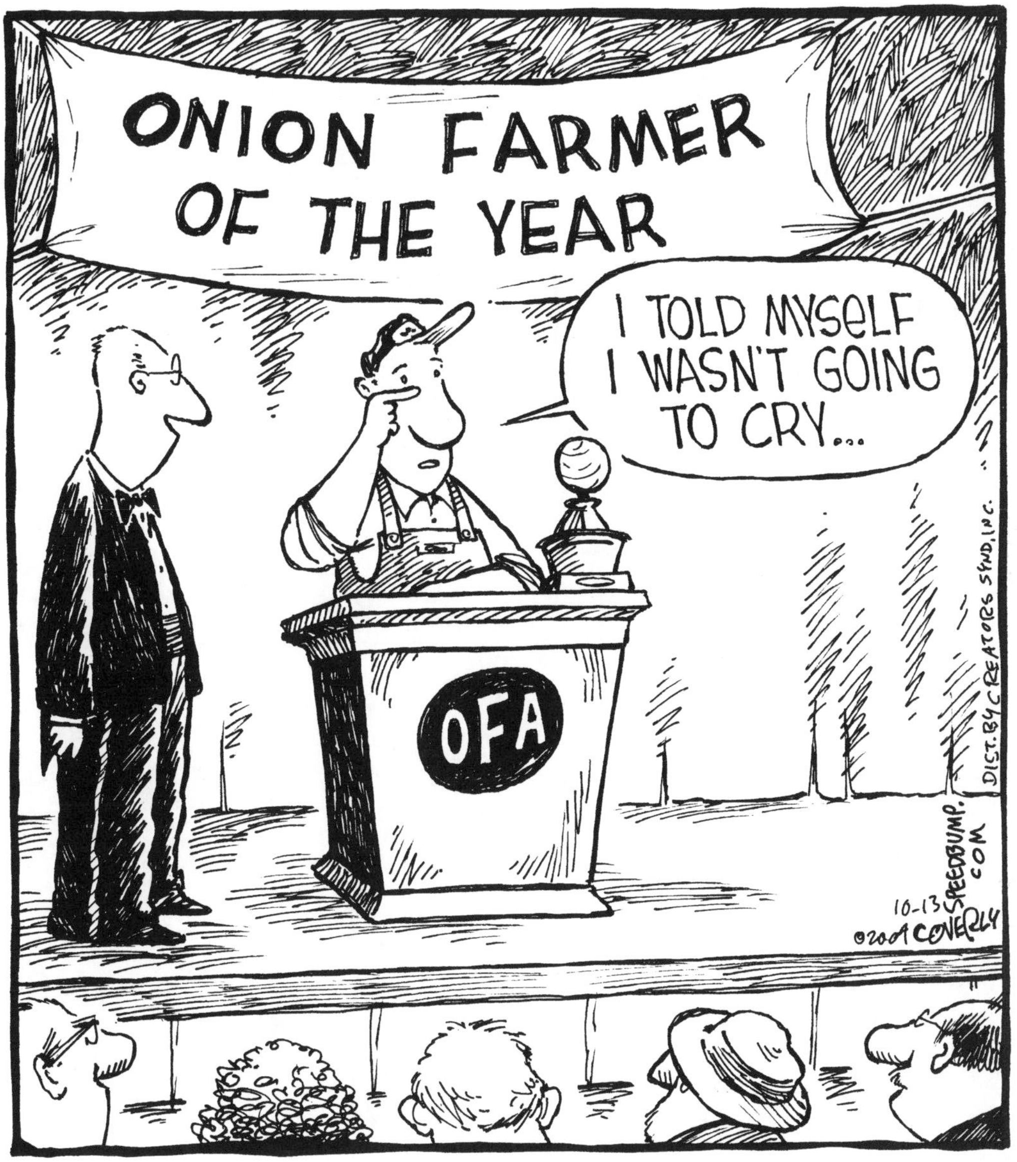
ONION FARMER OF THE YEAR
I TOLD MYSELF I WASN'T GOING TO CRY...
OFA
DIST. BY CREATORS SYND, INC.
SPEEDBUMP.COM
10-13
©2009 COVERLY

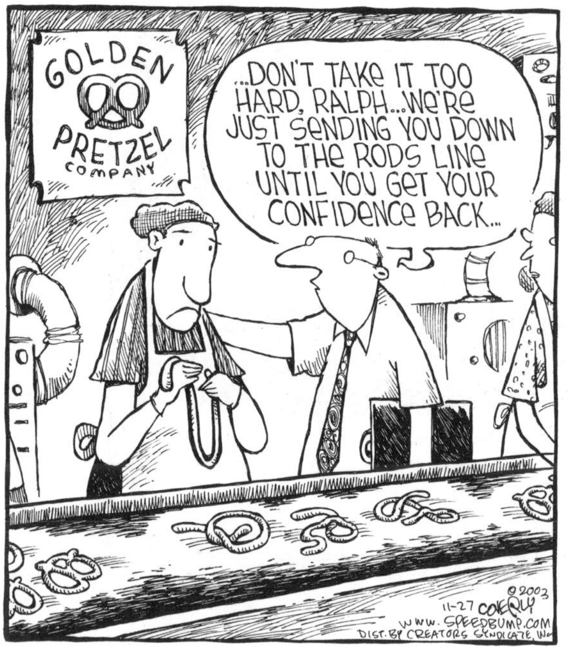
GOLDEN PRETZEL COMPANY
...DON'T TAKE IT TOO HARD, RALPH...WE'RE JUST SENDING YOU DOWN TO THE RODS LINE UNTIL YOU GET YOUR CONFIDENCE BACK...
©2003 11-27 COVERLY
WWW.SPEEDBUMP.COM
DIST. BY CREATORS SYNDICATE, INC.

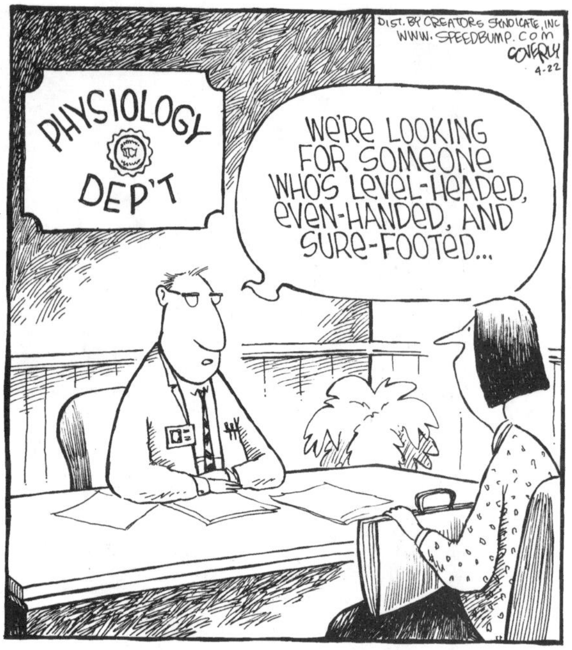
DIST. BY CREATORS SYNDICATE, INC.
WWW.SPEEDBUMP.COM
COVERLY 4-22
PHYSIOLOGY DEP'T
WE'RE LOOKING FOR SOMEONE WHO'S LEVEL-HEADED, EVEN-HANDED, AND SURE-FOOTED...

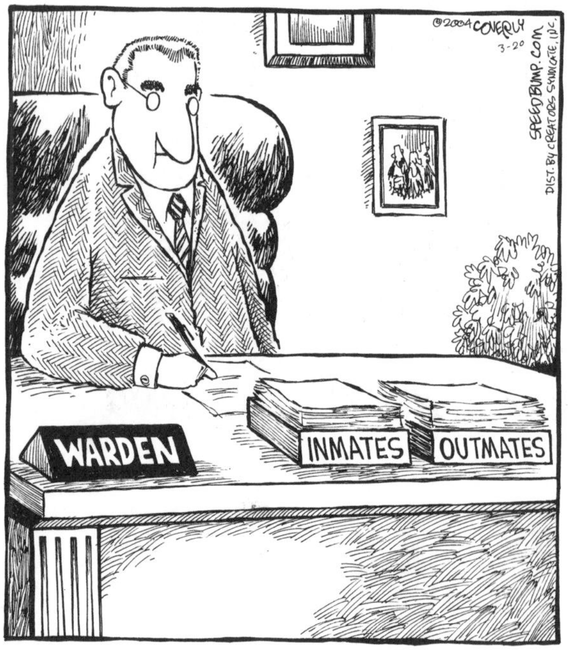
©2004 COVERLY 3-20
SPEEDBUMP.COM
DIST. BY CREATORS SYNDICATE, INC.
WARDEN
INMATES
OUTMATES

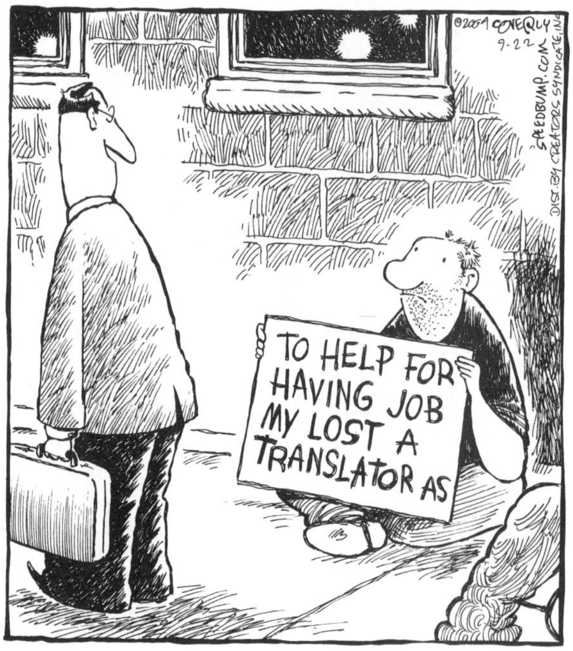
©2004 COVERLY 9-22
SPEEDBUMP.COM
DIST. BY CREATORS SYNDICATE, INC.
TO HELP FOR HAVING JOB MY LOST A TRANSLATOR AS

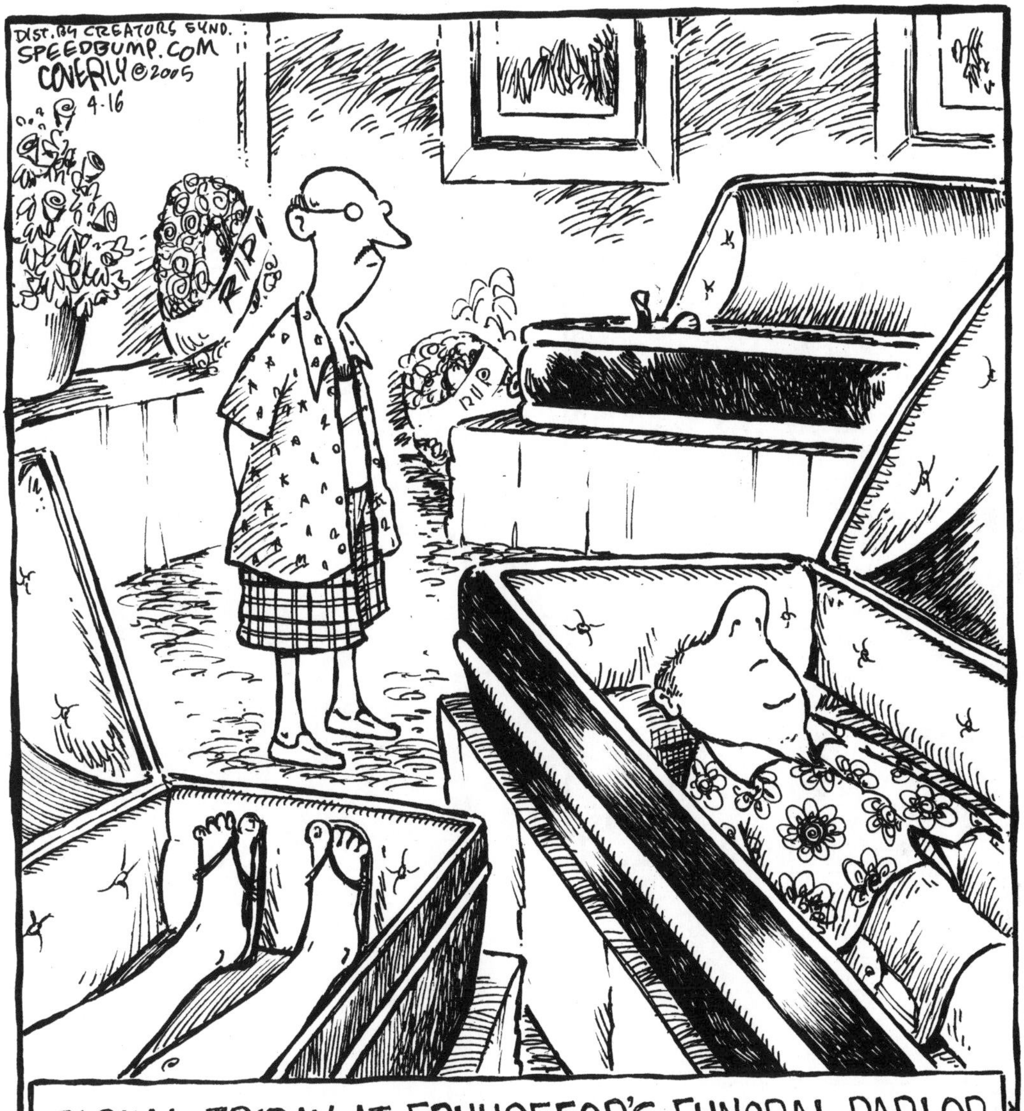
DIST. BY CREATORS SYND.
SPEEDBUMP.COM
COVERLY ©2005
4-16
RIP
RIP
CASUAL FRIDAY AT FRUHOFFER'S FUNERAL PARLOR

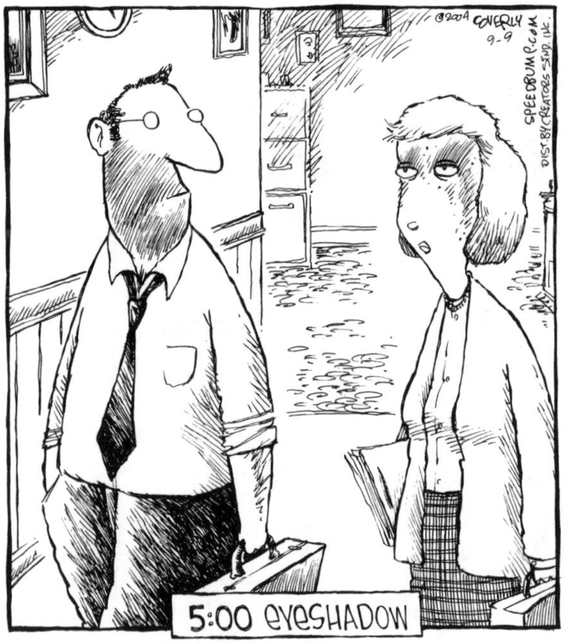
5:00 EYESHADOW
©2004 COVERLY 9-9
SPEEDBUMP.COM
DIST. BY CREATORS SYND. INC.

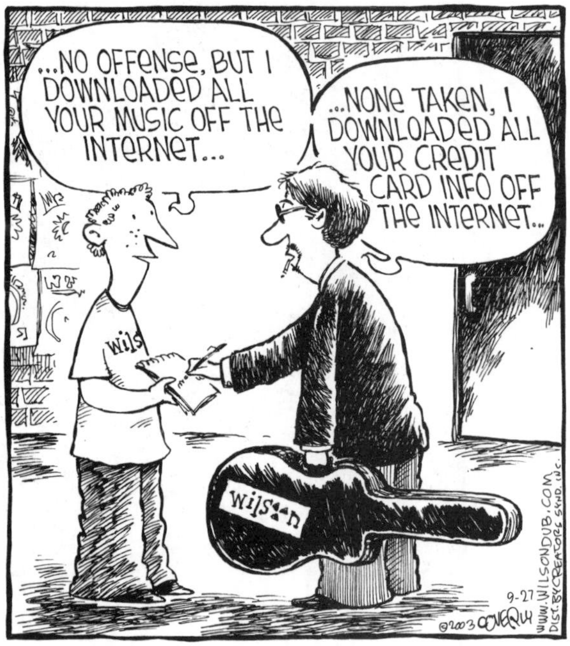
...NO OFFENSE, BUT I DOWNLOADED ALL YOUR MUSIC OFF THE INTERNET...
...NONE TAKEN, I DOWNLOADED ALL YOUR CREDIT CARD INFO OFF THE INTERNET...
9-27
©2003 COVERLY
WWW.WILSONDUB.COM
DIST. BY CREATORS SYND. INC.

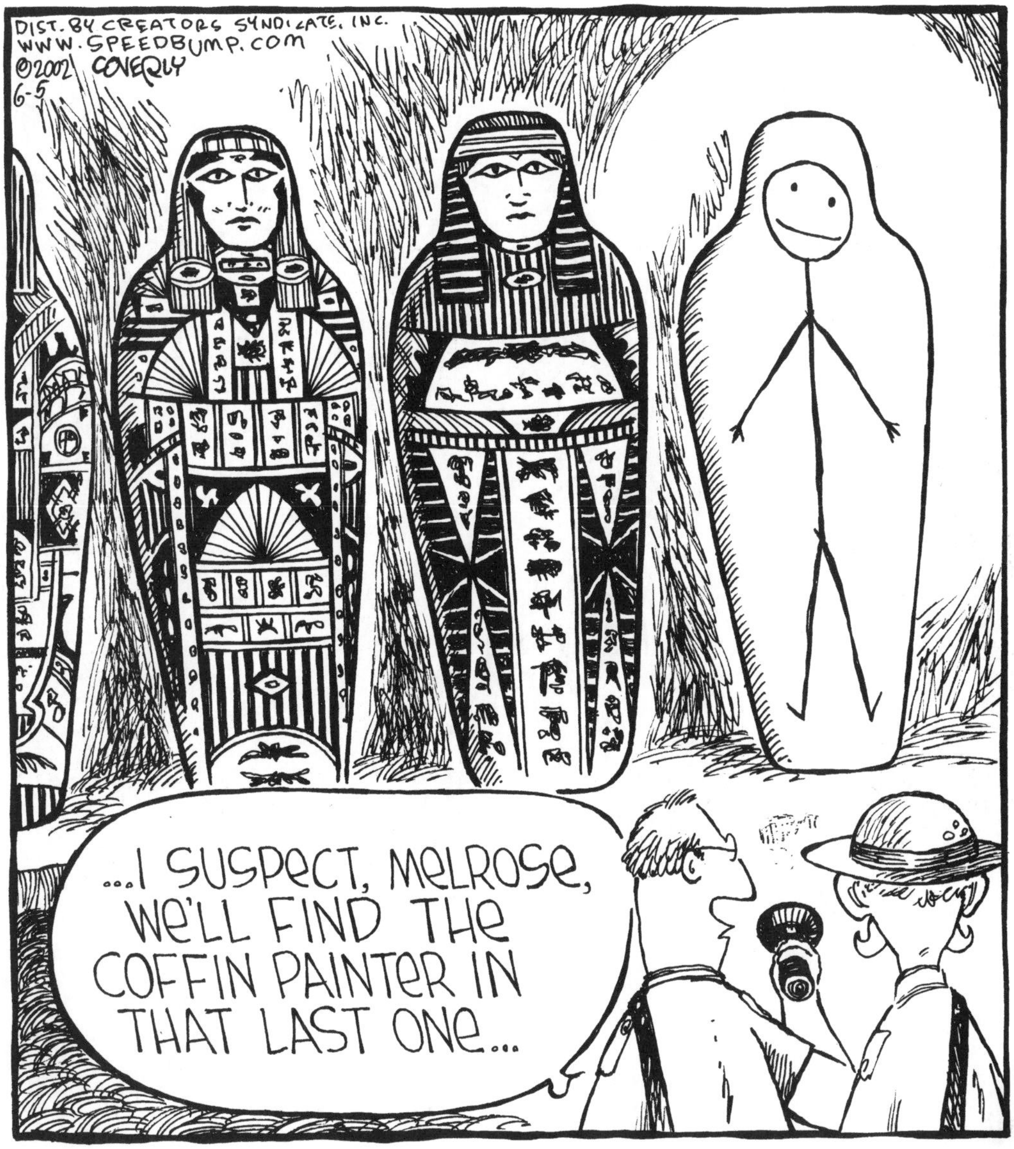
DIST. BY CREATORS SYNDICATE, INC.
WWW.SPEEDBUMP.COM
©2002 COVERLY
6-5
...I SUSPECT, MELROSE, WE'LL FIND THE COFFIN PAINTER IN THAT LAST ONE...

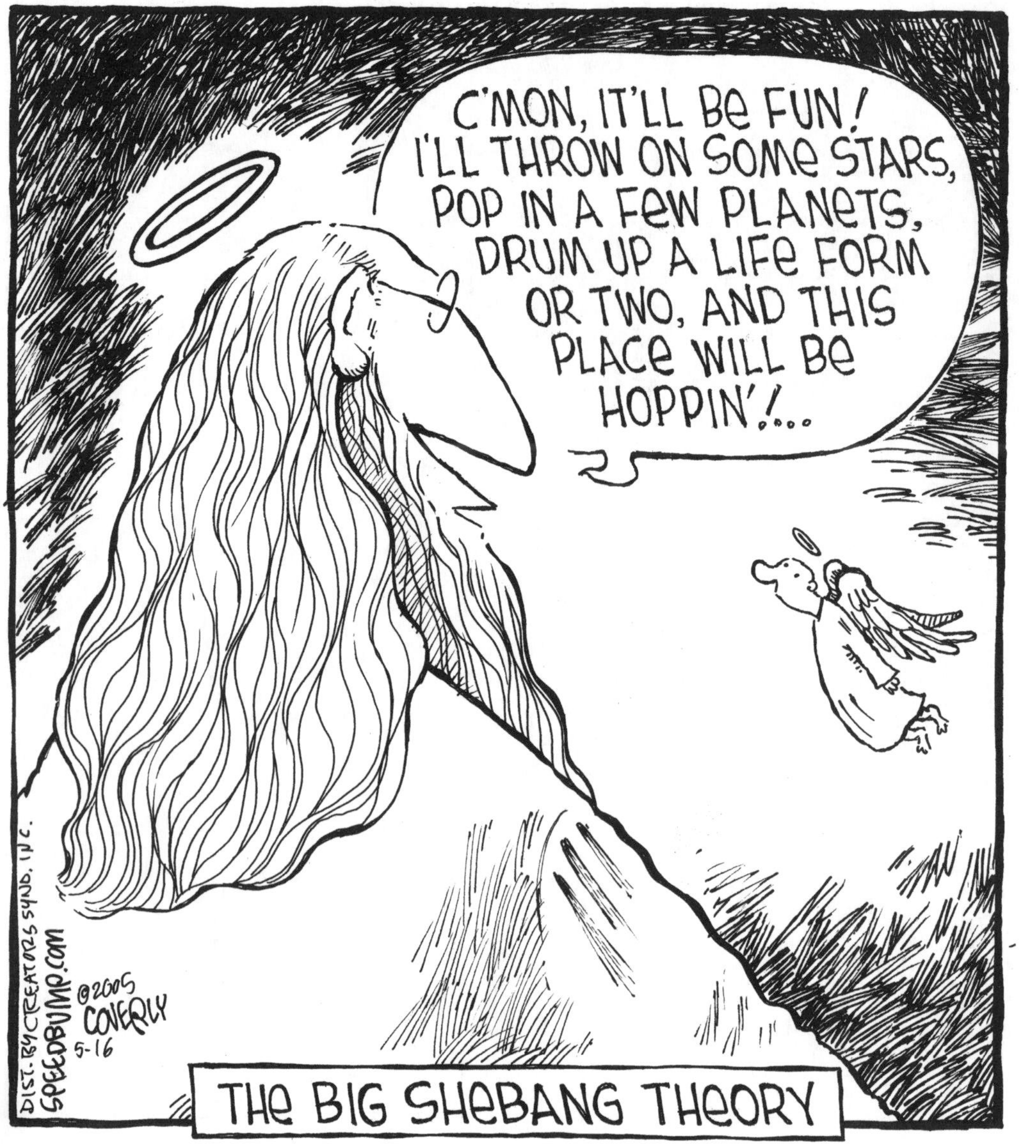
C'MON, IT'LL BE FUN! I'LL THROW ON SOME STARS, POP IN A FEW PLANETS, DRUM UP A LIFE FORM OR TWO, AND THIS PLACE WILL BE HOPPIN'!...
DIST. BY CREATORS SYND. INC.
SPEEDBUMP.COM
©2005 COVERLY 5-16
THE BIG SHEBANG THEORY

Meaning of Life*

*If you're looking for the meaning of life in a cartoon, you may want to get out more . . .

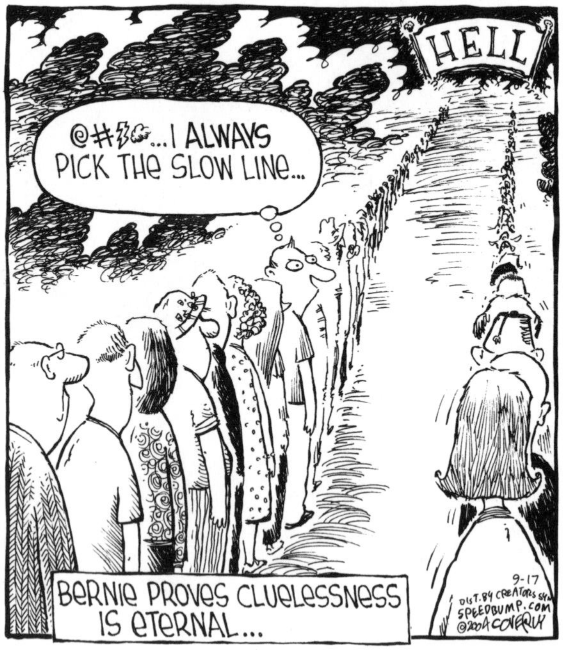
HELL
@#...I ALWAYS PICK THE SLOW LINE...
BERNIE PROVES CLUELESSNESS IS ETERNAL...
9-17
DIST. BY CREATORS SYN.
SPEEDBUMP.COM
©2004 COVERLY

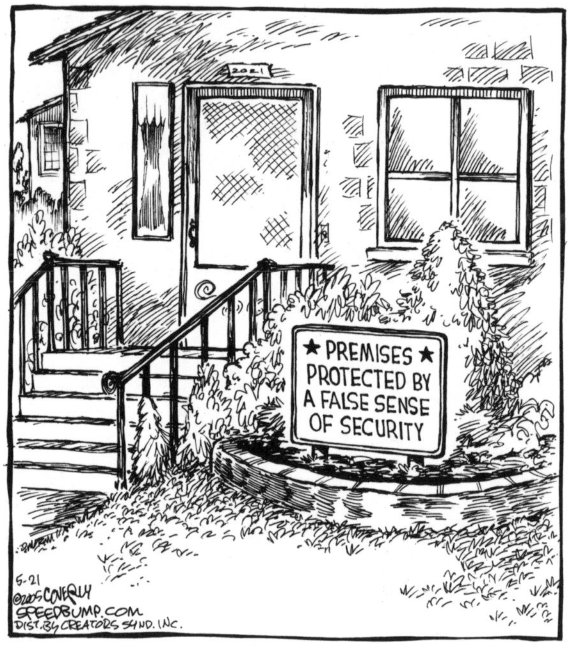
2021
★ PREMISES ★
PROTECTED BY
A FALSE SENSE
OF SECURITY
5-21
©2005 COVERLY
SPEEDBUMP.COM
DIST. BY CREATORS SYND. INC.

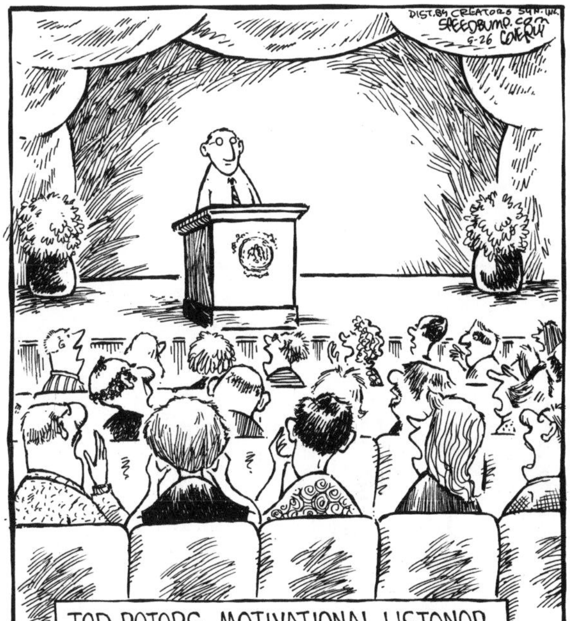
TED PETERS, MOTIVATIONAL LISTENER.

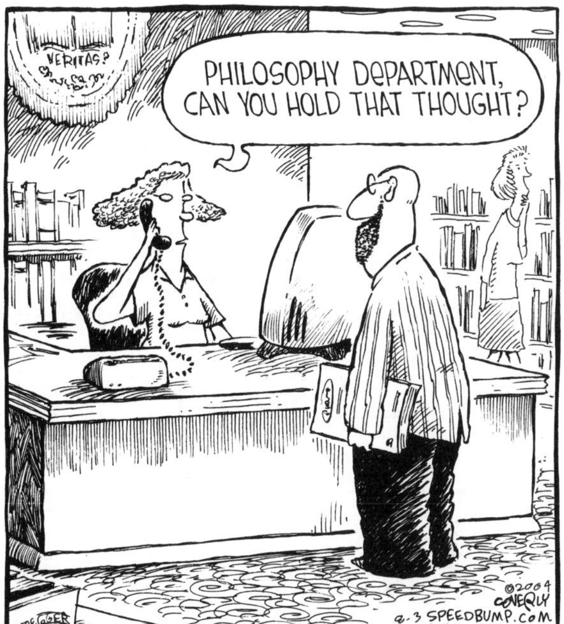
PHILOSOPHY DEPARTMENT, CAN YOU HOLD THAT THOUGHT?
VERITAS?
©2004 COVERLY
8-3 SPEEDBUMP.COM
DIST. BY CREATORS SYND. INC.

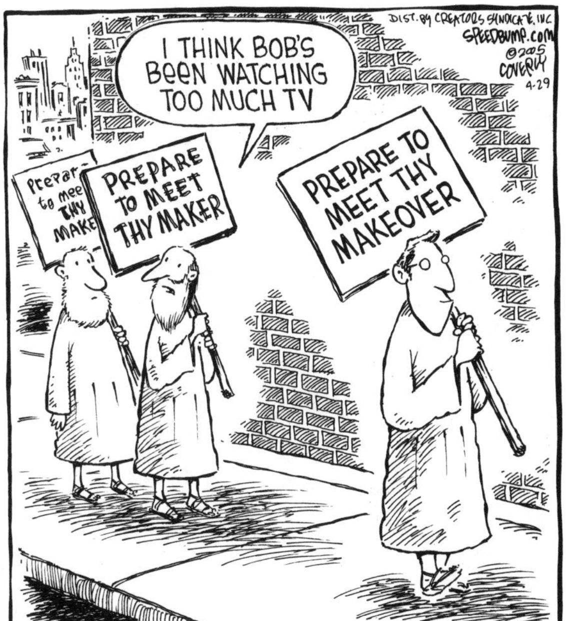
I THINK BOB'S BEEN WATCHING TOO MUCH TV
PREPARE TO MEET THY MAKER
PREPARE TO MEET THY MAKEOVER
DIST. BY CREATORS SYNDICATE, INC
SPEEDBUMP.COM
©2005 COVERLY
4-29

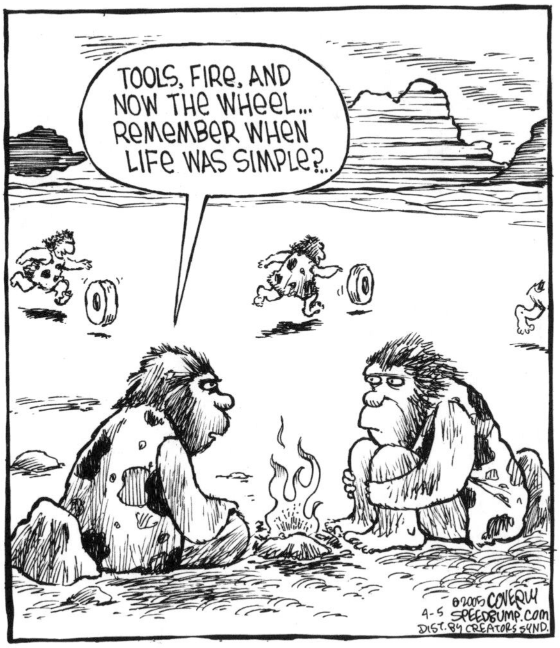
TOOLS, FIRE, AND NOW THE WHEEL... REMEMBER WHEN LIFE WAS SIMPLE?...
©2005 COVERLY
4-5 SPEEDBUMP.COM
DIST. BY CREATORS SYND.

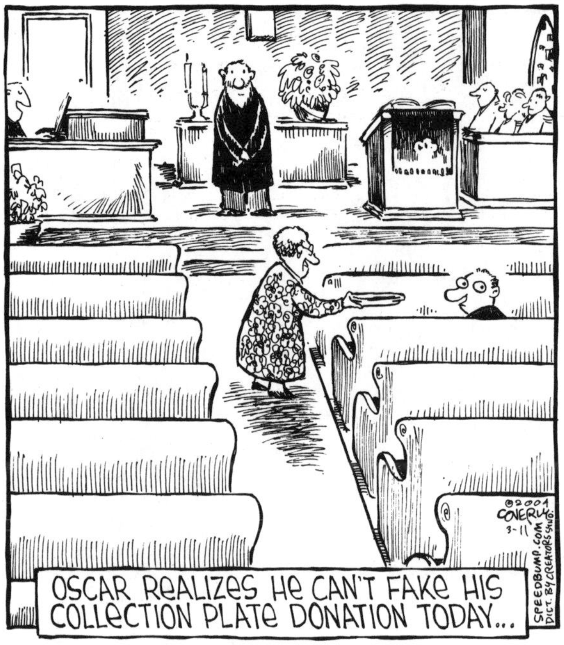
OSCAR REALIZES HE CAN'T FAKE HIS COLLECTION PLATE DONATION TODAY...
©2001 COVERLY 3-11
SPEEDBUMP.COM
DIST. BY CREATORS SYND.

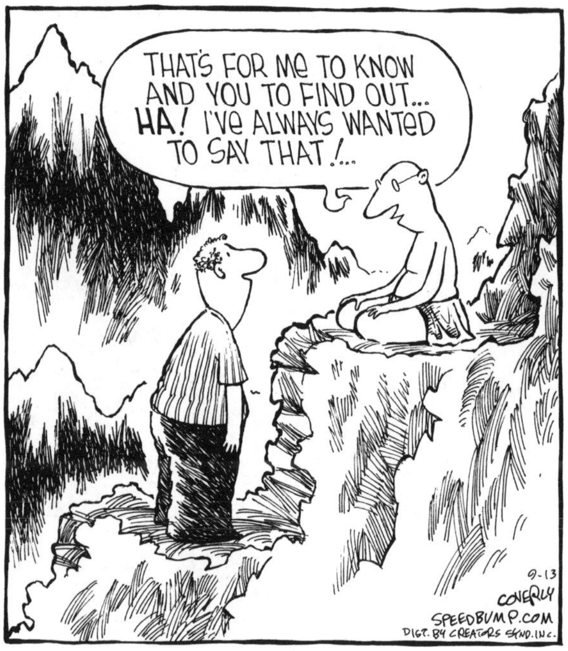
THAT'S FOR ME TO KNOW AND YOU TO FIND OUT... HA! I'VE ALWAYS WANTED TO SAY THAT!...
9-13
COVERLY
SPEEDBUMP.COM
DIST. BY CREATORS SYND. INC.

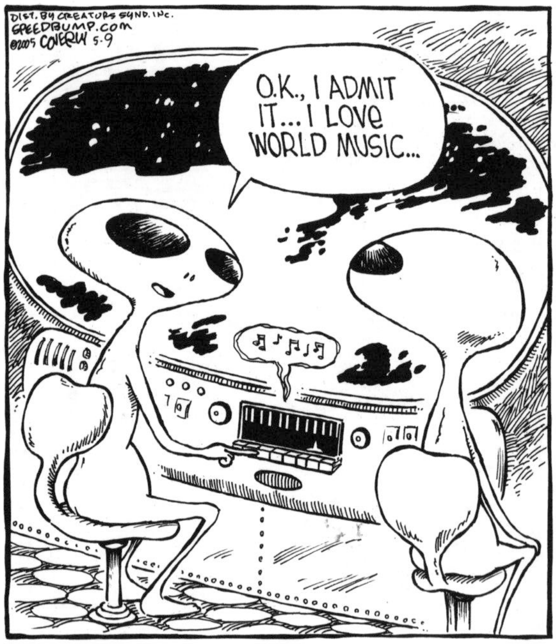
DIST. BY CREATORS SYND. INC.
SPEEDBUMP.COM
©2005 COVERLY 5-9
O.K., I ADMIT IT... I LOVE WORLD MUSIC...

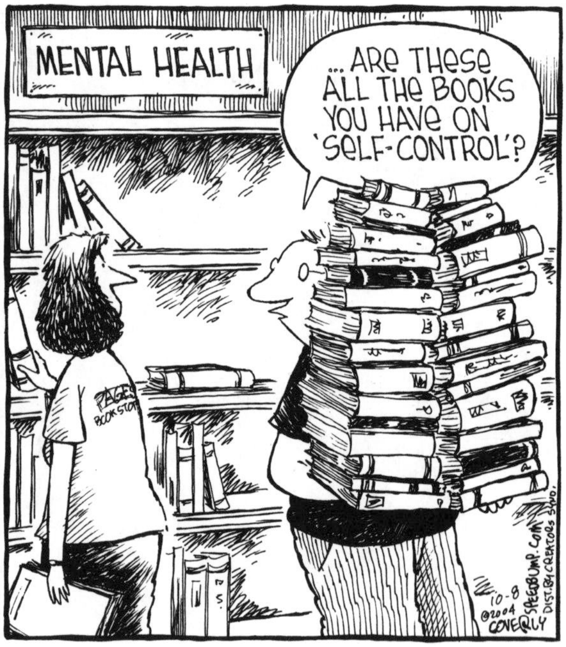
MENTAL HEALTH
...ARE THESE ALL THE BOOKS YOU HAVE ON 'SELF-CONTROL'?
10-8
©2004
COVERLY
SPEEDBUMP.COM
DIST. BY CREATORS SYND.

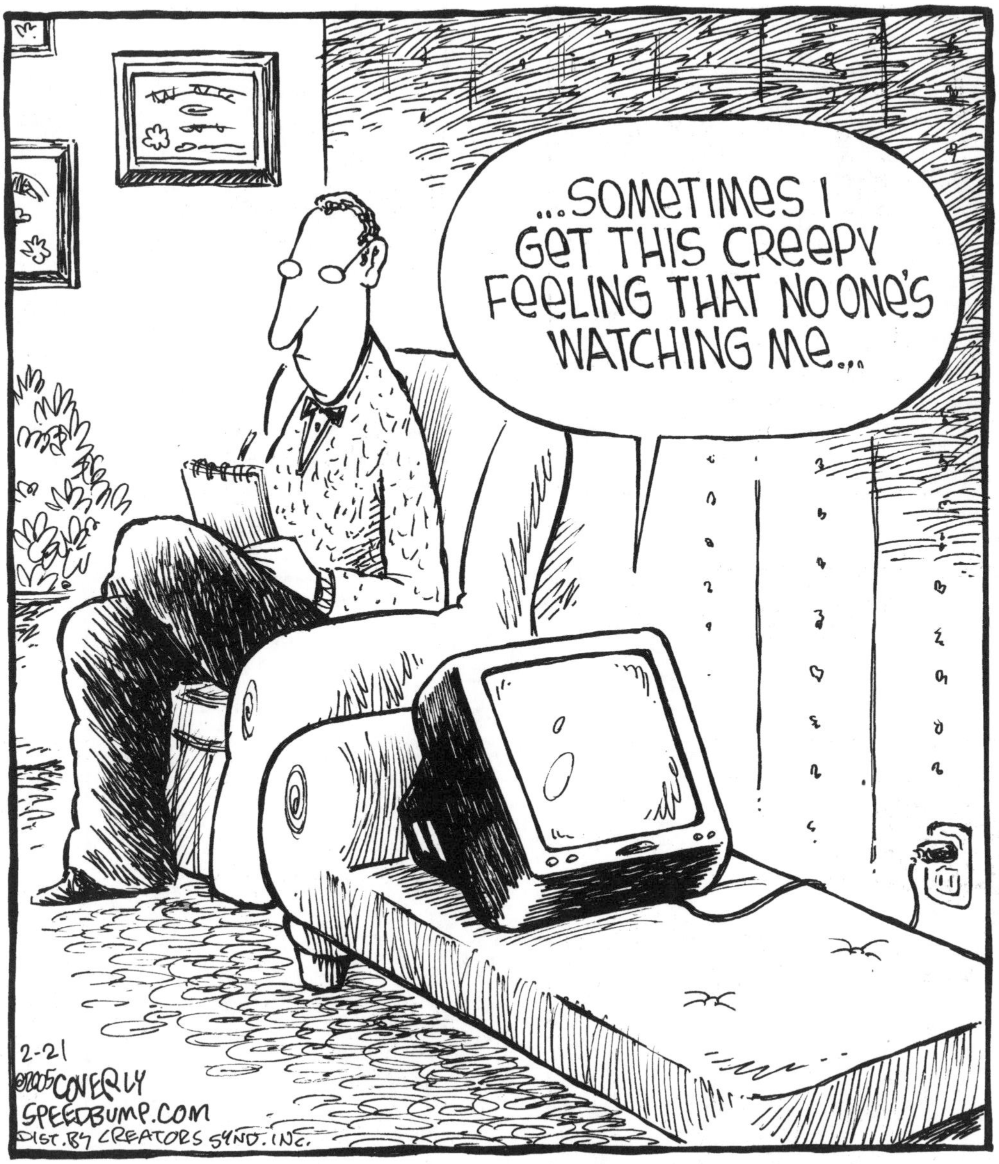
...SOMETIMES I GET THIS CREEPY FEELING THAT NO ONE'S WATCHING ME...
2-21
©2005 COVERLY
SPEEDBUMP.COM
DIST. BY CREATORS SYND. INC.

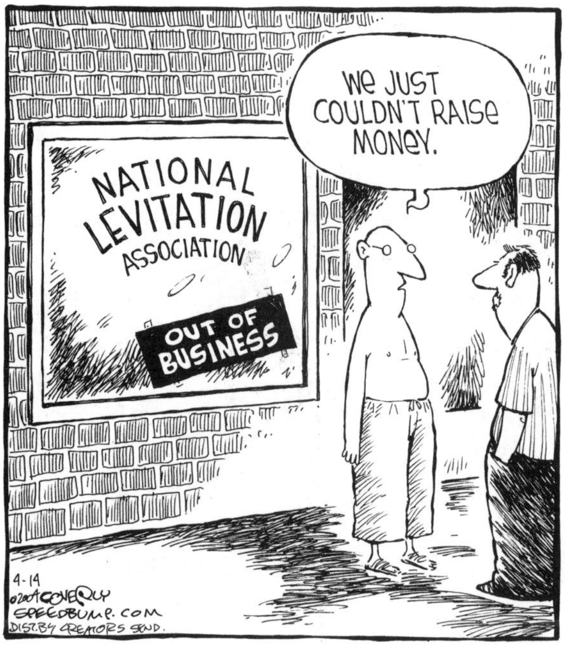
WE JUST COULDN'T RAISE MONEY.
NATIONAL LEVITATION ASSOCIATION
OUT OF BUSINESS
4-14
©2004 COVERLY
SPEEDBUMP.COM
DIST. BY CREATORS SYND.

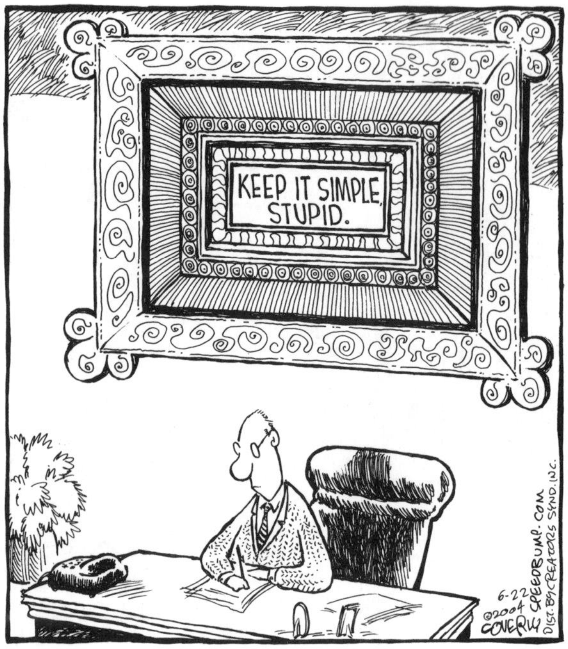
KEEP IT SIMPLE, STUPID.
6-22
©2004 COVERLY
SPEEDBUMP.COM
DIST. BY CREATORS SYND. INC.

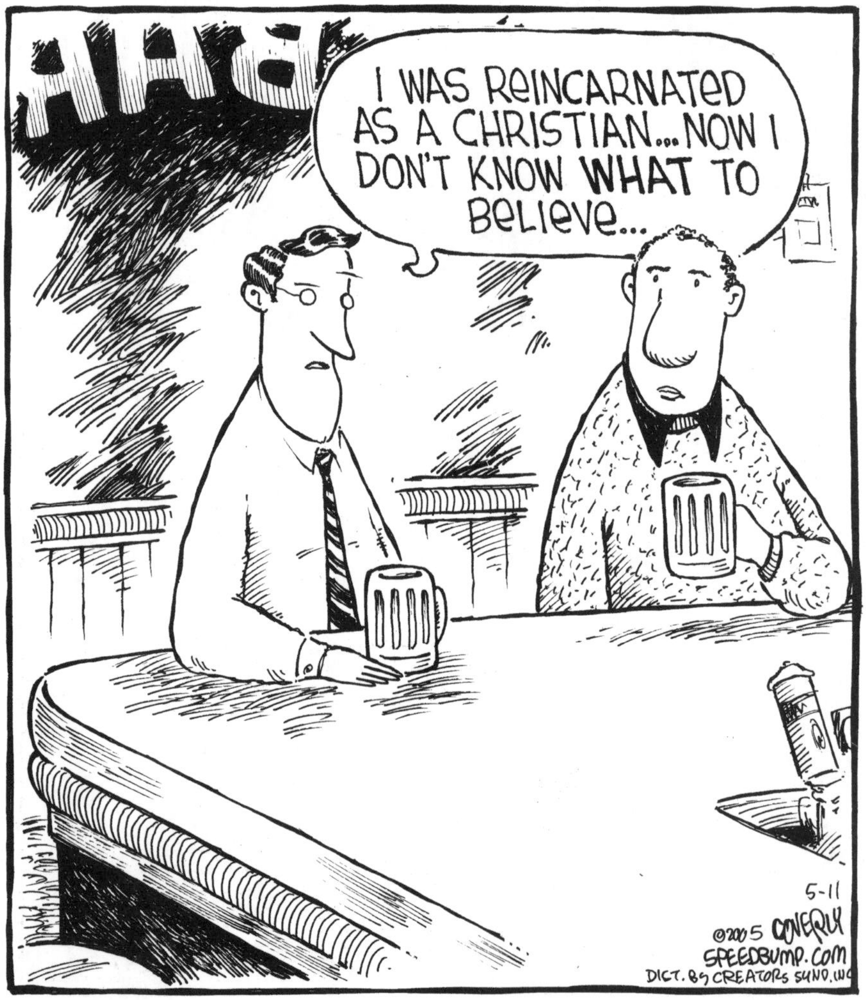
I WAS REINCARNATED AS A CHRISTIAN...NOW I DON'T KNOW WHAT TO BELIEVE...
5-11
©2005 COVERLY
SPEEDBUMP.COM
DIST. BY CREATORS SYND. INC

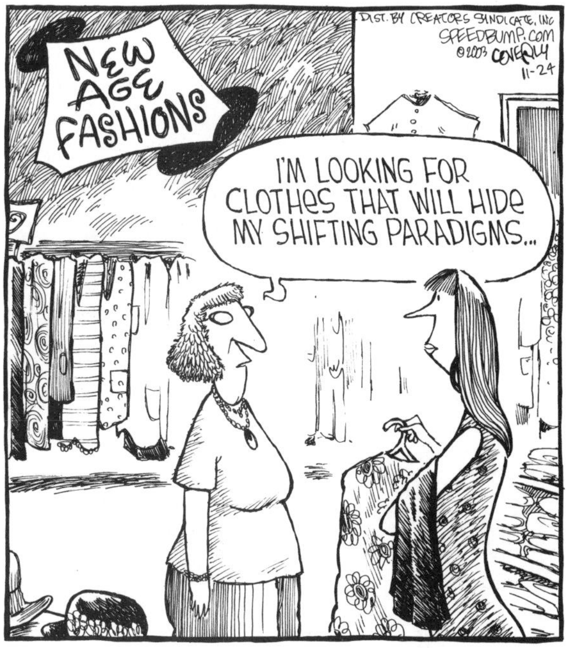
DIST. BY CREATORS SYNDICATE, INC
SPEEDBUMP.COM
©2003 COVERLY
11-24
NEW AGE FASHIONS
I'M LOOKING FOR CLOTHES THAT WILL HIDE MY SHIFTING PARADIGMS...

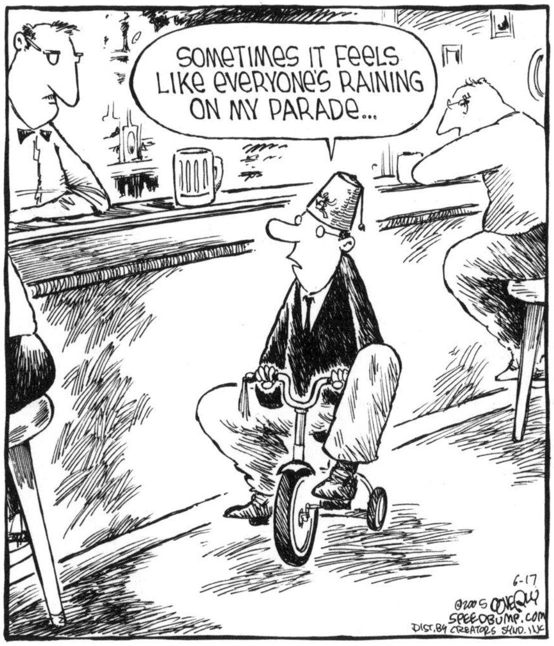
SOMETIMES IT FEELS LIKE EVERYONE'S RAINING ON MY PARADE...
6-17
©2005 COVERLY
SPEEDBUMP.COM
DIST. BY CREATORS SYND. INC

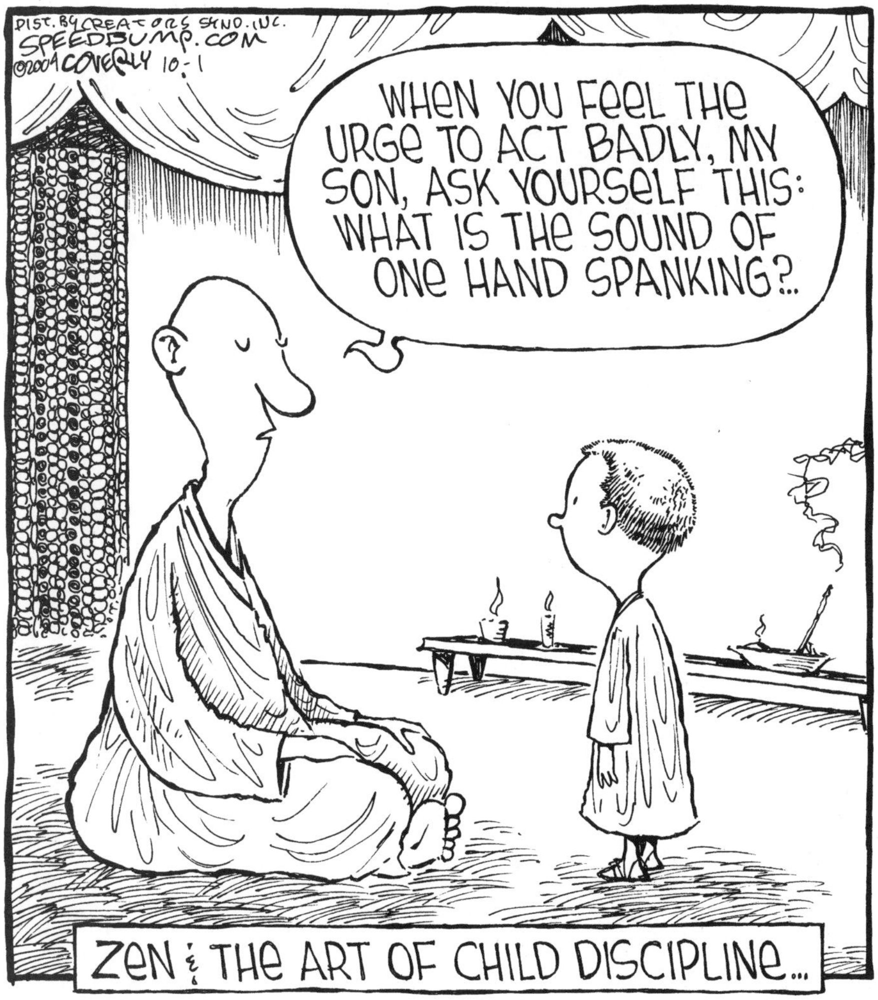
DIST. BY CREATORS SYND. INC.
SPEEDBUMP.COM
©2004 COVERLY 10-1
WHEN YOU FEEL THE URGE TO ACT BADLY, MY SON, ASK YOURSELF THIS: WHAT IS THE SOUND OF ONE HAND SPANKING?..
ZEN & THE ART OF CHILD DISCIPLINE...

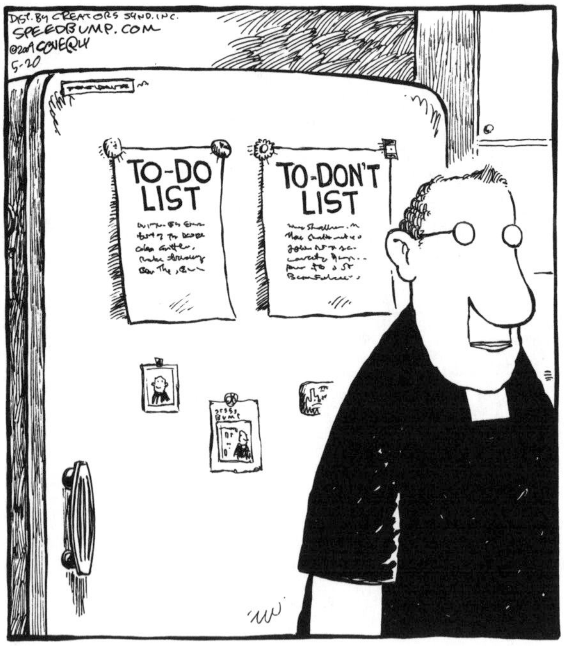
DIST. BY CREATORS SYND. INC.
SPEEDBUMP.COM
5-20
TO-DO LIST
TO-DON'T LIST

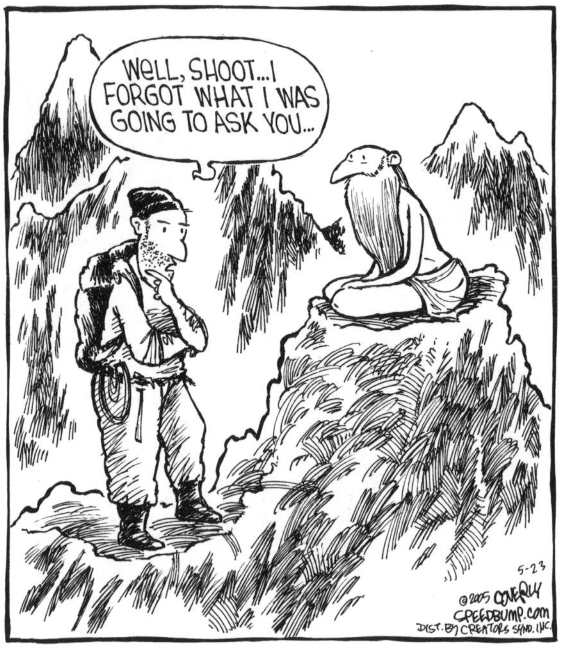
WELL, SHOOT...I FORGOT WHAT I WAS GOING TO ASK YOU...
5-23
©2005 COVERLY
SPEEDBUMP.com
DIST. BY CREATORS SYND. INC.

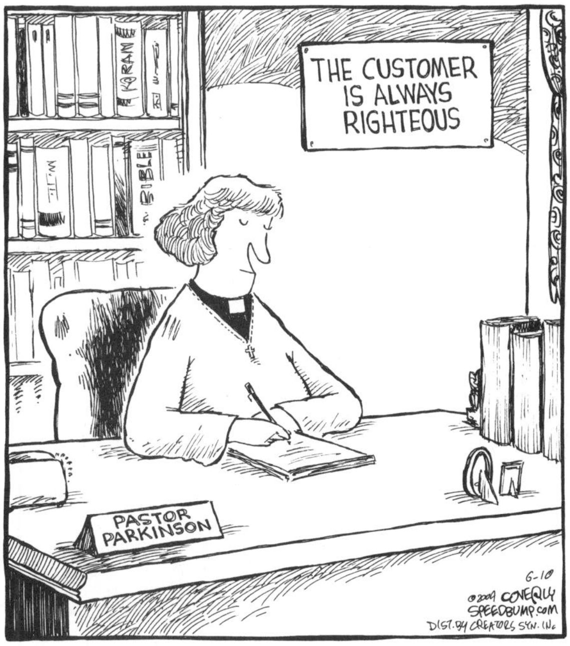
THE CUSTOMER IS ALWAYS RIGHTEOUS
KORAN
BIBLE
PASTOR PARKINSON
SPEEDBUMP.COM

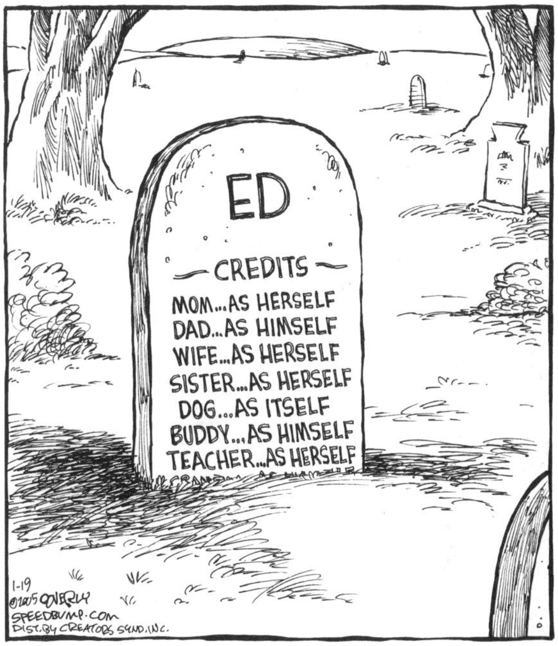
ED
CREDITS
MOM...AS HERSELF
DAD...AS HIMSELF
WIFE...AS HERSELF
SISTER...AS HERSELF
DOG...AS ITSELF
BUDDY...AS HIMSELF
TEACHER...AS HERSELF
SPEEDBUMP.COM
DIST. BY CREATORS SYND. INC.

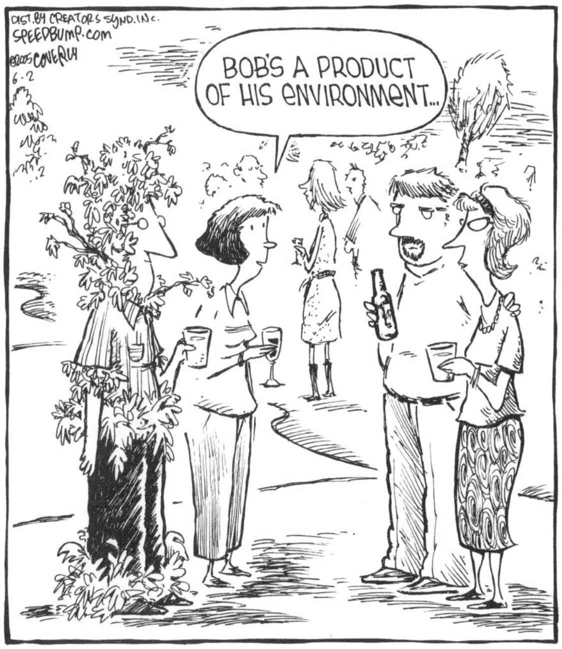
DIST. BY CREATORS SYND. INC.
SPEEDBUMP.COM
BOB'S A PRODUCT OF HIS ENVIRONMENT...

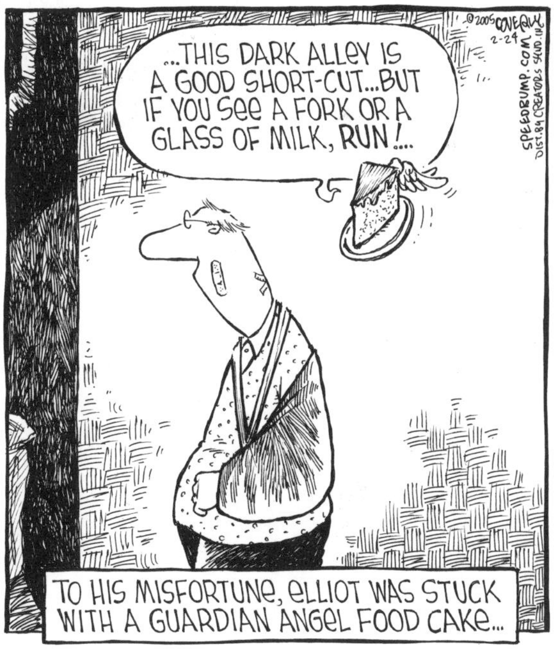
...THIS DARK ALLEY IS A GOOD SHORT-CUT...BUT IF YOU SEE A FORK OR A GLASS OF MILK, RUN!...
SPEEDBUMP.COM
TO HIS MISFORTUNE, ELLIOT WAS STUCK WITH A GUARDIAN ANGEL FOOD CAKE...

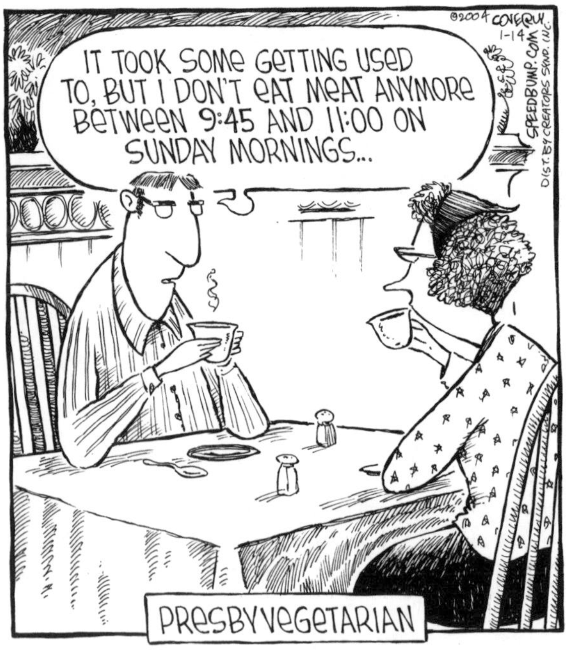
©2004 COVERLY 1-14
SPEEDBUMP.COM
DIST. BY CREATORS SYND. INC.
IT TOOK SOME GETTING USED TO, BUT I DON'T EAT MEAT ANYMORE BETWEEN 9:45 AND 11:00 ON SUNDAY MORNINGS...
PRESBYVEGETARIAN

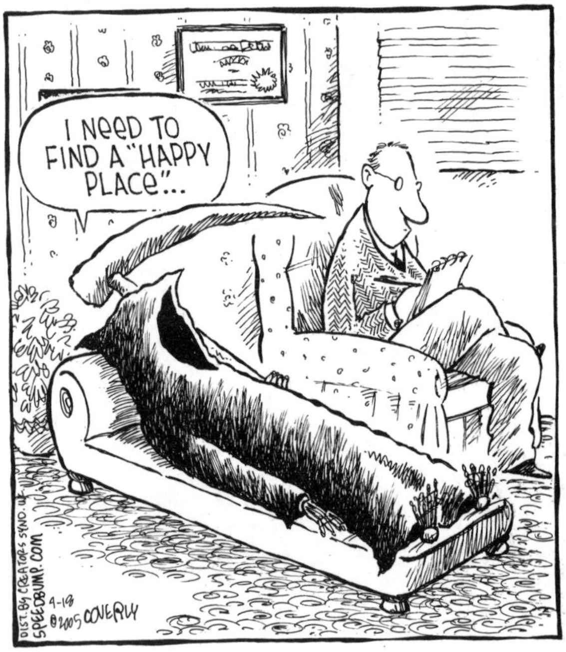
I NEED TO FIND A "HAPPY PLACE"...
DIST. BY CREATORS SYND. INC.
SPEEDBUMP.COM
4-18
©2005 COVERLY

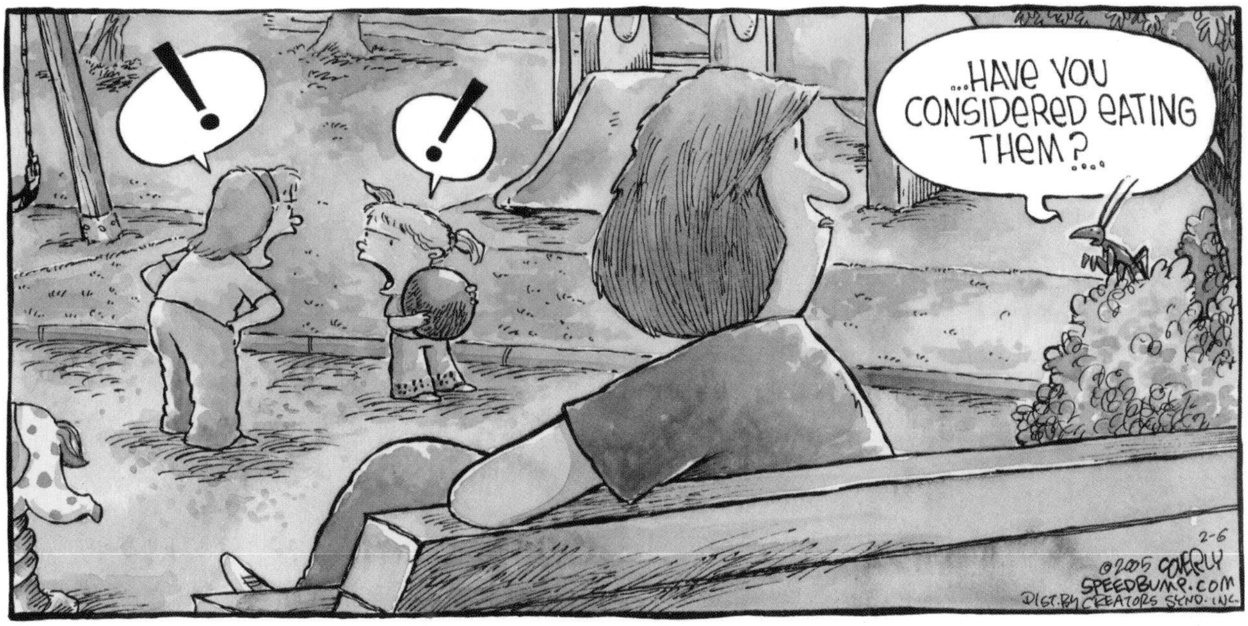
!
!
...HAVE YOU CONSIDERED EATING THEM?...
2-6
©2005 COVERLY
SPEEDBUMP.COM
DIST. BY CREATORS SYND. INC.

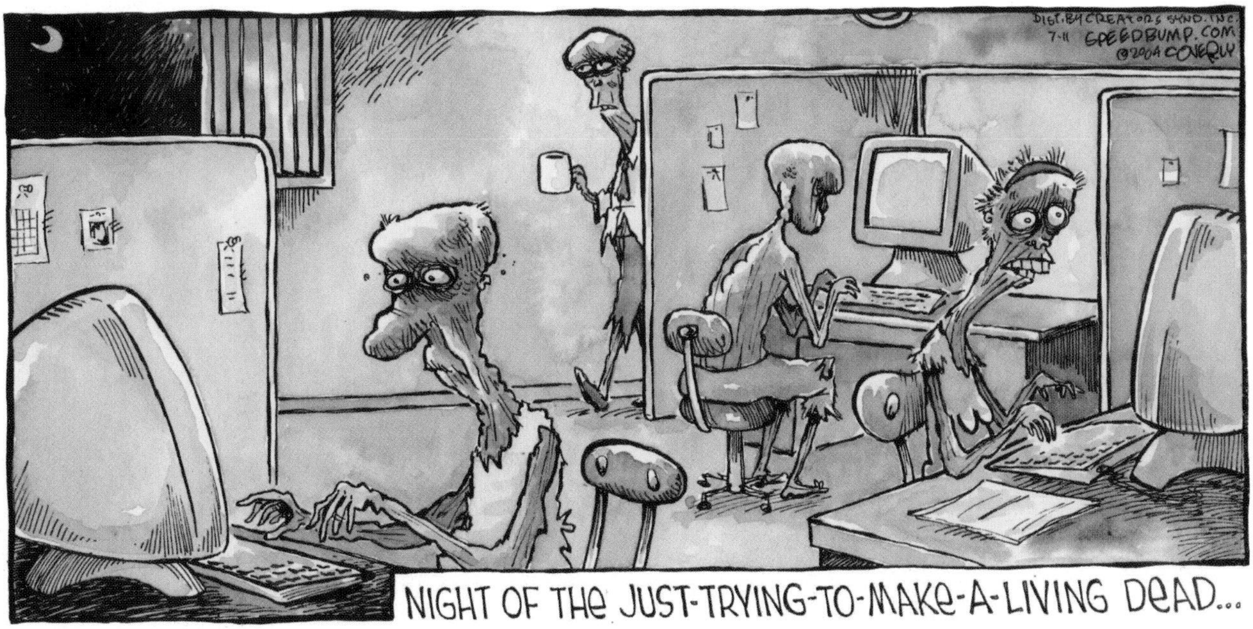
DIST. BY CREATORS SYND. INC.
7-11
SPEEDBUMP.COM
©2004 COVERLY
NIGHT OF THE JUST-TRYING-TO-MAKE-A-LIVING DEAD...

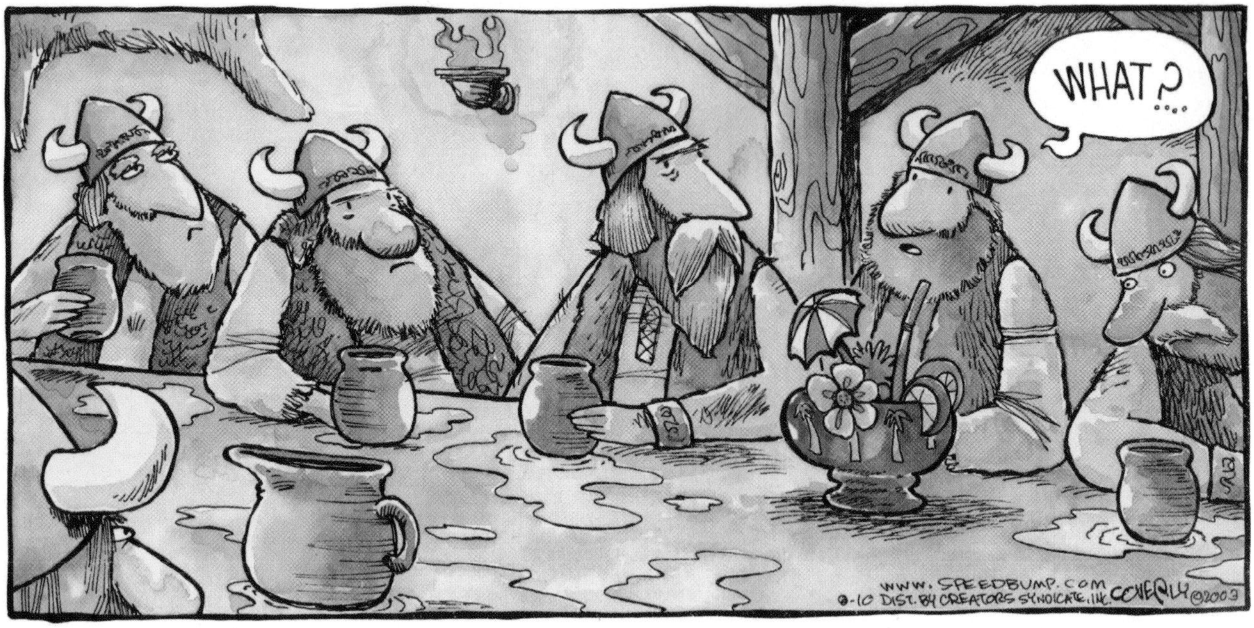
WHAT?....
WWW.SPEEDBUMP.COM
8-10 DIST. BY CREATORS SYNDICATE, INC. COVERLY ©2003

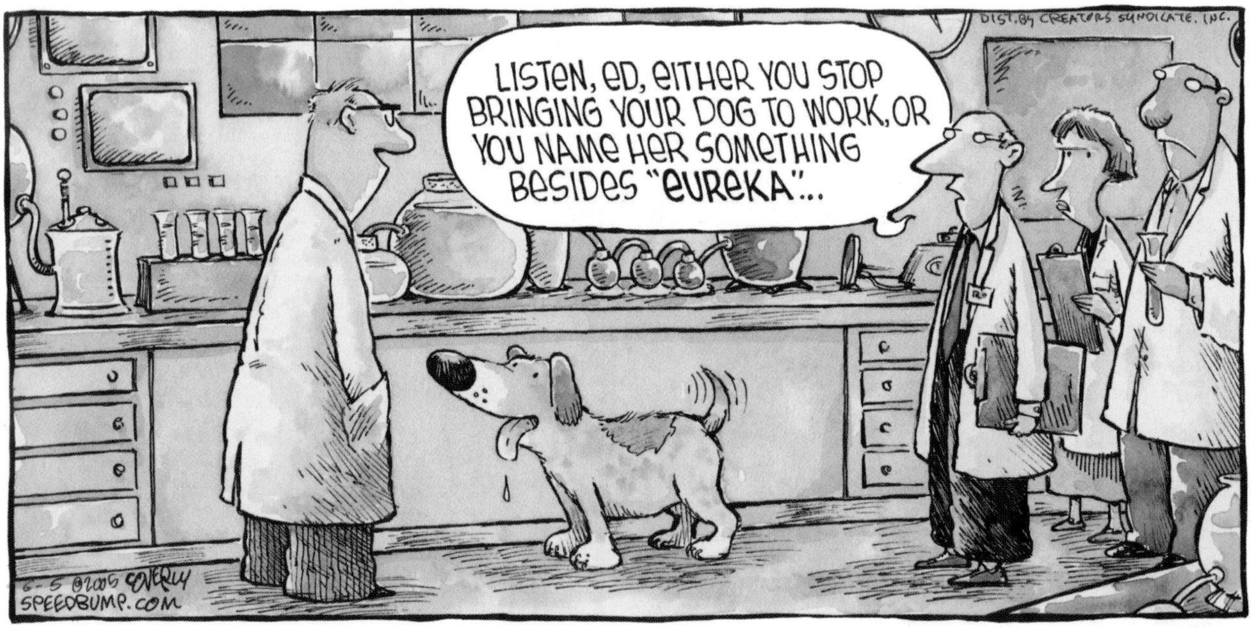
DIST. BY CREATORS SYNDICATE, INC.
LISTEN, ED, EITHER YOU STOP BRINGING YOUR DOG TO WORK, OR YOU NAME HER SOMETHING BESIDES "EUREKA"...
6-5 ©2005 COVERLY
SPEEDBUMP.COM

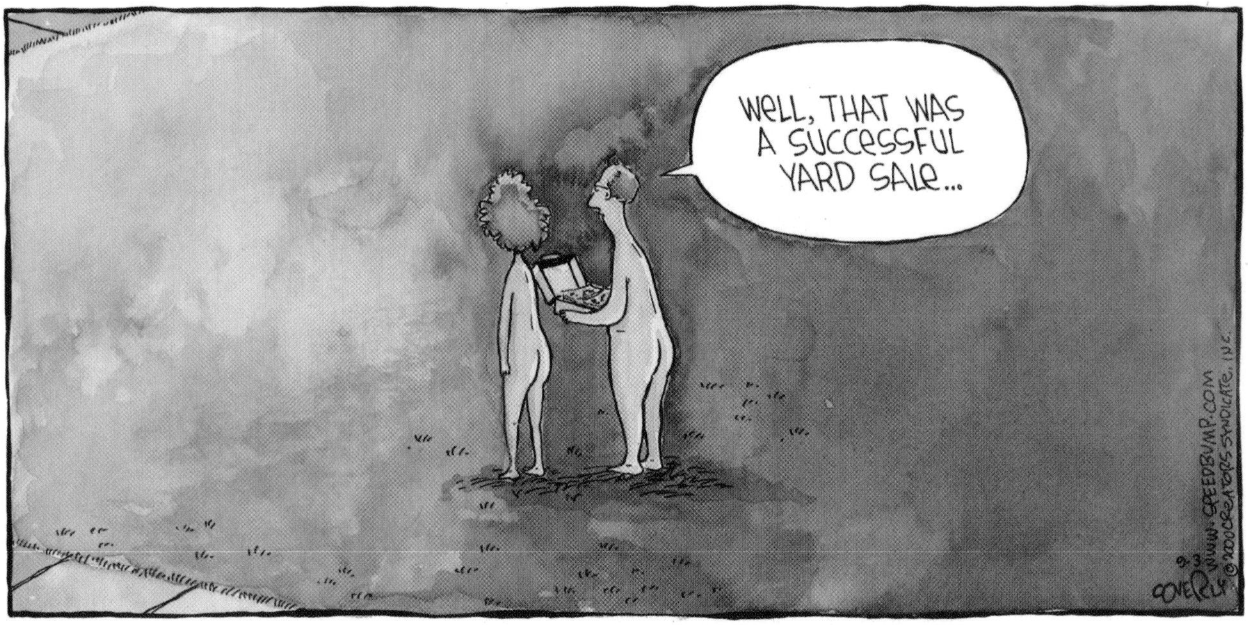
WELL, THAT WAS A SUCCESSFUL YARD SALE...
9-3
COVERLY
WWW.SPEEDBUMP.COM
©2000 CREATORS SYNDICATE, INC.

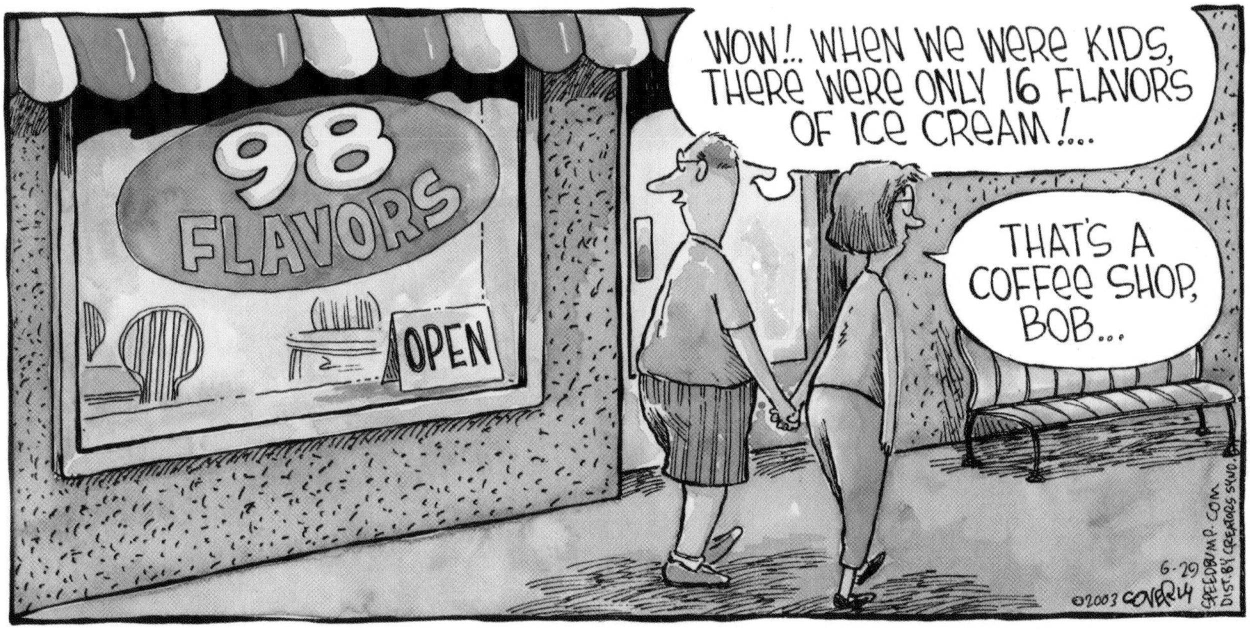
98 FLAVORS
OPEN
WOW!.. WHEN WE WERE KIDS, THERE WERE ONLY 16 FLAVORS OF ICE CREAM!...
THAT'S A COFFEE SHOP, BOB...
6-29
©2003 COVERLY
SPEEDBUMP.COM
DIST. BY CREATORS SYND.

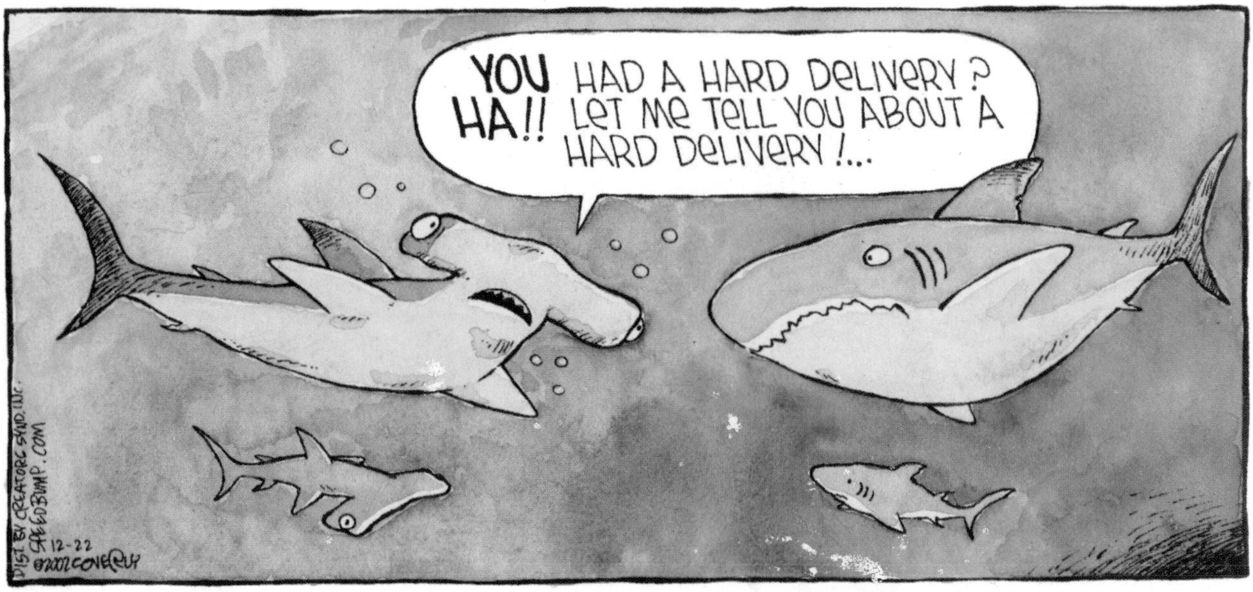
YOU HAD A HARD DELIVERY? HA!! LET ME TELL YOU ABOUT A HARD DELIVERY!...
DIST. BY CREATORS SYND. INC. SPEEDBUMP.COM
12-22 ©2002 COVERLY

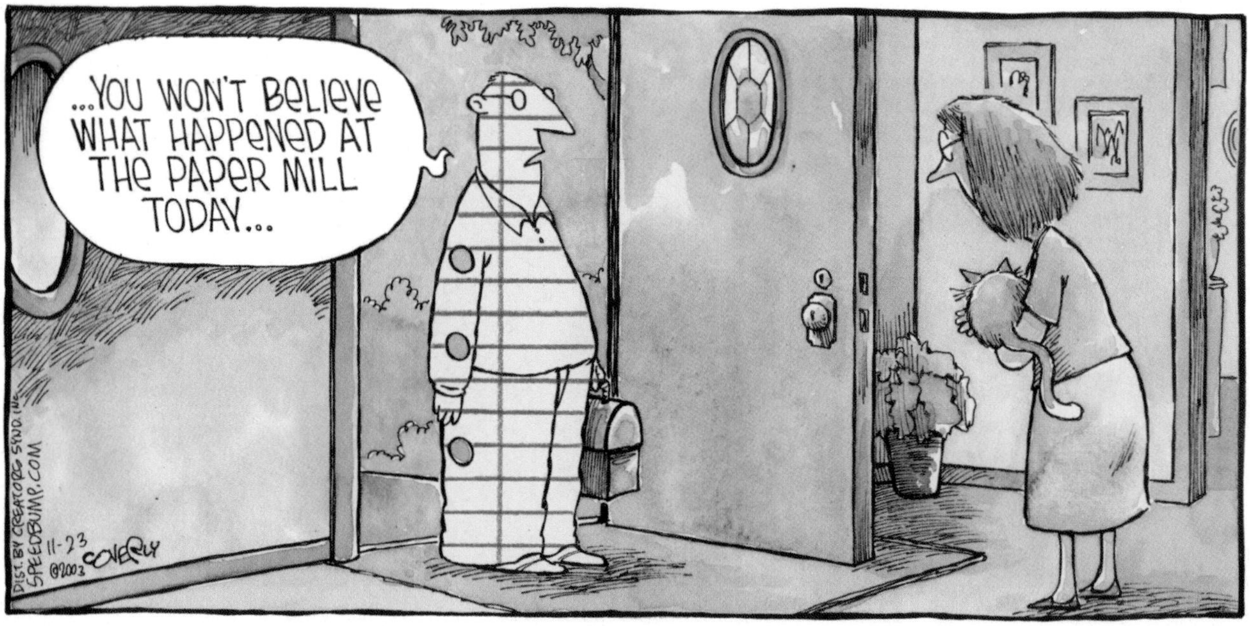
...YOU WON'T BELIEVE WHAT HAPPENED AT THE PAPER MILL TODAY...
DIST. BY CREATORS SYND. INC. SPEEDBUMP.COM
11-23 ©2003 COVERLY

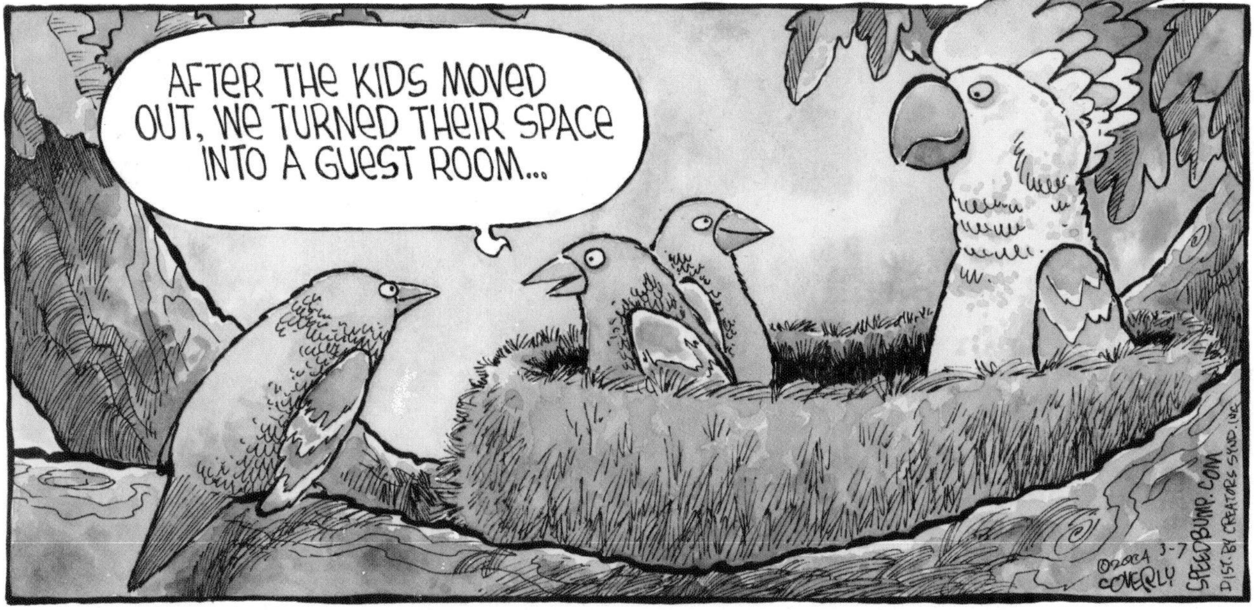
AFTER THE KIDS MOVED OUT, WE TURNED THEIR SPACE INTO A GUEST ROOM...
COVERLY
SPEEDBUMP.COM
DIST. BY CREATORS SYND. INC.

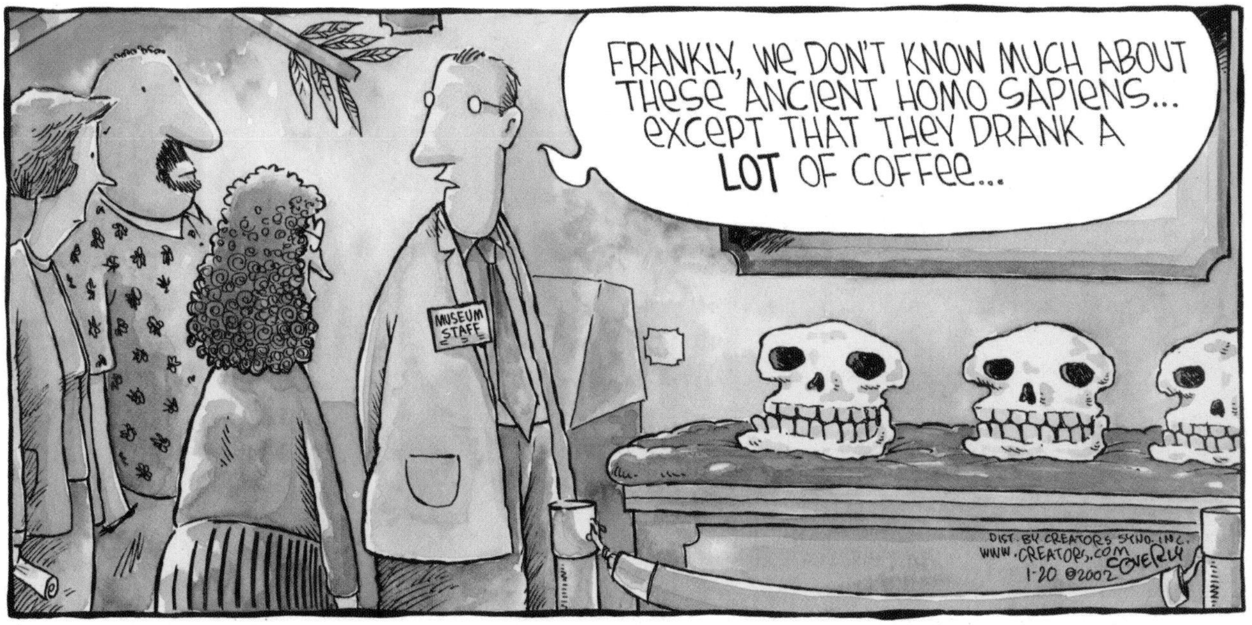
FRANKLY, WE DON'T KNOW MUCH ABOUT THESE ANCIENT HOMO SAPIENS... EXCEPT THAT THEY DRANK A **LOT** OF COFFEE...
MUSEUM STAFF
DIST. BY CREATORS SYND. INC.
WWW.CREATORS.COM
1-20 ©2002 COVERLY

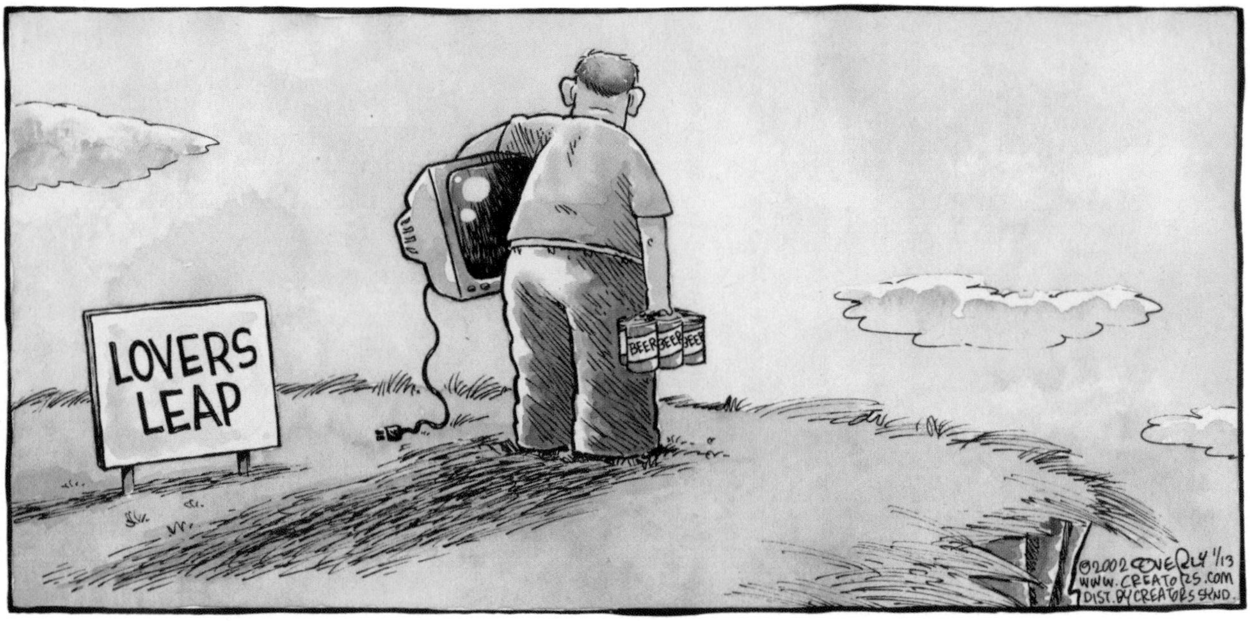
LOVERS LEAP
BEER BEER BEER
©2002 COVERLY 1/13
WWW.CREATORS.COM
DIST. BY CREATORS SYND.

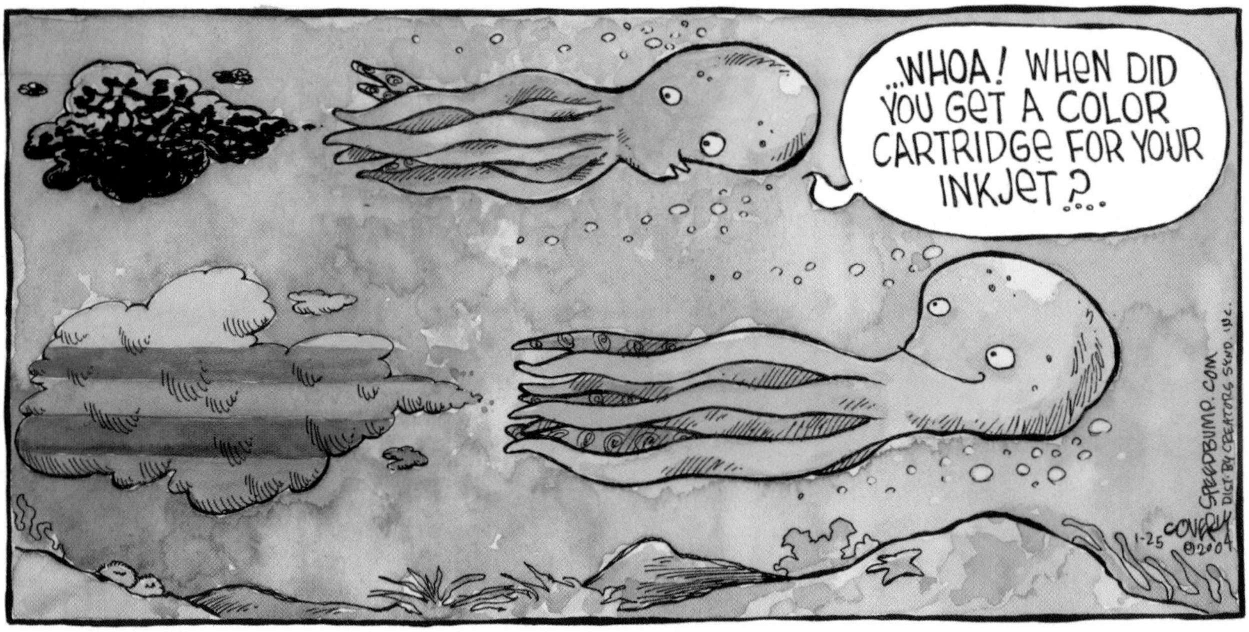
...WHOA! WHEN DID YOU GET A COLOR CARTRIDGE FOR YOUR INKJET?...
SPEEDBUMP.COM
DIST. BY CREATORS SYND. INC.
1-25 COVERLY ©2004

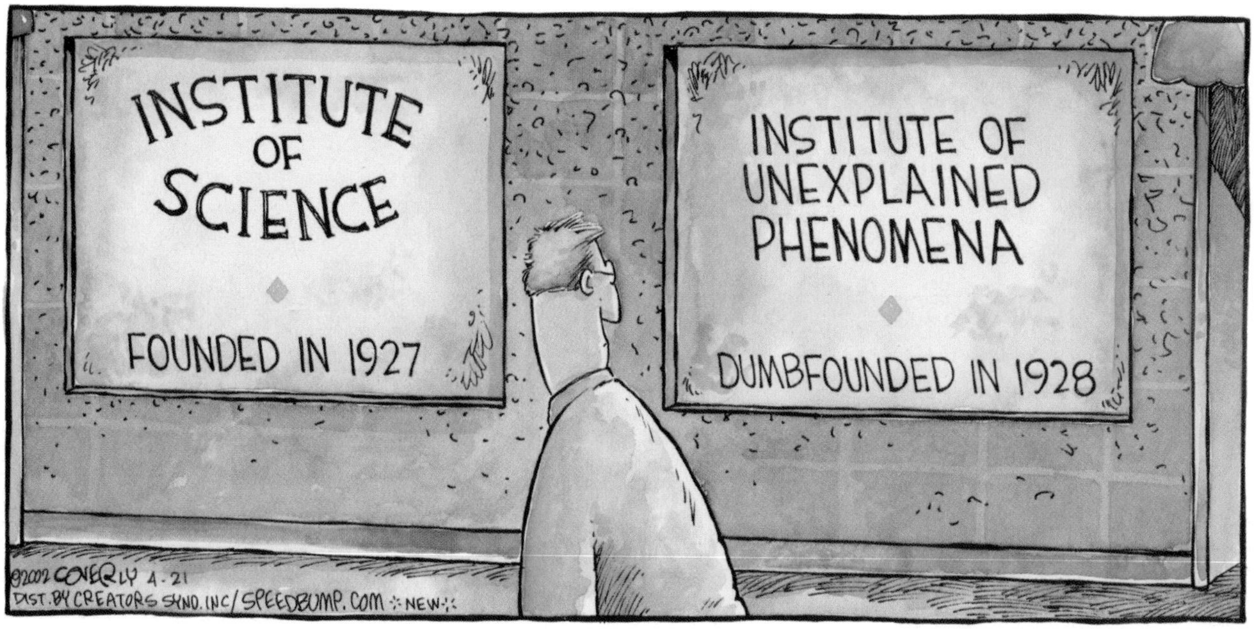
INSTITUTE OF SCIENCE
FOUNDED IN 1927
INSTITUTE OF UNEXPLAINED PHENOMENA
DUMBFOUNDED IN 1928
©2002 COVERLY 4-21
DIST. BY CREATORS SYND. INC/SPEEDBUMP.COM NEW

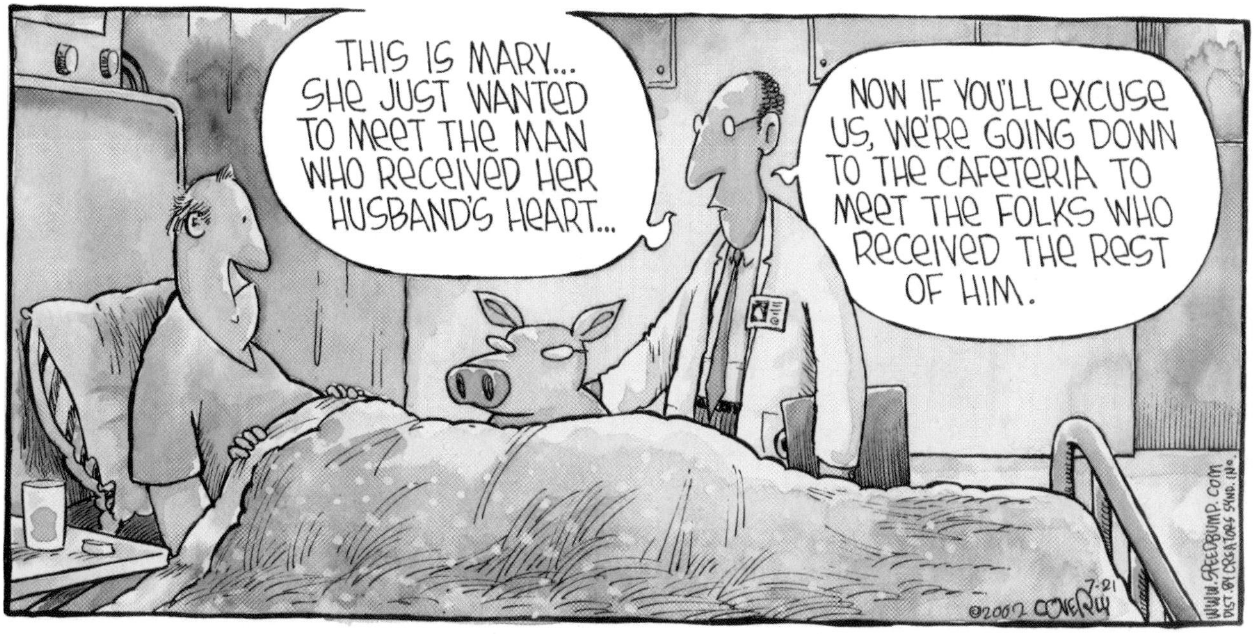
THIS IS MARY... SHE JUST WANTED TO MEET THE MAN WHO RECEIVED HER HUSBAND'S HEART...
NOW IF YOU'LL EXCUSE US, WE'RE GOING DOWN TO THE CAFETERIA TO MEET THE FOLKS WHO RECEIVED THE REST OF HIM.
©2002 COVERLY 7-21
WWW.SPEEDBUMP.COM
DIST. BY CREATORS SYND. INC.

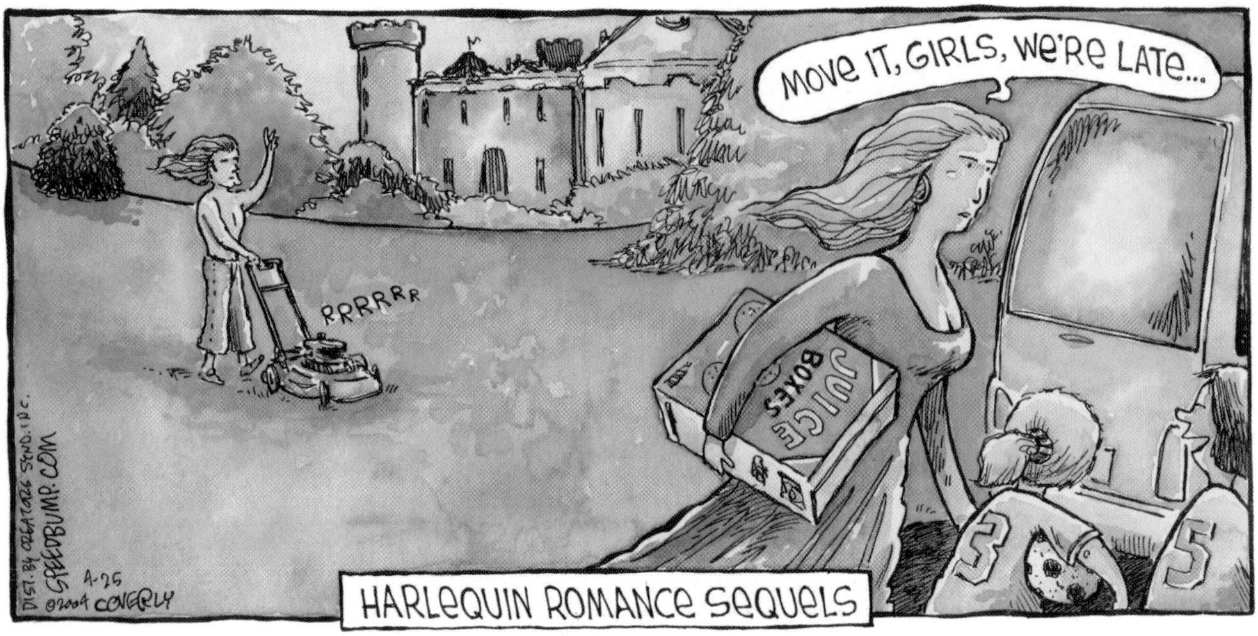
MOVE IT, GIRLS, WE'RE LATE...
RRRRRR
JUICE BOXES
DIST. BY CREATORS SYND. INC.
SPEEDBUMP.COM
4-25
©2004 COVERLY
HARLEQUIN ROMANCE SEQUELS

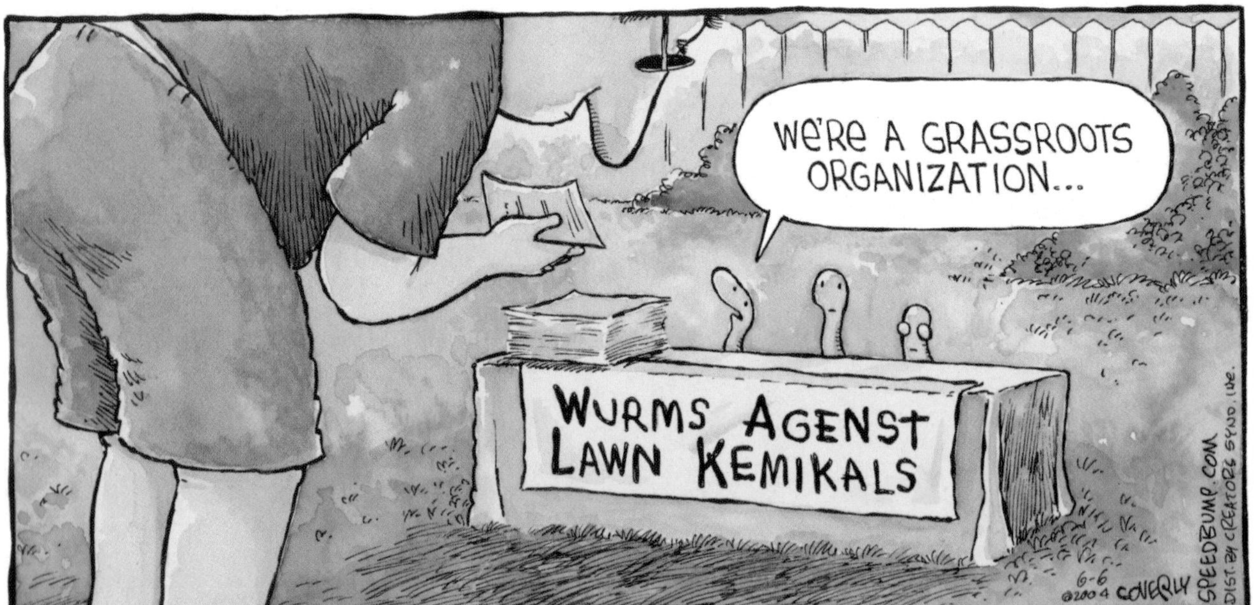
WE'RE A GRASSROOTS ORGANIZATION...
WURMS AGENST LAWN KEMIKALS
6-6
©2004 COVERLY
SPEEDBUMP.COM
DIST. BY CREATORS SYND. INC.

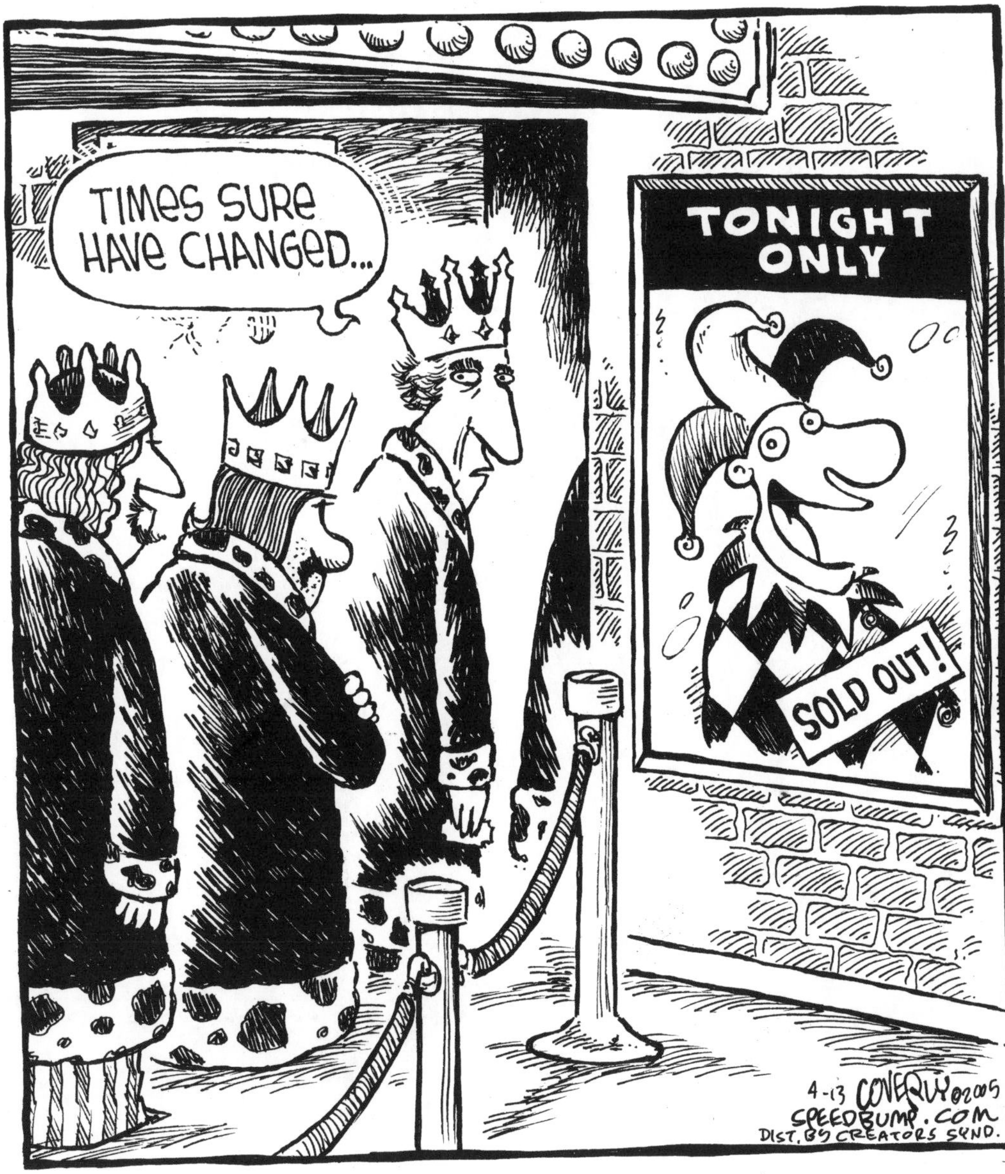
TIMES SURE HAVE CHANGED...
TONIGHT ONLY
SOLD OUT!
4-13 COVERLY ©2005
SPEEDBUMP.COM
DIST. BY CREATORS SYND.

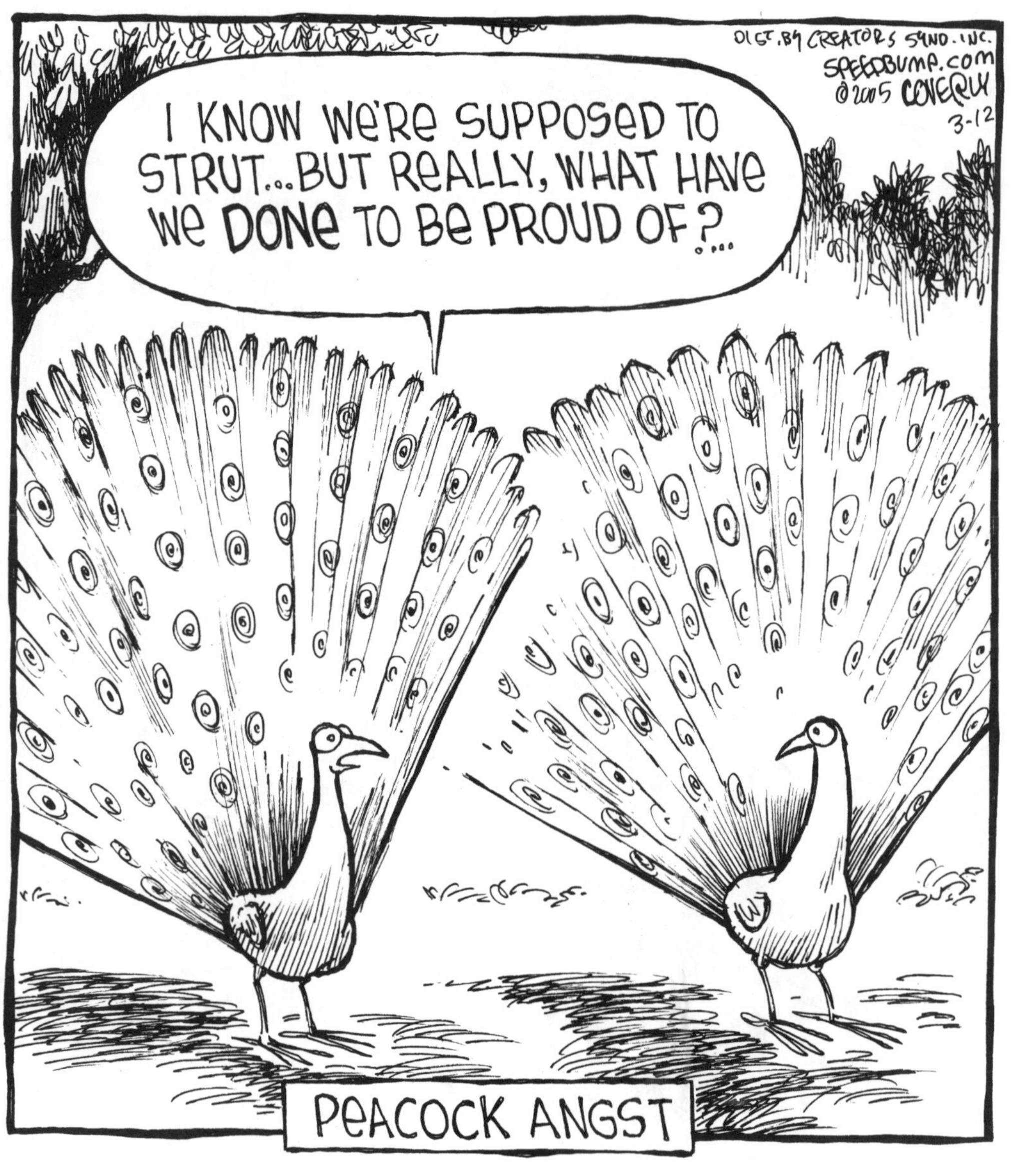
DIST. BY CREATORS SYND. INC.
SPEEDBUMP.COM
©2005 COVERLY
3-12
I KNOW WE'RE SUPPOSED TO STRUT...BUT REALLY, WHAT HAVE WE DONE TO BE PROUD OF?...
PEACOCK ANGST

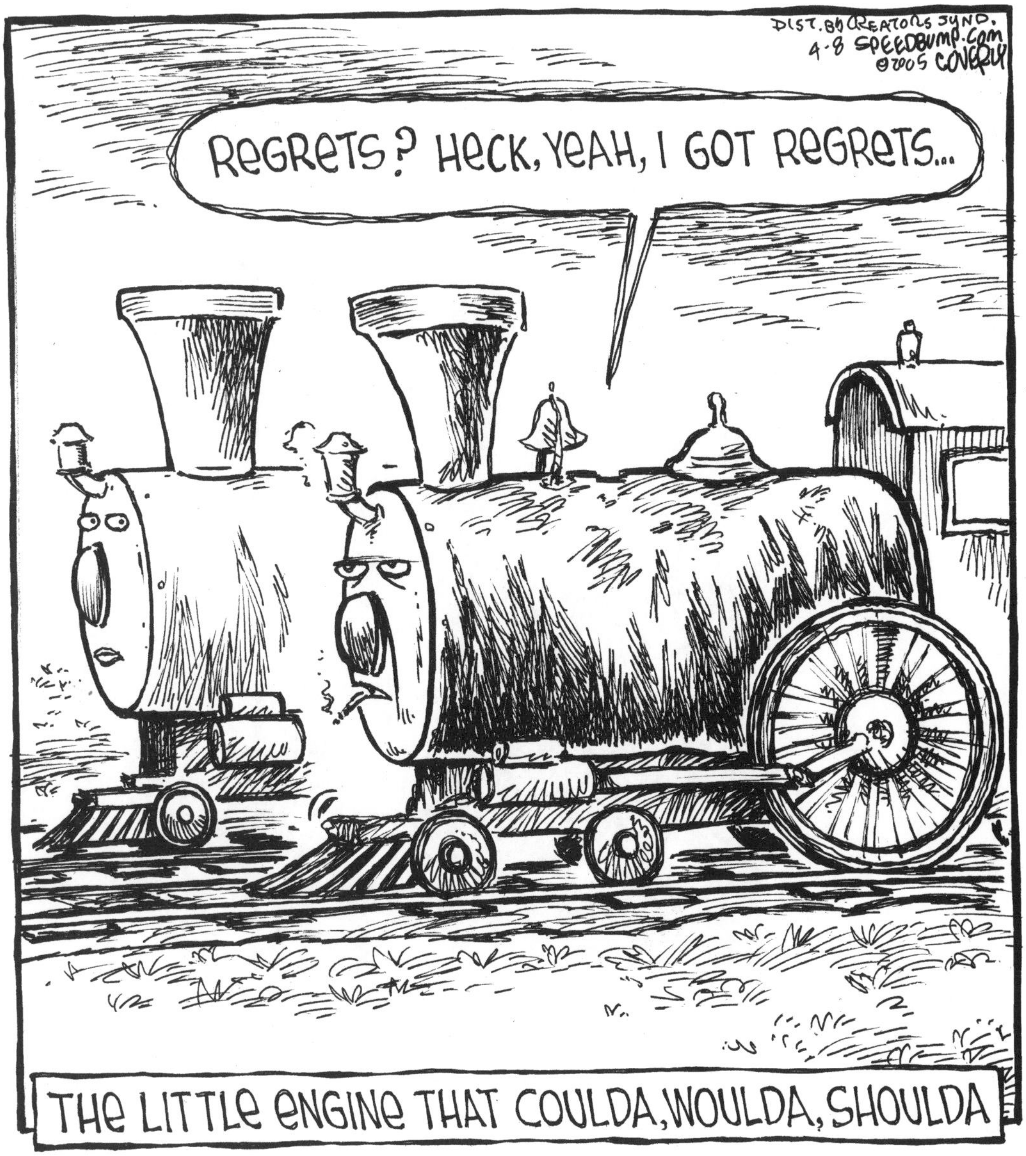
DIST. BY CREATORS SYND. 4-8 SPEEDBUMP.COM ©2005 COVERLY
REGRETS? HECK, YEAH, I GOT REGRETS...
THE LITTLE ENGINE THAT COULDA, WOULDA, SHOULDA

Odds 'n' Ends

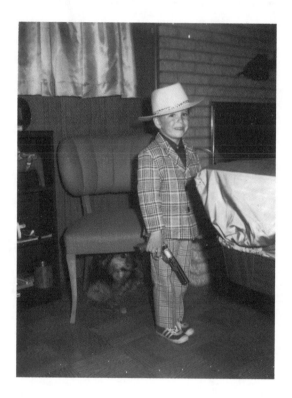

May 12, 1968. Southfield, Michigan.

Even my grandparents' dog, Teddy, would dive under a chair when I entered the room. Pool sharks feared me (see: cover on the pool table), tailors besieged me, milliners fell weeping at my feet.

I was an odd child, but no one dared tell me. Not when I was packing my pirate pistol, anyway.

Sadly this photo was taken just seconds before I shot a hole in my red suede shoe. However, due to the hammer-toes that are a Coverly curse, the bullet missed my foot and merely lodged in the linoleum.

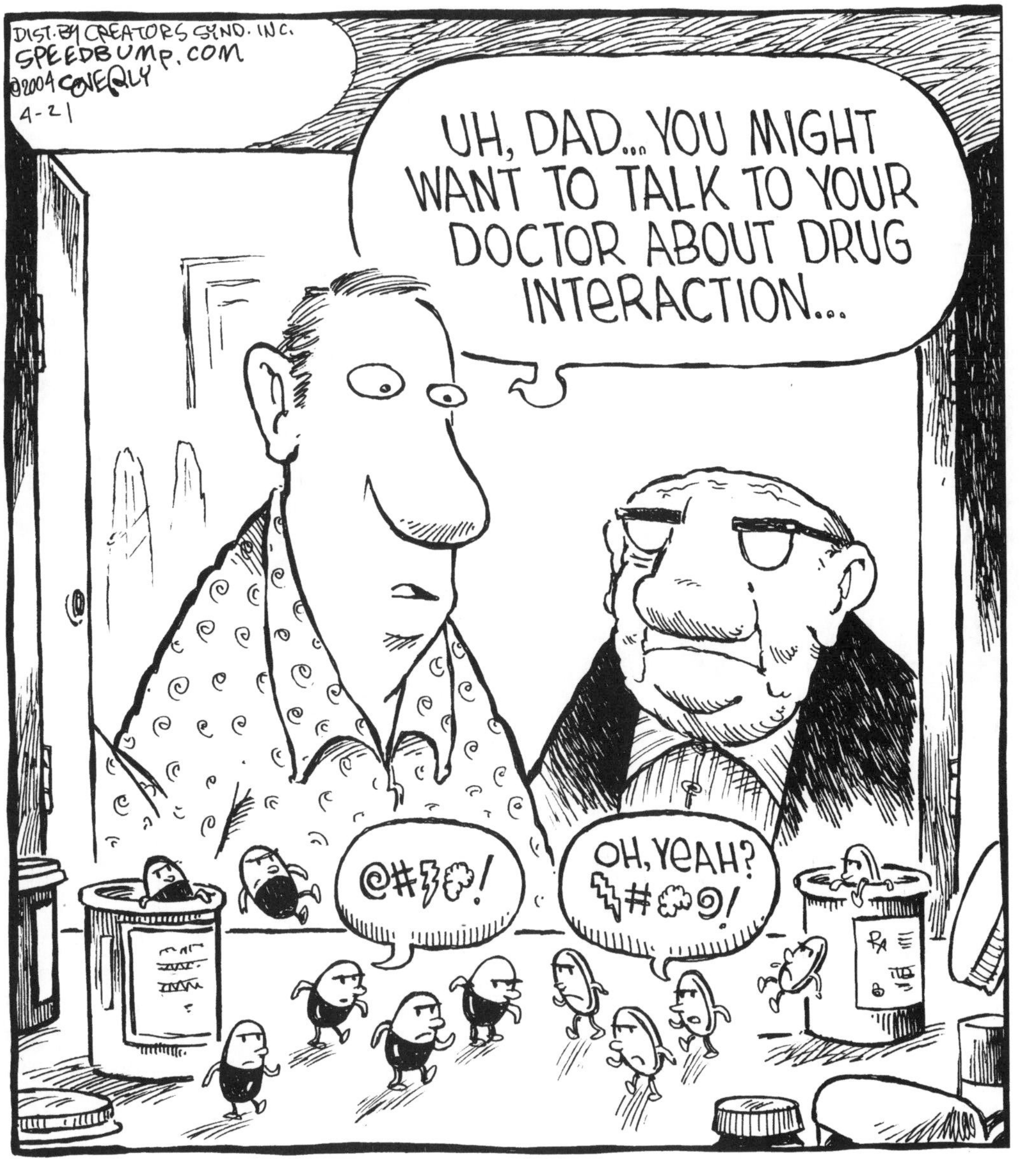
DIST. BY CREATORS SYND. INC.
SPEEDBUMP.COM
©2004 COVERLY
4-21
UH, DAD... YOU MIGHT WANT TO TALK TO YOUR DOCTOR ABOUT DRUG INTERACTION...
OH, YEAH?

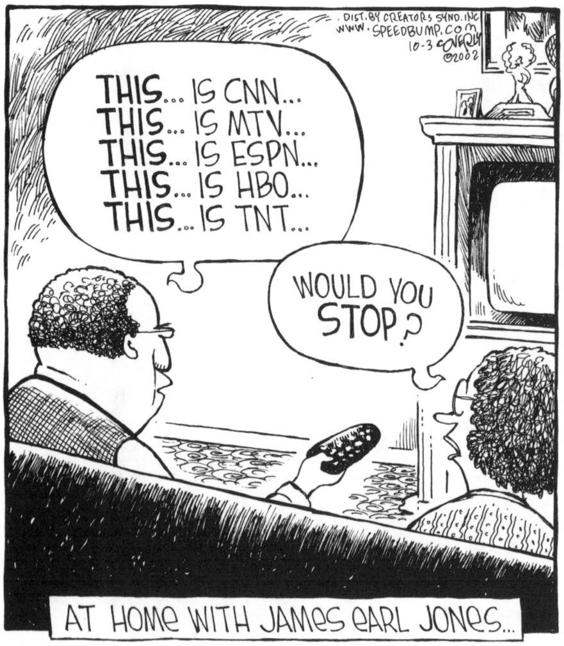
DIST. BY CREATORS SYND. INC
WWW.SPEEDBUMP.COM
10-3 COVERLY ©2002
THIS... IS CNN... THIS... IS MTV... THIS... IS ESPN... THIS... IS HBO... THIS... IS TNT...
WOULD YOU STOP?
AT HOME WITH JAMES EARL JONES...

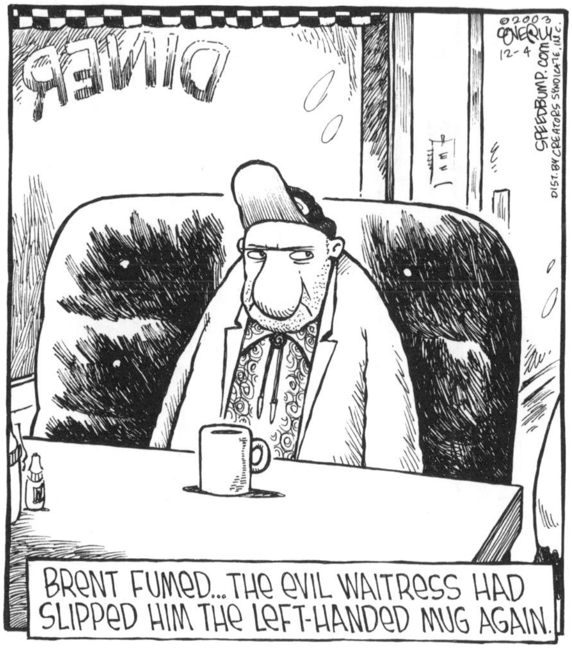
©2003 COVERLY 12-4
SPEEDBUMP.COM
DIST. BY CREATORS SYNDICATE, INC.
BRENT FUMED...THE EVIL WAITRESS HAD SLIPPED HIM THE LEFT-HANDED MUG AGAIN.

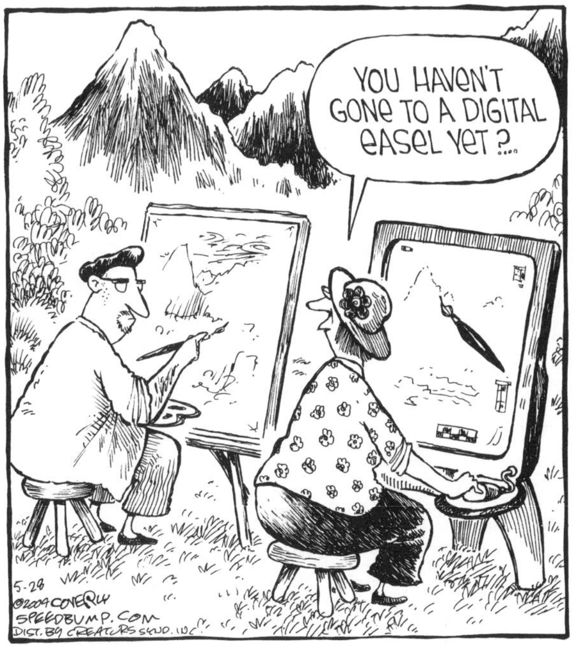
YOU HAVEN'T GONE TO A DIGITAL EASEL YET ?...
5-28
©2009 COVERLY
SPEEDBUMP.COM
DIST. BY CREATORS SYND. INC

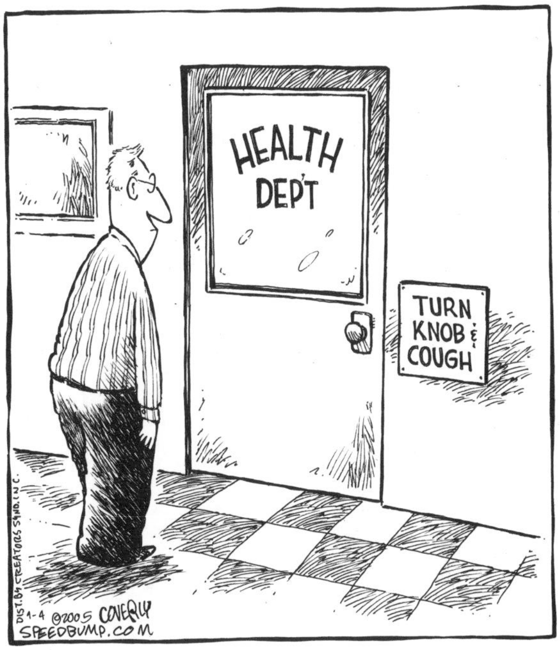
HEALTH DEPT
TURN KNOB & COUGH
©2005 COVERLY
SPEEDBUMP.COM
DIST. BY CREATORS SYND. INC.

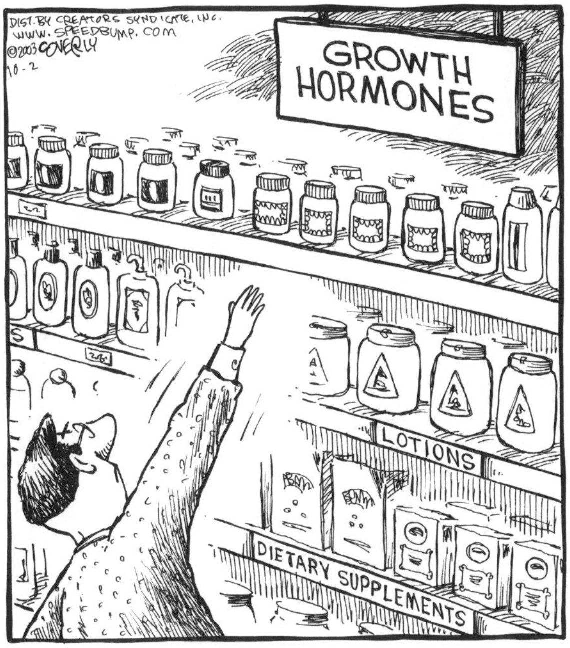
DIST. BY CREATORS SYNDICATE, INC.
WWW.SPEEDBUMP.COM
©2003 COVERLY
10-2
GROWTH HORMONES
LOTIONS
DIETARY SUPPLEMENTS

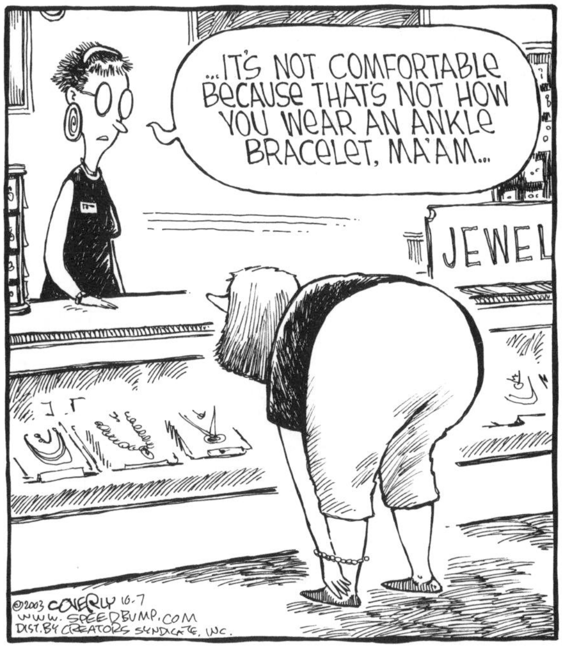
...IT'S NOT COMFORTABLE BECAUSE THAT'S NOT HOW YOU WEAR AN ANKLE BRACELET, MA'AM...
JEWEL
©2003 COVERLY 10-7
WWW.SPEEDBUMP.COM
DIST. BY CREATORS SYNDICATE, INC.

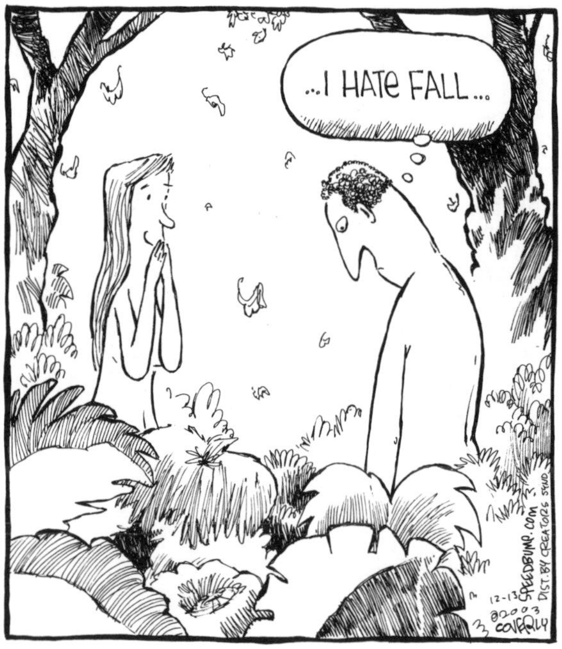
...I HATE FALL...
12-13 ©2003 COVERLY
SPEEDBUMP.COM DIST. BY CREATORS SYND.

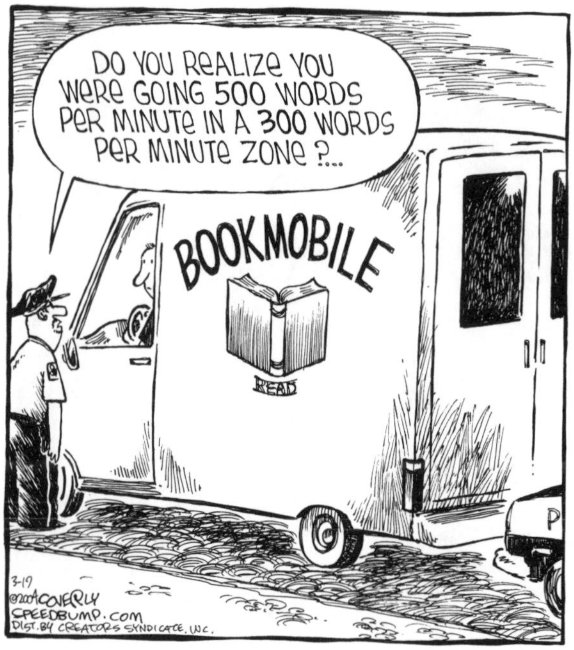
DO YOU REALIZE YOU WERE GOING 500 WORDS PER MINUTE IN A 300 WORDS PER MINUTE ZONE ?...
BOOKMOBILE
READ
3-19
©2004 COVERLY
SPEEDBUMP.COM
DIST. BY CREATORS SYNDICATE, INC.

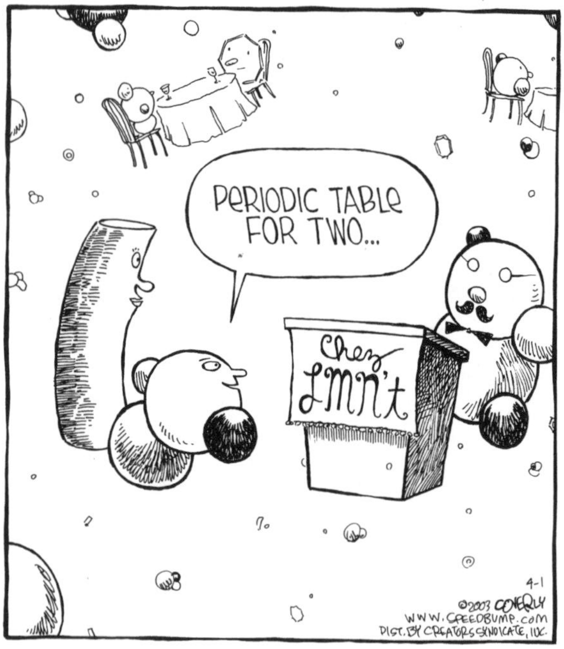
PERIODIC TABLE FOR TWO...
Chez LMN't
4-1
©2003 COVERLY
WWW.SPEEDBUMP.COM
DIST. BY CREATORS SYNDICATE, INC.

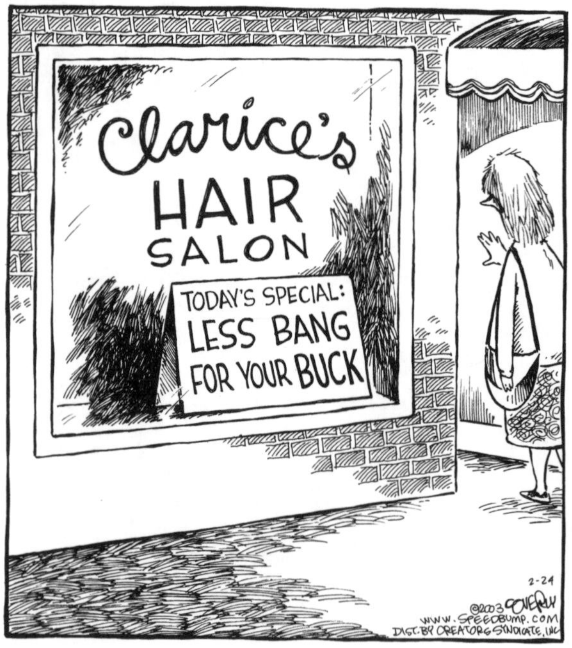
Clarice's
HAIR
SALON
TODAY'S SPECIAL:
LESS BANG
FOR YOUR BUCK
2-24
©2003 COVERLY
WWW.SPEEDBUMP.COM
DIST. BY CREATORS SYNDICATE, INC.

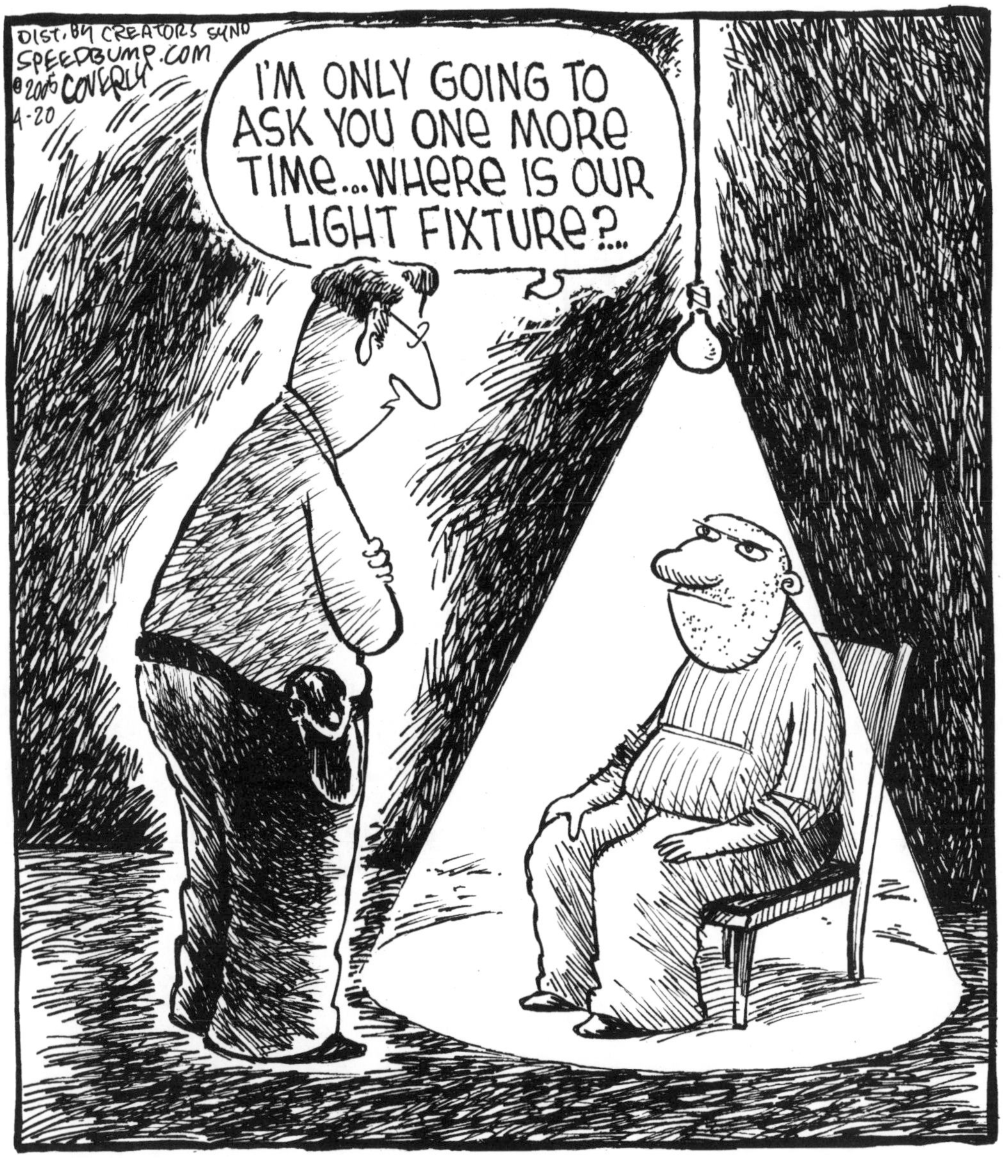
DIST. BY CREATORS SYND
SPEEDBUMP.COM
©2005 COVERLY
4-20
I'M ONLY GOING TO ASK YOU ONE MORE TIME...WHERE IS OUR LIGHT FIXTURE?...

UROLOGY
DIST. BY CREATORS SYND. INC.
4-7 SPEEDBUMP.COM
©2005 COVERLY
OF COURSE IT BURNS WHEN I GO...

...HOLY SCHMOLY, YOU'RE RIGHT... AND ALL THIS TIME I THOUGHT IT SAID "WOW"!..
MOM

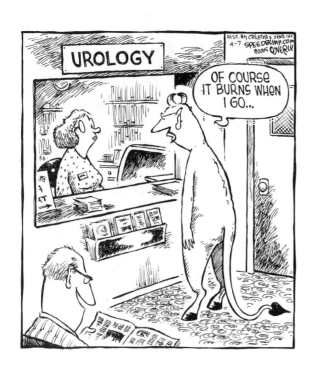

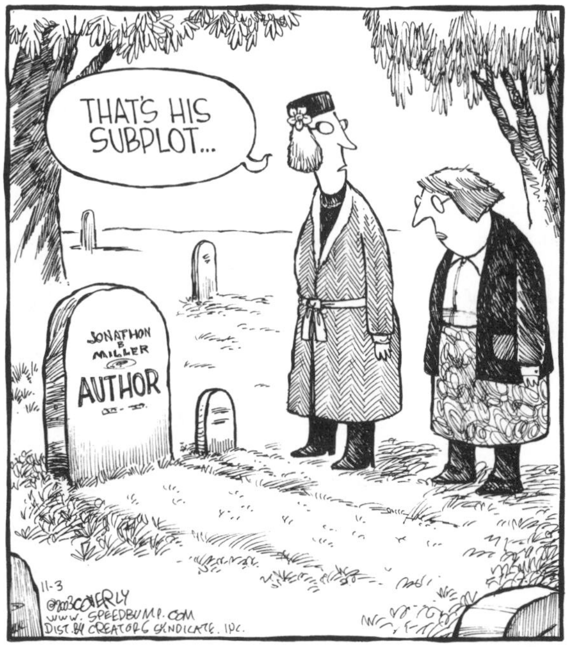
THAT'S HIS SUBPLOT...
JONATHON B MILLER
AUTHOR
11-3
©2003 COVERLY
www.SPEEDBUMP.COM
DIST. BY CREATORS SYNDICATE, INC.

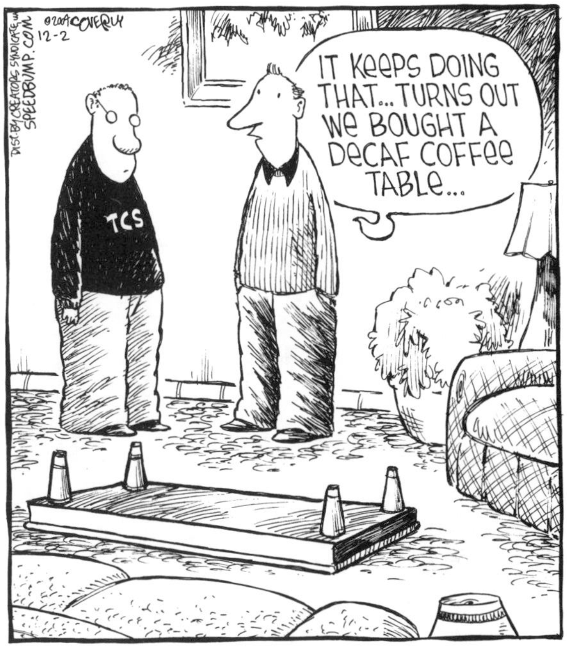
IT KEEPS DOING THAT... TURNS OUT WE BOUGHT A DECAF COFFEE TABLE...
TCS
©2004 COVERLY
12-2
SPEEDBUMP.COM

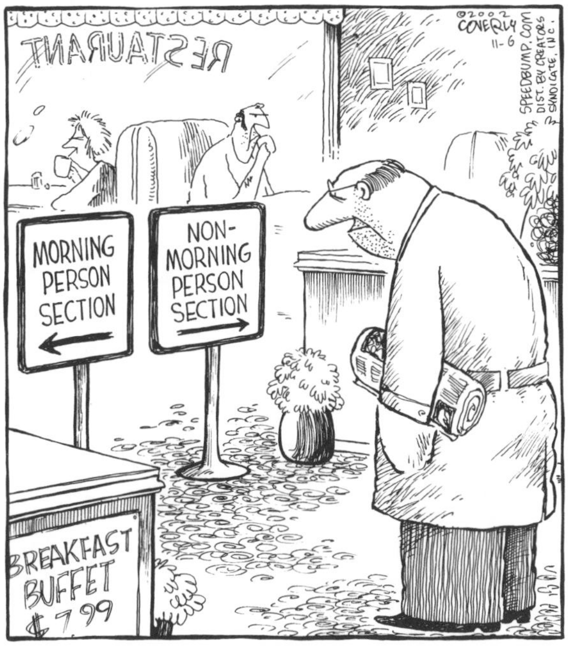
RESTAURANT
MORNING PERSON SECTION
NON-MORNING PERSON SECTION
BREAKFAST BUFFET $7.99
©2002 COVERLY
11-6
SPEEDBUMP.COM
DIST. BY CREATORS SYNDICATE, INC.

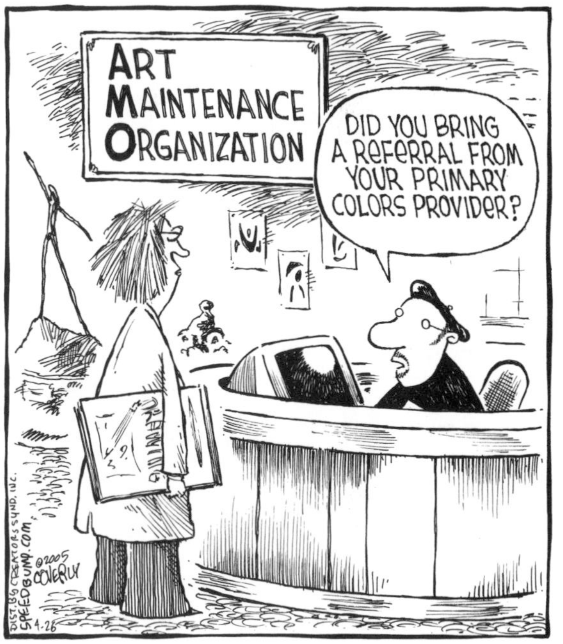
ART MAINTENANCE ORGANIZATION
DID YOU BRING A REFERRAL FROM YOUR PRIMARY COLORS PROVIDER?
©2005 COVERLY
SPEEDBUMP.COM
4-26

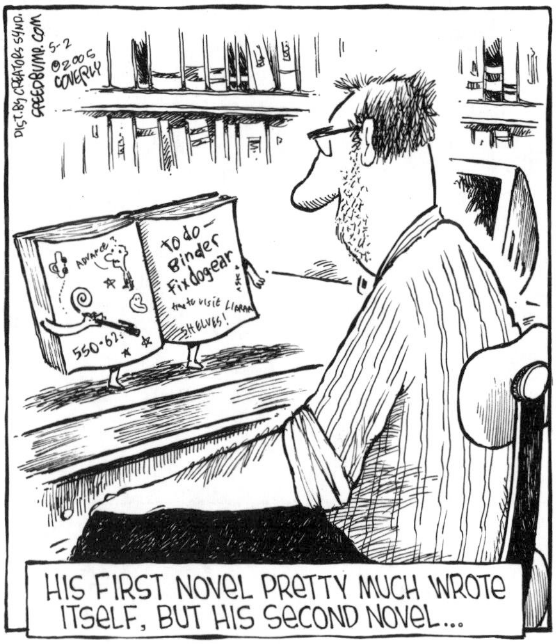
DIST. BY CREATORS SYND.
SPEEDBUMP.COM
5-2
©2005
COVERLY
HIS FIRST NOVEL PRETTY MUCH WROTE ITSELF, BUT HIS SECOND NOVEL...

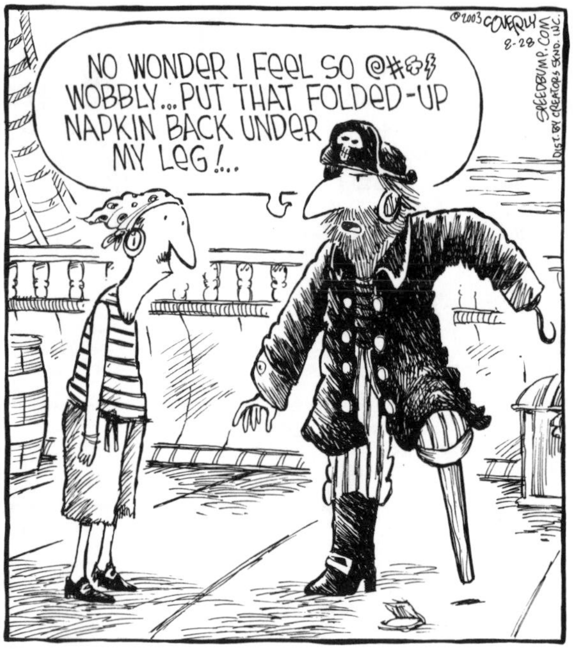
©2003 COVERLY
8-28
SPEEDBUMP.COM
DIST. BY CREATORS SYND. INC.
NO WONDER I FEEL SO @#&$ WOBBLY... PUT THAT FOLDED-UP NAPKIN BACK UNDER MY LEG!...

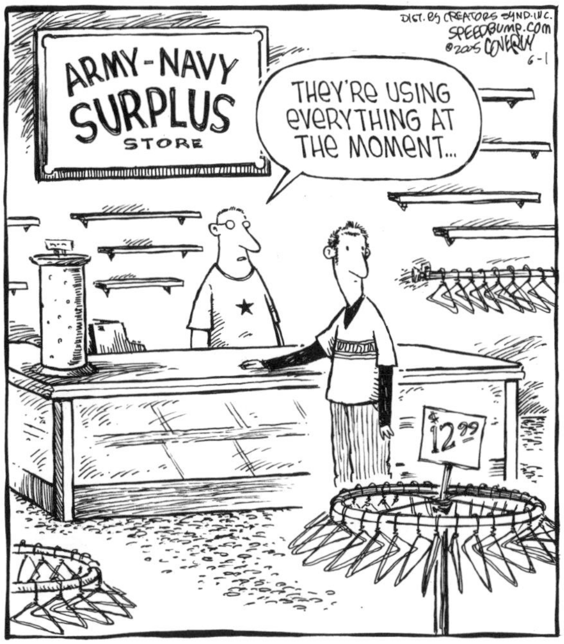
DIST. BY CREATORS SYND. INC.
SPEEDBUMP.COM
©2005 COVERLY
6-1
ARMY-NAVY SURPLUS STORE
THEY'RE USING EVERYTHING AT THE MOMENT...
$12.99

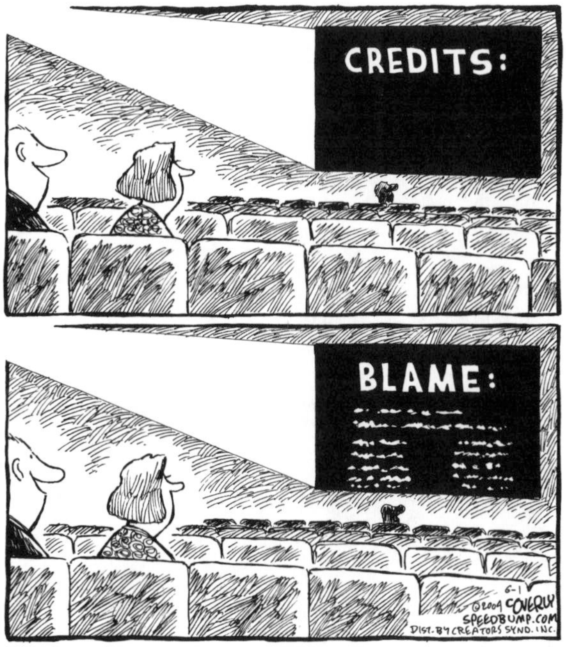
CREDITS:
BLAME:
6-1
©2004 COVERLY
SPEEDBUMP.COM
DIST. BY CREATORS SYND. INC.

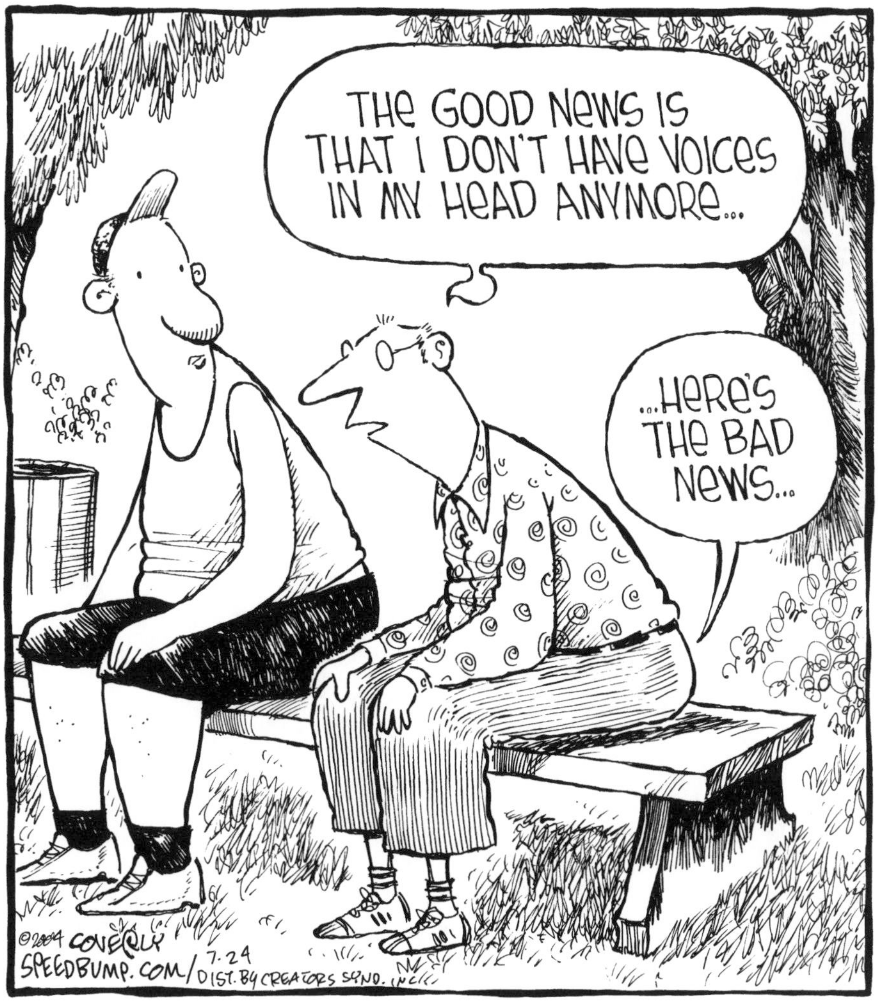
THE GOOD NEWS IS THAT I DON'T HAVE VOICES IN MY HEAD ANYMORE...
...HERE'S THE BAD NEWS...
©2004 COVERLY
SPEEDBUMP.COM/
7.24
DIST. BY CREATORS SYND. INC.

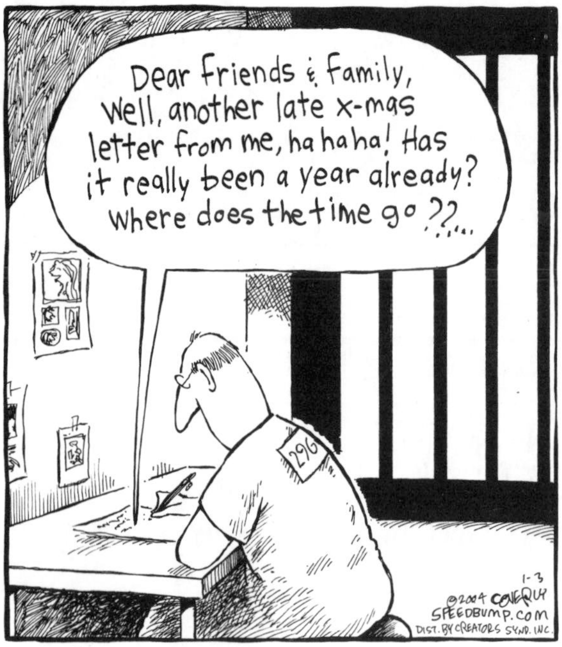
Dear friends & family,
Well, another late x-mas letter from me, ha ha ha! Has it really been a year already? Where does the time go ??...
296
1-3
©2004 COVERLY
SPEEDBUMP.COM
DIST. BY CREATORS SYND. INC.

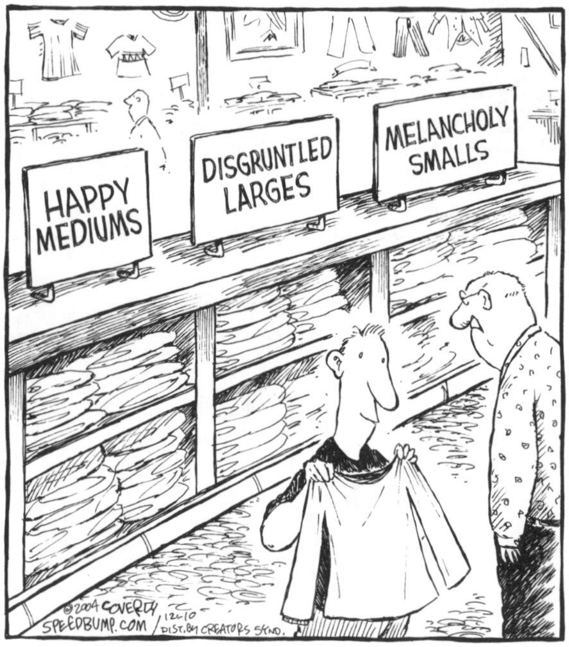
HAPPY MEDIUMS
DISGRUNTLED LARGES
MELANCHOLY SMALLS
©2004 COVERLY
SPEEDBUMP.COM
12-10
DIST. BY CREATORS SYND.

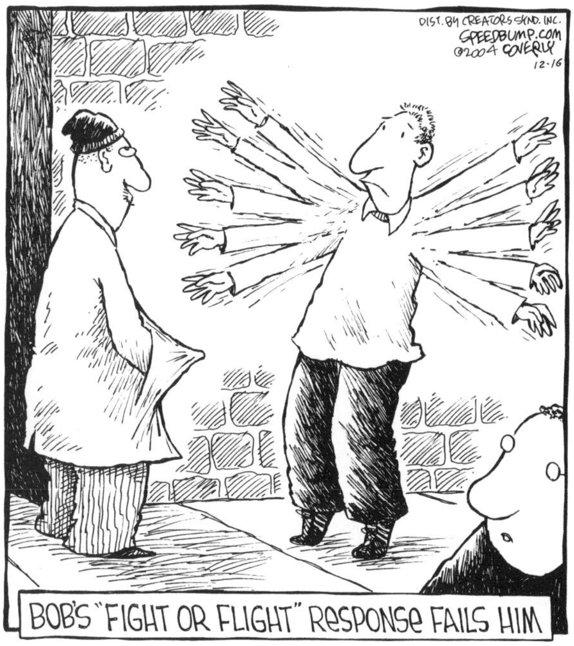
DIST. BY CREATORS SYND. INC.
SPEEDBUMP.COM
©2004 COVERLY
12-16
BOB'S "FIGHT OR FLIGHT" RESPONSE FAILS HIM

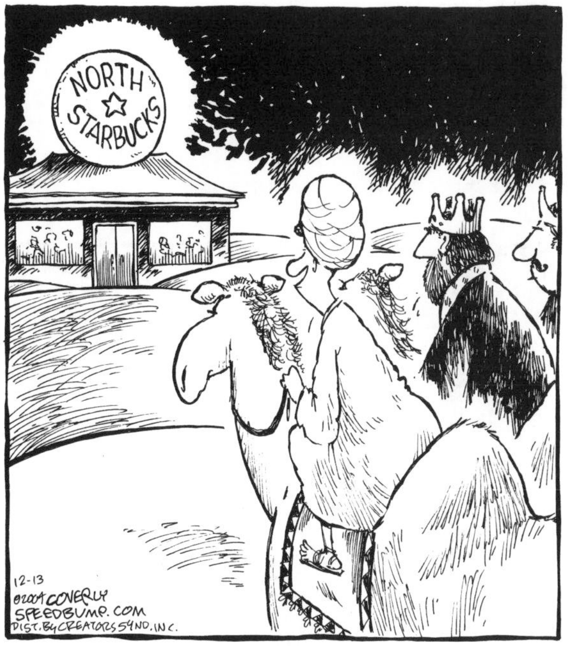
NORTH STARBUCKS
12-13
©2004 COVERLY
SPEEDBUMP.COM
DIST. BY CREATORS SYND. INC.

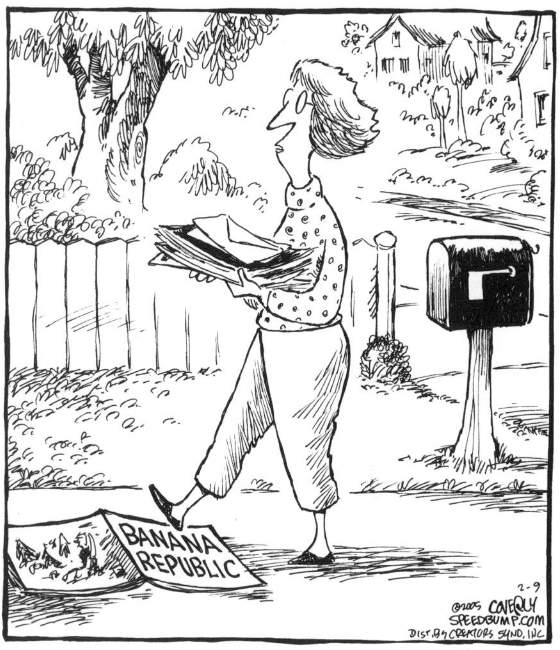
BANANA REPUBLIC
2-9
©2005 COVERLY
SPEEDBUMP.COM
DIST. BY CREATORS SYND. INC.

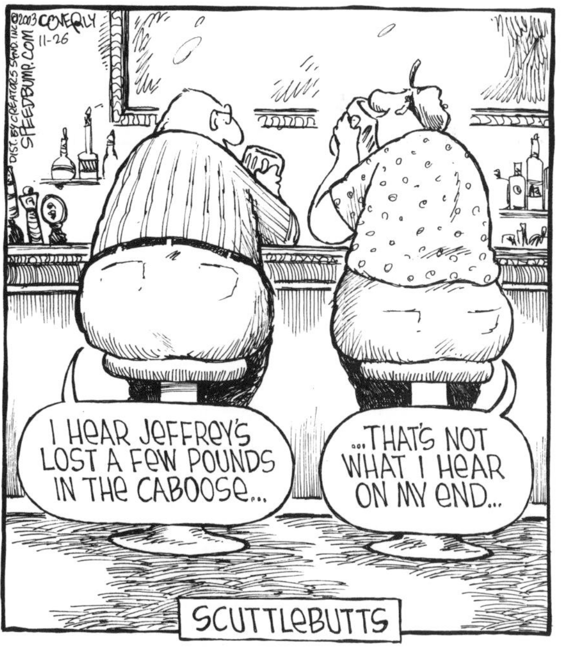
©2003 COVERLY
11-26
DIST. BY CREATORS SYND. INC.
SPEEDBUMP.COM
I HEAR JEFFREY'S LOST A FEW POUNDS IN THE CABOOSE...
...THAT'S NOT WHAT I HEAR ON MY END...
SCUTTLEBUTTS

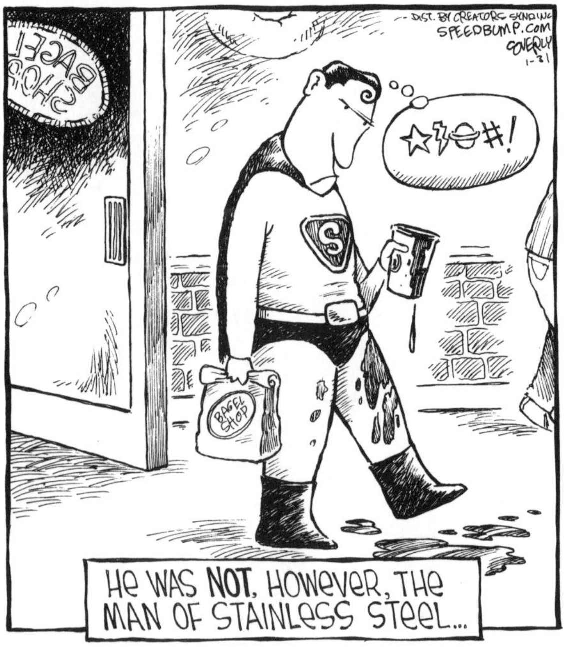
DIST. BY CREATORS SYND.INC
SPEEDBUMP.COM
COVERLY
1-31
BAGEL SHOP
He WAS **NOT**, HOWEVER, THE MAN OF STAINLESS STEEL...

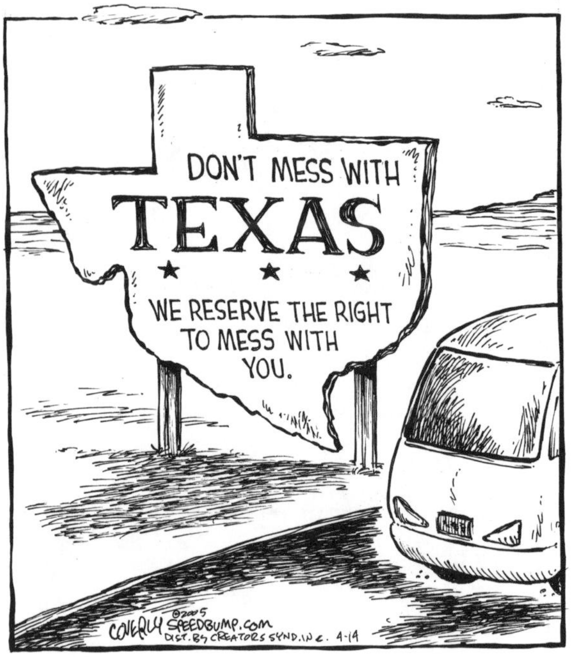
DON'T MESS WITH
TEXAS
WE RESERVE THE RIGHT TO MESS WITH YOU.
©2005
COVERLY SPEEDBUMP.COM
DIST. BY CREATORS SYND.INC. 4-14

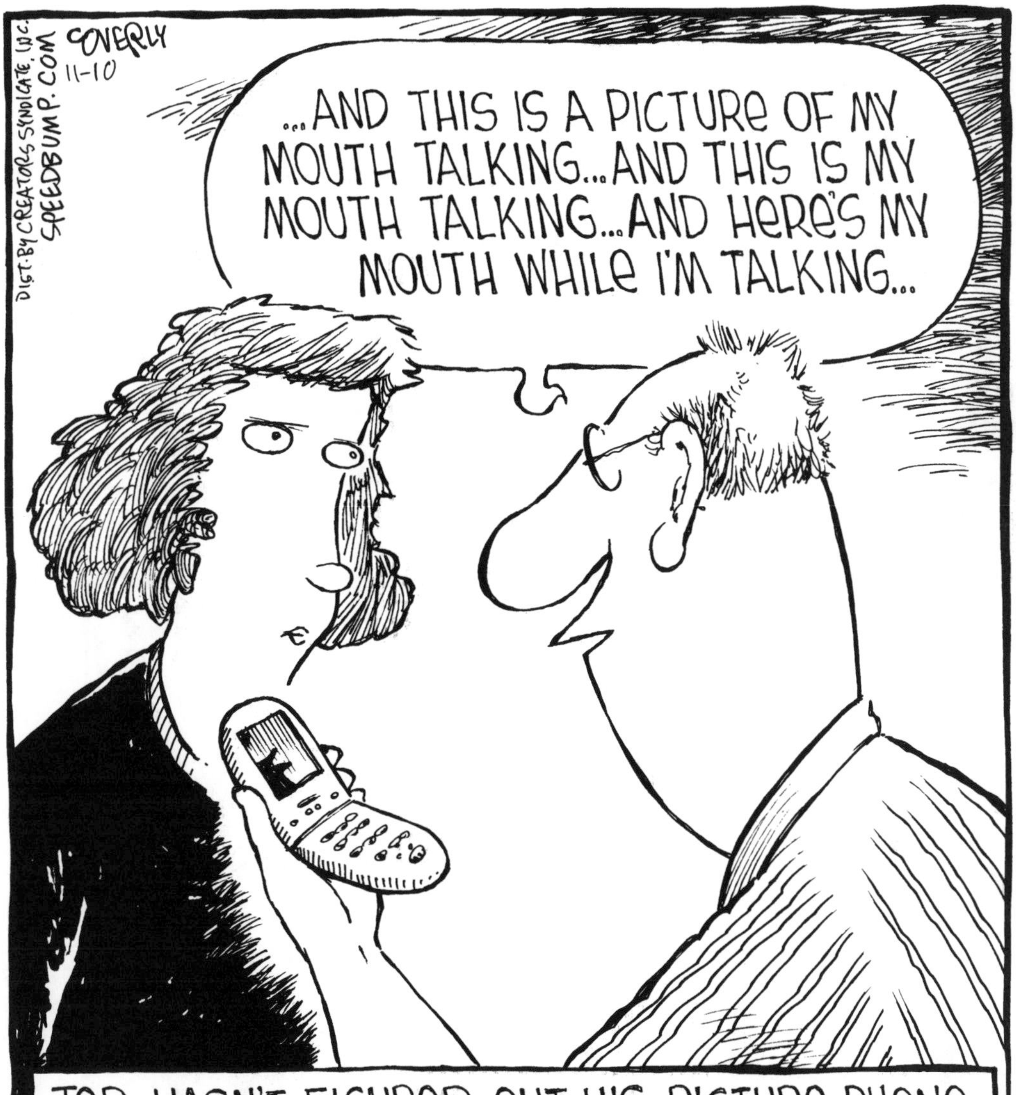
DIST. BY CREATORS SYNDICATE, INC.
SPEEDBUMP.COM
COVERLY
11-10
...AND THIS IS A PICTURE OF MY MOUTH TALKING...AND THIS IS MY MOUTH TALKING...AND HERE'S MY MOUTH WHILE I'M TALKING...
TED HASN'T FIGURED OUT HIS PICTURE PHONE...

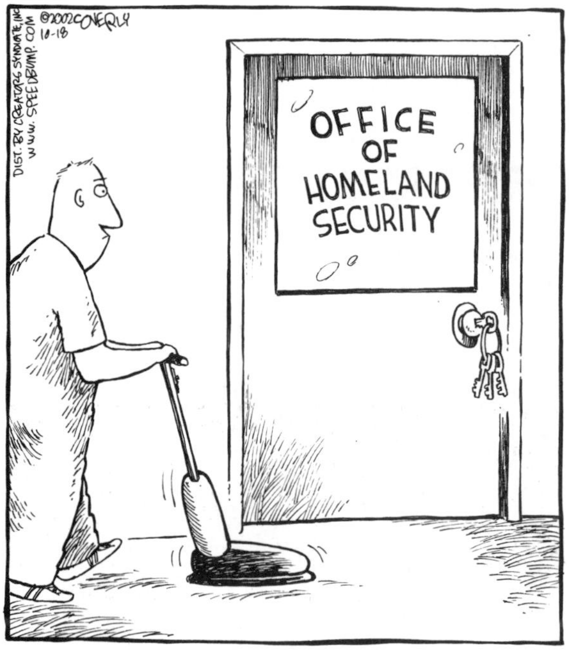
OFFICE OF HOMELAND SECURITY
©2002 COVERLY 10-18
DIST. BY CREATORS SYNDICATE, INC
www.SPEEDBUMP.COM

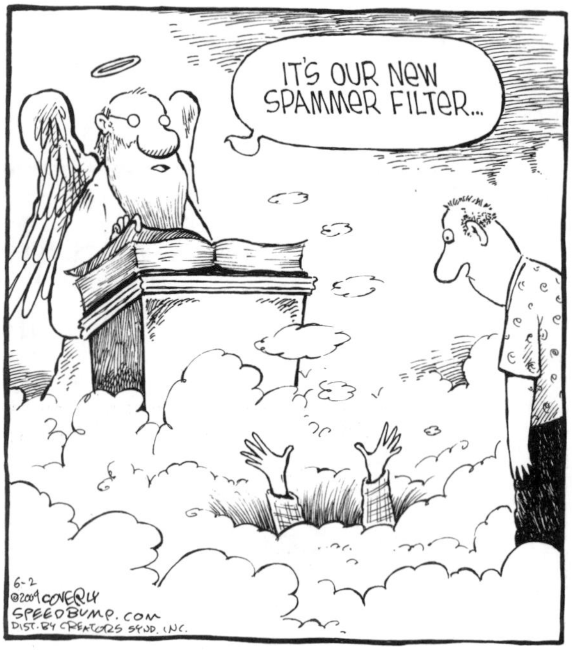
IT'S OUR NEW SPAMMER FILTER...
6-2 ©2004 COVERLY
SPEEDBUMP.COM
DIST. BY CREATORS SYND. INC.

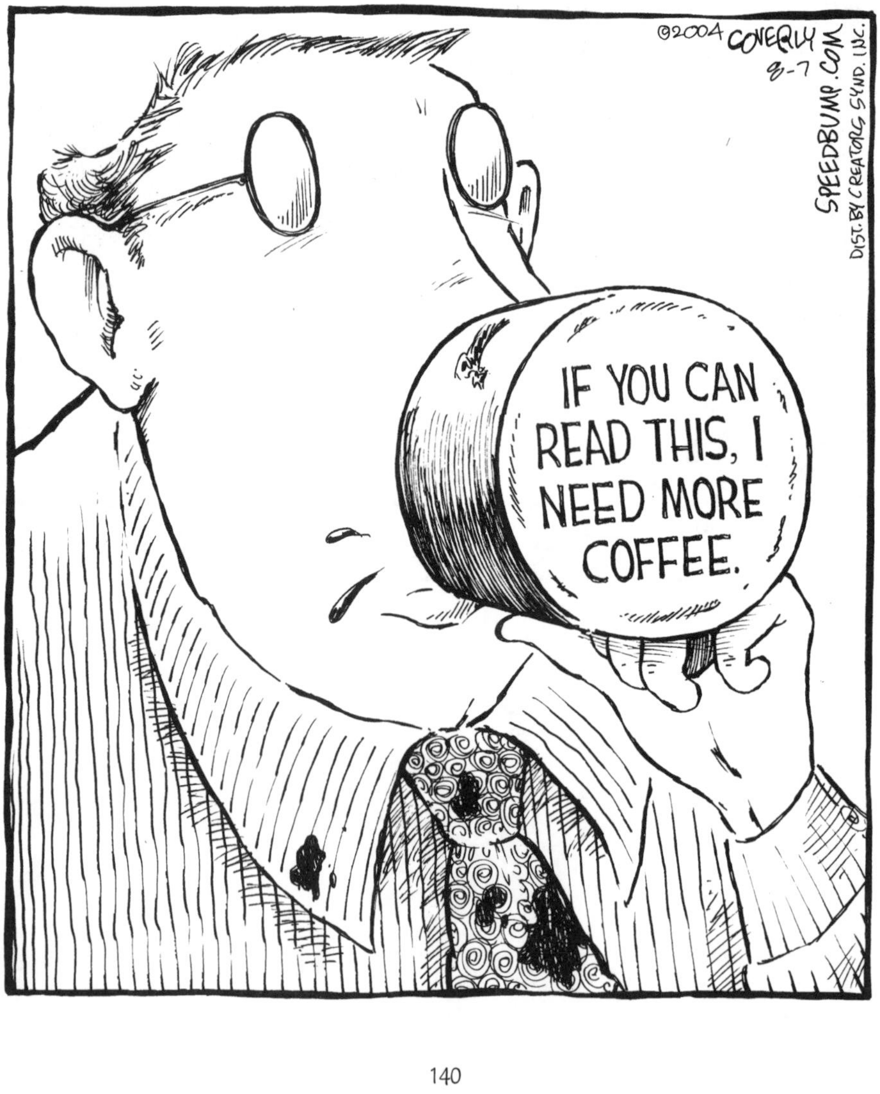
©2004 COVERLY 8-7
SPEEDBUMP.COM
DIST. BY CREATORS SYND. INC.
IF YOU CAN READ THIS, I NEED MORE COFFEE.

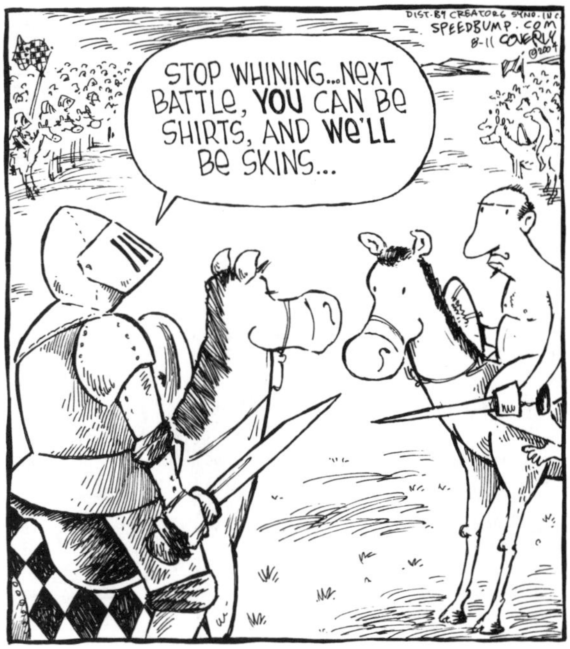
STOP WHINING...NEXT BATTLE, **YOU** CAN BE SHIRTS, AND **WE'LL** BE SKINS...

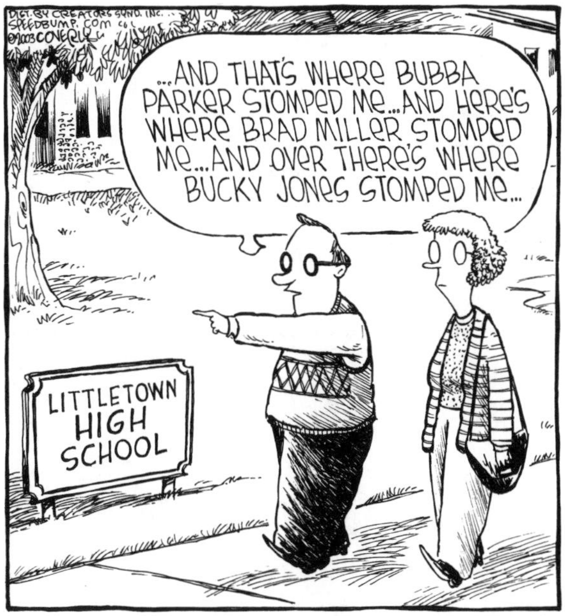
...AND THAT'S WHERE BUBBA PARKER STOMPED ME...AND HERE'S WHERE BRAD MILLER STOMPED ME...AND OVER THERE'S WHERE BUCKY JONES STOMPED ME...
LITTLETOWN HIGH SCHOOL

...TED RETURNS TO HIS OLD STOMPING GROUNDS.

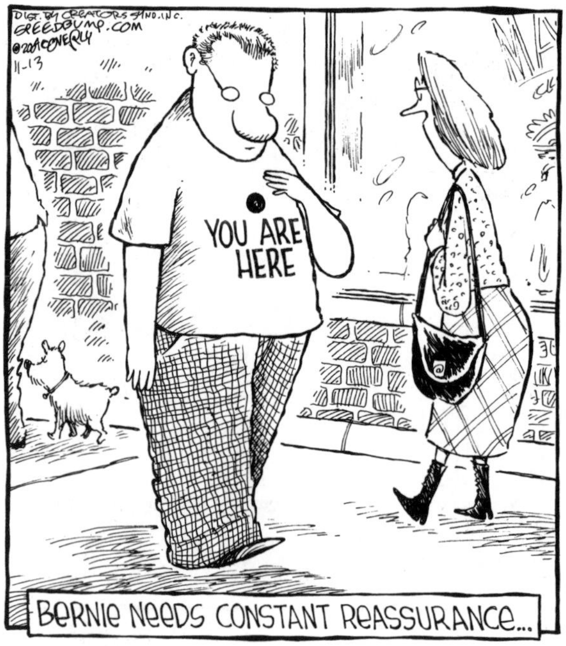
YOU ARE HERE
BERNIE NEEDS CONSTANT REASSURANCE...

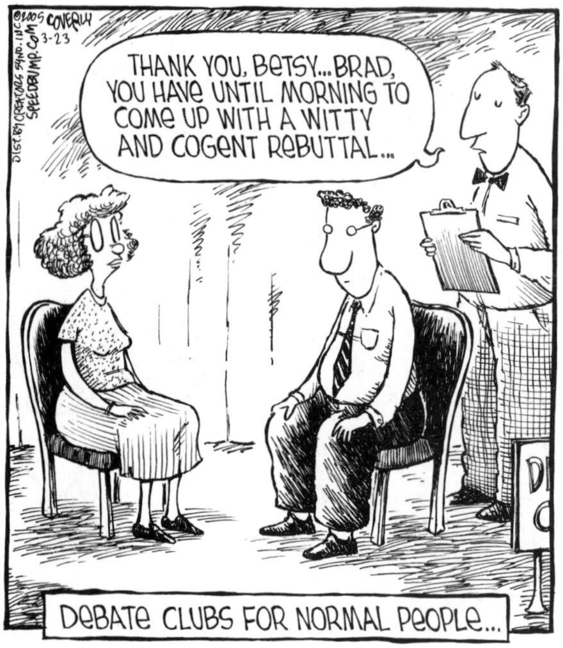
THANK YOU, BETSY... BRAD, YOU HAVE UNTIL MORNING TO COME UP WITH A WITTY AND COGENT REBUTTAL...
DEBATE CLUBS FOR NORMAL PEOPLE...

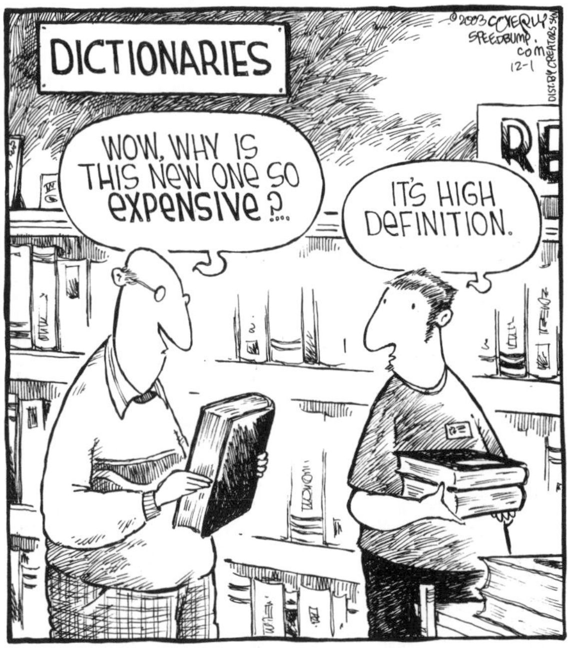
DICTIONARIES
WOW, WHY IS THIS NEW ONE SO EXPENSIVE?...
IT'S HIGH DEFINITION.

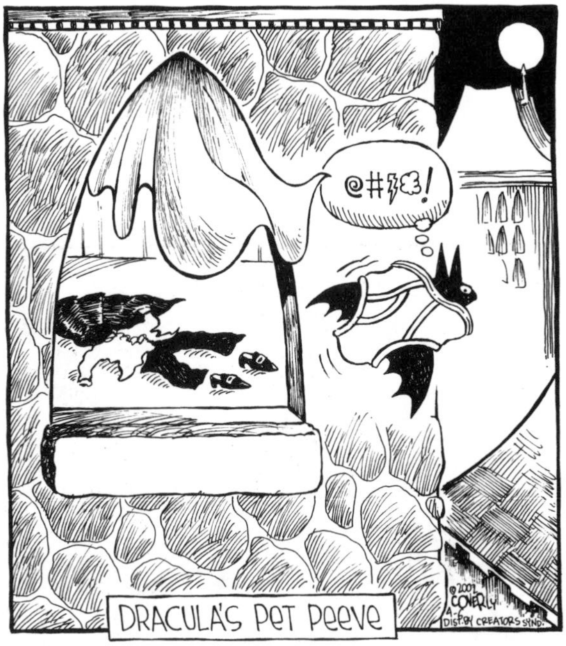
DRACULA'S PET PEEVE

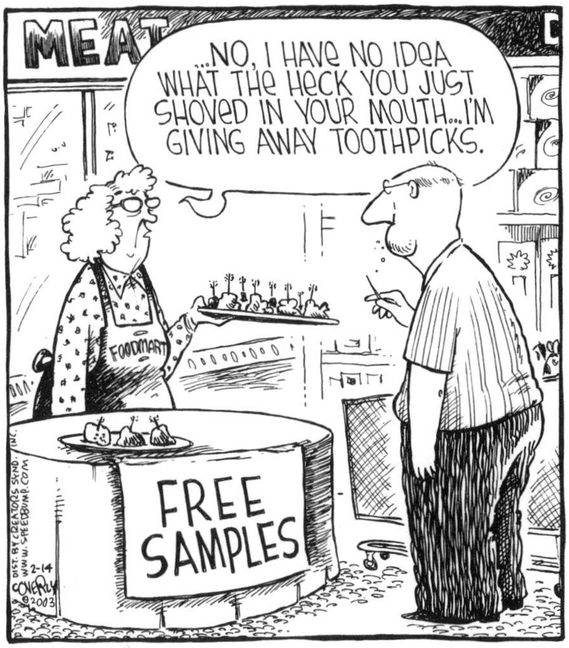
MEAT
...NO, I HAVE NO IDEA WHAT THE HECK YOU JUST SHOVED IN YOUR MOUTH...I'M GIVING AWAY TOOTHPICKS.
FOODMART
FREE SAMPLES

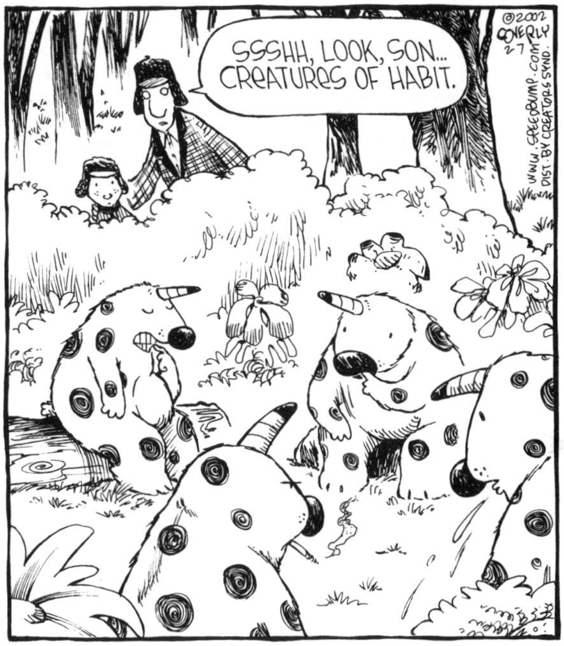
SSSHH, LOOK, SON... CREATURES OF HABIT.

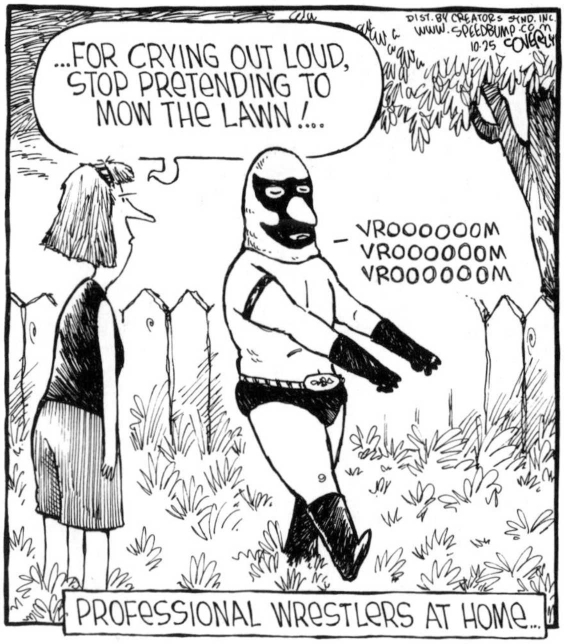
DIST. BY CREATORS SYND. INC
WWW.SPEEDBUMP.COM
10-25 COVERLY
...FOR CRYING OUT LOUD, STOP PRETENDING TO MOW THE LAWN!...
VROOOOOOM VROOOOOOM VROOOOOOM
PROFESSIONAL WRESTLERS AT HOME...

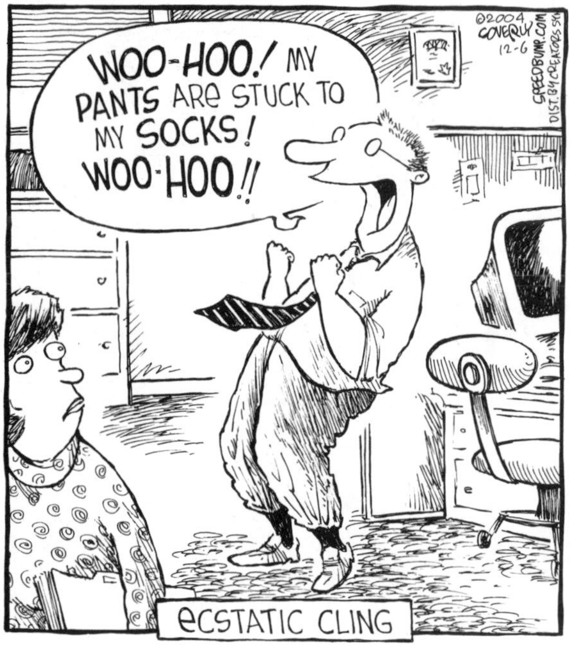
©2004 COVERLY 12-6
SPEEDBUMP.COM DIST. BY CREATORS SYN.
WOO-HOO! MY PANTS ARE STUCK TO MY SOCKS! WOO-HOO!!
ECSTATIC CLING

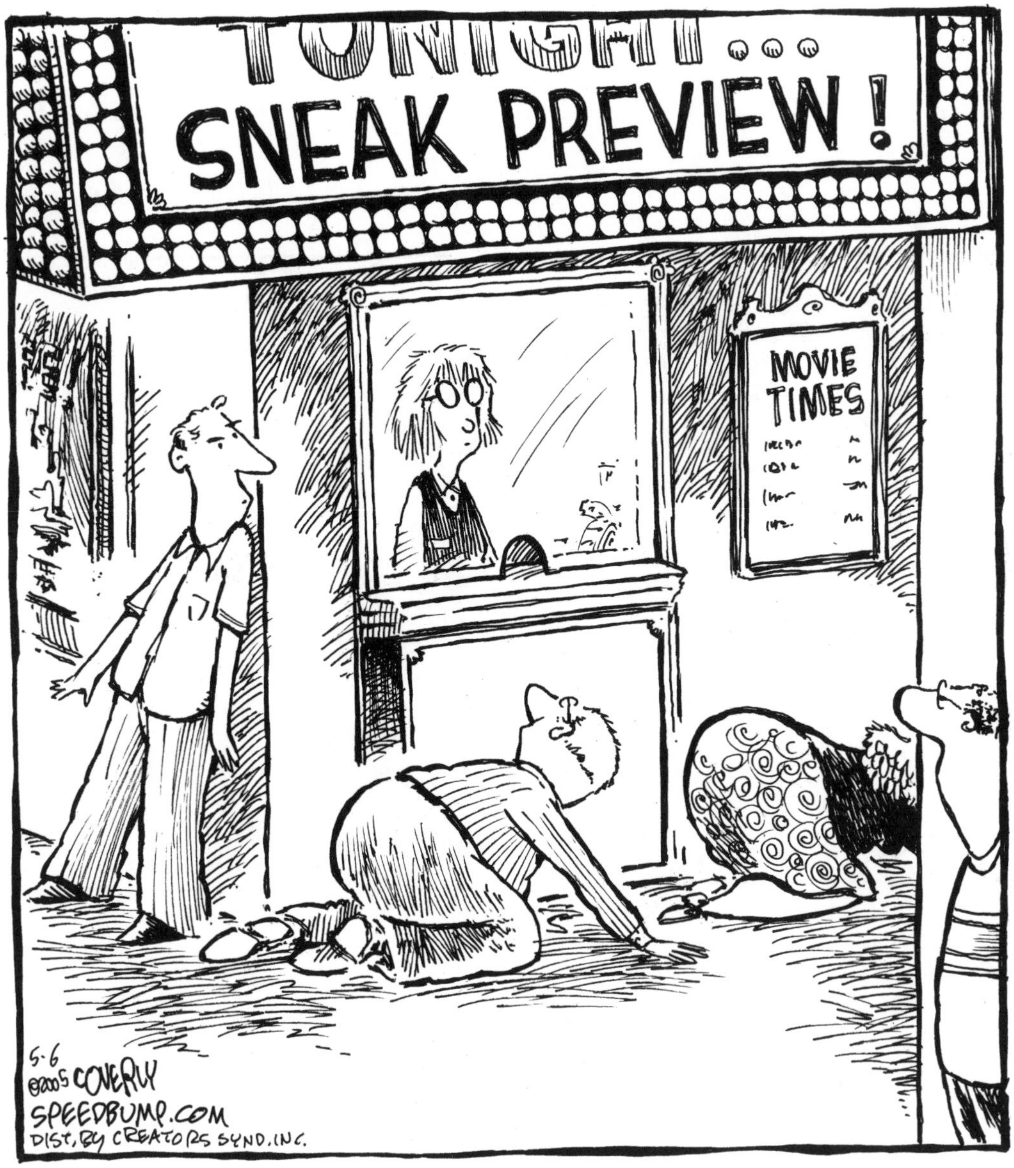
TONIGHT...
SNEAK PREVIEW!
MOVIE TIMES
5·6
©2005 COVERLY
SPEEDBUMP.COM
DIST. BY CREATORS SYND. INC.

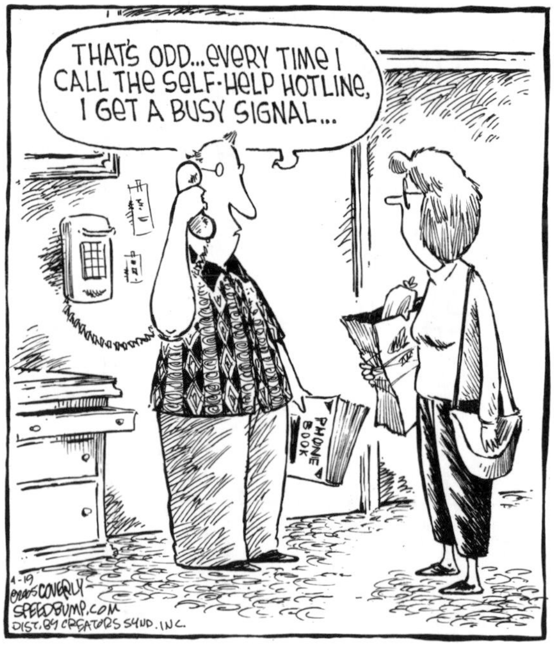
THAT'S ODD...EVERY TIME I CALL THE SELF-HELP HOTLINE, I GET A BUSY SIGNAL...
PHONE BOOK
SPEEDBUMP.COM
DIST. BY CREATORS SYND. INC.

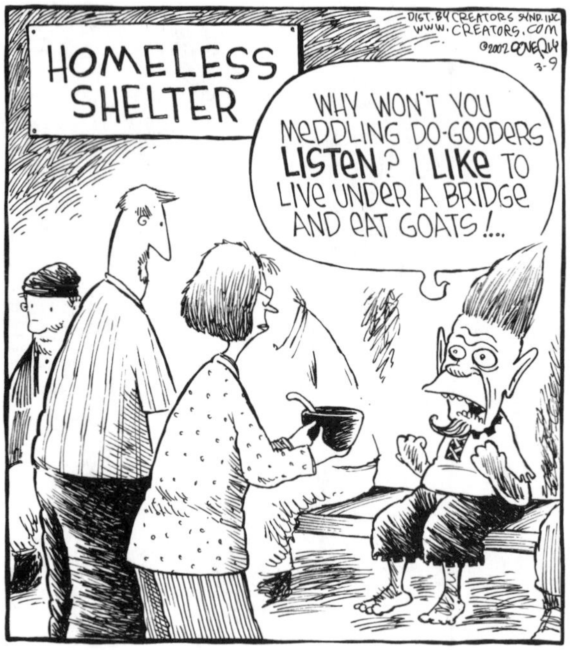
HOMELESS SHELTER
WHY WON'T YOU MEDDLING DO-GOODERS LISTEN? I LIKE TO LIVE UNDER A BRIDGE AND EAT GOATS!...
DIST. BY CREATORS SYND. INC
WWW.CREATORS.COM

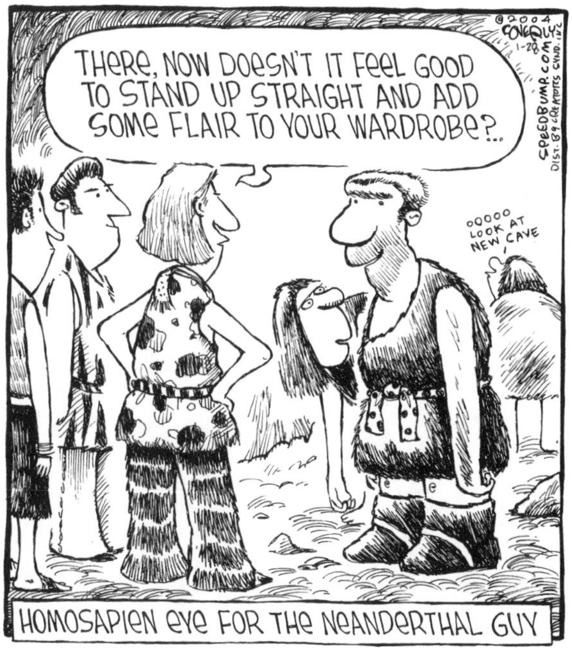
THERE, NOW DOESN'T IT FEEL GOOD TO STAND UP STRAIGHT AND ADD SOME FLAIR TO YOUR WARDROBE?..
OOOOO LOOK AT NEW CAVE
©2004 COVERLY SPEEDBUMP.COM DIST. BY CREATORS SYND. INC.
HOMOSAPIEN EYE FOR THE NEANDERTHAL GUY

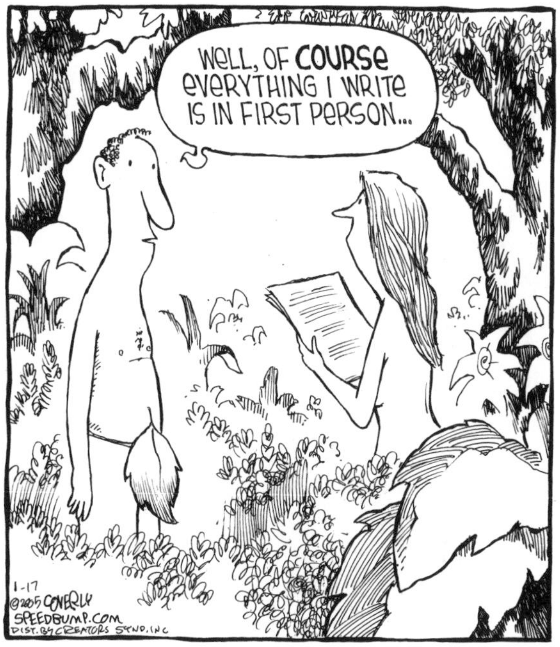
WELL, OF **COURSE** EVERYTHING I WRITE IS IN FIRST PERSON...
1-17 ©2005 COVERLY SPEEDBUMP.COM DIST. BY CREATORS SYND. INC

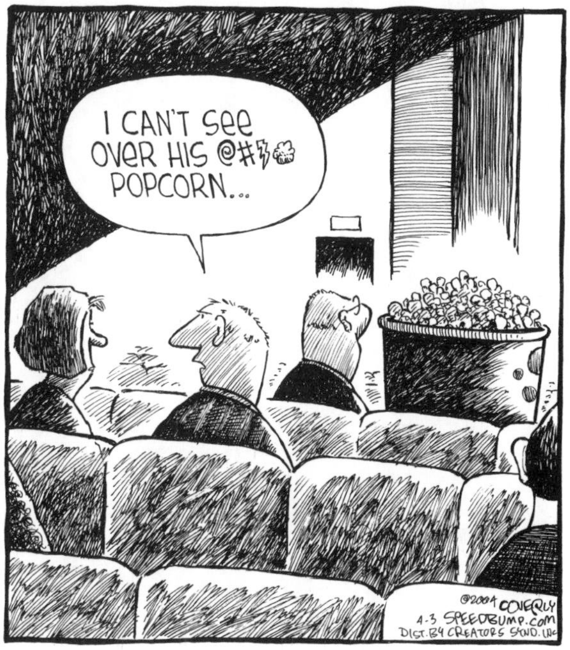
I CAN'T SEE OVER HIS @#$ POPCORN...
©2004 COVERLY 4-3 SPEEDBUMP.COM DIST. BY CREATORS SYND. INC

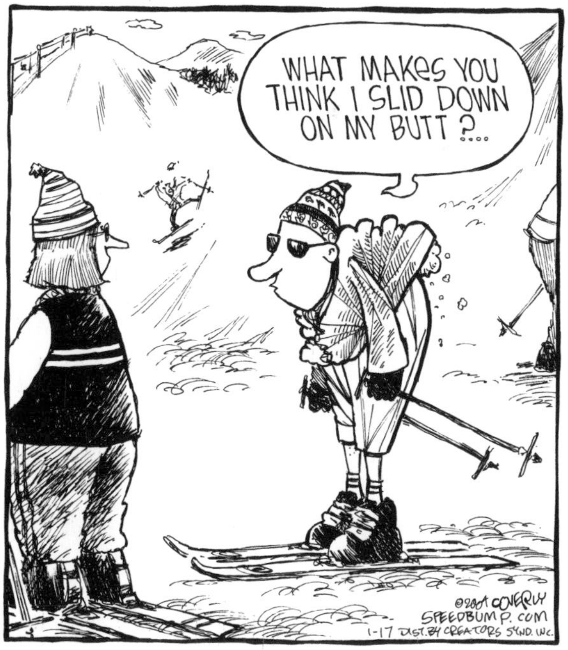
WHAT MAKES YOU THINK I SLID DOWN ON MY BUTT ?...
©2004 COVERLY SPEEDBUMP.COM 1-17 DIST. BY CREATORS SYND. INC.

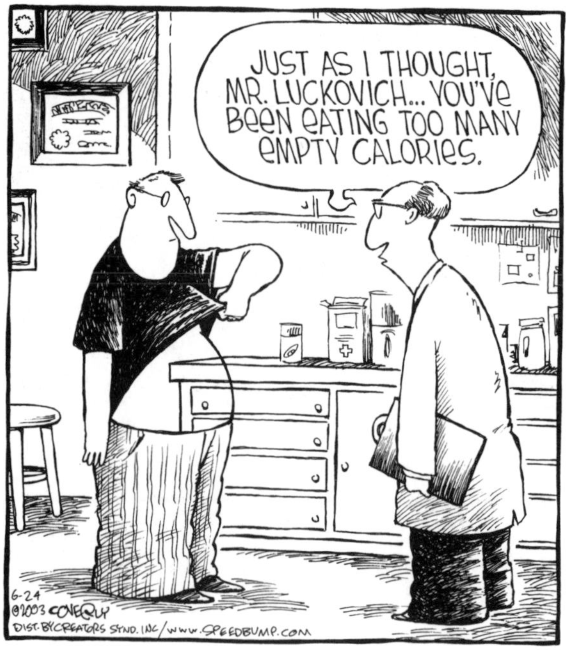
JUST AS I THOUGHT, MR. LUCKOVICH... YOU'VE BEEN EATING TOO MANY EMPTY CALORIES.
6-24
©2003 COVERLY
DIST. BY CREATORS SYND. INC/www.SPEEDBUMP.COM

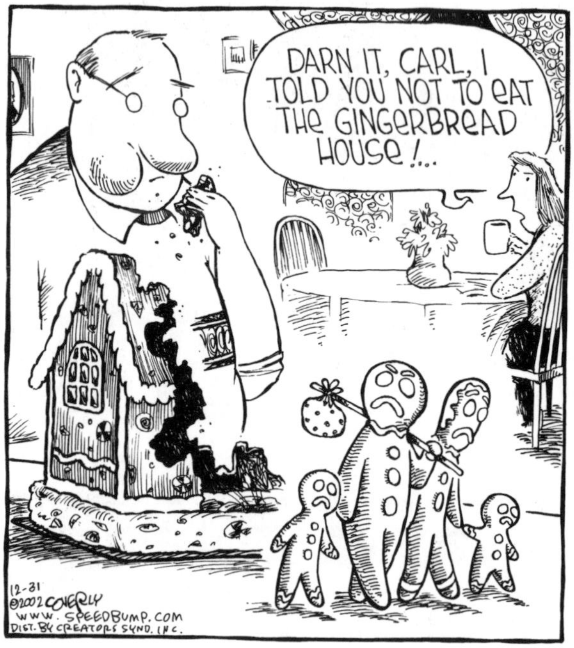
DARN IT, CARL, I TOLD YOU NOT TO EAT THE GINGERBREAD HOUSE!..
12-31
©2002 COVERLY
www.SPEEDBUMP.COM
DIST. BY CREATORS SYND. INC.

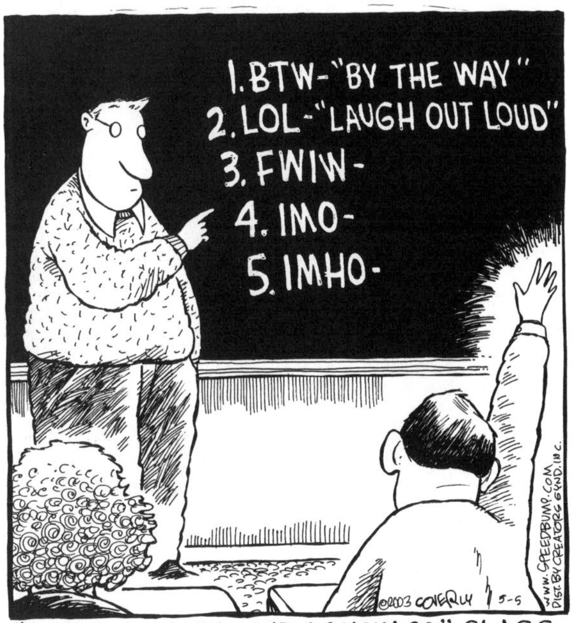
1. BTW- "BY THE WAY"
2. LOL- "LAUGH OUT LOUD"
3. FWIW-
4. IMO-
5. IMHO-
©2003 COVERLY 5-5
WWW.SPEEDBUMP.COM
DIST. BY CREATORS SYND. INC.
"E-MAIL AS A SECOND LANGUAGE" CLASS

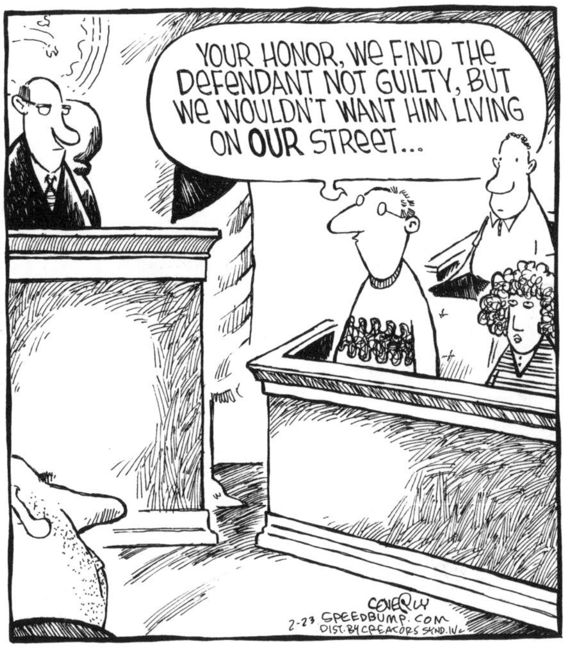
YOUR HONOR, WE FIND THE DEFENDANT NOT GUILTY, BUT WE WOULDN'T WANT HIM LIVING ON **OUR** STREET...
COVERLY
2-23 SPEEDBUMP.COM
DIST. BY CREATORS SYND. INC.

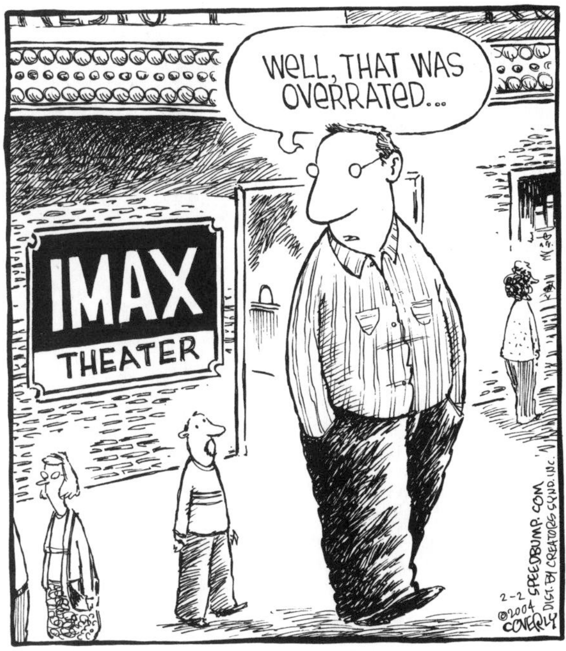
WELL, THAT WAS OVERRATED...
IMAX
THEATER
SPEEDBUMP.COM
DIST. BY CREATORS SYND. INC.
2-2
©2004
COVERLY

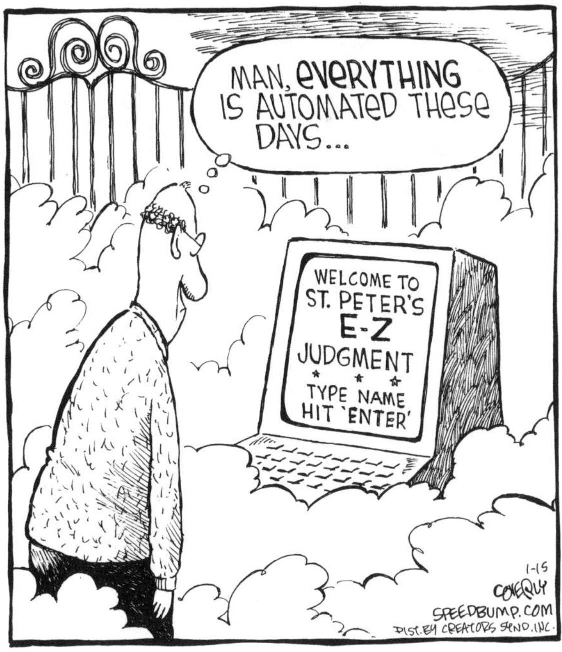
MAN, **EVERYTHING** IS AUTOMATED THESE DAYS...
WELCOME TO
ST. PETER'S
E-Z
JUDGMENT
TYPE NAME
HIT 'ENTER'
1-15
COVERLY
SPEEDBUMP.COM
DIST. BY CREATORS SYND. INC.

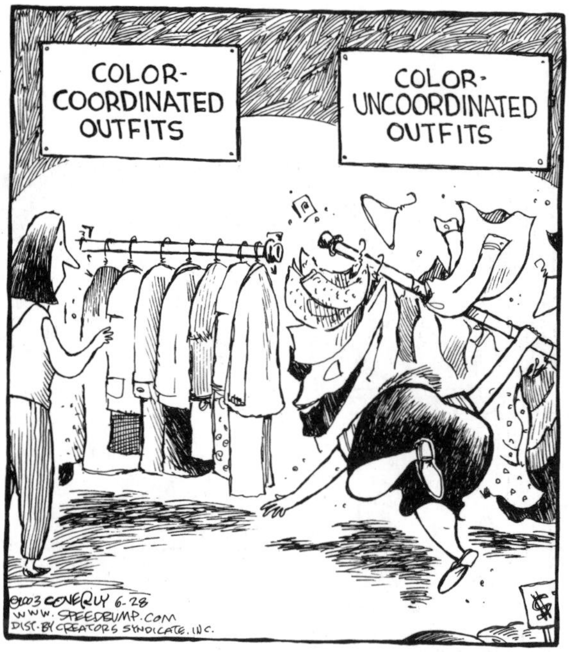
COLOR-COORDINATED OUTFITS
COLOR-UNCOORDINATED OUTFITS
©2003 COVERLY 6-28
WWW.SPEEDBUMP.COM
DIST. BY CREATORS SYNDICATE, INC.

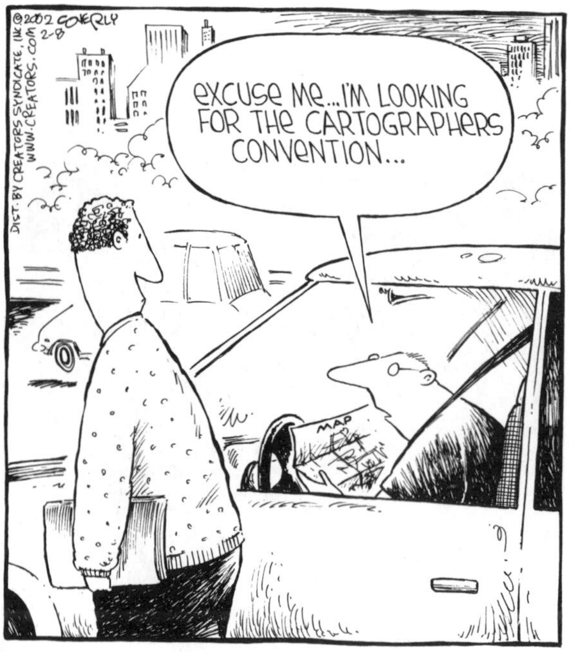
©2002 COVERLY 2-8
DIST. BY CREATORS SYNDICATE, INC. WWW.CREATORS.COM
EXCUSE ME...I'M LOOKING FOR THE CARTOGRAPHERS CONVENTION...
MAP

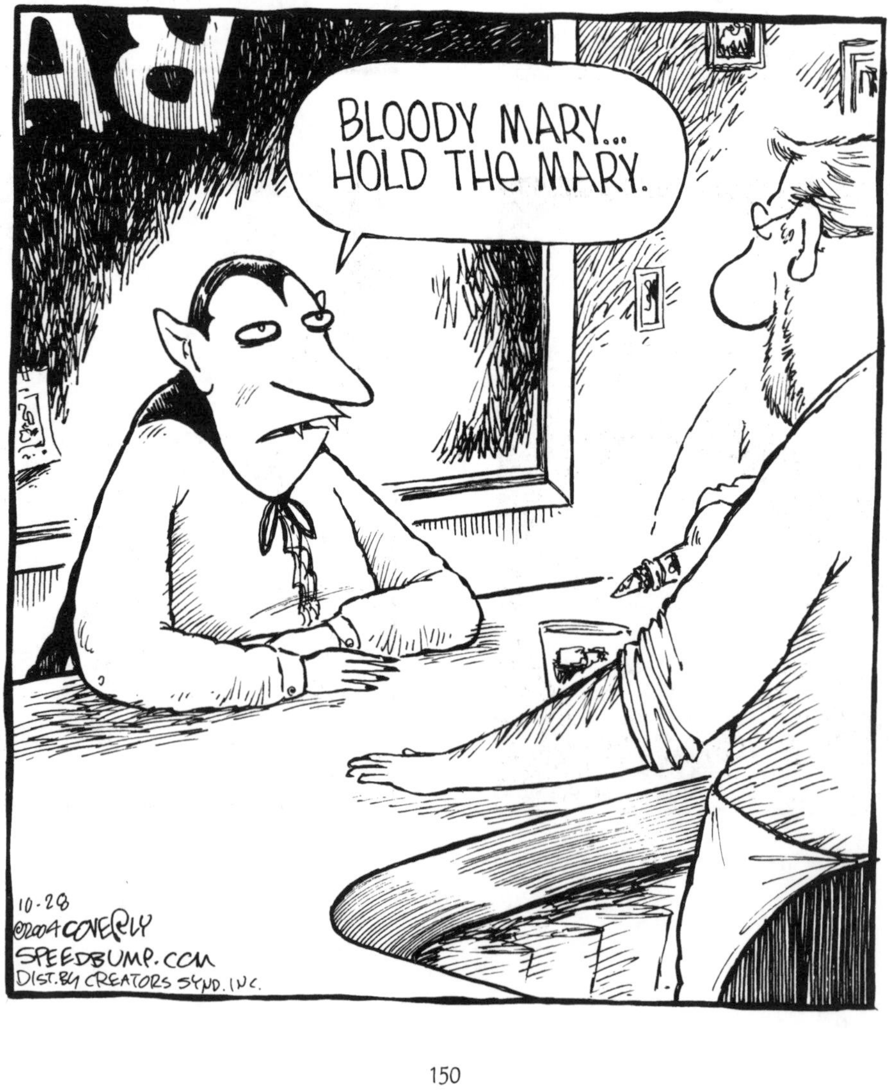
BLOODY MARY... HOLD THE MARY.
10-28
©2004 COVERLY
SPEEDBUMP.COM
DIST. BY CREATORS SYND. INC.

COMMUNITY SERVICE CHARITY RUN
I STILL SAY IT'S UNFAIR... "HEAD START" WINS EVERY YEAR!...
SAFE HOUSE
UNITED WAY
HABITAT FOR HUMANITY
©2002 5-1 COVERLY SPEEDBUMP.COM DIST. BY CREATORS SYND.

HE'S NOT MUCH OF A CHEF, BUT IF YOU WANT YOUR PIZZA SLICED PERFECTLY, ISOSCELES IS YOUR MAN...
©2005 COVERLY 3/31
SPEEDBUMP.COM DIST. BY CREATORS SYND. INC.

HEY DUDE, IT'S CHAD! I JUST GOT INTO TOWN!...
EXCELLENT! COME ON BY, BUD!...
COVERLY ©2003
5/3
DIST. BY CREATORS SYND, INC., WWW.SPEEDBUMP.COM
COMMUNICABLE DISEASES

IT LOOKS LIKE A COLD SORE.
4-8 ©2003 COVERLY WWW.SPEEDBUMP.COM DIST. BY CREATORS SYNDICATE, INC.

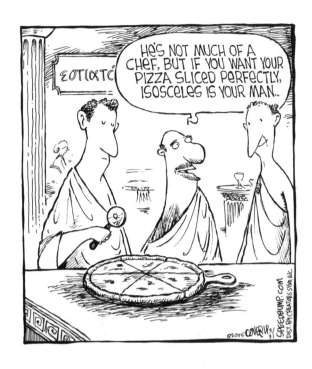

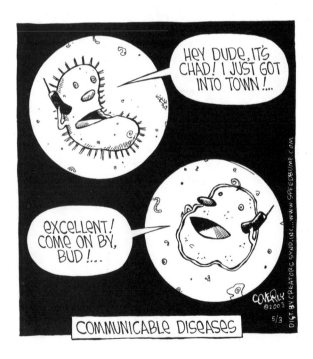

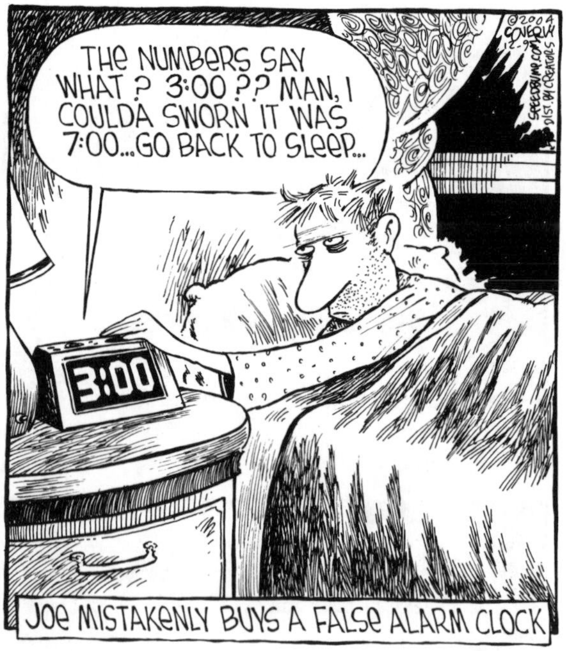
THE NUMBERS SAY WHAT? 3:00?? MAN, I COULDA SWORN IT WAS 7:00...GO BACK TO SLEEP...
3:00

JOE MISTAKENLY BUYS A FALSE ALARM CLOCK

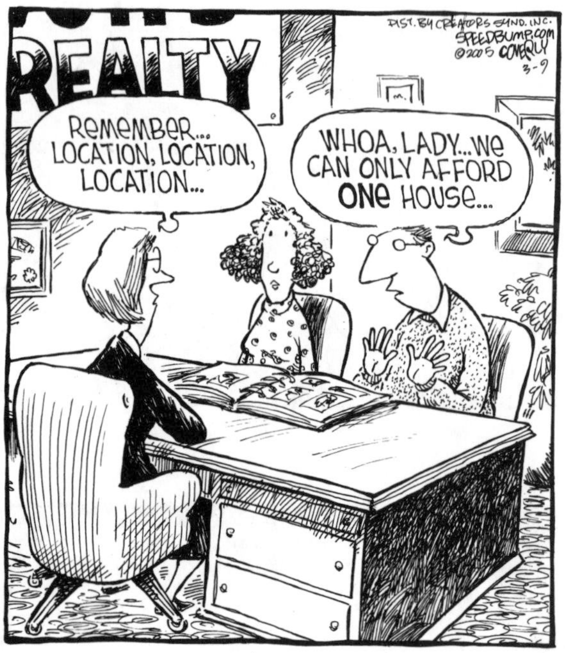
REALTY
REMEMBER... LOCATION, LOCATION, LOCATION...
WHOA, LADY...WE CAN ONLY AFFORD **ONE** HOUSE...

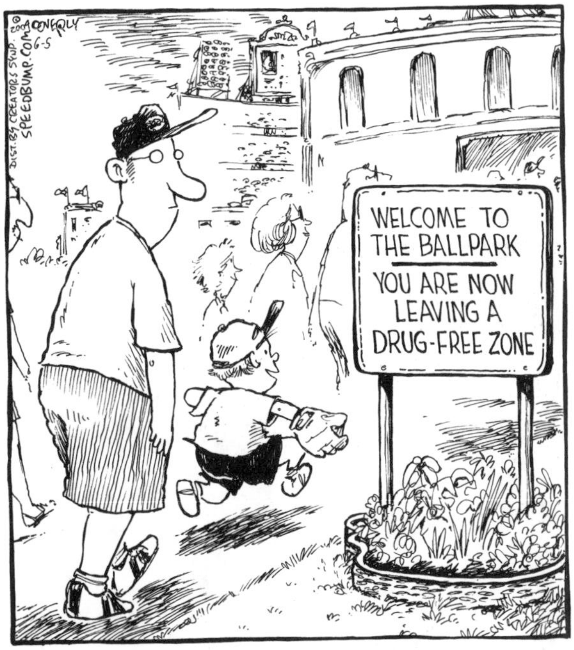
WELCOME TO THE BALLPARK
YOU ARE NOW LEAVING A DRUG-FREE ZONE

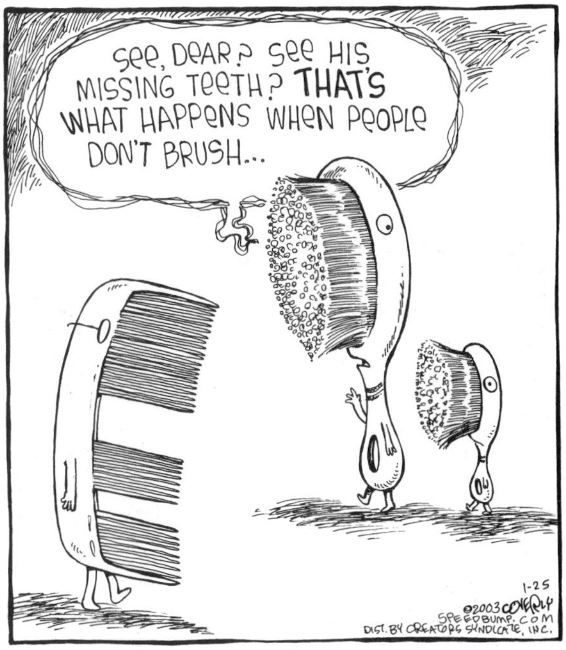
SEE, DEAR? SEE HIS MISSING TEETH? THAT'S WHAT HAPPENS WHEN PEOPLE DON'T BRUSH...

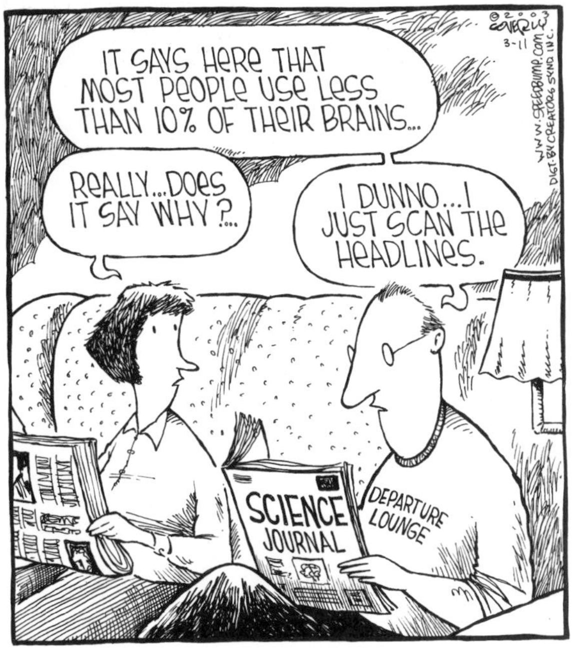
IT SAYS HERE THAT MOST PEOPLE USE LESS THAN 10% OF THEIR BRAINS...
REALLY...DOES IT SAY WHY?...
I DUNNO...I JUST SCAN THE HEADLINES.
SCIENCE JOURNAL
DEPARTURE LOUNGE

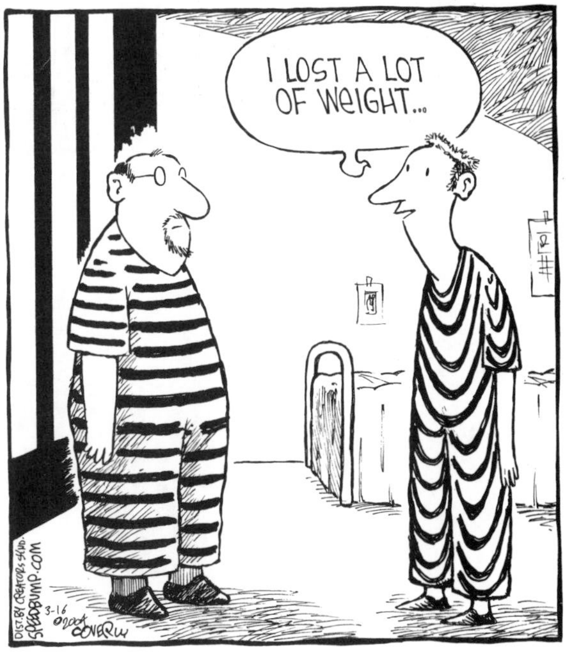
I LOST A LOT OF WEIGHT...

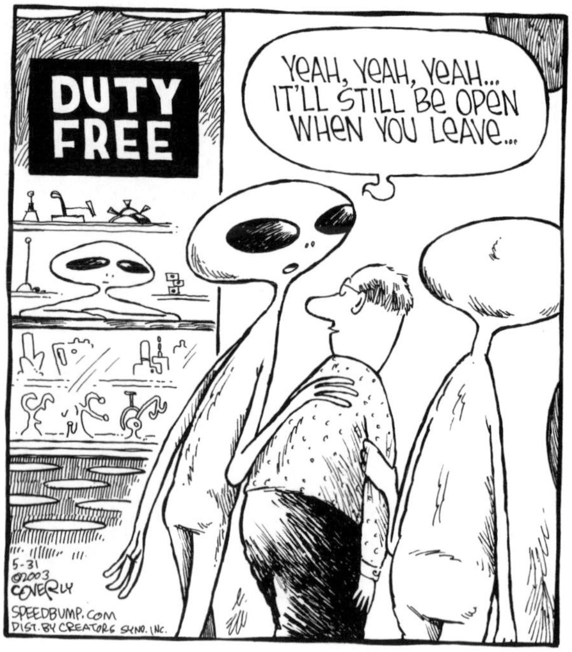
DUTY FREE
YEAH, YEAH, YEAH... IT'LL STILL BE OPEN WHEN YOU LEAVE...
5-31 ©2003 COVERLY
SPEEDBUMP.COM
DIST. BY CREATORS SYND. INC.

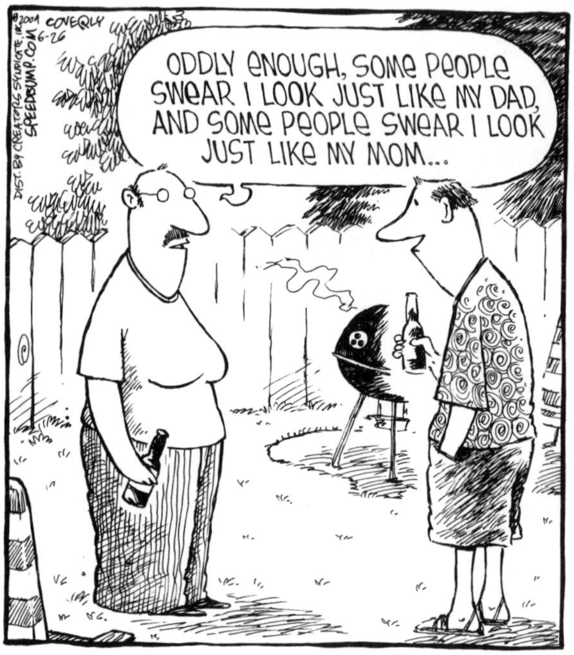
©2004 COVERLY 6-26
DIST. BY CREATORS SYNDICATE INC.
SPEEDBUMP.COM
ODDLY ENOUGH, SOME PEOPLE SWEAR I LOOK JUST LIKE MY DAD, AND SOME PEOPLE SWEAR I LOOK JUST LIKE MY MOM...

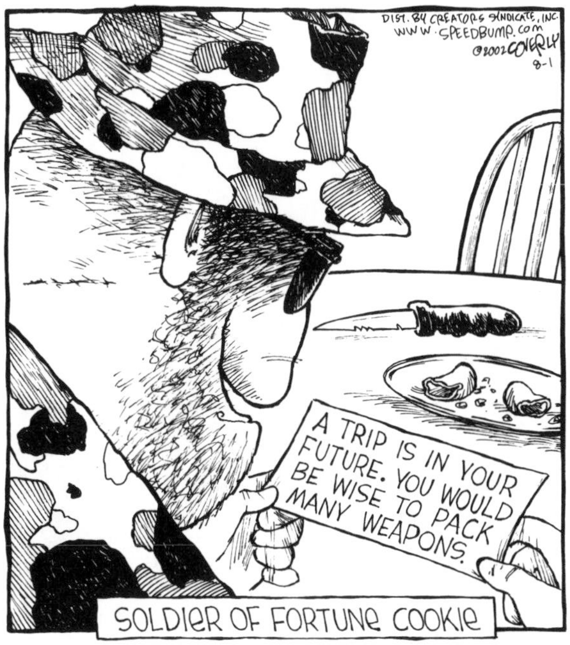
DIST. BY CREATORS SYNDICATE, INC.
WWW.SPEEDBUMP.COM
©2002 COVERLY
8-1
A TRIP IS IN YOUR FUTURE. YOU WOULD BE WISE TO PACK MANY WEAPONS.
SOLDIER OF FORTUNE COOKIE

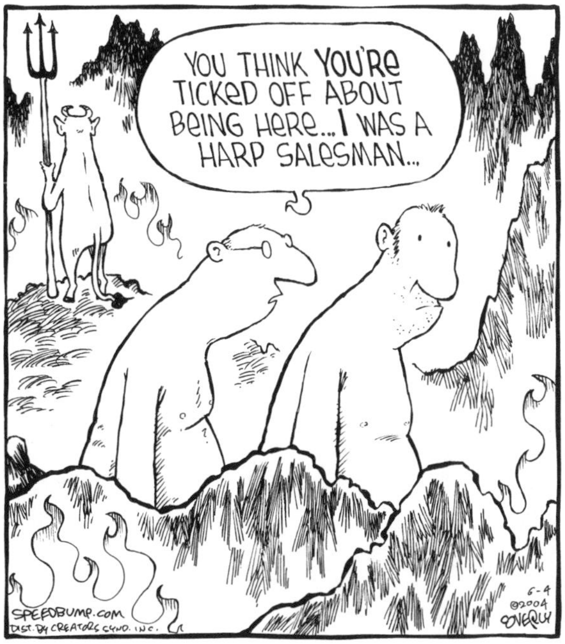
YOU THINK YOU'RE TICKED OFF ABOUT BEING HERE... I WAS A HARP SALESMAN...
SPEEDBUMP.COM
DIST. BY CREATORS SYND. INC.
6-4
©2004
COVERLY

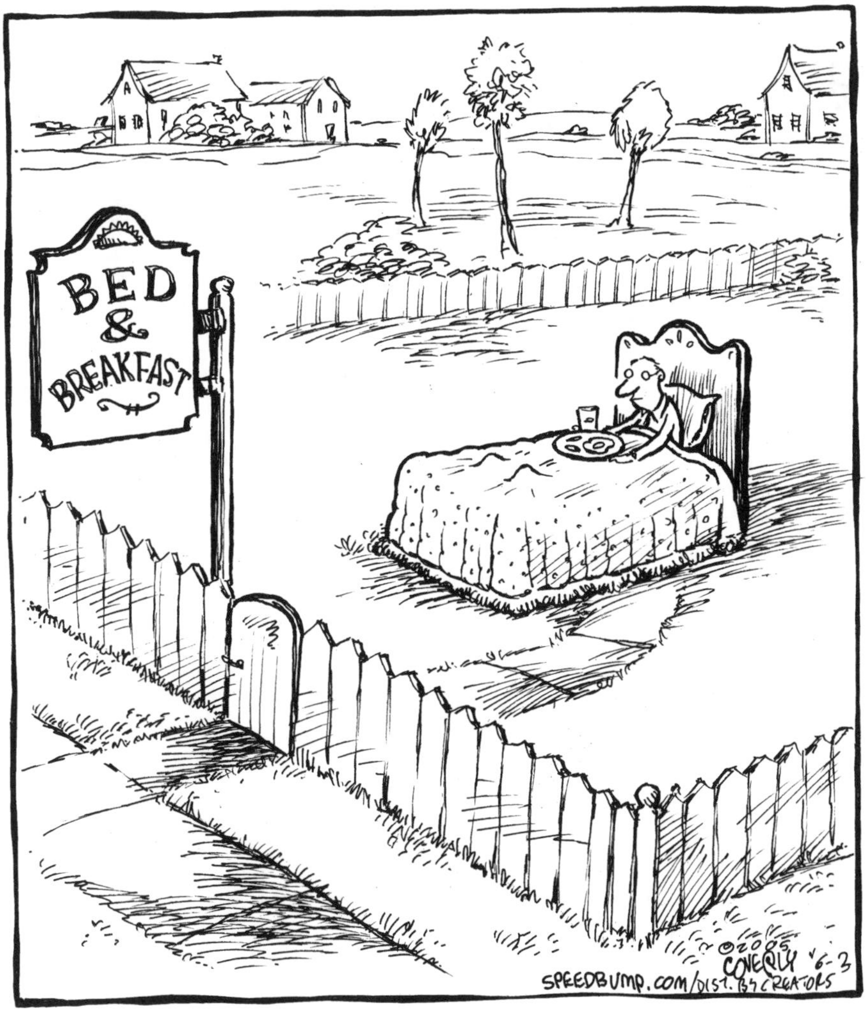
BED & BREAKFAST
©2005
COVERLY
6-3
SPEEDBUMP.COM/DIST. BY CREATORS

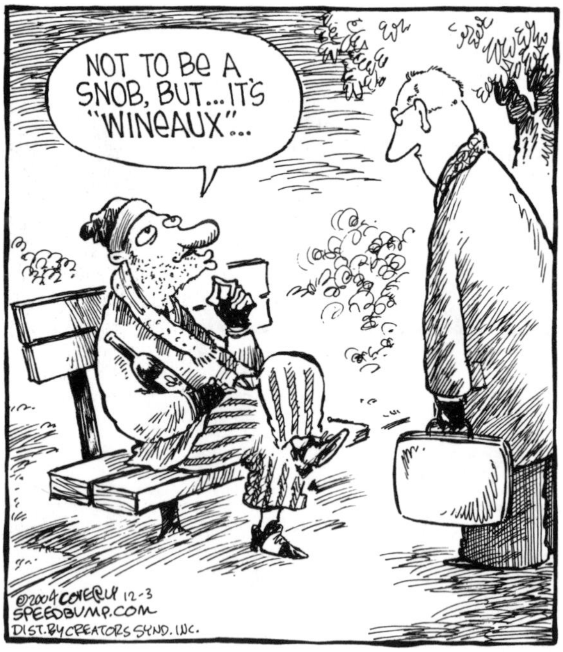
NOT TO BE A SNOB, BUT... IT'S "WINEAUX"...
©2004 COVERLY 12-3
SPEEDBUMP.COM
DIST. BY CREATORS SYND. INC.

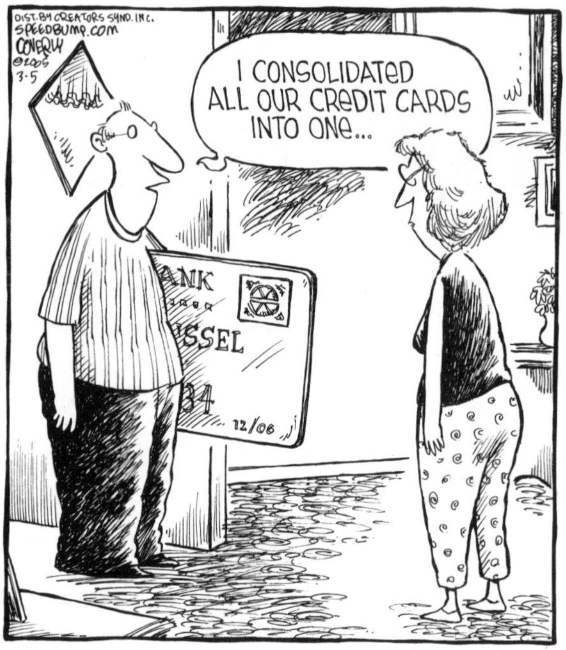
DIST. BY CREATORS SYND. INC.
SPEEDBUMP.COM
COVERLY
©2005
3-5
I CONSOLIDATED ALL OUR CREDIT CARDS INTO ONE...

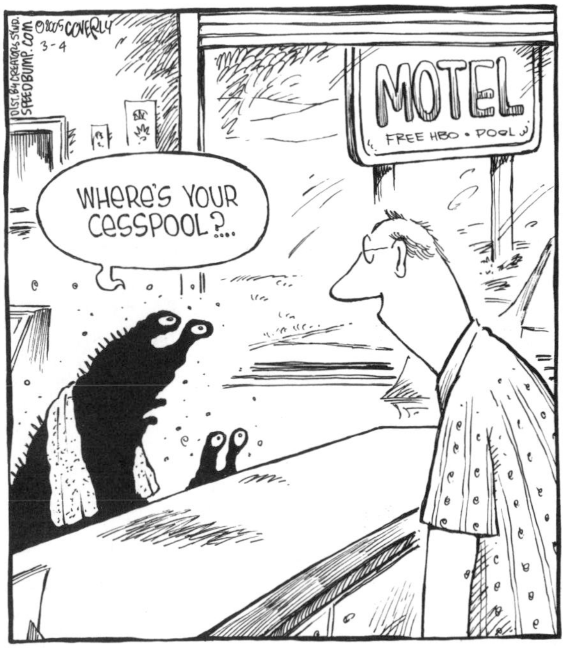

©2005 COVERLY 3-4
DIST. BY CREATORS SYND. SPEEDBUMP.COM
MOTEL
FREE HBO • POOL
WHERE'S YOUR CESSPOOL?...

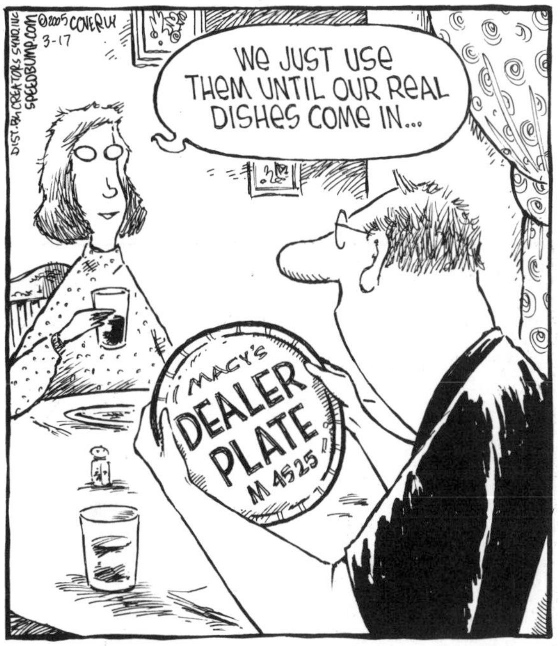

©2005 COVERLY 3-17
DIST. BY CREATORS SYND. INC. SPEEDBUMP.COM
WE JUST USE THEM UNTIL OUR REAL DISHES COME IN...
MACY'S
DEALER PLATE
M 4525

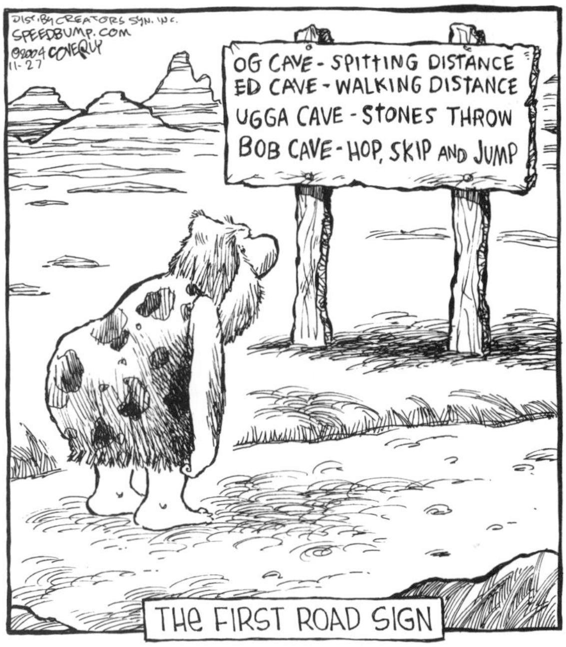

DIST. BY CREATORS SYN. INC.
SPEEDBUMP.COM
©2004 COVERLY 11-27
OG CAVE - SPITTING DISTANCE
ED CAVE - WALKING DISTANCE
UGGA CAVE - STONES THROW
BOB CAVE - HOP, SKIP AND JUMP

THE FIRST ROAD SIGN

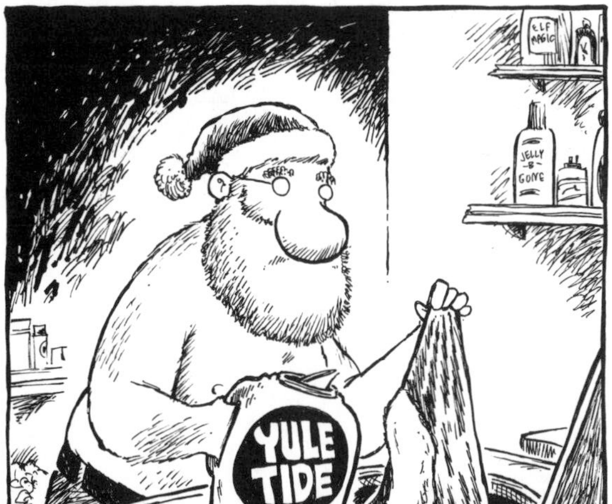

ELF MAGIC
JELLY B GONE
YULE TIDE
12-17 ©2004 COVERLY
DIST. BY CREATORS SYND. INC./ SPEEDBUMP.COM

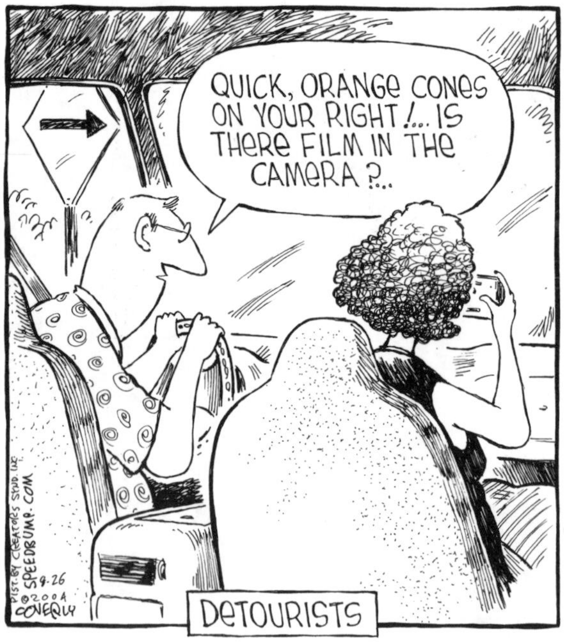
QUICK, ORANGE CONES ON YOUR RIGHT!... IS THERE FILM IN THE CAMERA?...
DETOURISTS
DIST. BY CREATORS SYND. INC.
SPEEDBUMP.COM
9-26
©2004
COVERLY

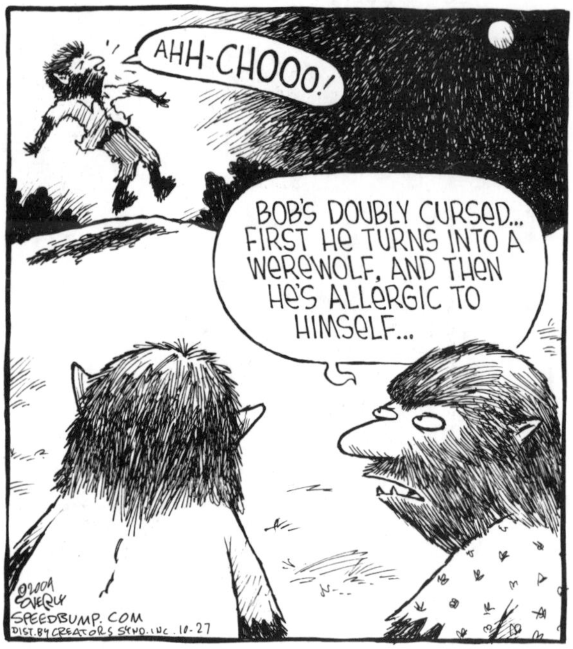
AHH-CHOOO!
BOB'S DOUBLY CURSED... FIRST HE TURNS INTO A WEREWOLF, AND THEN HE'S ALLERGIC TO HIMSELF...
©2004
COVERLY
SPEEDBUMP.COM
DIST. BY CREATORS SYND. INC. 10-27

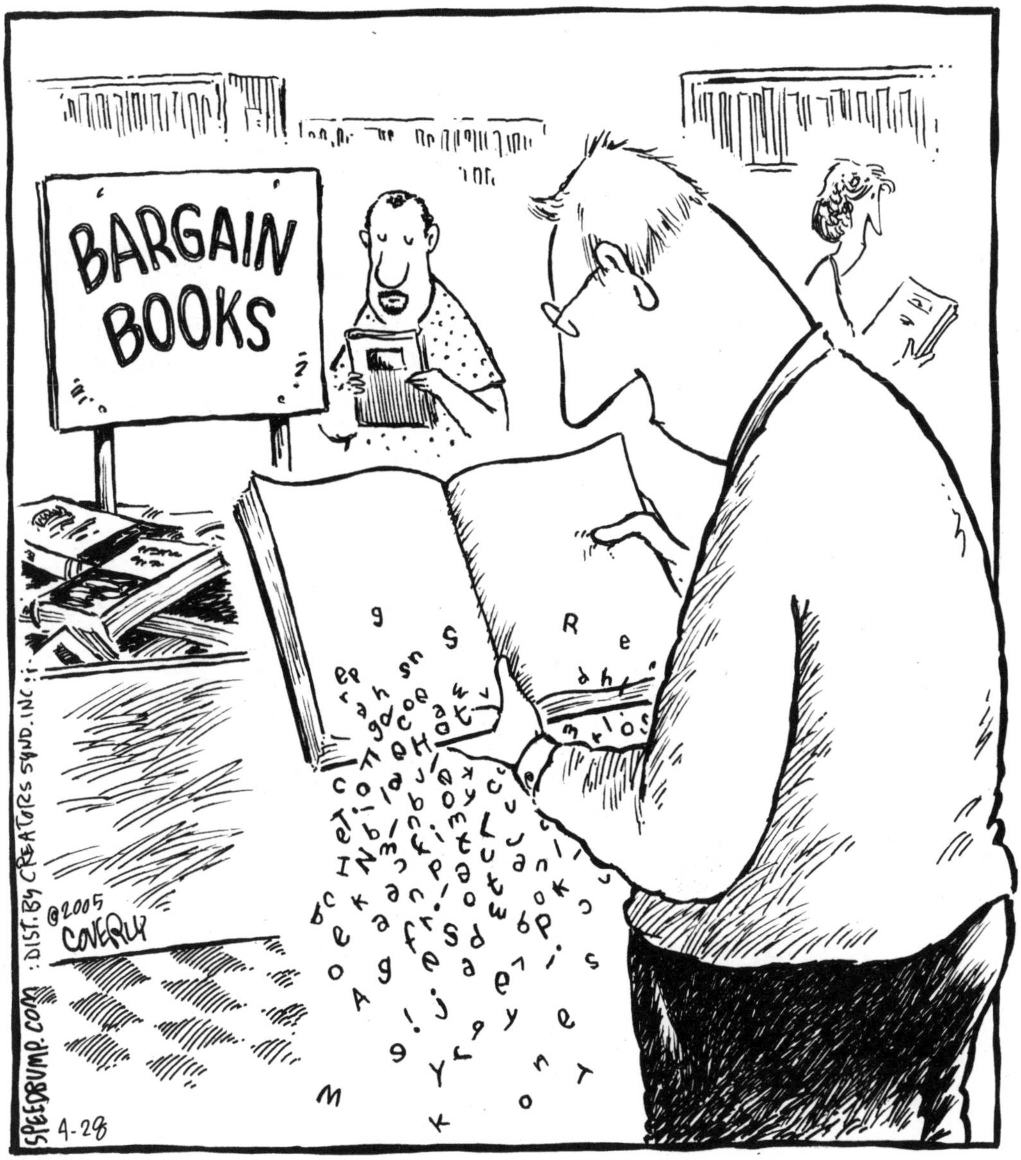
BARGAIN BOOKS
SPEEDBUMP.COM : DIST. BY CREATORS SYND. INC.
©2005 COVERLY
4-28

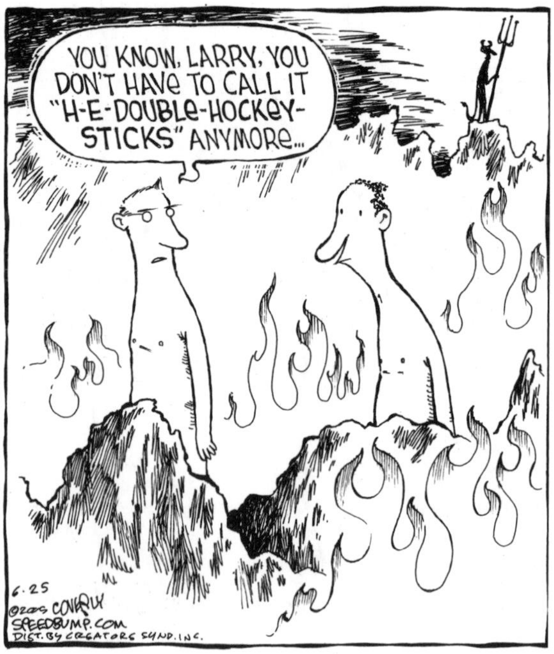
YOU KNOW, LARRY, YOU DON'T HAVE TO CALL IT "H-E-DOUBLE-HOCKEY-STICKS" ANYMORE...
6-25
©2005 COVERLY
SPEEDBUMP.COM
DIST. BY CREATORS SYND. INC.

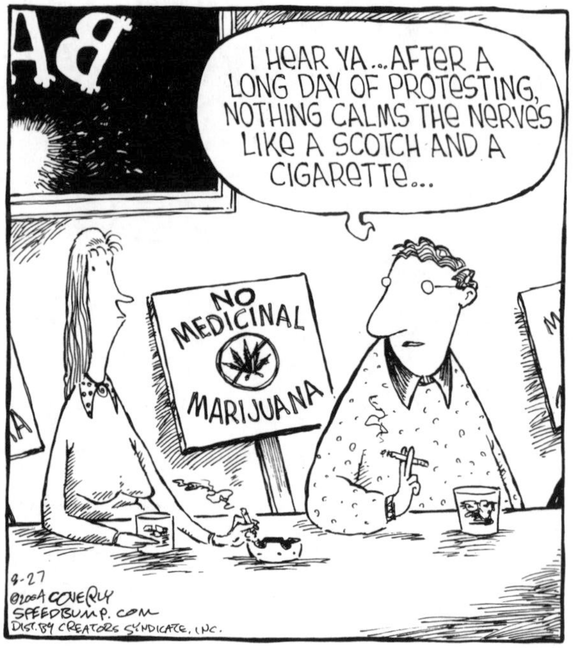
I HEAR YA... AFTER A LONG DAY OF PROTESTING, NOTHING CALMS THE NERVES LIKE A SCOTCH AND A CIGARETTE...
NO MEDICINAL MARIJUANA
8-27
©2004 COVERLY
SPEEDBUMP.COM
DIST. BY CREATORS SYNDICATE, INC.

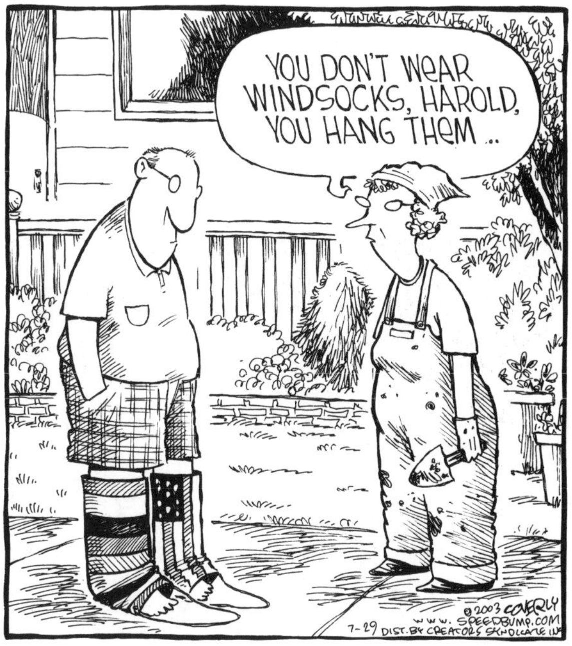
YOU DON'T WEAR WINDSOCKS, HAROLD, YOU HANG THEM...
©2003 COVERLY
7-29 WWW.SPEEDBUMP.COM
DIST. BY CREATORS SYNDICATE INC

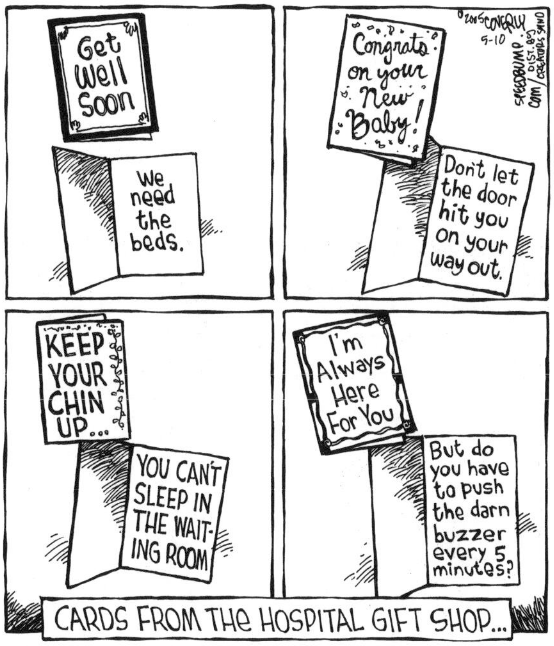
Get Well Soon
We need the beds.
Congrats on your New Baby!
Don't let the door hit you on your way out.
KEEP YOUR CHIN UP...
YOU CAN'T SLEEP IN THE WAIT-ING ROOM
I'm Always Here For You
But do you have to push the darn buzzer every 5 minutes?
CARDS FROM THE HOSPITAL GIFT SHOP...

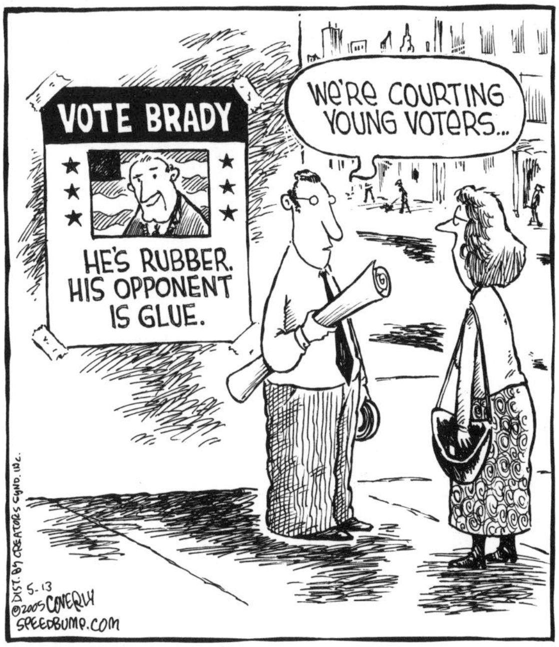
VOTE BRADY
HE'S RUBBER. HIS OPPONENT IS GLUE.
WE'RE COURTING YOUNG VOTERS...
5-13
©2005 COVERLY
SPEEDBUMP.COM

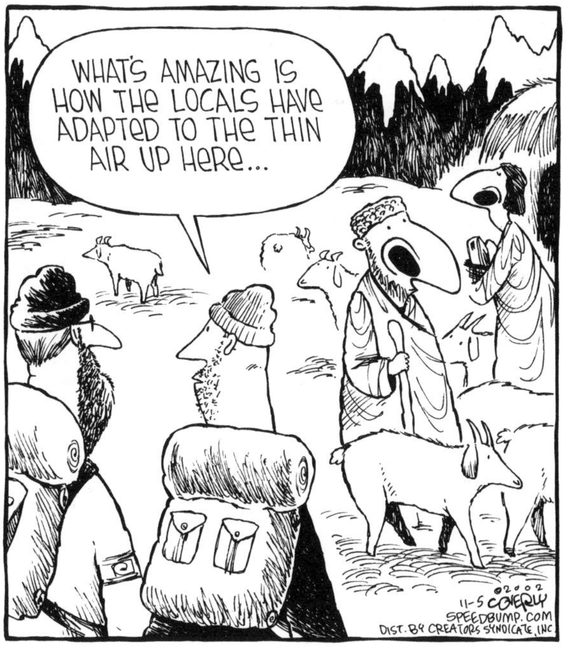
WHAT'S AMAZING IS HOW THE LOCALS HAVE ADAPTED TO THE THIN AIR UP HERE...
11-5 ©2002 COVERLY
SPEEDBUMP.COM
DIST. BY CREATORS SYNDICATE, INC

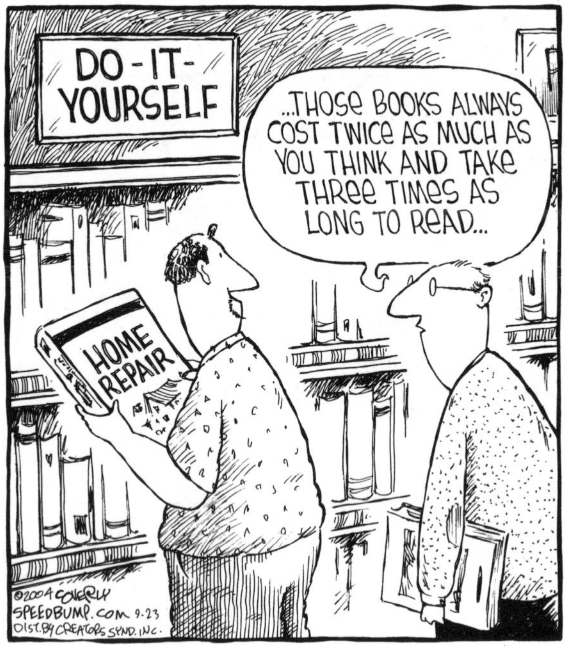
DO-IT-YOURSELF
...THOSE BOOKS ALWAYS COST TWICE AS MUCH AS YOU THINK AND TAKE THREE TIMES AS LONG TO READ...
HOME REPAIR
©2004 COVERLY SPEEDBUMP.COM 9-23 DIST. BY CREATORS SYND. INC.

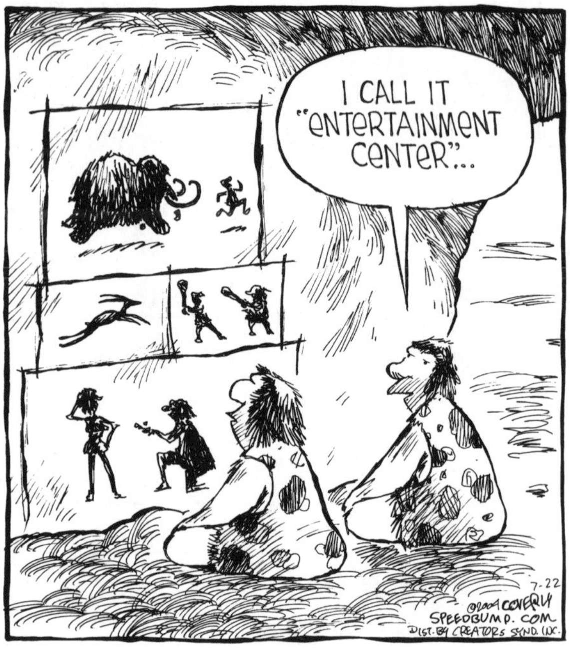
I CALL IT "ENTERTAINMENT CENTER"...
7-22 ©2004 COVERLY SPEEDBUMP.COM DIST. BY CREATORS SYND. INC.

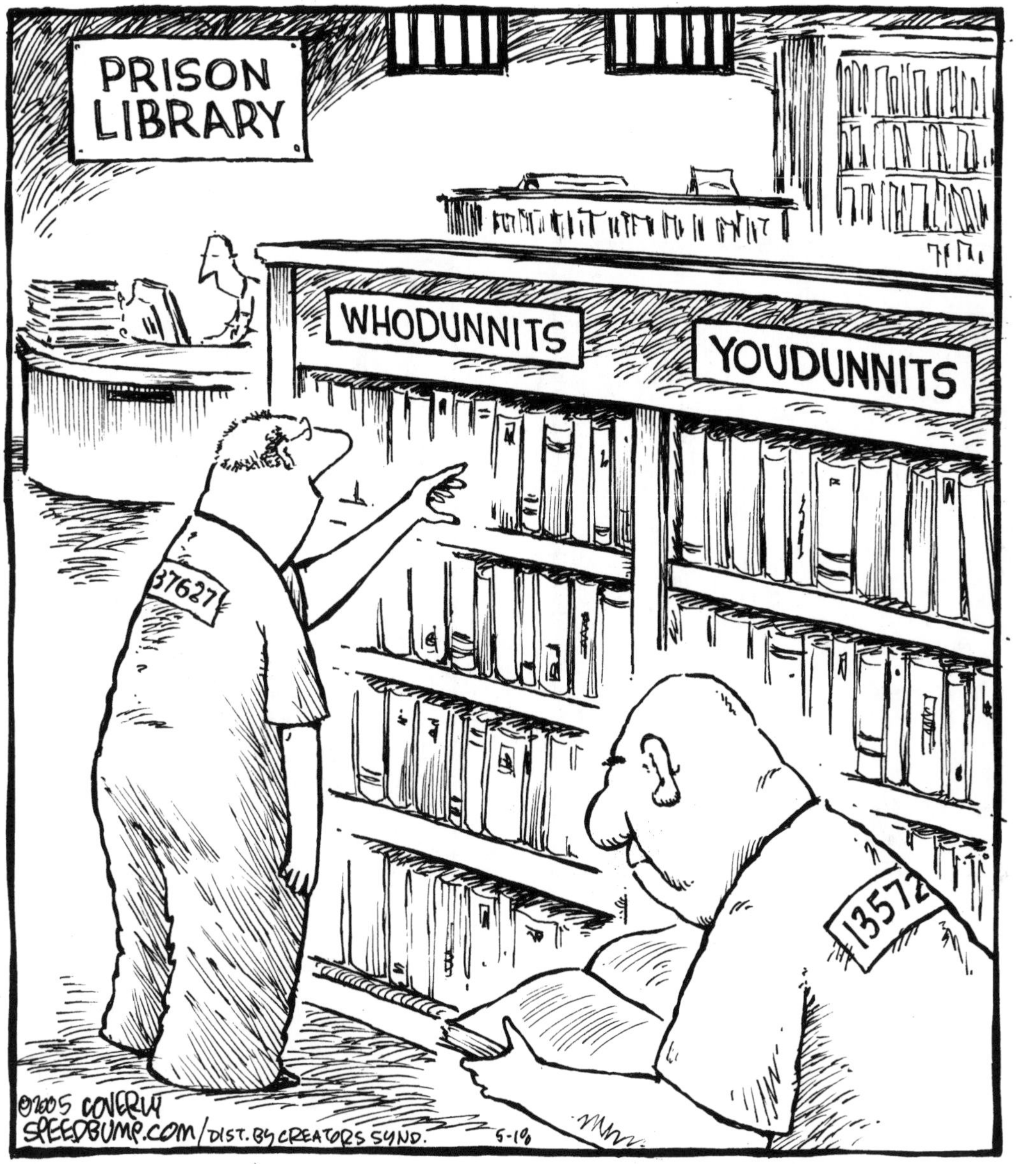
PRISON LIBRARY
WHODUNNITS
YOUDUNNITS
37627
13572
©2005 COVERLY
SPEEDBUMP.COM/DIST. BY CREATORS SYND.

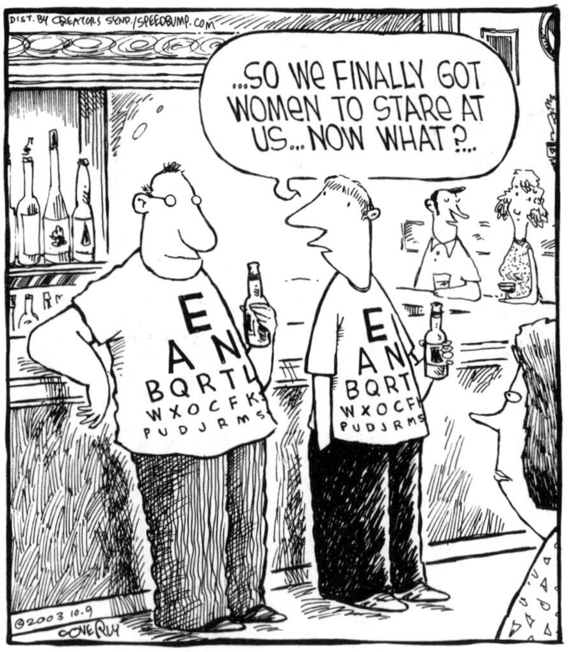
DIST. BY CREATORS SYND./SPEEDBUMP.COM
...SO WE FINALLY GOT WOMEN TO STARE AT US...NOW WHAT?...
E
AN
BQRTL
WXOCFK
PUDJRMS
©2003 10-9
COVERLY

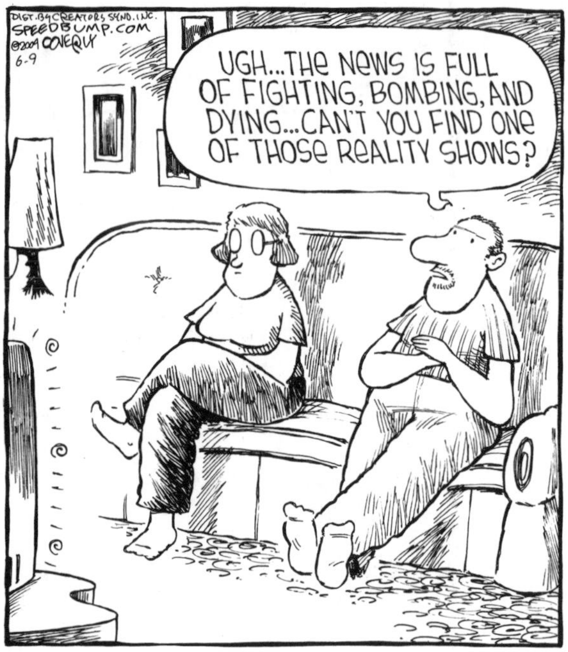
DIST. BY CREATORS SYND. INC.
SPEEDBUMP.COM
©2004 COVERLY
6-9
UGH...THE NEWS IS FULL OF FIGHTING, BOMBING, AND DYING...CAN'T YOU FIND ONE OF THOSE REALITY SHOWS?

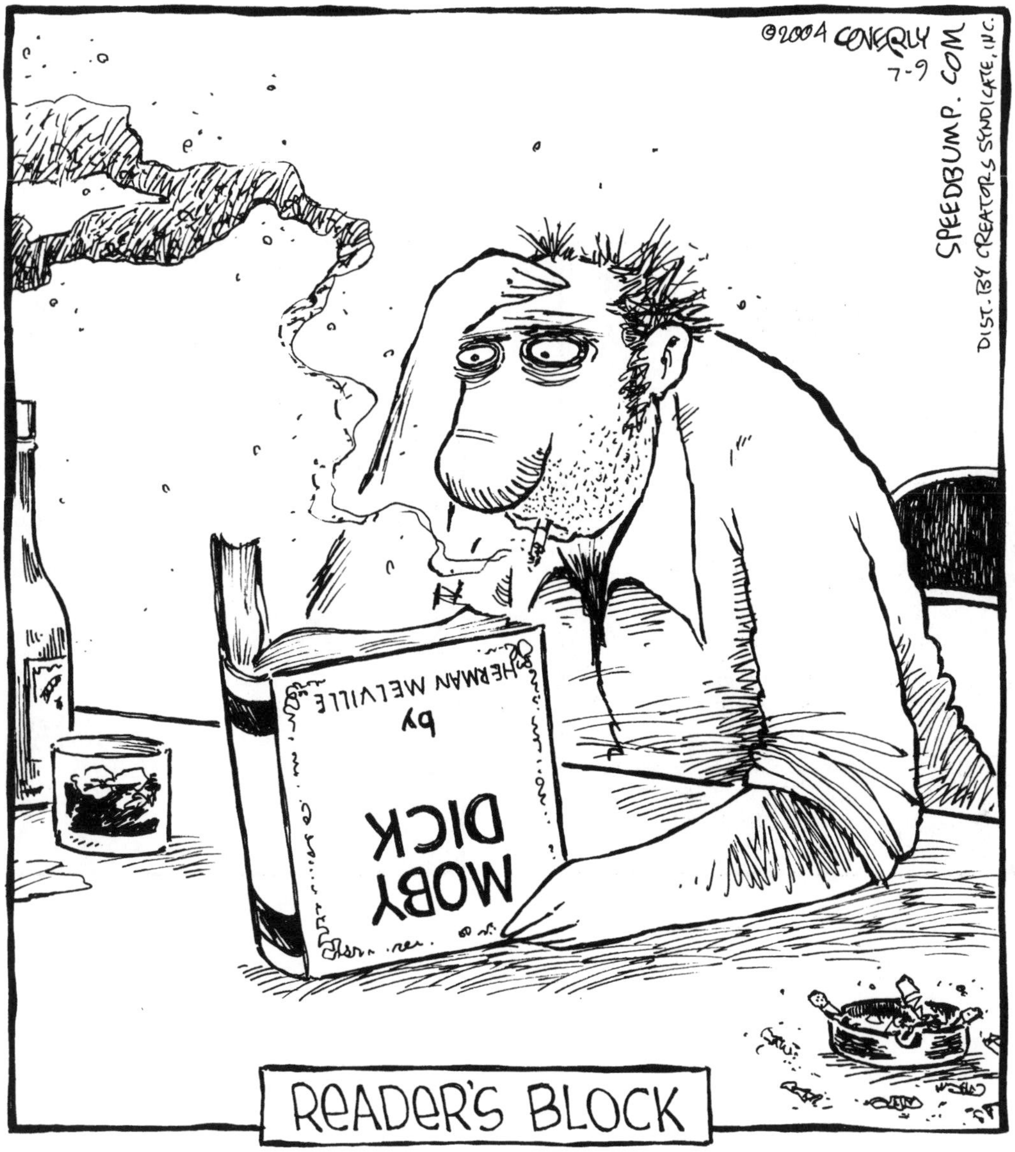
©2004 CONERLY
7-9
SPEEDBUMP.COM
DIST. BY CREATORS SYNDICATE, INC.
MOBY DICK
by
HERMAN MELVILLE
READER'S BLOCK

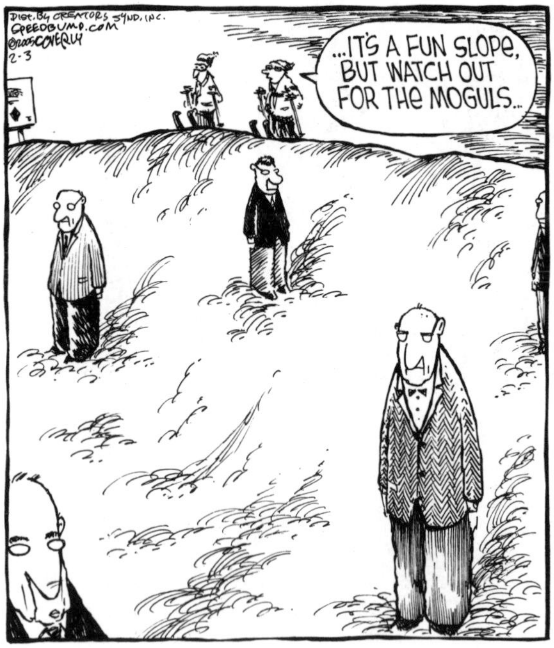
...IT'S A FUN SLOPE, BUT WATCH OUT FOR THE MOGULS...

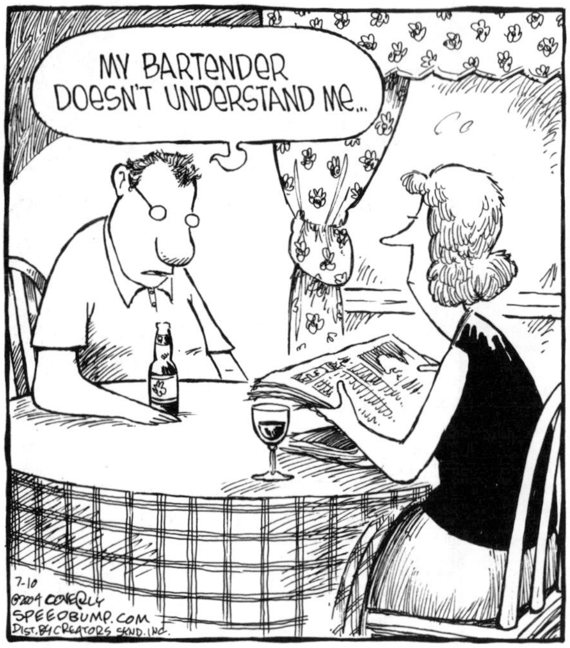
MY BARTENDER DOESN'T UNDERSTAND ME...

11TH ANNUAL
TASTE OF
DOWNTOWN
©2009
COVERLY 9-19
SPEEDBUMP.COM
DIST. BY CREATORS SYND. INC.

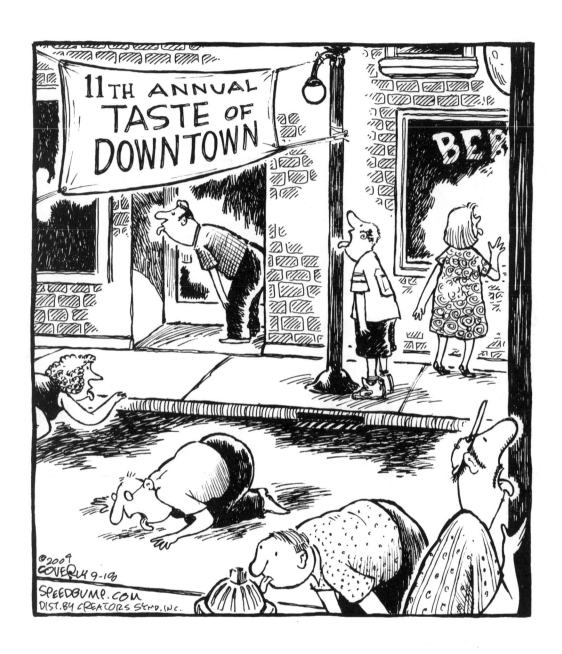

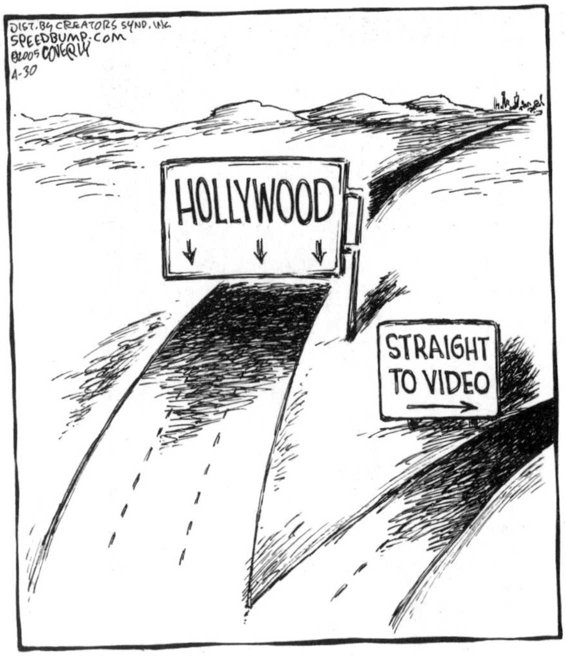
DIST. BY CREATORS SYND. INC.
SPEEDBUMP.COM
©2005 COVERLY
4-30
HOLLYWOOD
STRAIGHT TO VIDEO

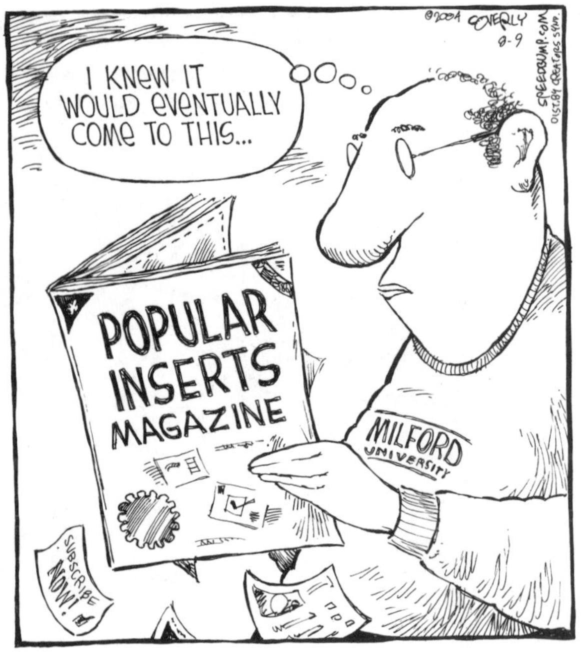
©2004 COVERLY
8-9
SPEEDBUMP.COM
DIST. BY CREATORS SYND.
I KNEW IT WOULD EVENTUALLY COME TO THIS...
POPULAR INSERTS MAGAZINE
MILFORD UNIVERSITY
SUBSCRIBE NOW!

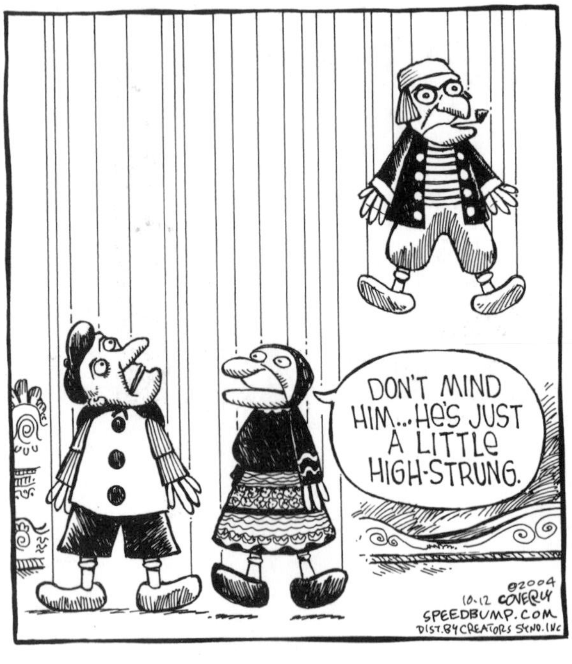
DON'T MIND HIM...HE'S JUST A LITTLE HIGH-STRUNG.
©2004
10-12 COVERLY
SPEEDBUMP.COM
DIST. BY CREATORS SYND. INC

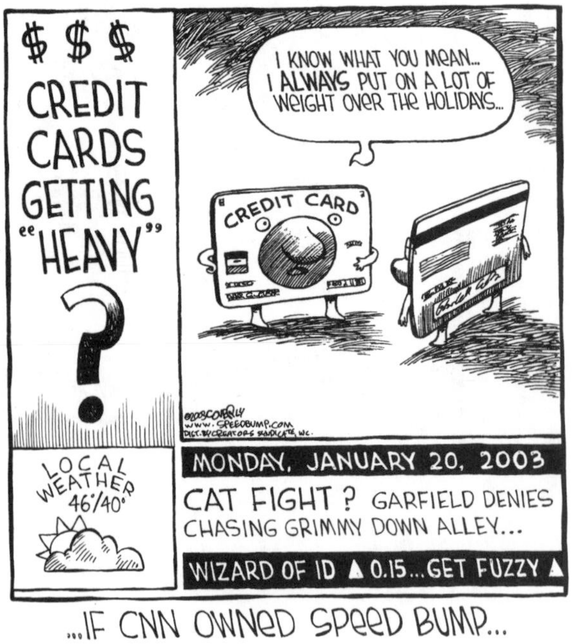
$ $ $
CREDIT CARDS GETTING "HEAVY" ?
I KNOW WHAT YOU MEAN... I ALWAYS PUT ON A LOT OF WEIGHT OVER THE HOLIDAYS...
CREDIT CARD
LOCAL WEATHER 46°/40°
MONDAY, JANUARY 20, 2003
CAT FIGHT ? GARFIELD DENIES CHASING GRIMMY DOWN ALLEY...
WIZARD OF ID ▲ 0.15...GET FUZZY ▲

...IF CNN OWNED SPEED BUMP...

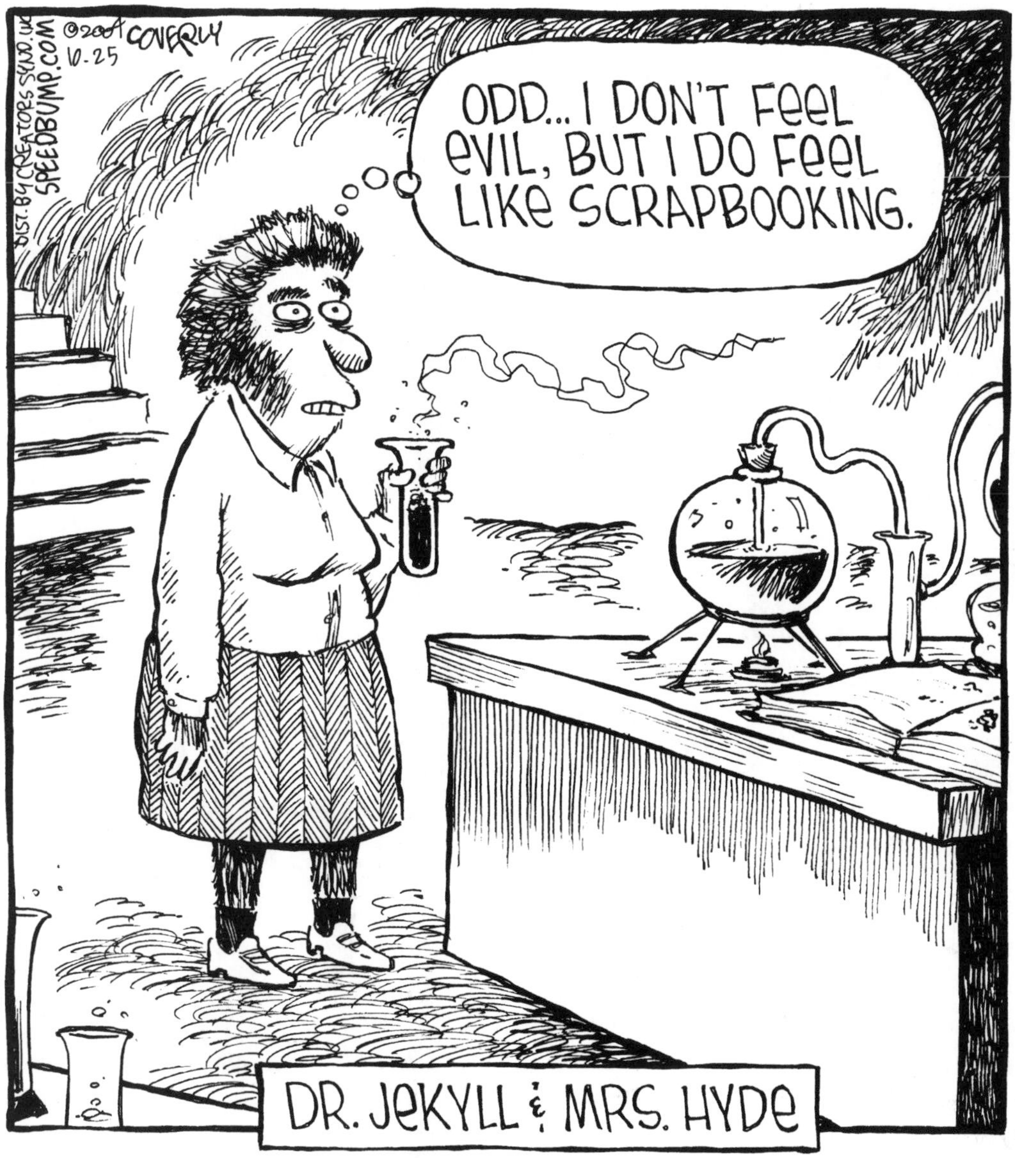
©2004 COVERLY
10-25
DIST. BY CREATORS SYND. INC
SPEEDBUMP.COM
ODD... I DON'T FEEL EVIL, BUT I DO FEEL LIKE SCRAPBOOKING.
DR. JEKYLL & MRS. HYDE

Caption Contest II

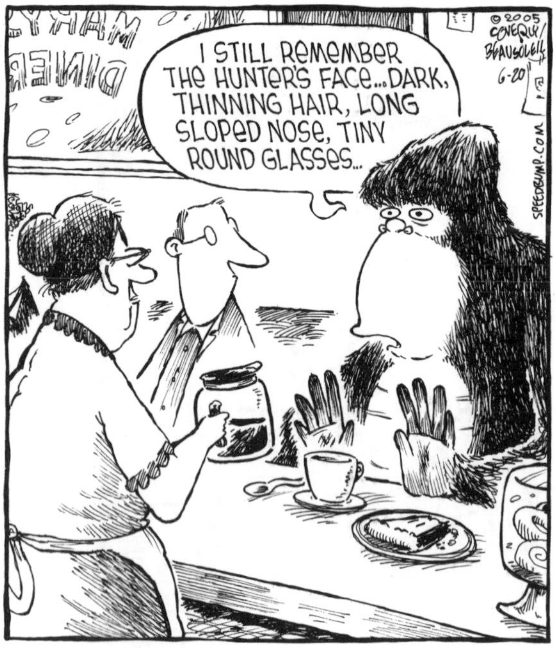
I STILL REMEMBER THE HUNTER'S FACE...DARK, THINNING HAIR, LONG SLOPED NOSE, TINY ROUND GLASSES...
SPEEDBUMP.COM

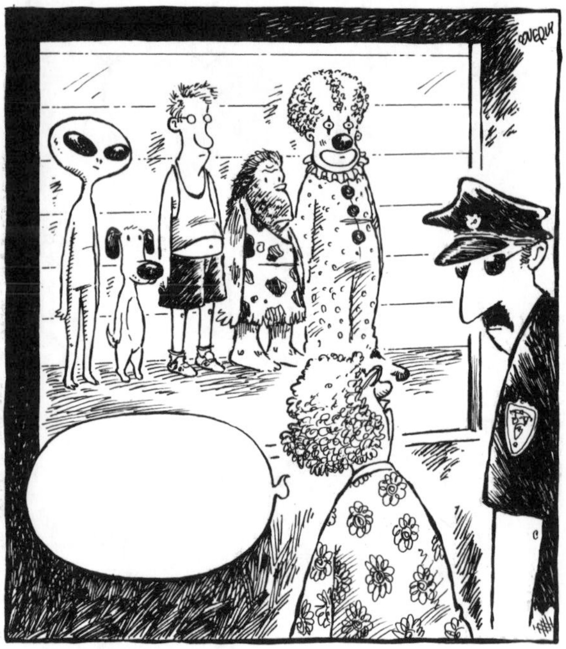

Thanks a million to everyone who entered our little contest. And actually, it wasn't so little – more than 3,200 of you entered! I personally read every single one of them, much to the chagrin of my eyes, neck, and buttocks, and was pleased to discover that *Speed Bump* readers are witty, intelligent, and smell good (I'm assuming the last part).

The winner, hailing from Albuquerque, New Mexico, is Michael Beausoleil.

I love this caption for a few reasons: it's subtle yet direct, it has an ominous feel of impending violence, and it uses a character in the drawing that is not a part of the action, which leads to the surprise element of the punchline.

Bravo, Sir Beausoleil!

You may enter the new caption contest in either of the following ways:

By email: **speedbumpcomic@comcast.net**
(put Caption Contest in the subject line)
By post: **Speed Bump Caption Contest**
Box 8115, Ann Arbor, MI 48107

For more information, please visit **www.speedbump.com**.
Deadline is April 7, 2006.
The winning entry will receive three inscribed books, the original artwork, and some sort of Speed Bump product . . . and, of course, will appear in hundreds of newspapers. . . . Good luck!
